NOT MY KID 2:

PROTECTING YOUR CHILDREN FROM THE 21 THREATS OF THE 21ST CENTURY

NOT MY KID 2:

PROTECTING YOUR CHILDREN FROM THE 21 THREATS OF THE 21ST CENTURY

DR. MARY E. MUSCARI

Scranton: The University of Scranton Press

Library of Congress Cataloging-in-Publication Data

Muscari, Mary E.
  Not my kid 2 : protecting your children from the 21 threats of the 21st cen-
try / by Mary E. Muscari.
    p. cm.
  Includes bibliographical references and index
  ISBN 1-58966-068-4 (pbk.) -- 1-58966-069-2
  1. Children's accidents–Prevention. 2. Safety education. I. Title: Not my
kid two. II. Title.
  HV675.72.M87 2004
  613.6–dc22   2003065771

DISTRIBUTION:

**The University of Scranton Press
445 Madison Avenue
Scranton, PA 18510
Phone: 1-800-941-3081
Fax: 1-800-941-8804**

PRINTED IN THE UNITED STATES OF AMERICA

CONTENTS

Section Three:
Checklists

ACKNOWLEDGMENTS

The author would like to thank the following people without whose help and support this book would not have been possible:

Richard W. Rousseau, SJ, AB, MA, STL, PhD, STD
Director, University of Scranton Press

Patricia Mecadon, BS
Production Manager, University of Scranton Press

Patricia Harrington, EdD, RN
Chairperson, Department of Nursing

Abigail Byman, JD
General Counsel

DEDICATION

To parents everywhere, especially my own, Joseph and Mary Muscari, and to my sister, Joanne and her husband, Joey; my brother Joe and his wife Kathy; and my brother Chris and his wife Ann Marie—for realizing that parenting is the most important job in the world and working so hard at it.

For waiting so patiently while I worked:
Mystique, Chelsea, Sabrina, Effie, Shelby, Arielle, Mona, Norman, Travis, Zoe, Bubba, Xena, Rocky, Dakota, and Gus.

And, of course, my high school writing teacher,
Vera Michener.

FOREWORD

Every year in the United States:

- 3000 to 5000 children are abducted by people who are not family members.
- More than 300,000 children are sexually abused.
- 1 in 5 youths receive a sexual approach or solicitation over the Internet.
- Accidental gunshots account for 27% of all firearm deaths among children under 12.
- Nationwide, 17.4% of high school students carry a weapon to school; 5.7% carry a gun.
- As many as 1 in 10 children ages 6 through 12 experience depressive symptoms.
- 25% of all children suffer an injury severe enough to warrant medical attention or miss school.
- Thousands of children develop infectious diseases that could be prevented by immunizations.
- Unintentional injury remains the leading cause of death in children ages 1 to 21.

The new millennium brings the promise of a brighter future, but it also brings dangers that past generations couldn't even fathom: Internet predators, abductions, dating violence, terrorist attacks on US soil, extreme weather, and school shootings. Today's children face these perils, as well as the ongoing hazards created by vehicles, fire, water, poisons, drugs, stress, and infectious diseases.

You can't be with your children 24/7, so this book gives you the tools you need to protect them from these and other dangers. And it does so without your feeling the need to put them inside a bubble for the rest of their lives—there's a whole chapter dedicated to fear. Compiled from research, statistics, expert advice, and common sense, *Not My Kid 2: Protecting Your Children from the 21 Threats of the 21st*

Century arose from the questions of parents across the country: How can I prevent my child from being abducted? How can I tell if my daughter has anorexia? My son just got his driver's license, help! Just how prevalent is date rape and what can I do to protect my daughter? Which video games are bad for my kids?

The 21 Threats address the problems that most frequently cause injury to children, as well as those issues that create the most fear. Stranger abductions, for instance, are rare. But statistics are meaningless when it comes to your child, so you want to know how to protect her no matter what the numbers say—and this book tells you how.

In addition to the 21 Threats, this book provides bonus sections that give you tips for special circumstances, such as home alone kids and babysitter safety, as well as extra tips for children with disabilities and rural kids, even though these terrific kids are addressed throughout the book. It also provides home and age-specific checklists, and a chapter on disaster preparedness.

There's everything you need to protect your children from the 21 Threats, so that you can concentrate more time on the more positive and fun things in life!

Yes, there's plenty of information out there on how to keep your children safe, but do you really have the time to look for it all? Considering the amount of time it took to compile it for this book, I can guarantee the answer is no. So keep this on the coffee table, or near the phone or computer, since it also gives you plenty of resources to check out for more information. And let it help you do your best to keep your kids safe and secure.

ABOUT THE AUTHOR

Former Yonkers, NY city slicker, now Pocono, PA country bumpkin, Dr. Mary Muscari has worked with thousands of children from tots to teens. An Associate Professor of Nursing at the University of Scranton, she is a certified pediatric nurse practitioner, a certified psychiatric clinical nurse specialist (therapist), and a forensic nurse. Besides writing the *Not My Kid* books and two pediatric nursing books, she writes chapters for academic textbooks and numerous articles for scholarly journals and regional newspapers. Her writing centers on child and adolescent health issues.

Dr. Muscari also serves as Editor-in-Chief of the University of Scranton's upcoming on-line magazine, "Healthy Lifestyles for Today's Families." A prolific writer who credits much of her writing success to her high school writing teacher Vera Michener, Dr. Muscari graduated U.C.L.A.'s Professionals Screenwriting Program and is currently utilizing this talent to write and produce educational videos, including the teen violence prevention video created to accompany her first *Not My Kid* book.

An experienced, fascinating speaker, she has presented her work at numerous academic and professional forums, as well as community groups and PTAs. Her down-to-earth, no-nonsense approach on the topical issues that face today's parents and children typically results in high praise from her audiences and requests for repeat performances. It's from those parenting groups that this book evolved.

Now completing a post-master's certificate in forensic nursing at Duquesne University, Dr. M earned a Ph.D. in nursing from Adelphi University, where she also earned a post-master's certificate in psychiatric nursing. She holds a master's degree in pediatric nursing from Columbia University and a bachelor's degree in nursing from Pace University. She earned her RN from the Cochran School of Nursing at St. John's Riverside Hospital in Yonkers, following the footsteps of her grandfather who worked there as a nurse and nurtured her career with hospital stories and chocolate milk.

If you wish to contact Dr. Muscari, please e-mail her at Muscarim1@scranton.edu.

DISCLAIMER

The author and the University of Scranton attempt to provide quality child safety information to the public. We strive for accuracy and timeliness in all of our materials, and this book underwent a rigorous editorial process.

As child safety advice should be tailored to meet the specific needs of each child, and as health care information is constantly changing and expanding, nothing in this book should be used as a substitute for your child's health care provider. This book is intended for use with the guidance of your child's health care provider.

The author, the University of Scranton and its trustees, officers, agents and employees, and the University of Scranton Press, will not be responsible or liable for any damages whatsoever resulting from use or inability to use material in this book or resources notes in this book whether such cause of action is based on contract, tort, warranty, or any other legal theory, and whether the University of Scranton is advised of the possibility of such damages.

SECTION ONE

THE 21 THREATS OF THE 21ST CENTURY

BITES AND STINGS

NEW JERSEY, 1998:
Three pit bulls injure fifteen 6- and 7-year-old students.

SOME STATS

- Over 1 million dog bites occur every year with 10 children, usually by the family or neighborhood dog.
- An estimated 400,000 cat bites occur annually, accounting for 5% to 15% of all animal bites. More than half of these occur in children.
- 45,000 snake bites occur every year; 8,000 from poisonous snakes.
- 250,000 human bites occur every year.
- Approximately 12,500 cases of Lyme disease, caused by tick bites, were reported annually from 1993 to 1997.
- Thousands of people are stung by bees every year, and 40 to 50 of these people die from an allergic reaction to the sting.

Bites can be inflicted by animals, insects, or humans. While the majority of bites are not fatal, many result in local inflammation, infection, or a serious systemic disease, such as rabies. Very young children and children with HIV/AIDS and other immunosuppressive disorders, and diabetes—and children who are receiving cancer or other treatments that affect the immune system—are most at risk for an infection from a bite.

The good news is that most bites can be prevented.

HUMAN BITES

Kid-to-kid bites typically occur between siblings during a scuffle or tykes in day care. The actual occurrence of day care biting incidents isn't known, but studies show bite rates of 5% – 51% from all injuries reported by day care staff. According to the Canadian Pediatric Society, most bite injuries take place in September during mid-morning. The incidence rate varies according to the age of the child, with toddlers, age 13 to 30 months, being bit most often, followed by infants and preschool children. Only four in 224 bites broke the skin.

Bites are classified as either occlusal injuries or clenched-fist injuries. Occlusal injuries occur with actual biting, typical of siblings and day care kids, but also occurring accidentally (or not so accidentally) during sporting events and rough sex. Clenched-fist injuries develop when a closed fist, usually belonging to a teenager, hits a person's teeth during a fight. These injuries tend to be more serious because the knuckle joints can be penetrated by the teeth, increasing the chance that bone, joint, or tendon become infected with germs from the punchee's mouth. The wound looks small, and the injury may be ignored until infection and pain develop.

Human bites can cause more serious infections than dog and cat bites because the human mouth contains many species of bacteria. The most common infectious organisms associated with human bites are *Viridans streptococci, Staphylococcus aureus, Eikenella corrodens, Haemophilus influenzae*, and beta-lactamase-producing bacteria. Infections vary from cellulitis (tissue infection), to osteomyelitis (bone infection) or septic arthritis (joint infection). Before the days of antibiotics, 20% of human bite cases required amputation. Today, up to 5% of these bite cases may still warrant amputation because of compromised blood flow or infectious complications.

The transmission of viral illnesses, such as hepatitis B and the human immunodeficiency virus (HIV), are rare. Most children are now immunized for hepatitis B. However, the risk for infection persists if a non-immunized child is bitten by a child who tests positive for hepatitis (HBsAg-positive), or if the unprotected child bites the HBsAg-positive child—with either case resulting in broken skin. In those cases, the unprotected child should receive proper protective measures from the child's health care provider. Fortunately, most children of day care age are immunized against hepatitis B.

The transmission of HIV via a bite is extremely unlikely. In 1997 the Centers for Disease Control and Prevention (CDC) published findings that suggested blood-to-blood transmission of HIV by a human bite, as did other reports in the medical literature. However, severe trauma with extensive tissue tearing and damage and the presence of blood were reported in each of these instances. Biting isn't a usual way of transmitting HIV. In fact, there are numerous reports of bites that did not result in HIV infection. Therefore, the transmission of HIV through a biting incident in day care, even when minor skin breakage is involved, is extremely unlikely.

PREVENTING HUMAN BITES

If your child bites, decrease his risk of biting other children by:

1. Helping him to avoid stressful and frustrating situations.
2. Firmly telling him "NO" when he bites and simply explaining the impact of his misconduct.
3. Using disciplinary measures, such as time-outs for biting behavior and positive reinforcement of appropriate behavior.

Frequent biting isn't likely to stop using the above measures. If your toddler continues to bite regularly or if your child is still biting past the age of 2½, consult your health care provider. Persistent biting can indicate anger, a high frustration level, or language delay.

WHAT TO DO IF YOUR CHILD IS BITTEN

If your child is bitten:

- Remain calm.
- Reassure your child that you can help.
- Contact your health care provider for specific treatment.
- If the skin isn't broken, clean it with mild soap and water and apply a cool compress to soothe the child.
- If the skin is bleeding, allow a little gentle bleeding to flush the area.
- If the bite is bleeding more than slightly, apply pressure to the area with a clean bandage or towel to stop the bleeding.
- Wash the bite wound with mild soap and water under pressure from a faucet for at least five minutes. Don't scrub because this may bruise the tissue.
- Dry the wound and cover it with a sterile bandage. Don't use tape or butterfly bandages to close the wound. These can trap harmful bacteria in the wound, increasing the risk of serious infection.
- Apply a mild antiseptic.
- Human bites may need treatment with antibiotics to prevent infection. Call your child's health care provider to find out if additional treatment or a tetanus booster is needed.

COMPANION ANIMAL (PET) BITES

Although many parents believe that children are usually bitten by strange or wild animals, most children are bitten by an animal the child knows, including the family pet. Injuries are often minor, but bites can cause serious wounds, facial damage, emotional problems, rabies, and even death.

DOG BITES

Children run a higher risk of being bitten simply because of their natural behaviors—running, yelling, grabbing, hitting, quick and darting movements, and maintaining eye contact. The proximity of a child's face to the dog also increases their risk for head and neck injuries.

Large dogs have powerful jaws with teeth designed for tearing and exerting more than 450 pounds of pressure per square inch—resulting in a crush injury with lacerations, avulsions, and puncture wounds. The majority of dog bite fatalities occur in children and on the owner's own property. Most involve large, intact (not neutered) male dogs, and although some breeds have been reported to bite more often than others, over 25 different breeds have been involved in 238 fatalities over the past 20 years, demonstrating that breed-specific legislation isn't the answer.

Small dogs, including the toy breeds, can also bite and cause injury. Wolf hybrids, a mix of canine and wolf, can be quite dangerous. Their behavior is unpredictable, and they are usually treated as wild animals by state and local statutes, many veterinarians, and by this book.

Most dog bites occur in boys, ages 5 to 9, during the spring and summer months. About one-half to one-third of bites are provoked, and more commonly occur when the dog feels threatened. Dogs may bite when they are in pain or are fearful, or when their territorial boundaries are violated. Strays rarely attack, and unprovoked attacks typically involve large, young, intact male dogs. Most bites are inflicted by the family or neighbor's pet.

Attacks on infants occur during sleep and are unprovoked. Bites in older children usually involve an extremity, because they are likely to reach out to interact with the dog or use their extremity as a defense. Severe bites chiefly occur in young male children with a high incidence of head and neck injuries. Infection occurs in up to 20% of dog bite cases.

CAT BITES

About 400,000 cat bite cases occur each year, and more than half of these occur in children, usually girls under age 6. Most cases involve young cats who are known to the child and roaming unrestrained, off their owner's property. The bites typically occur when the child picks up a cat that perceives the situation as potentially harmful. Seventy-five percent of cat bites involve the upper extremities, usually the hand; others may involve injuries to the head and neck, especially the eye area.

Which bite is more infectious, a dog bite or a cat bite? If you guessed cat bite, you're correct. Although dog bites are more common, only 20% of them get infected. Fifty percent or more of cat bites become infected. Cat teeth are small and sharp, and therefore more likely to penetrate deeply, even into a joint capsule or bone. The list of bacteria is similar to that found in dog bites, but cat bites also include *Pasteurella mulocida*. This bacterium can cause a tissue infection that develops in less than 24 hours, causing fever and a pus-filled discharge. Cases of meningitis and blood infection have been reported. Tularemia, a bacterial disease associated with both animals and humans, has been noted in rural areas where cats feed off rabbits and rodents. Symptoms of tularemia vary from diarrhea and vomiting to pneumonia-like symptoms. Therefore, you should always contact your health care provider if your child is bitten by a cat.

Cat bites—as well as cat scratches—can also result in an illness know as "Cat Scratch Disease." This infection, caused by the germs *Afipia felis* and *Bartonella benselae*, is usually a self-limiting problem that resolves in less than 2 months. More severe infections may need treatment with an antibiotic. The symptoms of Cat Scratch Disease include a red bump that appears about 3 to 10 days following the injury, swollen glands, and fever. These symptoms also appear in serious illnesses, including leukemia; therefore, you should contact your health care provider immediately should they occur in your child.

FERRET BITES

Over a half-million homes contain ferrets. These little critters warrant special consideration as they are very different from traditional companion animals. They are not easy to care for and require a high level of commitment to be cared for responsibly and humanely. Like all mammals, ferrets can carry and transmit rabies.

Ferrets may be small, but they can cause significant injury with their quick, sharp teeth. Nearly one-third of ferret bites involve children under 10 years old, and more than one-fourth involve children ages 10 to 19. Ferrets can also bite infants because they are attracted to the smell of milk. Bites are almost always unprovoked, occurring when the animal is allowed to run freely without adult supervision or when it escapes from its cage. Ferrets induce multiple puncture wounds and lacerations, chiefly around the head and neck. When infants are attacked about the head and neck, 25% of them require plastic surgery.

PREVENTING COMPANION ANIMAL BITES

Having a pet should be a terrific experience for your family, especially your children. Pets become productive members of your family by:

- Providing your children with the opportunity to practice respect, nurturing, and love.
- Teaching your children responsible behavior when caring for the pet.
- Reinforcing good pet behavior helps your children develop self-esteem.
- Encouraging trusting relationships with others.
- Giving your children an outlet for their secrets.
- Teaching your children life lessons about reproduction, birth, sickness, and death.

To provide a rewarding experience for your family and the pet, keep your child safe from bites, and keep your pet from biting:

- Recognize animals as living, feeling beings—they are not disposable items.
- Decide when it's the right time to get a pet. Is your child ready for the responsibility of caring for the pet, particularly a dog? If not, wait until he's ready.
- Realize that you, the adult, are still ultimately responsible for the well-being of the pet.
- Choose the pet that works best for your family.

- Decide which species you want: Dog? Cat? Ferret? Other?
- Realize that most dog breeds have been bred for a purpose: guarding, herding, hunting, lap sitting.
- Read about the breed you're interested in to see if it's appropriate for children and your family lifestyle. What is the breed's typical temperament? How much time and energy do you have to devote to a pet? Some dogs require much more time than others for exercising and/or grooming.
- Utilize your local kennel club or the American Kennel Club (www.akc.org) to learn more about dog breeds and to find a responsible breeder. For cats, contact the Cat Fancier's Association (www.cfainc.org/).
- DON'T buy from a pet store. The dogs may be cute, but they are not bred by responsible breeders—good breeders always want to know who is getting their pups! Pet store dogs usually come from puppy mills, and they may have health or behavioral problems.
- Consider getting a pet from a rescue organization. Most breeds have national rescues with local contacts (www.petfinder.org). And rescue groups tend to be very helpful in connecting you to the right pet.
- DON'T forget about your local animal shelter. They have both purebreds and mixed breeds. Ask the shelter personnel about the dog's temperament.
- Puppies and kittens are cute, but they are also more active and more likely to bite. Your better choice is an older animal with a gentle disposition that was raised in a home with children. If you do get a puppy or kitten, adopt after it's at least 6 to 8 weeks old.
- Provide your pet with appropriate nutrition, water, shelter, and love. Pets need socialization. If you intend to leave the dog chained outside all day with little or no human contact—don't get one! Besides being unfair to the animal, lack of socialization may lead to aggression.
- If required, get your pet licensed.
- Secure the services of a reputable veterinarian so that your pet can have lifelong medical care.
- Immunize your dog/cat/ferret against rabies and other harmful diseases.
- Get your animal neutered or spayed. That makes them less likely to bite and healthier. Teach your dog basic obedience. If you are not sure how to do that, contact your local kennel club. The Petsmart (www.petsmart.com) chain provides basic obedience

and puppy socialization classes at a reasonable cost. Dogs are pack animals, and they need to learn that you're the leader of the pack.

- Never leave pets alone with small children.
- Keep pets on a leash when in public.
- Teach your children to respect animals, and never to mistreat or hurt an animal.
- Tell your children not to bother animals that are eating, drinking, sleeping, or quietly playing with their toys.
- Tell your child never to take food, water, or toys away from an animal.
- Teach your child not to pet animals when they have babies—of course, you will have your pet spayed to avoid that problem in the first place!
- Avoid rough play and wrestling with the puppy or dog as it encourages aggression.
- Cats love warm, soft places—so keep them away from cribs.
- Cats may also react aggressively to newborns because a baby's cry is similar to other cats and small prey. Never leave your baby alone with the cat.
- Keep your cat's nails trimmed and dull to decrease injury—as well as destroyed walls and furniture.

If your baby arrives AFTER you already own a pet:

1. Allow your dog to investigate the new baby's room before you bring the baby home.
2. Practice leaving the animal outside the baby's room if the pet won't be allowed in once the baby arrives.
3. Bring home blankets with the baby's scent to get the pet used to the "smell."
4. Anticipate changes in your pet (increased barking; urinating outside the litter box) as a form of "sibling rivalry."
5. When you bring the baby home, allow your pet to sniff the baby's feet at a safe distance while leashed. Gradually introduce them to each other.
6. Never leave the baby alone with the pet.
7. Make sure you still give your pet adequate attention, and the two of them will grow to be best friends.
8. As your child grows, allow him to help care for the pet, but keep small pet objects away from toddlers since they could choke on them.

WILD ANIMAL BITES

SMALL WILD ANIMALS, such as mice, rats, moles, gophers, chipmunks, prairie dogs, and rabbits—as well as pet gerbils, hamsters, and guinea pigs, are considered to be rabies-free. But there is a small risk of getting other infections, such as Monkey Pox from prairie dogs. Therefore, contact your health care provider if your child is bitten by a small animal.

Bites from RABIES-PRONE WILD ANIMALS, including bats, skunks, raccoons, foxes, coyotes, and large wild animals, are especially dangerous. Rabies can be present in any wild—or stray—animal, but should be suspected in wild animals that appear ill, attack when unprovoked, or act in an unusual manner (nocturnal animals roaming in the daytime). Even scratches and scrapes that come into contact with the infected animal's saliva can expose your child to the disease.

RABIES

Rabies is a viral infection (*Rhabdoviridae* family) that attacks the central nervous system (CNS). Once symptoms develop, the disease is 100% fatal in animals if left untreated. In this country, rabies primarily occurs in skunks, raccoons, foxes, and bats. In the mid-Atlantic states, woodchucks can be rabid. Affected wild animals can infect domestic cats, dogs, and livestock.

Rabies enters the body via a cut or scratch, or through mucous membranes, and travels to the CNS. Once established in the brain, the virus travels down the nerves and attacks other organs. The salivary (saliva) glands are a key source of contamination. Scratches are dangerous because the affected animal licks its claws, depositing virus-ridden saliva on them.

The incubation period in humans (time from exposure to symptoms) varies from five days to more than a year, but averages two months. Common symptoms include:

Stage 1:
- vague symptoms for 2 to 10 days (fever, headache, tiredness, decreased appetite, vomiting)
- pain, itching, or numbness at site of the bite or scratch

Stage 2:

- difficulty swallowing ("foaming at the mouth") due to inability to swallow saliva
- even the sight of water may terrify the child ("hydrophobia")
- agitation and disorientation or paralysis
- immediate death or coma resulting in death

There is no known treatment for rabies once symptoms appear. Fortunately, there is a new vaccine that provides immunity to rabies when administered after exposure. It can also be used as a preventive measure for persons who work with animals, such as veterinarians and animal handlers.

If a wild animal bites your child, call the police or sheriff so that a report can be filed and the animal can be properly contained to be examined for rabies. Contact your health care provider, or bring the child to the nearest emergency center for treatment. Any contact with a bat, even if it's just in the same room, should be reported to animal authorities and your child's health care provider.

PREVENTING WILD ANIMAL BITES

To keep your child safe:

- Never keep wild animals as pets, no matter how cute and calm they seem.
- Always treat wild animals with caution—even adorable little bunnies.
- Tell your children not to play with wild, sick, or unknown animals.
- Don't let your child separate fighting animals.
- Don't let your children chase or capture wild animals.
- Let your children know that ANY animal can bite when frightened or cornered.

IF THREATENED BY AN ANIMAL:

- Stay calm
- Stand still
- Don't run
- Avoid direct eye contact
- Talk softly to the animal
- Back away slowly

SNAKE BITES

Approximately 7,000 to 8,000 poisonous snake bites are re-ported every year; 5 to 15 of these result in fatalities. Children, teen-agers, people under the influence of alcohol or drugs, and snake han-dlers are the most common victims. Every state, except Maine, Alaska, and Hawaii, calls itself home to at least one of 20 domestic poisonous snakes, but these snakes are most common in the Appalachian region and western and southern states. To learn which snakes inhabit your area, visit the web site "Geo-Outdoors" and scroll down to the "poisonous reptiles by state": www.geo-outdoors.info.

Two families of poisonous snakes live in the United States. Most are pit vipers from the *Crotalidae* family. This group includes rattlesnakes, copperheads, and cottonmouths (water moccasins). Pit vipers earn their name from the small pit between their eyes and nos-tril, which deflects heat and allows them to sense their prey at night. These snakes inject their venom through two fangs, which retract at rest and rapidly spring into biting position when striking.

Almost all the bites in the United States come from pit vipers. Some, such as the Mojave rattlesnake or the canebrake rattler, carry a neurotoxic venom that affects the brain and spinal cord. Copperheads, however, have a milder and less dangerous venom that sometimes doesn't require antivenom, an antidote to snake venom, but still war-rants medical attention.

The second family is the *Elapidae*, which includes coral snakes found chiefly in southern states, as well as the much more dan-gerous Asian cobras. Coral snakes have small mouths and short teeth, giving them a less efficient venom system than pit vipers. Bite victims lack the characteristic fang marks, sometimes making the bite harder to detect. Coral snake bites are rare in the United States, but their neu-rotoxic venom can still be dangerous. Fatalities are not usual; howev-er, respiratory paralysis can occur.

Any snake that has a large triangular head with a slit pit is poi-sonous, and baby snakes are poisonous at birth.

DIFFERENTIATING POISONOUS FROM NONPOISONOUS SNAKES

If you have great vision, and nerves to go with it, you should be able to tell the difference between poisonous and nonpoisonous snakes:

POISONOUS	NONPOISONOUS
Elliptical pupil of the eye	Round pupil of the eye
Pit between eye and nostril	No pit between eye and nostril
Undivided scales on the underside of tail	Divided scales on underside of tail

Since it's difficult to spot the underside of a snake's tail, and because nonpoisonous snake bites can become infected, all victims of snake bites should be rushed to the nearest emergency facility.

PREVENTING SNAKE BITES

Snake bites can be deadly to small children, especially when you factor their small size against the amount of injected venom compared to that of an adult. To prevent snake bites, teach your children the following:

- Treat all snakes with respect; they serve a purpose on this planet.
- Leave snakes alone—don't kill them, catch them, or scare them.
- Don't play with apparently dead snakes. Snakes may play dead, then strike when you attempt to touch them.
- Stay out of tall grass, unless you wear thick leather boots and jeans.
- Step onto rocks and logs, not over them, because snakes like to sun themselves on the sides of rocks and logs.
- Don't put your hand into crevices and other areas you can't see.

BUG BITES AND STINGS

Insects may be tiny and seemingly harmless, but bee stings can be fatal to those allergic to them, ticks spread Lyme disease, and we certainly can't forget the West Nile virus, spread by mosquitoes.

BEE AND WASP STINGS

Stinging insects, including bees and wasps, belong to the order *Hymenoptera*. Their stinger is actually a modified egg-laying device; therefore, only females can sting. Most hymenopteras live solitary lives and would rather flee than fight. Social hymenopteras—yellow jackets, bumble bees, and honey bees—live in a colony where members function to defend the nest. If someone disturbs the nest, these bees or wasps defend it vigorously. Foraging members may also sting if someone disturbs or injures them as they go about their activities. Some, like yellow jackets, tend to be more likely to attack then others.

The Africanized honey bee (killer bee) is related to the European honey bee, which people use in agriculture for crop pollination and honey production. Both these bee types look and behave the same. Neither stings unless provoked, and both can sting only once with the same type of venom. However, the Africanized bees can be more defensive and less predictable, and they are more likely to defend a larger area around their nest. They also respond faster and in greater numbers than the European honey bee.

Stingers act as effective weapons because their venom causes immediate pain due to the chemical melittin, which stimulates the nerve endings of pain receptors in the skin. The pain feels sharp at its onset, lasts for a few minutes, and then turns to a dull ache. The sting site may be swollen, warm, and sensitive for up to a few days. If the child is stung again by the same type of insect, the body recognizes the venom and triggers an immune response to get rid of it. This response can cause extreme swelling at the sting site or all over the body, as well as itching. If the child scratches the area and breaks the skin, infection may develop.

If the sting is caused by a honey bee, the stinger remains in the skin because it's barbed. The stinger should be removed immediately because it continues to release venom for up to 60 seconds after the sting.

Almost everyone has been stung by an insect at one time or another, and for most people it results in nothing more than temporary discomfort. However, a small portion of the population, including children, suffers severe allergic reactions. As many as 40 to 50 people die each year due to sting allergies.

Allergic reactions can happen anywhere on the body. Non-life-threatening reactions include swelling, hives, nausea, vomiting, abdominal cramps, and headaches. Life-threatening reactions encompass dizziness, shock, unconsciousness, difficulty breathing, and laryngeal blockage from swelling in the throat. These symptoms begin immediately to 30 minutes after the sting and require prompt medical attention.

Anaphylaxis develops as a sudden, severe allergic reaction that occurs when you're exposed to a substance that your body was sensitized to during a previous exposure. It occurs when a sudden release of chemicals, including histamines, dilates the blood vessels—lowering blood pressure—and causes the blood vessels to leak fluid, leading to swelling and hives, especially around the face and throat. These chemicals also act on the lungs, causing an asthmatic-like reaction, resulting in constriction of the lung's airways and obstructed breathing. Anaphylactic shock becomes fatal in as quickly as ten minutes if not treated immediately.

Anaphylaxis can be reversed when epinephrine (adrenaline) is injected into the body. Children with known sting allergies should carry epinephrine in a regular syringe (premeasured in a bee sting kit) or an auto-injector (Epi-Pen) whenever they may encounter the offending insects. These medications are available by prescription from your health care provider. If your child is allergic, he should also wear a MedicAlert bracelet (1-800-ID-ALERT; www.medicalert.org).

If you suspect that your child may be allergic to stings, contact your health care provider for allergy testing. If your child tests positively, discuss the possibility of having him desensitized. Desensitization treatment, known as allergy shots, exposes your child to a series of injections that contain increasing amounts of the venom to which he's allergic, minimizing the chance of allergic reaction should your child be exposed to another sting. Desensitization is fairly effective, working up to 95% of the time.

Occasionally, people may be stung by large numbers of bees. Although it takes a significant number to cause severe harm to an adult, it takes considerably less to harm a small child. Even so, most deaths from multiple stings occur in people over 70 who already have poor heart and lung functioning.

PREVENTING BEE AND WASP STINGS

Bees and wasps are attracted to specific scents and colors; therefore it's possible to decrease your child's chance of being stung:

- Avoid the use of perfumes, shampoos, deodorants, and scented soaps and body creams.
- Wear clean, light-colored clothing—avoid bright colors and patterns.
- Cover his body with as much clothing as possible.
- Avoid walking barefoot in vegetation; always wear shoes and socks.
- Keep areas clean as wasps thrive in places where humans discard garbage. Be observant for nests, especially in July,

August, and September. Yellow jackets nest in old logs, walls, and in the ground in dirt mounds. Honey bees live in hives. Hornets nest in trees, bushes, and on buildings.

- Use insect screens on windows and doors during the warmer weather.
- Remove insect-attracting plants from your home.
- If a single bug is flying around, remain still and cover your face. Swatting will make it sting.
- If attacked by a swarm, run away as more insects will likely be on the way. If possible, jump into water or go indoors.
- If a bee enters your vehicle, slow to a stop and open the windows to let it out.

TICK BITES

Most ticks are harmless, but some cause serious illnesses, particularly Lyme disease and Rocky Mountain Spotted Fever. Other diseases include tularemia (plague-like disease), ehrlichiosis (abrupt fever, rash, nausea, vomiting and weight loss), and relapsing fever. In 1999 alone, more than 16,000 cases of Lyme disease, 579 cases of Rocky Mountain Spotted Fever, and 302 cases of ehrlichiosis were reported in the United States.

Ticks live in wooded areas, low-growing grasslands, seashores, and backyards. They feed on blood, transmitting disease as they eat. Favorite hosts include mice, deer, raccoons, birds, and opossums, but they will also feed on dogs, cats, and humans.

Lyme disease, the most common tick-borne illness, is a multi-stage, multisystem infection caused by the *Borrelia burgdorferi*, which is transmitted by a tick bite. The disease gets its name from Lyme, Connecticut, where the illness was first identified in 1975. Lyme disease is a year-round problem, but occurs most commonly from April through October during tick season. Cases have been reported in 45 of the 50 states, as well as in large areas of Europe and Asia.

Lyme disease has numerous symptoms, and each individual experiences it differently. It may start with a red rash that appears several days after the person is infected, lasts a few hours or several weeks, and may be very small or large. The rash can mimic hives, sunburn, poison ivy, and even flea bites. It may itch, feel hot, or not bother the victim. It can even disappear and return several weeks later. Flu-like symptoms develop, including fatigue, fever and chills, headache, stiff neck, swollen glands, aches and pains, sore throat, and poor appetite. Later problems include arthritis, heart problems, skin disorders, neurological disorders, hepatitis, eye problems, severe fatigue, weakness, and poor motor coordination.

Rocky Mountain Spotted Fever is caused by rickettsia bacteria carried mainly by the wood tick, *Dermacentor Andersoni*, in the Rocky Mountain states and the dog tick, *Dermacentor Variabilis*, in the eastern states. Like the ticks that cause Lyme disease, these ticks are most active during the spring and summer. Rocky Mountain Spotted Fever is most common in the southeast (Virginia, Georgia, and the Carolinas), but occurs as far north as Massachusetts and westward into Tennessee, Kentucky, Arkansas, and Oklahoma.

Rocky Mountain Spotted Fever begins suddenly with a high fever, chills, muscle aches, and a severe headache. The child's eyes can become red, muscles may be tender to the touch, and the body may swell. The spotted rash that gives the disease its name begins anytime from 1 to 10 days after the headaches start, but usually appears on the third to fifth day. The rash consists of small, red blotches or spots that begin on the palms, wrists, ankles, and soles. It then spreads up the arms and legs, changing in appearance to look more like bruising. Left untreated, the illness can cause damage to the lungs, kidneys, and liver, and finally death. Therefore, early treatment with antibiotics is critical.

PREVENTING TICK BITES

To prevent tick bites:

- Be more cautious in areas where ticks like to hide: near birdbaths and feeders; on outdoor pets; in woodpiles, brushpiles, stone or rock walls; treehouses and swing sets in the woods; on the clothes of landscapers, utility line workers, farmers, and other outdoor occupations; in association with outdoor recreation—freshwater fishing, camping, hunting, hiking.
- Wear light-colored clothing that makes ticks easier to see.
- Wear long-sleeved shirts, long-legged pants, and socks with closed shoes.
- Tuck pants into socks.
- Avoid shrubby areas and tall grass.
- Get rid of brush piles.
- Mow the grass.

- Wear tick repellent.
- Check pets regularly for ticks.
- Check your children for ticks:
  —All body parts that bend (knees, elbows, fingers, toes, under-arms)
  —Belly button, in and behind ears, neck, hairline, top of head
  —Pressure points (where underwear elastic meets the skin; pant and shirt bands)
  —Visually check, and run your fingers over the skin
- Shower after being outdoors.

TICK REMOVAL

- If you find a tick, remove it as soon as possible because it needs to feed for several hours before disease is transmitted:
- Don't use your bare hands.
- Use tweezers to remove it. Grab it firmly by its head as close to the skin as possible.
- Pull up slowly and steadily, without twisting.
- Don't squeeze the tick, and don't use petroleum jelly, solvents, knives or matches to kill it.
- Save the tick in a plastic container so it can be tested for disease, if needed.
- Wash the bite area well with soap and water, and apply an antiseptic.
- Call your health care provider to find out about testing and treatment.

MOSQUITO BITES

Although mosquito bites proved deadly in other countries, we thought of them as just another inconvenience that interfered with summer fun. But now numerous cases of West Nile Virus are cropping up in New York City and elsewhere, and parents worry about allowing their children to play outside, fearing they would contract the disease from a mosquito bite.

The West Nile Virus is a flavivirus found mostly in Africa, Western Asia, and the Middle East. Closely related to the St. Louis encephalitis virus found in the United States, it can affect mosquitoes, birds, horses, other mammals, and humans. Until 1999 the virus had not been documented in the Western Hemisphere.

Most infected persons have no symptoms of illness. Twenty percent develop West Nile fever, a mild form of the disease in humans, characterized by flu-like symptoms: fever, headache, body aches, swollen glands, and occasionally, a rash. It usually lasts only a few days and doesn't appear to cause any lasting effects.

More severe forms of the disease include West Nile encephalitis (an inflammation of the brain), meningitis (inflammation of the membranes surrounding the brain), or meningoencephalitis (inflammation of both brain and surroundings). Symptoms include high fever, headache, stiff neck, muscle weakness, disorientation, seizures, tremors, coma, and paralysis. It's estimated that 1 in 150 persons infected with the West Nile Virus will develop a severe form of the disease.

PREVENTING MOSQUITO BITES

To minimize the risk of mosquito bites to your children:

- Get rid of all sources of stagnant water:
  —Pool covers, tarps, and other covers that allow water to pool on their surface
  —Gutters
  —Leaf piles
  —Old tires
  —Old flower pots
  —Birdbaths
  —Outdoor pet water and food dishes
- Avoid going outdoors at dawn, dusk, and early evening—peak mosquito biting times.
- Install or repair window and door screens.
- Wear long-sleeved shirts and long-legged pants.
- Use mosquito netting over infant carriers and carriages when outdoors.
- Use a mosquito repellent that contains DEET, and follow the recommendations of the American Academy of Pediatrics:
  —Read label carefully and follow directions
  —Don't use near food
  —Don't apply to infants under 2 months
  —Apply sparingly to exposed skin and clothes, not under clothes
  —Never use on irritated skin or over cuts and wounds
  —Don't place near eyes or mouth; apply sparingly around ears
  —Don't spray directly on the face
  —Don't let children handle repellents, and don't apply to their hands

—Don't spray in enclosed areas

—Once back indoors, wash treated skin

—If child has a reaction to the repellent, discontinue use

SPIDER BITES

The arachnid family boasts at least 50,000 spider species. To qualify as a spider, the animal must have eight legs, no wings, no antennae, and only two body sections—the thorax and abdomen. The vast majority of spiders do us a world of good by spending their days catching and eating other insects.

All spiders have hollow fangs and venom of varying degrees of potency. They use their fangs to inject their prey with venom and to aid in digestion. Most are not dangerous to humans because their fangs are either too short or too fragile to penetrate human skin.

Fewer than 5000 cases of spider bites are reported each year, with only the bites of two spiders reported as serious—the female Black Widow and the Brown Recluse. Unfortunately, the bites of these spiders can be very serious in young children, and the bite of any spider can be problematic if the child is sensitive to the venom.

Black Widow spiders usually live in closets, attics, trash, woodpiles, garages, and other dark places. They are common in California, particularly the warmer Central Valley and Southern California regions. The Black Widow is a shiny, inky black spider with a large round abdomen. Counting the legs, its length generally measures from one-half to one inch in length. A red-colored, hourglass-shaped marking is usually found on its underbelly.

The bite of the Black Widow looks like a bull's-eye with a pale area surrounded by a red ring. Within two hours, the victim develops severe muscle pain and cramps that start in the back, shoulders, abdomen, and thighs. This is followed by headache, weakness, anxiety, sweating, itching, nausea, vomiting, difficulty breathing, and increased blood pressure. Young children are at high risk from developing symptoms from a black widow bite. No one has died from the bite of a Black Widow in over ten years, but you should wash the area with soap and water, and bring your child to the nearest emergency center.

The Brown Recluse earned its name from hiding in dark corners. Also known as the violin spider or fiddle-back spider, because of a violin-shaped marking, the Brown Recluse is about one-half inch long, including the legs, and solid light brown in color. This spider is native to Kansas, Texas, Oklahoma, and Mississippi.

The bite of the Brown Recluse causes pain, burning, and itching for the first ten minutes. The bite takes on the appearance of a target, with a center blister surrounded by a flaming red ring and then a blanched white ring. The blister pops, leaving an ulcer that scabs over. The ulcer can enlarge and erode surrounding tissue and muscle. Other symptoms include a generalized itchy red rash, fever, chills, nausea, vomiting, muscle aches, and hemolytic anemia (an anemia where red blood cells are destroyed). There is no special treatment for the bite of the Brown Recluse, but if your child is bitten, wash the area with soap and water and contact your health care provider.

PREVENTING SPIDER BITES

The best prevention against spider bites is vigilance. A spider bite usually occurs when a person accidentally invades its space—for example, a child picking up and wearing an old article of clothing from the attic. Be careful when unpacking long-stored boxes, and wear gloves when doing so.

DRUGS

NEW JERSEY, 2002:
High School senior dies after an apparent heroin overdose.

SOME STATS

According to the 2001 Youth Risk Behavior Surveillance from the Centers for Disease Control and Prevention:

- 63.9% of students have tried cigarette smoking; 21% smoked before age 13.
- 15.2% smoked cigars.
- 8.2% used smokeless tobacco.
- 67.2% who purchased or attempted to purchase cigarettes at a store or gas station were not asked to show proof of age.
- 78.2% had one or more drinks during their lifetime; 29.9% drink five or more drinks on occasions; 29.1% had first drink before age 13.
- 14.7% had used inhalants.
- 42.4% had used marijuana; 23.9% used it one or more times in the 30 days before the survey; 10.2% tried marijuana before age 13.
- 9.4% had used cocaine (crack or freebase).
- 3.1% had used heroin.
- 9.8% had used methamphetamines (speed).
- 5% had used steroids.

Your children face exposure to drugs every day. You take medicine. Classmates use asthma inhalers. The media inundates them with commercials plugging pharmaceuticals, celebrities being arrested for drug abuse and driving while intoxicated, and dramas touting the "glamorous side" of the drug world. All this makes for a very confusing message for your child.

Most teens limit their experimentation to tobacco, alcohol, and marijuana, but a small number try other drugs. The good news is that most adolescents who use drugs and alcohol will, when they assume adult roles and responsibilities, spontaneously quit using drugs and develop controlled patterns of alcohol use. The bad news is that some kids will be seriously affected by drug abuse and its associated consequences, including addiction, withdrawal, school failure, diseases such as HIV/AIDS, unwanted and unprotected sex, motor vehicle accidents, violence, and suicide. The younger a child uses drugs, the more likely she's to develop a drug problem.

The new wave of club and designer drugs, such as GHB (gamma hydroxybutyrate), rohypnol, MDMA/Ecstasy (methylenedioxymethamphetamine), ketamine (ketamine hydrochloride), and LSD (lysergic acid diethylamide), is making the rounds at high school gatherings and college campuses. These drugs are cheaper than cocaine and heroin, and they are relatively easy to obtain, many cooked up right in a kitchen. Most are odorless and tasteless, leaving no telltale evidence for you to detect. They can be addictive, and when mixed with alcohol, they can be deadly.

All drugs can cause harm, and small amounts of certain drugs can kill brain cells, which don't regenerate. Once a brain cell dies, it's gone forever. Glue sniffing can cause permanent blindness, and just one hit of cocaine can cause a fatal heart attack.

Think you live in a nice, safe neighborhood, free of the worry of your child accessing drugs? Think again. She can get them right in your own home—under the kitchen sink and over the Internet. Many household chemicals serve as inhalants for both children and young teens. Your child can sniff your fabric protector or degreaser to get high. A few clicks of her mouse, and her drug of choice lands right in your mailbox. She can access online connections to drug labs for supplies, or easily find detailed, step-by-step recipes, complete with ingredients and the necessary supplies for mixing up GHB right in your own kitchen.

DRUG ABUSE

The term drug or substance abuse denotes a persistent pattern of use of any substance that affects the mind or body despite adverse psychological, medical, or social consequences. This pattern can be intermittent, and it can occur with or without tolerance (need for increasingly larger doses of a drug to get same desired effect) and physical dependence (physical need for repeated use of a drug). Physical dependence causes withdrawal symptoms when the user stops using certain drugs, particularly alcohol, opiods, sedatives, amphetamines, cocaine, and caffeine. Addiction refers to a group of thinking, behavioral, and physical symptoms that occurs in a person who continues to use a substance despite its consequences, leading to significant impairment.

Teens use and abuse drugs for a number of reasons, including curiosity, peer pressure, need for acceptance, imitation of family members, rebellion, escape, unhappy home life, feelings of alienation, and attempts at sophistication. No single factor determines who will use drugs and who won't, but there are some predictors: poor school performance, aggressive and rebellious behaviors, excessive influence by peers, lack of parental support and guidance, substance abusing family members or friends, and behavior problems at an early age.

Drugs, including alcohol, depress the cerebral cortex of the brain (a still immature intellectual and reasoning center in teens) and release inhibitions in the limbic system: the center of pleasure, anger, and other emotions. The limbic system craves instant and constant gratification and contributes to the teen's sense of boredom. Thus some teens go to extremes in seeking alcohol, hard drugs, and aggressive outlets.

GIRL TALK

Got girls?

Girls have come a long way—but sometimes in the wrong direction. More than 25% of high school girls smoke cigarettes; 45% drink alcohol; more than 25% binge drink; and 20% use marijuana. According to the National Center on Addiction and Substance Abuse at Columbia University (CASA), girls use cigarettes, alcohol, and other drugs for reasons different than boys, and they are more vulnerable to substance abuse, addiction, and the consequences that come with these problems.

The risks and consequences of smoking, alcohol and other drug use identified by the CASA are:

- Girls who experience early puberty have a higher risk of using substances more frequently and in greater quantities than later maturing peers.
- Girls are more like to be sexually abused and to have eating disorders and depression than boys, and all of these put them at risk for substance abuse.
- Girls become addicted more quickly than boys.

- Girls who use alcohol and other drugs are more likely to commit suicide than those who don't use substances.
- Girls are more likely to experience adverse health effects (greater lung damage from cigarettes, more likely to get alcohol-induced brain, heart, and liver damage).
- Girls are more likely to abuse prescription medications than boys.
- Transition times—from elementary to middle school, from middle school to high school, and from high school to college—mark times of increased substance abuse risk for girls.
- Girls are more likely to be offered substances from other girls or a boyfriend, and in private settings, whereas boys are more likely to be offered substances from other boys, a parent or a stranger, and in public settings.
- Religion provides more protection for girls than boys.
- Girls who drink coffee are more likely to smoke and drink, and to do so at earlier ages.

WHAT IS OUT THERE?

Any drug can be abused, and most can harm your child while she goes through her formative years. Alcohol and nicotine are sanctioned by society, but are still drugs nonetheless. The type of drug preferred varies according to geographic location, socioeconomic status, and various historical periods. What is popular with one generation of teens may not be fashionable to another. Changing trends influence teenagers' search for experiences.

TOBACCO

(Cigarettes: Cigs, Butts)
(Cigars: Ropes, Stogies)
(Smokeless: Chew, Dip, Sniff, Snuff, Spit)

At $3.50 per pack and one carton of ten packs per week, cigarettes cost $1,820 per year. That could buy a lot of books, food, CDs, or sports equipment.

Approximately 90% of tobacco users started before they were 18 years old—if your kids can stay smoke-free, they most likely won't smoke as adults. Cigarettes contain nicotine, which is highly addictive. Most teens who smoke are addicted; they may want to quit, but they can't. Smokers tend to do poorer in school, and smoking can be the gateway to other drugs.

Kids smoke for a number of reasons—to look older, to look "cool," to make themselves "good-looking," to look like a movie, sports, or rock star—none of which make any sense, although cigarettes certainly do age those who smoke them. They also smoke because their peers or parents smoke.

According to the Centers for Disease Control and Prevention (CDC), the short-term health effects of smoking on teenagers include damage to the respiratory system, addiction to nicotine, and the associated risk of other drug use. Long-term health consequences develop since most young people who smoke regularly continue to smoke throughout adulthood

Smoking effects:

- Smoking can hamper a young person's rate of lung growth and the level of maximum lung function.
- Smoking decreases young people's physical fitness in terms of both performance and endurance—even among young people trained in competitive running.
- Regular smoking is responsible for cough and increased frequency and severity of respiratory illnesses.
- The younger people start smoking cigarettes, the more likely they are to become strongly addicted to nicotine.
- Teens who smoke are 3 times more likely than nonsmokers to use alcohol, 8 times more likely to use marijuana, and 22 times more likely to use cocaine.
- Smoking is associated with a host of other risky behaviors, such as fighting and engaging in unprotected sex.
- Smoking is associated with poor overall health and a variety of short-term adverse health effects in youths, and may also be a marker for underlying mental health problems, such as depression. High school seniors who are regular smokers and began smoking by grade nine are:
  —2.4 times more likely than their nonsmoking peers to report poorer overall health
  —2.4 to 2.7 times more likely to report cough with phlegm or blood, shortness of breath when not exercising, and wheezing or gasping
  —3.0 times more likely to have seen a doctor or other health professional for an emotional or psychological complaint.
- Between 1000 to 3000 youths who begin smoking every day will prematurely die of a tobacco-related disease.

- Young adult smokers are 1.43 times more likely to have a stroke than their nonsmoking peers.
- Smoking is connected to lung cancer, as well as other lung diseases and heart disease.

Cigar smoking has become increasingly popular among high school and college students. But tobacco is tobacco is tobacco, thus cigar smoking can lead to nicotine addition. Cigars come in many sizes, but they generally contain 7 times more tar and 4 times more nicotine than cigarettes. They also produce 30 times more carbon monoxide, demonstrating that cigar smoking is far from a safe substitute for cigarette smoking. Inhaling cigar smoke isn't required for someone to become addicted to nicotine or to get lung cancer; oral membranes directly absorb the nicotine in cigars whether the cigar is smoked or just held in the mouth. Cigar smoke causes cancers of the lip, tongue, mouth, throat, larynx, esophagus, and lung, and like cigarette smoke, cigar smoke leads to heart disease, chronic cough, emphysema, and dental problems.

The shredded tobacco used for pipes comes in a loose leaf form and may be aged and sprayed with chemicals or flavorings. Pipe smoking, although not favored by kids at this writing, shares all the negative effects of the other forms of tobacco use, and it has a higher incidence of chronic cough and lip cancer.

Secondhand smoke, also known as passive smoking or environmental tobacco smoke (ETS), is just as deadly as smoking. It contains more than 43 known carcinogens and 200 known poisons, including ammonia, formaldehyde, hydrogen cyanide, arsenic, carbon monoxide, and benzene.

Children are the most affected. Because their bodies are still developing, exposure to the poisons in secondhand smoke puts them in danger of severe respiratory diseases and can hinder the growth of their lungs—effects that can last a lifetime.

Home ventilation systems can't filter and circulate air well enough to eliminate secondhand smoke. Blowing smoke away from children, going into another room to smoke, or opening a window may help reduce children's exposure, but won't protect them from the dangers of secondhand smoke.

Secondhand smoke:

- Increases your baby's risk of dying from Sudden Infant Death Syndrome (SIDS, Crib Death)

- Increases the risk of lung cancer and asthma
- Causes 26,000 healthy U.S. children develop asthma every year because of secondhand smoke
- Causes between 150,000 and 300,000 children 18 months or younger suffer from lower respiratory infections (like bronchitis and pneumonia)
- Results in 700,000 and 1.6 million visits to the doctor for children 18 months and younger for childhood ear infections

Smokeless tobacco (chewing tobacco, dip. chew, snuff, spit), which is as addictive and harmful as smoked tobacco, has become popular among youths; 14.8% of high school boys and 1.9% of high school girls currently use it. In some states the numbers of male users are higher—Arkansas (24.9%), Montana (25.2%), Wyoming (28.6%), and West Virginia (33%).

Despite common belief to the contrary, smokeless tobacco is dangerous to your child's health:

- Smokeless tobacco causes serious dental and gum disease, which can lead to tooth and bone loss.
- Smokeless tobacco users are more likely to use marijuana, inhalants, alcohol, and cocaine than nonusers.
- Smokeless tobacco causes leukoplakia (white patches in the mouth), a precursor to cancer, that can appear as early as 3 to 4 months after the first use.
- Smokeless tobacco can cause cancer of the mouth, pharynx, larynx, esophagus, stomach, and pancreas. Smokeless users are 50 times more likely to get mouth cancers than nonusers.
- Smokeless tobacco increases the risk of heart disease, including heart attack.

INHALANTS

(Airblast, Bang, Bullet bolt, Discorama, Hippie Crack, Huff, Medusa, Moon Gas, Oz, Poor Man's Pot)

Inhalants, substances that are often frequently found right in your home, are among the most popular and deadly substances kids abuse. More than 20% of children report having used inhalants by the eighth grade, and about 6% try inhalants by the time they reach the fourth grade. Users sniff or "huff" (breathe through the mouth) ordinary products like whipped cream, nail polish remover, gasoline, and spray paint. Since inhalants starve the body of oxygen, they can cause severe, irreversible brain damage and even death.

Most inhalant abuse indicates the deliberate inhaling or sniffing of common products found in homes and schools to get high. Products are inhaled by wanging (sniffing), huffing, (placing an inhalant soaked rag in the mouth), or bagging (inhaling fumes from a plastic bag). Some children soak their sleeves in solvent and sniff away all day; others paint their nails with typewriter fluid and sniff their fingers. Sniffing is accessible, cheap, and intense, and it doesn't leave needle marks or other obvious evidence.

The immediate negative effects of inhalants include fatigue, sneezing, coughing, nosebleeds, loss of appetite, nausea, and lack of coordination. Solvents decrease heart and breathing rates, and impair judgment. The nitrites cause rapid pulse, headaches, and loss of bladder and bowel control. Long term use produces weight loss, electrolyte (body salt) imbalance, and muscle fatigue, while repeated sniffing of concentrated vapors may lead to permanent brain damage. When deeply inhaled or used in a short period of time, inhalant use may result in disorientation, violent behavior, unconsciousness, or death.

Inhalant abuse claims young lives every year and can lead to permanent brain damage, loss of muscle control, and destruction of the heart, liver, kidneys, blood, and bone marrow. Sudden Sniffing Death can occur without warning during or right after sniffing, even in first-time users. The heart overworks, beating too fast and unevenly—causing cardiac arrest.

Three categories of inhalant abuse exist: volatile solvents, including adhesives and aerosols; nitrites, such as butyl nitrite and amyl nitrite; and anesthetics, including chloroform and nitrous oxide (laughing gas). Over 1,000 different products are abused, mostly solvents, aerosols, and glues. Some examples are model airplane glue, rubber cement, household glue, hair spray, spray paint, paint thinner, cleaning fluid, lighter fluid, air freshener, spot remover, degreaser, deodorant, fabric protector, typewriter correction fluid, nail polish, nail polish remover, marking pens, fabric protectors, vegetable cooking spray, aerosol whipping cream, gasoline, air conditioning coolants, propane, butane, helium, and the commercial spray used to clean keyboards and electronic devices. Unfortunately, the ease of availability of these products adds to the chance that they can land right under your child's nose.

COUGH SYRUP

(Codeine cough syrup: AC/DC, Barr)
(DXM cough syrup and cold tablets: Dex, DXM, Robo, Tussin)

Codeine, while noted in the narcotic section, more frequently passes through youthful lips in the form of prescriptive cough syrup. Codeine cough syrups can also be purchased illegally at "syrup houses." The cough syrup may be taken undiluted or combined with alcohol or soft drinks to improve the taste. Some teens also coat marijuana joints with it. Codeine cough syrups produce the same effects as other narcotics (see narcotic section), and may also cause reactions from other ingredients found in the syrup.

DXM, or dextromethorpan, is found in over-the-counter cough and cold products, making it cheap and easy to obtain. DXM is legal and usually effective as a cough suppressant, but potentially deadly when misused—and the abuse of DXM is rising among adolescents.

Many teens combine DXM with marijuana, ecstasy, and alcohol. Most DXM cough syrups taste nasty, so teens turn to cold tablets containing DXM, which adds to the problems, as these pills contain other medications, including acetaminophen (Tylenol) and/or antihistamines. High doses of acetaminophen, especially when combined with alcohol, can cause liver damage.

The effects of DXM vary, depending on body weight and composition and the degree of tolerance to the drug. Unfortunately, there are web sites that provide your teen with calculators for her to plug in her weight to figure out how much she needs to take to get high. Short-term effects include sweating, flushing, nausea, vomiting, abdominal pain, diarrhea, high blood pressure, seizures, confusion, an irregular heartbeat, hyperactivity, and hallucinations. The latter signifies the main reason the drug is abused—to get a psychedelic experience with euphoria. However, they may also get the unexpected results—loss of consciousness, brain hemorrhages, stroke, and permanent brain damage.

ALCOHOL

(Firewater, Gut-warmer, Reviver, Skee)
(Beer: Act of Congress, Never Fear, Roadies, Skit, Toby)

(Liquor: Hallelujah Syrup, Nose Paint, Snake Water, Social
        Lubricant, Valley Tan, Whoopie Water)
(Champagne: Laughing Water)
(Gin: Cat's Water, Deadeye, Old Tom, Stiff Naked)

Alcohol remains the drug of choice for teenagers because of
its social acceptance, easy accessibility, and the peer pressure to use it.
Teens may be afraid of hard drugs, but they feel comfortable with
alcohol, a drug that is relatively inexpensive, can be purchased legally by adults, and is part of a meal.

The average age to start drinking has dropped from 14 to 12,
and 80% to 90% of teenagers have used alcohol by age 18. Intake
peaks between 18 and 22, and binge drinking–drinking large quantities in a small amount of time–plagues college campuses. Estimates
show that 4.6 million teens between the ages of 14 and 17 have significant alcohol problems. Teens that do have alcohol problems have
marked mood changes and become difficult to live with. They have
trouble with their memory, judgment, and learning abilities. Even
though the majority of adolescents are not heavy users, social drinking remains a problem due to its problem effects. Drunk driving is the
number one killer of teens and young adults, and over 38% of
drowning accidents are alcohol-related. Alcohol often acts a factor in
fights, assaults, and murders.

Alcohol causes several behavior changes. Low doses significantly impair the judgment and coordination required to safely drive a
car. Low to moderate amounts can increase the incidence of aggressive acts. Moderate to high doses cause significant impairment of
mental functions, severely impairing the user's ability to learn and
remember information. Very high amounts can cause respiratory
depression and death.

The American Academy of Pediatrics lists three stages of alcohol use:

Stage 1:
        Uses alcohol just for fun or to be part of the group
        Most use on weekends
        Usually no change in behavior
Stage 2:
        Alcohol used to feel better during stressful times
        Use occurs during the week
        Behavior changes occur:

Spends more time alone
Decreased communication with family members
Frequent arguing and a high level of secretiveness
Changes in dress or grooming
Hangs out with different friends
Problems sleeping
Lack of energy
Bloodshot eyes
Moodiness—irritable, depressed
Runs away from home
Attempts suicide

Stage 3:

Preoccupied with alcohol
Almost total loss of control over its use
Can have withdrawal symptoms
Alcohol may disappear from home
Family possessions may disappear to get money to support habit
May get in trouble with the law

Continued use leads to dependence. Abrupt cessation of a steady intake causes withdrawal symptoms including severe anxiety, tremors, hallucinations, and convulsions. The long term effects, especially when combined with poor nutrition, lead to organ damage, chiefly the brain and liver. In addition, when taken during pregnancy, alcohol may create fetal alcohol syndrome resulting in an infant born with mental retardation and other irreversible abnormalities. Research also indicates that children born to alcoholics are at greater risk than other children for becoming alcoholics themselves.

Alcohol abuse, particularly binge drinking, has become an increasing problem on college campuses, with consequences rising in destructiveness and cost. These consequences can affect your child—whether or not she drinks. The National Institute of Alcohol Abuse and Alcoholism notes the following on college students ages 18 to 24:

- 2.1 million drove under the influence of alcohol
- 1,400 die each year of alcohol-related accidents, including motor vehicle crashes
- 500,000 are injured
- 600,000 are assaulted by another student who has been drinking
- 70,000 are victims of alcohol-related sexual assault or date-rape

- 400,000 engage in unprotected sex
- 100,000 report being too intoxicated to know if they consented to sex
- 25% report alcohol-related academic consequences
- More than 150,000 develop alcohol-related health problems, with 1.2–1.5% attempting suicide
- 11% damaged property while under the influence of alcohol
- About 5% get involved with campus security or the police
- About 110,000 are arrested for alcohol-related violations
- 31% meet the criteria for a diagnosis of alcohol abuse
- 6% meet the criteria for alcohol dependence

You're the best influence on your college-bound child. To decrease your child's chances of alcohol-related problems:

Choose the right school –

- Ask about their alcohol policies
- Ask how they enforce underage drinking prevention
- Ask what counseling services are available
- Ask about alcohol-free dorm/housing arrangements
- Ask if they employ adults or RAs (residential advisors) to monitor dorms
- Ask if there are fraternities or sororities on campus, and inquire about their influence (fraternity and sorority houses have the highest drinking rates)
- Ask if the school offers Friday classes to minimize early weekend party behavior
- Ask about the number of liquor law violations
- Consider the location of the college and how this may affect the atmosphere
- Stay involved
- Keep in touch with what she's doing, especially the first 6 weeks—too much free time can equal too much partying
- Ask if she attended the school's orientation to campus policies
- Ask about her roommates
- Make sure she understands the penalties for underage drinking.

You can find college alcohol policies at: www.collegedrinkingprevention.gov/policies.

MARIJUANA

> (Acapulco Gold or Red, Ace, African, Airplane, Ashes,
> Bammy, Bash, Blonde, Blue Sage, Cannabis Tea, Dry
> High, Finger Lid, Griefs, Light Stuff, Mary Jane, Mu,
> Rip, Weed)

Marijuana is the most used illegal drug in this country, and today's marijuana isn't the same stuff that baby boomers experimented with in their youth. Thinking, "well it did not hurt me, so my kid can use it," can lead to potential disaster. Today's marijuana is four times stronger than what was used in the 1960s. It can seriously interfere with your child's ability to concentrate, or to perform well in school or in sports. Heavy users do even worse in school, often dropping out altogether, and no one knows the long-term health effects of chronic marijuana use.

Marijuana hails as a crude preparation of the Indian hemp plant which grows in most parts of the world. Marijuana's main ingredient is THC, tetrahydrocannabinol, the level of which gives marijuana its potency. Hashish, a potent preparation made from the resin of the plant leaves, may contain up to 14% THC. Most users smoke marijuana; others ingest it.

As a psychoactive drug, the effects of marijuana are influenced by both the user's expectations and past experiences. People use marijuana because it produces euphoria, heightened sensory experiences, and a laid-back feeling. But it also creates increased heart rate and appetite, impaired or reduced short-term memory function and comprehension, disturbed thought patterns, and decreased attention. Motivation and thinking may be altered, making the acquisition of new information difficult. Marijuana gives the user a sense of depersonalization where the mind seems to separate from the body. Long-term users may develop psychological dependence and view the drug as the center of their lives.

Lung damage occurs because users frequently inhale deeply from unfiltered marijuana products and then hold it in their lungs. As few as five joints (marijuana cigarettes) a week exposes the user to as many cancer causing chemicals as smoking a pack of cigarettes every day for a week, and long term male users risk low sperm counts, while females risk menstrual problems.

KHAT

(Chat, Kat, Mirra, Quat, Abyssinian Tea, African Tea, and African Salad)

Khat (pronounced "cot") contains an ephedrine-like compound and comes from the Catha Edulis plant found in eastern Africa and southern Arabia. This natural stimulant is chewed like tobacco, providing a mild cocaine or amphetamine-like euphoria. Used since antiquity as a recreational and religious drug by natives of eastern Africa, the Arabian peninsula, and throughout the Middle East, this drug tends to be popular in the U.S. among immigrants from Yemen, Somalia, and Ethiopia. However, it's illegal here. Compulsive use can result in manic behavior with grandiose delusions, or in a paranoid disorder that may be accompanied by hallucinations. So far it has not become a popular street drug, but a synthetic form called Methcanthinone has been discovered in illegal drug labs.

METHCANTHINONE

(Bathtub Speed, Cadillac, The C, Wild Cat, Wonder Star, Gaggers, Goob, Jeff)

This dangerous and addictive drug is a lovely mix of drain cleaner, battery acid and over-the-counter asthma medication. It's so cheap and easy to make that your child could whip it up in the kitchen sink. Most users snort this drug, but some drink it in coffee or soft drinks, others inject it or smoke it in a crack pipe or in a tobacco or marijuana cigarette. Users also typically use methcathinone in binges that last from two to six days, using the drug repeatedly.

Short-term affects include: feeling of euphoria and increased alertness, loss of appetite, and stimulation of the heart rate and respiration. Due to the newness of this drug, the long-term effects are not yet known. However, reports have demonstrated a range of problems similar to those seen with other stimulant type drugs: anxiety and depression, paranoia, delusions, hallucinations, loss of appetite, weight loss and malnutrition, nose bleeds, tremors, and seizures. Intoxication can result in death, and manufacturing accidents can result in serious injury.

COCAINE

(Cocaine: Angie, Beam, Big C, Big Rush, Candy C, Coke,
Lady, Line, Sleigh Ride, Teenager)
(Crack Cocaine: Apple Jacks, BJs, Badrock, Basing, Coke,
Glo, Groceries, White Ghost)

A stimulant, cocaine is extracted from the leaves of the cocoa bush which grows primarily in South America. It's sold on the streets as a fine, white crystalline powder that is usually diluted with corn starch, sugar, talcum powder, amphetamines, and quinine. The actual cocaine content is usually 5 to 50%, but may be as high as 80%.

Users snort (inhale through a straw, rolled up dollar bill, or coke spoon), freebase (smoke in a water pipe filled with rum instead of water), ball (implant vaginally), or mainline (inject into vein) cocaine to feel its fast, intense effects or "rush." That rush only lasts 5 to 30 minutes and is followed by a crash or a feeling of depression.

Others use the processed, ready-to-smoke form of cocaine known as crack or rock, available in small beads or pellets (rocks). Users smoke crack in a glass pipe or tin can by inhaling the vapor from the heated crack. They may mix it with marijuana or PCP (angel dust), the latter called space blasting. Crack is easier to use and comes in smaller, less expensive doses, and is extremely potent and highly addictive—the user can become addicted with the first use or in a matter of weeks. The user may become paranoid and psychotic as well as violent toward family and friends.

The immediate effects of cocaine include dilated pupils and elevated blood pressure, heart rate, respiratory rate, and body temperature. Occasional use may cause a stuffy or runny nose, while chronic use creates ulcerations in the nasal mucous membrane. Injecting cocaine with a contaminated needle can cause hepatitis, HIV/AIDS, or other diseases. The preparation of freebase, performed with solvents, can result in injury or death from fire or explosion. Sudden death results when large doses of cocaine are absorbed in the bloodstream causing convulsions, respiratory collapse, irregular heartbeat, lack of oxygen to the heart, heart attack, and stroke.

Babies born to cocaine users have multiple defects including facial malformations, organ defects, mental retardation, and low birth weight. Later in life they are at higher risk for Sudden Infant Death Syndrome (SIDS), and possibly learning disorders and conduct problems.

AMPHETAMINES

(Amp, Back Dex, Bennie, Blacks, Brownies, Bumblebees, Co-pilot, Nugget, Sweets)

Sometimes used to curb appetite, amphetamines stimulate the central nervous system so that the user feels more alert, wide-awake, and less fatigued and bored. Less expensive and longer acting than cocaine, methamphetamine (crank, crystal, meth) is snorted, injected, swallowed, or smoked. Acute intoxication causes violent, aggressive behavior or psychotic episodes manifested by paranoia and uncontrollable agitation. Abuse typically starts with an attempt to cope with a temporary situation, like cramming for exams. Tolerance develops, and the user requires larger doses.

Stimulants dilate pupils, decrease appetite, and increase blood pressure, pulse and respiratory rate. Users may also experience sleeplessness, anxiety, headache, blurred vision, sweating, and dizziness. If injected in high doses, amphetamines may cause a sudden rise in blood pressure that could lead to a stroke or heart failure. Injection creates feelings of euphoria and vigor that lasts for hours. Once these feelings wear off, the user experiences feelings of irritability and vague uneasiness. Long-term use creates paranoia, hallucinations, delusions, and incoherence.

SEDATIVES (DEPRESSANTS)

(Barbies, Blues, Downer, Idiot Pills, Nebbies, Strawberries, Tooles, Yellow Jackets)

Three varieties of drugs fall into the sedative category: barbiturates or downers (amobarbital, secobarbital, pentobarbital), tranquilizers (Valium, Xanax, Librium) and nonbarbiturates (placidyl, quaaludes). Rohypnol, the date rape drug, recently found its place in adolescent drug experimentation—it's treated in this book under CLUB DRUGS USED AS DATE RAPE DRUGS.

Sedatives create effects similar to those of alcohol. They reduce anxiety and cause mood changes and drowsiness, impair muscular coordination, and slur speech. Sedatives affect mental functioning, but the degree varies from person to person. Small amounts produce feelings of relaxation, calmness and sleepiness, and relaxed muscles. Large amounts create slurred speech, staggering walk, and altered perception. Large doses can cause respiratory depression, coma, and death. When combined with alcohol, these drugs cause a profound depressant effect, sometimes proving fatal.

Regular use can lead to dependence and addiction. Once the user becomes dependent, abrupt cessation of use can lead to withdrawal symptoms, including anxiety, insomnia, tremors, delirium, convulsions, and death. Babies born to depressant abusers may be dependent on the drugs and show withdrawal symptoms shortly after birth. Birth defects and behavioral problems may also result in children born to addicted mothers.

NARCOTICS

(Heroin: Aries, Bin Laden, Black Pearl, Diesel, Horse, Nice and Easy, Noise, Skag, Smack)
(Opium: Aunti, Big O, Chinese Tobacco, Dreams, O, Pox, Toys, Zero)
(Fentanyl: Apache, China Girl or Town, Dance Fever, Friend, Jackpot, King Ivory)

Legal restrictions did not exist on the importation or use of opium until the early 1900s. In the United States, the unrestricted availability of opium, the influx of opium-smoking immigrants from eastern Asia, and the invention of the hypodermic needle contributed to the more severe variety of compulsive drug abuse seen at the turn of the 20th century. Back then, medicines often contained opium without a warning label. Today there are state, federal, and international laws governing the production and distribution of narcotic substances.

Although opium is used in the form of paragoric to treat diarrhea, most opium imported into the United States is broken down into its alkaloid constituents. Also called opioids, narcotics come in both natural and synthetic forms, and include heroin, morphine, methadone, codeine, and meperidine. Normally prescribed to relieve pain, they become drugs of abuse because of their euphoric effect. Heroin use has decreased over the years, but periodic increases among young users appear occasionally. This, along with its use by rock stars and fashion models—both role models to teenagers—creates concern.

Fentanyl, a potent drug used as both an analgesic and anesthetic, started its illicit use in the mid-1970s and continues to be a problem in the United States. Twelve different analogs of the drug pass through drug traffic in forms for ingestion, injection, and intradermal (skin patch) use. The drug can also be snorted or smoked, making it far too versatile. The effects of the drug include dizziness, light-headedness, weakness, shortness of breath, anxiety, restlessness, and confusion. Other effects and overdose are similar to those seen in heroin and morphine.

Narcotic users initially experience feelings of euphoria, followed by drowsiness, nausea, and vomiting. They may develop constricted pupils, watery eyes, and itching. Overdose produces slow and shallow breathing, clammy skin, convulsions, coma, and possible death. Tolerance develops quickly, and dependence is almost a certainty. Infants born to addicted mothers may be stillborn, premature, or addicted with severe withdrawal symptoms. Users who utilize contaminated needles risk HIV/AIDS, hepatitis, and endocarditis.

CLUB DRUGS

> (LSD: Acid, Animal, Battery Acid, Conductor, Electric Kool Aid, Ghost, Micro Dot, Wedge)
> (MDMA: Bens, Blue Kisses, Clarity, Disco Biscuit, E-bombs, Love Pill, Snackies, Wheels)
> (PCP: Angel Dust, Aurora Borealis, Black Whack, Columbo, Fresh, Horse Tracks, Snorts)
> (Ketamine: Jet, Ket, Kit Kat, Super Acid, Super C, Vitamin K)
> (Mescaline: Buttons, Cactus, Chief, Mesc, Mecz, Moon, Peyote)

Hallucinogens alter the user's feelings, perceptions, and thoughts. Typically ingested or smoked, they include: LSD (lysergic acid diethylamide), STP (dimethoxymethyl amphetamine), DMT (dimethyltryptamine), MDMA (3, 4-methylene-dioxmethamphetamine), PCP (phencyclidine), mescaline, and psilocybin. Also called club drugs, and some "designer drugs," they are popular at "raves" (all-night dance parties usually designed to enhance a hallucinogenic experience through music and lights).

LSD (lysergic acid diethylamide) appears to be having a revival, as rates of use among high school students rose in 1990. In 1995, more than 10% of high school seniors reported trying LSD. Even tiny doses of LSD produce noticeable effects, such as an altered sense of time, visual disturbances, enhanced hearing, mood changes, and distortions on how the user perceives her body. Larger doses cause depersonalization and reality distortions. Some users report flashbacks, perceptual distortions, and bizarre thoughts that occur long after the drug has been eliminated from the body.

PCP (phencyclidine, aka/angel dust, hog, peace pill), interrupts the section of the brain that controls intellect and keeps instincts in check. It creates sensory deprivation and agitation. Users experience a sense of distance and estrangement, as time and body movements slow down and muscular coordination and senses become dulled. Speech becomes blocked and incoherent. Chronic users often experience hallucinations and exhibit paranoid and violent behavior. Because PCP blocks pain receptors, violent episodes can result in self-inflicted injuries. Large doses may cause convulsions and coma, as well as heart and lung failure.

Other hallucinogens also produce hallucinations and illusions, as well as negative physical effects. Ketamine (Special K, New Ecstasy) creates effects similar to PCP, and large doses cause a near-death-like experience. MDMA (Ecstasy, X) causes increased feelings of closeness to other people. The ceremonial drug of the Native American Church, mescaline (peyote) produces different effects than LSD and is quite expensive. Thus most street mescaline is really diluted LSD. Other products that cause hallucinogenic effects include certain mushrooms (psilocybe or magic mushrooms), nutmeg, jimsonweed, and certain morning glory seeds. Luckily, the unpleasant side effects of these botanicals limit their popularity.

CLUB DRUGS ALSO USED AS "DATE RAPE" DRUGS

GAMMA HYDROXY BUTRATE (GHB)

(G, Georgia Home Boy, Scoop, Woman's Viagra, Grievous Body Harm, Easy Lay, Thunder Nectar, Midnight Blue, Serenity, Plant Food, Paint Stripper)

With more than 80 known names, GHB remains a deadly drug that depresses the central nervous system. First synthesized in France as an anesthetic, GHB lost legal status in most countries due to its undesirable side effects. It can be easily manufactured at home with a simple recipe found or purchased on the Internet. Colorless and odorless, GHB has been reported in several cases of date rape because it produces euphoric and disinhibiting effects. It's popular at dance clubs and "rave" parties, and it's used by exotic dancers seeking a "sexier" performance, and by bodybuilders and athletes.

Combined with drugs like alcohol, GHB can produce nausea and difficulty breathing; with higher doses, coma and death may result. GHB can also cause withdrawal symptoms, such as insomnia, anxiety, sweating, and tremors.

ROHYPNOL

(Date Rape Drug, Forget Pill, Roach, Rope, Rophies, Rophy, Ropies, Row-shay, Wolfies)

Rohypnol (flunitrazepam) has created great concern due to its abuse as a date rape drug. The perpetrators, who could be under 18, slip the drug into the intended victim's alcoholic beverage to incapacitate her so that she can't resist—or remember—sexual assault. Ro-hypnol may also be abused personally for its sedative-hypnotic effects, which include muscle relaxation and amnesia. It can also produce physical and psychological dependence, and it can be lethal when mixed with alcohol and/or other depressants.

HERBAL ECSTASY

(Cloud 9, Rave Energy, Ultimate Xphoria, X)

Marketed as a natural high, Herbal Ecstasy is a combination of herbs that are legal, cheap, and potentially deadly. Since it's legal, Herbal Ecstasy can even be found in enticing little packages at the counter in drugstores, music stores, and other shops across the country.

The key drug in Herbal Ecstasy, ephedrine, stimulates the central nervous and cardiovascular systems and may cause serious reactions in youths who have high blood pressure, diabetes, and other conditions. Vulnerable youths can suffer liver damage, seizures, heart attacks, or strokes when taking the drug. Some states have banned its sale following reports of deaths.

**TIPS FOR YOUR TEENS ON CLUB DRUGS
FROM THE NATIONAL INSTITUTE ON DRUG ABUSE**

Club drugs are made in illegal laboratories, so you can't tell how strong they are or what else is in them.

Club drugs destroy brain cells, impairing memory, judgment, sensation, and coordination.

Club drugs damage your body, and can cause blurred vision, loss of muscle control, and seizures.

Club drugs can take away your self-control, causing you to become unconscious and immobilized, and making it easier for others to take advantage of you.

Club drugs can kill you.

ANABOLIC STEROIDS

(Roids, Juice)

A group of powerful compounds developed in the 1930s, anabolic (derived from the Greek word for build up) steroids are closely related to the male sex hormone, testosterone. They are not the same as the steroid medications prescribed for numerous childhood illnesses, such as asthma and inflammatory bowel disease. Anabolic steroids are rarely prescribed today and are usually obtained illegally.

Anabolic steroids are used by teens and adults interested in bodybuilding, because they believe that they contribute to body weight and muscle strength. They want to run faster, jump higher, hit farther, lift heavier weights, or have more endurance. The drugs are taken orally or by injection, usually in cycles of weeks or months (cycling), rather than continuously. Users typically take different types of steroids to maximize their effectiveness and minimize the side effects (stacking).

Steroid abuse can cause serious side effects, including hair loss, jaundice (yellowing of the skin), severe acne, fluid retention, high blood pressure, increased LDL (bad cholesterol) and decreased HDL (good cholesterol), trembling, heart enlargement, heart attacks, strokes, kidney tumors, and liver tumors or cancer. Other side effects are gender or age related:

- Males: baldness, breast enlargement, withering testicles, sterility, impotence, and an increased risk for prostate cancer.
- Females: facial hair growth, male-pattern baldness, deepened voice, breast shrinkage, clitoral enlargement, and changes in or cessation of the menstrual cycle.
- Teenagers: premature halting of growth through early skeletal maturation and accelerated puberty. Thus, teens risk being short for life if they take anabolic steroids prior to their growth spurt.
- Youths who inject steroids also run the risk of contracting and transmitting hepatitis and HIV/AIDS.

Aggression and other psychiatric side effects can develop. Psychological effects include depression and the occurrence of very aggressive behavior, labeled "roid rage," which affects both sexes. Many users also suffer from paranoid jealousy, extreme irritability, delusions, and impaired judgment stemming from feelings of invincibility. Other users turn to other drugs to alleviate the negative effects of steroids, including opioids to counteract irritability and insomnia.

PRESCRIPTION DRUG ABUSE

(ANY PRESCRIPTION DRUG CAN BE ABUSED. THOSE LISTED HERE ARE THE ONES MOST COMMON AT THE TIME OF THIS WRITING. PLEASE KEEP IN MIND THAT SOME OF THE PREVIOUSLY MENTIONED DRUGS ARE ALSO PRE-SCRIPTION MEDICATIONS.)

Addiction rarely occurs in those children who need medication for pain relief or for the treatment of disorders, such as Attention Deficit Hyperactivity Disorder. However, estimates from 1999 note that 2% of the population—or 4 million—ages 12 and over use prescription drugs non-medically. Girls are more likely than boys to abuse prescription drugs, and they are more likely to misuse sedatives, anti-anxiety medications, or hypnotics. They're also twice as likely to become addicted.

OXYCONTIN

(40, 40-bar, Kicker, Killers, OC, Oxy, Oxycotton)

OxyContin, or oxycodone HCL controlled-release, is an opioid analgesic—a narcotic painkiller found in Percodan and Percocet, prescription medications used for arthritis, low back conditions, injuries, and cancer. Unfortunately, it has become popular for abuse these past few years.

Unlike other painkillers that are taken every three to six hours, OxyContin tablets are coated to last 12 hours. Abusers remove the sustained-release coating to get a rush of euphoria similar to that of heroin. They may chew the tablets, crush them for snorting, or even boil them in water for injection.

Common side effects include headache, dizziness, nausea, vomiting, constipation, sweating, dry mouth, weakness, and sedation. When the sustained-release coating is destroyed, a potentially deadly overdose can occur, causing respiratory depression.

RITALIN

(Kibbles and Bits, Pineapple, Vitamin K)

Ritalin (methylphenidate) exerts both a calming effect on hyperactivity and a focusing effect on inattention for children with ADHD, but it's actually a stimulant with effects similar to but less potent than those experienced with amphetamines or cocaine. Children with ADHD don't get addicted to Ritalin—it becomes an abuse problem for people for whom the drug isn't prescribed.

When abused, Ritalin can cause nervousness, insomnia, loss of appetite, weight loss, abdominal pain, nausea and vomiting, dizziness, palpitations, headaches, heart rate and blood pressure changes, itching and skin rash, psychotic episodes, drug dependence, and severe depression on withdrawal. Long-term effects can bring malnutrition, life-threatening heart irregularities, paranoia, hallucinations, and delusions.

STREET TERMS FOR THE DRUG TRADE

TERM	DEFINITION
2-for-1 sale	Promotion to increase crack sales
A-boot	Under the influence of drugs
Abe	$5 worth of drugs
Acid head	Person who uses LSD
Agonies	Withdrawal symptoms
All lit up	Under the influence of drugs
All-star	Person who uses multiple drugs
Amped	High on amphetamines
Amping	Accelerated heartbeat
Are you anywhere?	Do you use marijuana?
Artillery	Equipment for injecting drugs
Author	Doctor who prescribes illegal prescriptions
B-40	Cigar laced with marijuana & dipped in malt liquor
Baby habit	Occasional use of drugs
Back door	Residue left in pipe
Bad bundle	Inferior quality heroin
Bag	Container or package for drugs
Bag man	Person who transports drugs
Bagging	Using inhalants
Banging, Buzz	Under the influence of drugs
Bedbugs	Fellow addicts
Bender	Drug party
Bingo	To inject drugs
Body packer	One who ingests bags of heroin/cocaine for transport
Bong	Pipe used to smoke marijuana
Boost	To steal
Boot	To inject a drug
Break night	All-night cocaine binge
Broker	Go-between in a heavy drug deal
Buffer	Woman who performs oral sex for cocaine
Bull	Narcotics agent or police officer
Burned	Purchased faked drugs
Cafeteria use	Use various drugs simultaneously
Carry	To be in possession of drugs
Channel swimmer	One who injects drugs
Cook down	Process to liquefy heroin for use
Clear up	Stop drug use
Cooker	Person who manufacturers amphetamines
Crash	Sleep off the effects of drugs
Cut	Adulterate drugs
Deuce	$2 worth of drugs

Dinosaurs	Heroin users in their 40s and 50s
Disease	Drug of choice
Dog	Good friend
Dollar	$100 worth of drugs
Dump	Vomiting after taking drugs
Fire	Crack and methamphetamine
Following that cloud	Searching for drugs
G	$1000 or 1 gram of drugs
Get a gift	Obtaining drugs
Get lifted	Under the influence of drugs
Geezer	To inject a drug
Gimmick	Drug injection equipment
Glading	Using inhalant
Gluey	Person who sniffs glue
Give wings	Teach someone to inject
Hand to hand	Direct delivery and payment
Head shop	Store specializing in drug paraphernalia
Hitch up the reindeers	To inhale cocaine
Holding	Possessing drugs
Hot load/shot	Lethal dose of a narcotic
Huffer	Inhalant abuser
Ice cream habit	Occasional use
Jonesing	Need for drugs
Juggler	Teenage street dealer
Junkie	Addict
Kiddie dope	Prescription drugs
Klingons	Crack addicts
Lemonade	Poor quality drugs
Lipton tea	Poor quality drugs
Loused	Covered with sores from injections
Monkey	Drug dependency; cigarette of tobacco and cocaine paste
Make up	Need to find more drugs
Mule	Carrier of drugs
Nickel bag	$5 worth of drugs
Nix	Stranger among the group
On a mission	Searching for crack
Panic	Drug not available
Pepsi habit	Occasional use of drugs
Piggybacking	Injecting two drugs simultaneously
Plant	Hiding place for drugs
Rap	Criminally charged
Raspberry	Girl who trades sex for crack or money to buy crack
Razed	Under the influence of drugs
Res	Potent residue from smoking crack
Roach	Butt of a marijuana cigarette
Rockette	Female who uses crack

Rollers	Police
Runners	People who sell drugs for others
Score	Purchase drugs
Server	Crack dealer
Set	Place where drugs are sold
Sewer	Vein in which drug is injected
Sharps	Hypodermic needles
Shotgun	Inhaling marijuana forced into mouth by another's exhaling
Slanging	Selling drugs
Snotballs	Rubber cement rolled into balls, burned and inhaled
Split	Adulterated drugs
Spoon	1/16 ounce of heroin; paraphernalia used to prepare heroin
Stash	Place to hide drugs
Stoned	Under the influence
Strung out	Heavily addicted to drugs
Swishers	Cigars in which marijuana replaced the tobacco
Tools	Equipment used for injecting drugs
Totally spent	Hangover feeling from MDMA
Tracks	Rows of needle marks
Turned on	Introduced to drugs
Turf	Place where drugs are sold
Twists	Small plastic baggies of heroin with twist-tie
Viper	Marijuana smoker
Wigging	Odd behavior from mind-altering drugs
Working	Selling crack
Works	Equipment for using drugs
Yen sleep	Drowsy state after LSD use
Zombie	PCP; heavy user of drugs
Zonked	Extremely high on drugs

(From the Office of National Drug Control Policy: Drug Policy Information Clearing-house. For more terms and definitions visit: www.whitehousedrugpolicy.gov; 1-800-666-3332).

DRUG-PROOF YOUR CHILD

Nearly half of the middle- and high- school children recently surveyed by the National Center on Addiction and Substance Abuse at Columbia University reported that their parents never talked to them about the dangers of drugs. This "don't ask, don't tell" attitude can prove devastating to your child's health.

No one is immune to alcohol and drug problems. You may be the best parent in the world with the world's greatest kid. But circumstances can put your child in the wrong place at the wrong time. You're your child's most important source of information when it comes to drugs and alcohol. To prevent her from abusing alcohol and drugs, start at an early age, and continue open communication throughout her development.

1. Get the facts. You need to know about drugs and alcohol so that you can provide your child with correct and current information. Know what is out there, and know their effects on the body. Get familiar with the street names of drugs and drug using. Know what drugs look like. Learn the signs of alcohol and drug use, and know how to get help if you suspect that your child is using drugs.

2. Set family standards and rules on drug and alcohol use. Be specific. Explain the rules, what behavior is expected, and what the consequences will be if she breaks them. Be consistent; keep the rules the same at all times—at home, in school, at friends' houses, anywhere she goes. Be reasonable; the punishment should fit the crime—if rules are broken. Make sure to tell her the rules early in grade school and repeat them often.

3. Set an example. Actions speak louder than words, and you will not be too effective telling her not to use tobacco and alcohol when you sit there with a cigarette in one hand and a beer in the other. Follow your own rules, and demonstrate your attitude towards drugs and alcohol. Don't use illicit drugs. Use prescription drugs and other pharmaceuticals properly. Avoid alcohol, but if you do drink, drink responsibly.

4. Let your child know that there are consequences for breaking the rules, and be sure to set up and clarify the consequences before rules are broken.

5. Foster her self-esteem. Strong self-esteem minimizes the chances for your child abusing substances. Help her to set realistic goals for her academic, athletic, social, and other activities. Praise her when she does well and get excited about the things she cares about.

6. Do things as a family. Have family meetings to discuss important family issues, and let her have her say. Discuss responsibilities, hers and yours. Make your home a happy, safe, positive place.

7. Keep the lines of communication open, and create a warm, caring environment that tells her she can come to you whenever

she has questions or wants to talk about her feelings. Make time everyday to talk to her about her life, how her day went, her feelings, and what she thinks. Talk to her about the future. Make sure to listen and show her that you care.

8. Be nosy. Get to know her friends. Ask questions. Know where she's, who she's with, and what she's doing. Make sure she knows that you ask questions because you love her, not because you don't trust her. Limit the time she spends without adult supervision, and realize that the hours between 4 and 6 P.M. are the most dangerous times for her to be on her own. Peer pressure and boredom can too easily lead to an after-school drug habit.

9. Get involved. Know what she learns in school about drugs and alcohol. If they have an antidrug program, join it. Know your neighborhood. Different communities have different trends in drug use.

TALK TO YOUR CHILD ABOUT DRUGS AND ALCOHOL

Be open and straightforward. Remember that more than half of all children try alcohol by the time they reach the eighth grade. Start your discussions early.

UNDER 4:

Attitudes and habits that form during the preschool years may greatly influence your child later on. Little ones may not understand statistics, but they can develop the baseline for the problem-solving and decision-making skills they will have when they get older.

1. Allow her to make small decisions, like what she wants to wear. Don't worry if her choices don't match, just let her know that she's able to make good decisions.
2. Encourage her to help around the house as best she can, and let her know what a big help she is.
3. Be careful about the messages you send. Don't ask her to get you a beer, and then praise her for it. You don't want her to associate drinking with praise.

4 TO 6:

At this age your child still thinks and learns primarily from experience, and she doesn't understand things that will happen in the future. Focus on the present, and people and places she knows.

1. Talk to her about how she has to take medicine when she gets sick because the doctor said so, and therefore, she should only take the medicine that the doctor tells her to take.

2. Instruct her to say no if a stranger offers her candy and to tell you or another adult she trusts about it. Role-play scenarios with you being the stranger to allow her to practice this skill.

3. Watch for teachable moments, such as when you both see someone smoking or drinking on television. Bring up the topic about these chemicals, and that they can harm her body.

6 TO 9:

Your child loves school and the new opportunities that it provides. She loves to learn, but she still learns by experiences and still lives in the present. Keep discussions in the here and now.

1. She will be interested in how her body works so discuss ways to maintain good health (brushing her teeth, washing her hands before eating, and eating nutritious food) and to avoid things that may be harmful (smoking, drugs, drinking to excess).

2. Adults are important role models, and your child is generally trusting, believing that all decisions adults make for her are right. Talk to her about the ones she can trust. Create a file of people she can rely on—with their phone numbers: relatives, family friends, neighbors, teachers, religious leaders, the police and the fire department. Remind her not to talk to strangers.

3. Discuss how advertisers try to persuade children to buy their products, such as toys and candy bars. This will prepare her for the advertising pressures for tobacco and alcohol when she gets older.

4. Talk about the differences between medicine and illicit drugs. Medicine helps her get better, illicit drugs make her sick. However, she should also know that medicines are drugs that can be harmful if misused.

5. Ask if she knows anyone in her school who smokes or uses alcohol or other drugs. Springboard into a basic discussion of the effects of these products, especially tobacco, inhalants, and alcohol. Talk about incidents in the news. For example, in Media, PA, five girls were killed when their car plowed off the road into a utility pole. The girls had been huffing a commercial spray duster used for cleaning keyboards. When tragic events like this happen, use them to start a discussion with your child.

6. Practice ways for your child to say no. Describe simple situations that would make her uncomfortable, like eating live

worms. Practice the following steps to make it easier for her to turn down an offer of alcohol or drugs. Tell her to:

a   Ask questions when something is offered. "What is it, and where did you get it?"

b. Say no. No arguments or discussions. Say no and show them that you mean it.

c. Give a reason if the person persists. The old, "My parents would kill me if I did," line still works today.

d. Suggest other things for them to do when a friend offers alcohol or drugs. Propose going to the movies, working on a project, going to the mall, playing a game or sport. This way she rejects the drugs, not the friend.

e. When all else fails, leave. Get out of the situation. Go home. Go to school. Join a group of friends or talk to someone else.

10 TO 12:

Even more energy goes into learning at this age. Your child loves to learn facts, especially weird ones, and she wants to know how things work and what sources of information are available to her. Friends become very important, and her interests will be greatly influenced by what her peer group thinks. Her self-image is partly determined by the extent to which she's accepted by her friends. Because of this, if she's a follower, she may be unable to make independent decisions and choices. Keep her out of the follower position by teaching her decision-making skills.

Preadolescence is the most important time to focus on drug and alcohol prevention. Crucial decisions about drugs and alcohol crop up at this age. Your child is at the greatest risk to start smoking in the sixth or seventh grade, and research shows that the earlier children start to use alcohol or drugs, the more likely they are to have a real problem.

1. Give her a clear no-use message, factual information, and strong motivation to resist the pressures to use drugs and alcohol. Provide the following information:

    a. how to identify specific drugs, including alcohol, tobacco, inhalants, marijuana, and cocaine, in all their various forms

    b. the short and long term effects of substances and the con sequences of their use, including criminal prosecution

since drugs are illegal, as is drinking alcohol under the age
of 21

   c.   the effects of drugs on the growing body

   d.   the effects of drug and alcohol abuse on the family and
      society

2. Encourage your child to participate in positive activities. Limit
"free-time," which often leads to experimentation with alcohol
and other drugs.

3. Discuss the advertising pressures of drugs and alcohol, not for-
getting TV shows and song lyrics that glorify their use. Separate
the myths from the realities.

4. Continue to practice ways of saying no. Sixth graders are
offered cigarettes and beer, and most of them know other children who smoke and drink.

5. Encourage her to join a school or local antidrug group, or peer
assistance group that encourages drug-free activities.

6. Scan the newspaper or news with your child and discuss drug-
related crime. Talk about the influence it has on society and
individuals.

7. Get together with her friends' parents so that you can reinforce
each others' efforts to teach good personal and social habits.

13 TO 14:

Your young teen begins to deal with abstractions and the
future. She understands that actions have consequences, and she
knows that her behaviors affect others. She still has a shaky self-image
that is strongly influenced by friends, causing her to be unsure
whether she's normal. She's often in conflict with you, isn't sure
where she's heading, and tends to see herself as "not okay." This
rocky ground paves the way for experimentation. Young people who
use drugs including alcohol typically begin during this age period.

1. Emphasize the immediate effects of drug use, not what will
happen over time. Instead of talking about lung cancer, tell her
about bad breath, yellow teeth and burned clothes.

2. Bring up the topic of steroids. You can start by discussing their
use by professional sports players. Talk about their negative
effects, and discuss body image issues.

3. Offset peer influence with parent influence. Reinforce your no-
use rules. When she counterattacks with "but everyone else
does it," inform her that everyone doesn't do it. Emphasize
how unpredictable drug use can be, that even though some

users appear to function properly, drug use remains risky and that their effects may not always be readily apparent.

4. Make sure she knows the following:
    a. the characteristics of specific drugs and drug interactions (such as deadly effects of mixing sedatives and alcohol)
    b. the effects of drugs on the cardiac, respiratory, nervous, and reproductive systems
    c. the stages of chemical dependency and how they vary from person to person
    d. the way drugs affect daily activities such as driving and sports participation
    e. your family history, especially if alcoholism or drug addiction is a problem
5. Monitor her whereabouts.
6. Role play several variations on how to say no until you're confident she knows how.
7. Continue to spend private time with her to allow her to discuss her fears and feelings.
8. Review and revise household rules on issues such as chores and curfews. Reinforce the rules on drugs and alcohol.
9. Plan supervised no-alcohol parties for your child in your home. Similar adult parties set good examples.
10. Discuss friendships, and make a point of stressing that real friends don't ask each other to do things that are wrong or harmful.

14 TO 17:

Peer influence remains strong, but your child develops an increasingly realistic understanding of adults. She begins to develop a broader outlook on life, and she becomes more interested in the welfare of others.

1. Focus on the long-term effects of alcohol and other drugs during these years. They can ruin her chance of getting into college, being hired for certain jobs, and being accepted into the military.
2. Remind her that she serves as a role model for her younger siblings.
3. Minimize her unsupervised hours at home. Lunchtime and after school (3 P.M. to 6 P.M.) are times that teens are likely to experiment.

4. Encourage her to volunteer to help out at a drug prevention program or a hot-line call service, or to volunteer as a peer counselor.

5. Keep her busy with school, sports, clubs, volunteer work, religious activities, trips to museums and the library, film festivals, work, arts and craft—anything constructive. Plan activities for vacation and holiday times. The busier she is, the less chance for her to get bored and seek an outlet in drugs.

6. Cooperate with other parents to keep get-togethers and parties drug and alcohol free.

7. Discuss drinking and driving. Chances are she will drive herself or have friends who drive, and she will know other kids who use alcohol and other drugs. Talk about the legal issues, and impress the possibility of an accident where someone, including herself, may get killed.

8. Draw up a written contract on the conditions of using the car, and have her sign it. Promise to pick her up, no questions asked at any time, when she or the person who is giving her a ride is under the influence. Promise not to scream or yell, and say that you will talk about it the next day.

9. Set consequences for substance use in your car—her use or her friends.

10. If your child is giving a party or going to a party, follow the suggestions of the American Academy of Pediatrics:

If she's planning a party, plan ahead. Let her plan the guest list activities, but go over them with her. Keep it small, no more than 10 to 15 teens, and provide adult supervision without being intrusive. Set a time limit, restrict attendance to invited guests only, and don't allow people to leave the party and then return. Make rules—no tobacco, alcohol, or other drugs; lights on at all times; certain rooms are off limits—and stick to them. Realize that you're legally responsible for anything that happens to a minor who is served alcohol or other drugs at your home, and discuss this with your teen. If any teen arrives to the party intoxicated, call her parents to make sure she gets home safely.

If your child is going to a party, call the host's parents to verify they know about it. Ascertain that there will be no tobacco, alcohol, or other drugs at the party, and that a supervising adult will be present. Know where she's going; have the phone number and address handy, and ask her to call you if the location changes. Make sure you let her

know where you will be during the party in case she needs
to contact you. Be sure she has a way to get home. Let her
know she can call you for a ride at any time, and that she
NEVER rides with someone who has been drinking
alcohol or using other drugs. Finally, make sure you greet
her when she gets home so you can check the time, note her
sobriety level, and talk about the evening.

18 TO 21:

At this point she should be thinking more like an adult and
looking forward to a productive lifestyle. However, she still needs
your direction. Continue to discourage drug use, and promote responsible attitudes toward alcohol. Your budding young adult can enjoy her
leisure time without alcohol or drugs. Discuss the consequences of
drugs and alcohol, especially binge drinking.

Encourage responsible drinking when she reaches age 21. Tell
her to eat before drinking and never drink on an empty stomach; food
slows alcohol absorption. She should drink slowly, sip rather than
gulp, and absolutely avoid binge drinking. She should avoid carbonat-
ed mixers, especially when thirsty, because these drinks are more likely to be gulped. At parties, she should drink nonalcoholic drinks or
alternate alcoholic beverages with nonalcoholic ones. Most important-
ly, she should know her limit.

HOW TO TELL IF YOU CHILD IS USING DRUGS

Sometimes it's difficult to know the difference between normal teenage behavior and behavior caused by drugs. If your child
exhibits behavioral changes that are extreme or that last for more than
a few days, consider the possibility that she's abusing drugs.

The following suggest substance abuse in teens; however,
some may indicate a behavioral or psychological problem other than
drug use. Either way, get help.

1. Changes in personality, especially if sudden: lack of empathy,
    less affectionate, apathetic, withdrawn, apathetic, sullen, less
    attentive, depressed, irritable, uncooperative, unpredictable,
    easily provoked, hostile.
2. Becomes irresponsible. Forgets important occasions; doesn't
    do chores or homework; frequently late for school.

3. Secretive behaviors about personal possessions such as dresser drawers, pocketbook, or backpack.

4. Loss of interest in usual hobbies or activities. No longer participates in family activities, school or church functions, sports, or organizational activities.

5. Change in personal appearance; becomes deteriorated or imitates drug-related music stars (such as heavy metal). Dresses in T-shirts, belt buckles, jewelry, or other apparel with drug logos, or has magazines or bumper stickers with drug logos.

6. Change in vocabulary or music tastes to resemble drug culture.

7. Irregular school attendance and/or decreased school performance without a valid reason. You child may claim that her performance is poor due to boredom, not caring about school, or disliking her teacher. Be suspicious if she's unconcerned that her grades drop dramatically.

8. Becomes difficult to communicate with; refuses to talk about friends, school, or activities. Changes conversations to talk about adult bad habits, and/or defends rights of youths and/or use of drugs.

9. Change in friends, and new friends are unkempt and/or abrasive. Secretive about friends.

10. Behaves irrationally; reckless driving; explosive rage episodes.

11. Rebellious behavior; disrespect for authority, persistent lying; antisocial behaviors without remorse.

12. Preoccupation with the occult or cults, Satanism, witchcraft. Tattoos or drawings of satanic symbols such as "666," pentagrams, or upside down crosses.

13. Child can't or won't account for where all her money goes.

14. Missing household money, credit cards, checks, jewelry, heirlooms, other items of value.

15. Presence of drug paraphernalia: whiskey/beer bottles, marijuana plants or seeds, rolling papers, clips, hemostats, pipes (homemade pipes can even be made out of a glass jar with some aluminum foil on top), drug buttons, mirrors, small medicine bottles, eyedroppers, butane lighters, and razor blades.

16. Has physical signs: pale face, red eyes, dilated pupils; chews heavily scented gum; uses heavy cologne, aftershave or perfumes; hypersensitive to touch, taste, or smell; weight loss alone or despite increased appetite.

17. Has mental signs: disordered or illogical thinking; decreased ability to remember things; severe lack of motivation; rapid thought pattern.

18. Shows signs of specific drug use as noted in box.

SIGNS OF SPECIFIC DRUG USE

DRUG	SIGNS
ALCOHOL	Odor of alcohol on breath Unsteady gait Slurred speech Impaired judgment Loss of inhibitions Quarrelsomeness Aggressiveness Hostility
INHALANTS	Sits with pen or marker near nose Constantly smelling clothing sleeves Hides rags or empty containers Paint or stains on face, finger, or clothes Spots or sores around the mouth Red or runny eyes or nose Chemical odor on breath Nausea, loss of appetite Excitability/irritability Dazed appearance
MARIJUANA	Bloodshot eyes Dry mouth (excessive thirst) Increased appetite Difficulty concentrating Euphoria Mild intoxication Drowsiness
COCAINE	Dilated pupils Insomnia Loss of appetite Restlessness Hyperactivity Runny nose, nasal ulcerations Track marks (needle marks)

STIMULANTS

Dilated pupils
Decreased appetite
Insomnia
Moodiness
Restlessness
Anxiety
Agitation/hyperactivity
Increased alertness

DEPRESSANTS

Slurred speech
Staggering walk
Short attention span
Impaired judgment
Hyperexcitability (methaqualone)

NARCOTICS

Constricted pupils
Watery eyes
Itching
Drowsiness
Track marks (needle marks)

CLUB DRUGS

Hallucinations or other altered
  perceptions
Loss of appetite; increased
  appetite
Sleeplessness
Confusion
Panic, suspicion
Flashbacks

**DESIGNER DRUGS
(MDMA, MPTP)**

Nausea
Blurred vision
Chills or sweating
Faintness
Anxiety
Depression
Paranoia

```
┌─────────────────────────────────────────────────────────────┐
│  ANABOLIC STEROIDS                                          │
│                              Quick weight and muscle gain   │
│                              Aggressiveness and combative-  │
│                                ness                         │
│                              Jaundice                       │
│                              Unexplained darkening of the skin │
│                              Red or purple spots on the body │
│                              Swelling of hands and lower legs │
│                              Trembling                      │
│                              Unpleasant breath odor         │
│                                                             │
└─────────────────────────────────────────────────────────────┘
```

WHAT TO DO IF YOU SUSPECT YOUR CHILD IS USING DRUGS

Drug use may take place right in your own home, especially inhalant abuse, since so many of the abused inhalants are household products. If you suspect your child is sniffing or if you catch her in the act:

1. Stay calm and don't panic.
2. Don't excite or argue with her while she's under the influence. Excitement or stimulation can cause her to hallucinate or become violent.
3. If she's unconscious, call 911 (or use whatever mechanism necessary in your area to obtain emergency ambulance services), and start CPR. If you don't know CPR, learn it now—don't wait for an emergency like this or any other type. Contact your local emergency service, hospital, or the American Red Cross for the CPR class nearest you.
4. Don't stress her or create any unnecessary activity, because it can cause heart problems which may lead to Sudden Sniffing Death.
5. Find out what she used. Ask friends or family members who may have witnessed what she used, or look around the area for the evidence—brown paper or plastic bag, aerosol cans, etc.
6. Once she recovers, be frank and discuss the problem, and seek professional help as described below.

No matter the drug, and even when signs are clear, it's usually difficult for parents to admit that their child has a drug problem. You may feel anger, resentment, guilt, or a sense of failure as a parent. If your child is abusing substances, you first must admit it, and avoid blaming yourself for the problem.

You need to confront your child, but not while she's under the influence of alcohol or drugs. Wait until she's sober. Then discuss your suspicions firmly, calmly, and objectively. Bring in other family members to help, if needed. Impose whatever disciplinary measures you had decided on for violating the rules and stick to it. Whatever you do, don't give in because she promises to never do it again.

Many teenagers lie about their drug and alcohol use. If you think she's being dishonest and the evidence is strong, you may want to consider having her evaluated by an experienced professional, one who specializes in adolescents with substance abuse problems.

If your child has developed a pattern of drug or alcohol abuse, or if she's engaged in heavy usage, get professional help. If you're unsure of drug and alcohol treatment professionals or treatment centers in your area, consult with your doctor, nurse practitioner, religious leader, local hospital, or county medical or mental health association for a referral. Call the nearest college or university and ask their counseling department. Most school districts have substance abuse counselors or coordinators who can also refer you to treatment programs. Finally, you can ask other parents whose children were treated for substance problems for information.

RESOURCES AND ORGANIZATIONS

ALCOHOLICS ANONYMOUS: Fellowship of men and women who share their experiences to solve the problem of alcoholism and to help other alcoholics achieve sobriety. Check your phone book for the chapter nearest you.

AL-ANON: Resource for family and friends of alcoholics. Check your phone book for the chapter nearest you.

AMERICAN COUNSEL FOR DRUG EDUCATION: Provides information on drug use and offers films and curriculum materials for preteens. 1-800-488-DRUG/301-294-0600

FAMILIES ANONYMOUS: Offers 12-step program for family and friends of people with behavioral problems usually associated with drug abuse. Similar to Alcoholics Anonymous. 818-989-7841

INSTITUTE ON BLACK CHEMICAL ABUSE: Provides training and technical assistance to programs that want to serve African-American clients and other people of color. 612-871-7878

NAR-ANON: Similar to Al-Anon to provide support for family and friends of people with drug problems. 810-547-5800

NARCOTICS ANONYMOUS: Similar to Alcoholics Anonymous, a fellowship of men and women who meet to help each other with their drug dependency problems. 818-780-3951

NATIONAL CLEARING HOUSE FOR ALCOHOL AND DRUG INFORMATION: Resource for alcohol and other drug information. 1-800-SAY-NOTO/301-468-2600

TOLL-FREE HOTLINES

1-800-COCAINE–A COCAINE HOTLINE: Round-the-clock information and referral service.

1-800-NAC-CALL–NATIONAL COUNCIL ON ALCO-HOLISM INFORMATION LINE: provides referral service to families and individuals seeking help for alcohol and other drug problems.

1-800-622-HELP—NIDA HOTLINE: Referral service for cocaine users.

3

EXTREME WEATHER

WASHINGTON, DC, 1999:
2 ½-year-old boy dies after being left in a van on a hot day.

SOME STATS

National Weather Service's report of fatalities and injuries caused by severe weather in 2001:

Weather Event	Fatalities	Injuries
Lightning	44	371
Tornado	40	743
Thunderstorm wind	17	341
Hail	0	32
Extreme cold	4	0
Extreme heat	166	445
Floods	48	277
Coastal storms	53	96
Tsunami	0	0
Hurricane/Tropical storm	24	7
Winter storm	18	173
Drought	0	0
Mudslide	0	0
Volcanic ash	0	0

Fatalities by gender and age:

	Female	Male
0 to 9	10	16
10 to 19	17	28

If you think the weather has been a lot worse lately, you're right.

Natural disasters affect the lives of many thousands of people, including children, every year. Within minutes, a natural disaster can rip apart your home and community, changing your lives forever. However, people who understand disasters and know what to do before and after disaster strikes can significantly reduce disaster deaths and injuries, as well as property damage.

Extreme weather is part of life for most of us. Californians struggle with earthquakes, while northeasterners literally plow though winter storms. Others face tornadoes, hurricanes, floods, mudslides, and wildfires. Some even face volcanoes and tsunamis.

Whatever the weather event you face, all families should have access to weather information, preferably information that is current. A National Oceanic and Atmospheric Administration (NOAA) weather Radio—with a battery backup and a tone-alert feature that automatically alerts you when a watch or warning is issued—is a great way to receive the most up-to-date weather information. The NOAA provides continuous broadcasts of the latest weather information from local National Weather Service offices. They repeat weather reports every 4 to 6 minutes and routinely update them every 1 to 3 hours, or more frequently if a nearby hazardous environmental condition exists or the weather changes rapidly. Most of these stations operate 24 hours daily. For further information, or to check warnings online, go to: www.nws. noaa.gov.

GENERAL SAFETY TIPS

Always be prepared. Create a family disaster plan, determine a safe place to go when needed, and have your disaster kit ready. Refer to Chapter 29 to learn more on how to be prepared for disasters, including how to create your disaster kit.

Take a basic first aid course and learn CPR. If you have already completed these, take refresher courses to keep yourself current. Your knowledge of CPR and first aid may mean the difference between life and death when disaster strikes.

Work together with your neighbors to create a plan to protect each others' children in the event of a disaster, and discuss disaster preparation with your neighborhood watch or neighborhood association group. Plan for child care, pet care, and the care of elders and people with disabilities. And make sure your child knows where to go in case of emergency.

DETERMINING THREAT

How do you know the potential for severe weather on a given day? When conditions become favorable for severe weather, a severe thunderstorm or tornado advisory is issued. Here is the difference between watch and warning, from the NOAA.

WATCH means conditions are ripe for severe weather and severe weather is possible, but not definite. You should monitor local weather conditions for rapid changes and be prepared to act quickly when a warning is issued.

WARNING indicates that severe weather is imminent or that a tornado has been sighted by doppler radar or human observation. Remain calm, but move quickly to a safe shelter. Follow instructions given by the local media, and make sure you have access to the latest information via a NOAA or portable radio.

DROUGHT

Although no deaths or injuries from drought were reported in 2001, drought bears mention, since much of the western part of the country is in a severe to extreme drought at this writing, and the eastern part of the country recently experienced a moderate drought problem. Droughts are also underestimated because they have a slow rate of onset and less visual impact than other weather hazards. Yet, the long-term outcome of a drought can be very devastating.

Drought means that there is a water supply shortage—water supplies are less than the demand. The greater the demand, the more serious the drought. Droughts lower ground and reservoir levels, expose shoreline, and impair fish and wildlife habitats. Extended dry weather increases the risk of fires, and water quality problems may develop, especially if bacterial or other contaminants affect water supplies. Water costs increase, and public officials may need to enforce water usage restrictions.

TO CONSERVE WATER:

- Flush toilets less frequently. If possible, purchase and install water-saving toilets.
- Take short showers and avoid tub baths.
- Install water-saving shower heads.
- Put a bucket in your shower to collect water for your plants.
- Don't let the water run while shaving, brushing your teeth, washing your face or hair, handwashing clothes, or washing dishes.
- Use dishwashers and washing machines only when full.

- When handwashing dishes, use a basin to wash and rinse them.
- Use garbage disposals sparingly.
- Repair leaky faucets and toilets.
- Water gardens between 7 and 10 A.M. and only when needed.
- Don't water the lawn—brown grass is only dormant.
- Mulch gardens to hold more moisture.
- Keep water in the refrigerator instead of running it until cold.
- Consider installing an automatic water heater instead of running it until hot.
- Never waste water—save it for watering plants or cleaning.
- Avoid using recreational water toys or fountains that create constant water flow.
- Use a commercial car wash to clean your vehicles.

EARTHQUAKES

The shaking ground of an earthquake is caused by the sudden breaking and shifting of large sections of the earth's rocky outer shell. Earthquakes are among the most powerful—and terrifying—events on earth, and a severe earthquake can release energy 10,000 times as great as that of the first atomic bomb.

An earthquake's force depends on how much rock breaks and how far it shifts. Powerful quakes can violently rattle firm ground for great distances. Yet, minor earthquakes cause vibrations that may be no greater than the shaking caused by a passing truck. Powerful quakes typically occur less than once every two years, with about 40 moderate quakes causing damage somewhere on earth each year. Scientists calculate that more than 8,000 minor quakes occur each day without causing damage, and only about 1,100 of these are strong enough to be felt.

Earthquakes can cause rock movements that make rivers change their course and landslides that cause great damage and loss of life. Large earthquakes beneath the ocean may create a series of vast, destructive waves called tsunamis (soo-NAH-meez) that flood coasts for miles.

Earthquakes rarely kill people directly. Death and injury result from falling objects and the collapse of buildings, bridges, and other structures. Other concerns include fire resulting from broken gas or power lines, and spills of hazardous chemicals.

According to the Federal Emergency Management Agency (FEMA), earthquakes occur most frequently west of the Rocky

Mountains. Most people equate California with earthquakes, but the state with the most major earthquakes is Alaska. The granddaddy of earthquakes occurred along the New Madrid Fault in Missouri where a 3-month-long series of quakes in 1811 and 1812 included three quakes that were felt over 2 million square miles.

All 50 states and all U.S. territories are vulnerable to earthquakes. At least 41 states or territories are at moderate to high risk. Generally, wherever earthquakes occurred in the past, they will happen again in the future. To learn whether earthquakes are a risk in your area, contact your local emergency management office, American Red Cross chapter, state geological survey, or department of natural resources.

IF YOU LIVE IN AN EARTHQUAKE-PRONE AREA, PLAN AHEAD. ELIMINATE POTENTIAL HAZARDS:

- Bolt bookcases, hutches, china cabinets, and other tall furniture to the wall, preferably to studs.
- Move heavy hanging objects, such as plants and pictures, away from chairs and beds.
- If you have mirrors on the walls, make sure they are fastened properly.
- Attach heavy wall clocks to studs.
- Move beds away from large windows.
- Don't hang lights or fans over beds, unless they can be secured with extra wire or chains.
- Fasten cabinet doors with latches.
- Strap the water heater to the wall studs.
- Replace rigid gas stove feed line with a flexible connector.
- Brace outside chimney to the house.
- Make sure your home's foundation is bolted.
- Keep your disaster kits ready.

SHOULD A QUAKE OCCUR:

When shaking begins:

- Drop, cover, and hold on. Stay indoors, away from windows, until you're sure it's safe to go outside.
- If you're in bed, stay there and hold on, protecting your head with pillows.

- If you're outside, find a clear spot away from buildings, trees, and power lines, and drop to the ground.
- If you're in your car, slowly drive to a clear place and stay in your car until the shaking stops.

After the shaking stops:

- Check yourself and your children for injuries. Provide first aid, if needed.
- Protect you and your family from further harm by putting on long-sleeved shirts, long legged pants, work gloves, and sturdy shoes.
- Check for and extinguish small fires. Turn off the gas if you suspect a leak.
- Check your home for damage. If your house is unsafe, get everyone out.
- Listen to the radio for further instructions.
- Only use your phone for emergencies.
- Expect aftershocks—the smaller earthquakes that follow the main shock and can cause further damage to weakened buildings. Aftershocks can occur in the first hours, days, weeks, or even months after the quake.
- Realize that some earthquakes are actually foreshocks, and a larger earthquake might occur.

FLOODS

Floods are weather's biggest killer. Floods, particularly flash floods, kill more people each year than tornadoes, hurricanes, high winds, or lightning. More than half of all deaths occur when vehicles are swept away by moving water. Driving into apparently shallow water could land a vehicle in water two or three feet deep and float it away.

Floods are a part of life for people living along rivers. They occur seasonally with torrential rains associated with tropical storms. General flooding can also occur in urban areas with poor drainage after a heavy rain.

Flash floods result from heavy localized rainfall, usually from a slow moving thunderstorm. They typically rise from small creeks and streams that overflow and become raging torrents through city streets, and even river beds, canyons, valleys, and coastal sections, sweeping everything with them. Flash floods tend to occur within six hours of the heavy rain.

A report in *USA Today* demonstrated that specific factors help determine whether a flood is minor or major:

1. Deep snow cover can melt into a large amount of water; however, it rarely causes flooding by itself. Typically, heavy rains and rapid warm-ups combine with melting snow to cause major floods.

2. Frozen ground can't absorb water, thus intense rain and snow melt may cause flooding.

3. Saturated soil can't absorb water. Excess water becomes runoff that quickly flows into rivers and streams.

4. Full reservoirs can't absorb water from swollen rivers.

5. High river and stream levels become a precursor to flooding when they are at bankfull. Heavy rain or snow melt into an already full river causes it to overflow and flood nearby locations.

6. Ice-covered rivers create problems when the ice surface breaks into chunks that flow downstream. The chunks form a dam when they run into barriers, causing the water to rise rapidly behind them, and possibly causing flooding in upstream locations. If the dam suddenly breaks, the downstream areas may flood.

7. Widespread heavy rain is the most influential factor of all, because long periods of rain can cause flooding even in the absence of all other factors. Heavy rain can also cause some of the other factors.

The National Weather Service issues flood and flash flood advisories:

FLOOD (takes hours or days to develop):

WATCH: Flood is possible in your area. Be alert and prepared for possible flood emergency. Fill jugs, tubs, and sinks with water in case the water supply becomes contaminated. Bring outdoor belongings indoors. Move your furniture and valuables to higher floors in your home, and fill up your car's gas tank in case evacuation becomes necessary.

WARNING: Flooding is already occurring or will occur soon. Evacuate if told to do so.

FLASH FLOOD (can develop in a few minutes):

WATCH: Heavy rains may result in flash flooding in a specific area. Be alert and prepared for the possibility of a flood emergency which will require immediate action.

WARNING: Flash flooding is occurring or is imminent in a specific area. Move to safe ground if it's your area. Don't drive around barricades; they are there for your safety.

SHOULD YOU AND/OR YOUR CHILDREN LIVE IN A FLOOD-PRONE AREA, FOLLOW THESE SAFETY RULES:

- Know your area's flood risk—check with your local Red Cross chapter, emergency management office, or planning and zoning board if you're unsure. Ask if your property is above or below flood stage level, and learn about the history of flooding in your area.
- Practice an evacuation route to the safest shelter. Have several alternative routes.
- Stock up on emergency building materials, such as plywood, plastic sheeting, lumber nails, hammer, saws, shovels, and sandbags.
- If it has been raining heavily for several hours or steadily for several days, be alert for possible flooding.
- Install check valves in building sewer traps to prevent floodwater from backing up into sewer drains.
- Flash floods can occur without warning in hilly terrains, because distant rains can channel into gullies and ravines, changing a quiet stream into a raging gush in minutes. Don't camp on low ground near streams, since a flash flood could catch you in your sleep.
- Don't cross flowing streams on foot where the water is above your ankles.
- When driving, don't try to cross water-filled streets of unknown depths. If your car stalls, get out and get to higher ground immediately.
- Don't attempt to move vehicles stalled in water. This is a main cause of flood-related deaths.
- Don't try to outrun a flood on foot. Get to higher ground immediately if you see a flood coming.
- Be careful at night because water dangers are harder to recognize.

- Become familiar with land features where you live and work, and where your child attends school or plays. Any of these may be a low area, near a drainage ditch or small stream, or below a dam. Always be prepared.
- Stay tuned to your NOAA radio for the latest weather news.

Unfortunately, flood dangers persist after the water begins to recede. Damaged property and contaminated supplies continue to place your children in danger. To keep them safe after a flood, remain home or in your safe place until authorities indicate it's safe to leave, and follow these suggestions by the American Red Cross, SafeChild. net, the Consumer Product Safety Commission, and the Electrical Safety Foundation International:

1. When entering the building, wear sturdy shoes and use a flashlight.
2. Inspect your home's foundation for cracks and other damage. Check walls, floors, windows, and doors to make sure the building isn't in danger of collapsing. Beware of loose plaster and ceilings that can fall. If you have any doubt—don't enter the building!
3. Check for fire hazards, including submerged furnaces or electrical appliances, or flammable/explosive materials coming upstream. If any exist, get out, go to a safer place and contact your utility company or emergency service.
4. Watch for animals, especially poisonous snakes, that may have come into your home with the floodwater. Use a large stick to poke your way through the debris.
5. Air out the house to dry it and prevent mold from developing.
6. Throw out food, even canned goods that come into contact with floodwater.
7. Pump water from basement gradually—about one-third per day—to prevent structural damage.
8. Service damaged septic tanks, cesspools, and leaching systems as soon as possible because damaged sewer systems can become health hazards.
9. Carefully inspect for damage to your utilities. If uncertain, contact the utility office.
10. Don't use electrical appliances or toys that have been wet. Water can damage the motors, causing them to shock or overheat and catch fire.
11. Have affected electrical appliances and toys serviced by a qualified repairperson.

12. Check the wiring before flipping on any switches.
13. Use portable GFCIs (ground fault circuit interrupters) to help prevent electric shock. Buy these ahead of time and keep them with your disaster supplies.
14. Water damages circuit breakers and fuses, as well as GFCIs. Discard all that have been submerged.
15. Follow the manufacturer's instructions when using wet-dry vacuums or pressure washers to prevent electric shock.
16. Don't allow power cord connections to get wet, and never remove or bypass the ground pin on three-prong plugs.

HEAT WAVES

The term heat wave indicates a prolonged period of excessive heat and humidity. The National Weather Service typically alerts the public to these periods. The heat index is a number in degrees (Fahrenheit) that tells how hot it actually feels when relative humidity is added to the actual temperature. Full sunshine exposure can increase the heat index by as much as 15 degrees.

Most humans control their body temperature through sweating and radiating heat through the skin. However, under extreme circumstances, such as unusually high temperature or humidity, or vigorous exercise in hot weather, this system can fail, allowing body heat to build up to dangerous levels, causing heat cramps, exhaustion and even heat stroke. Children, particularly those with respiratory and heart conditions, are even more susceptible to heat-induced problems.

Heat cramps are muscle spasms and pains that occur during or after vigorous exercise. They tend to be brief and are not serious, but they are a sign that the body is having trouble handling heat. Children are especially susceptible to heat cramps when they don't drink enough fluids. Heat cramps rarely need treatment and usually respond well to rest, fluids, and a cool environment.

Heat exhaustion occurs when people work or exercise heavily in a hot, humid place where significant amounts of body fluids are lost through sweating. Blood flow increases to the skin and decreases to vital organs, resulting in a mild form of shock. Symptoms include dehydration, fatigue, weakness, and clammy skin. Your child may also suffer headache, or nausea and vomiting. Left untreated, heat exhaustion can turn into heatstroke.

If your child shows signs of heat exhaustion, bring him to a cool place immediately and encourage fluids. Loosen or remove his clothing, and give him a bath in cool (not cold) water. Call your health care provider for further instructions. If your child is too ill to eat or drink, he may need intravenous fluids.

Heatstroke is the most severe form of heat illness and it's a life-threatening emergency. It causes the body to lose its ability to regulate its own temperature. Your child's body temperature can soar to 105 degrees or higher, leading to brain damage or death if not treated promptly. Factors that can increase your child's risk for heatstroke include inadequate fluid intake with excessive exercise or overdressing during hot weather. Heatstroke can also occur when a child is left in a car on a hot day—even for a few minutes. Car temperature can soar to 125 degrees in minutes when the outside temperature is 93 degrees.

Call for emergency assistance if your child shows any of the signs of heatstroke:

> Hot, red skin
> Changes in his level of consciousness (drowsiness, confusion, irritability)
> Loss of consciousness
> Rapid, shallow breathing
> Seizure
> Temperature of 105 or more

As with most hazards, the best way to treat heat illness is to prevent it.

TRY THESE SUGGESTIONS TO PROTECT YOUR CHILD DURING HEAT WAVES:

- DON'T LEAVE CHILDREN OR PETS IN PARKED CARS ON HOT DAYS.
- Dress your child in lightweight, light-colored clothing. Light colors reflect some of the sun's energy away from your child's body.
- Stay out of the heat, especially during the hottest times of day (usually between mid-morning and mid-afternoon).
- Use an air conditioner. If you can't, stay in the coolest part of the house, keep it shaded and use fans. You can also go to air-conditioned public buildings or malls periodically to cool down.

- Make sure your child avoids vigorous activity or that he does it during the coolest part of the day (4A.M. to 7A.M.). If your child is young, or if he has a chronic heart or lung condition, don't allow him to participate in sports or exercise during a heat wave, especially when the humidity is high.
- Make sure he drinks plenty of water. Don't wait until he is thirsty—that is a sign of dehydration.
- Avoid salt tablets and caffeine.
- Have him eat small, frequent meals, instead of three large ones.
- Keep track of how long your child is outside, and use common sense to get him out of the sun when you think it's necessary.
- High humidity and heat still pose problems at the beach or pool. Use proper sunscreen and make sure your child spends enough time in the shade.

HURRICANES

A hurricane is a type of tropical cyclone—a term used for all circulating weather systems over tropical waters. They are classified as follows:

Tropical Depression indicates an organized system of thunderstorms and clouds with a defined circulation and maximum sustained winds of 38 mph or less.

Tropical Storm refers to an organized system of thunderstorms and clouds with a defined circulation and maximum sustained winds of 39 to 73 mph.

Hurricane designates an intense tropical weather system with a well-defined circulation and maximum sustained winds of 74 mph or higher. In the western Pacific they are referred to as typhoons, and in the Indian Ocean they are called cyclones.

Hurricanes begin to form around mid-May in the Pacific and June in the Atlantic, with the peak hurricane season in the U.S. running from mid-August to late October, even though the official hurricane season extends through November.

Hurricanes are categorized by the Saffir-Simpson Hurricane Scale on a scale from 1 to 5:

1 = Winds 74-95 mph with minimal damage
2 = Winds 96-110 mph with moderate damage
3 = Winds 111-130 mph with extensive damage

4 = Winds 131-155 mph with extreme damage
5 = Winds over 155 mph with catastrophic damage.

Hurricanes can produce water domes, often 50 to 100 miles high, that sweep across the coastline near where the hurricane makes landfall. This surge of high water topped by waves is devastating, causing threat to life and property. If the storm arrives during high tide, water height is even greater.

Winds of 74 mph or more can destroy poorly constructed buildings and mobile homes. Debris from signs, roofing material, siding, and small outside items become missiles during hurricanes, and gusts can down trees and power lines, causing mass disruption.

Torrential rains can produce floods, contributing to billions of dollars worth of damage and more lives lost. Hurricanes also produce tornadoes, which add to the destruction.

The United States faces a significant hurricane problem, as our shorelines attract larger numbers of people from Maine to Texas—living in homes and condominiums built on sand and waiting for the next storm threat. These higher populations add to greater property damage and lost lives. The warning system has always proved adequate in giving coastal people time to move inland when hurricanes threaten. But it's becoming more difficult to evacuate people, because many roads have not kept pace with the rapid population growth. Coastal areas are not the only affected areas. Many inland areas become hard hit by hurricanes—the Scranton-Wilkes-Barre area of Northeastern Pennsylvania was hard hit by Hurricane Agnes and the flooding that followed.

The National Weather Service continuously broadcasts updates on hurricane advisories on NOAA weather radios:

TROPICAL STORM WATCH: Tropical storm conditions are possible, usually within 36 hours.

TROPICAL STORM WARNING: Tropical storm conditions are expected, usually within 24 hours.

HURRICANE WATCH: Hurricane conditions possible, usually within 36 hours. Prepare to take immediate action to protect your family and property.

HURRICANE WARNING: Hurricane conditions are expected, usually in 24 hours. Complete all storm preparations and evacuate if directed to do so by local officials.

TO PROTECT YOUR FAMILY, BE PREPARED FOR HURRI-CANES, PARTICULARLY IF YOU LIVE IN A HURRICANE PRONE AREA

Before hurricane season hits:

- Know the hurricane risks in your area.
- Learn the safe routes inland.
- Learn where shelters are located.
- Keep nonperishable food and water on hand.
- Purchase hurricane shutters, or buy precut ½ inch outdoor plywood for each window. If using plywood, install anchors and predrill holes so that you can put it up easily.
- Clear and repair clogged and loose rain gutters and downspouts.
- Remove diseased and damaged limbs from trees and strategically remove branches so that wind can blow through them.
- Keep shrubs trimmed.
- Keep extra cash on hand.

During the storm:

If you're in a watch area:

- Listen to NOAA weather radio or your local radio or TV broadcast for bulletins on the storm's progress.
- Service and fuel the family vehicles.
- If you live in a mobile home, inspect and secure the tie-downs.
- Stock up on batteries, canned food, first aid and medical supplies, and water.
- Prepare to bring in outdoor furniture and objects, such as garbage cans, plants, and decorations.
- Prepare to install shutters or plywood on windows; don't use tape, as it doesn't prevent window breakage.

Plan to evacuate if:

- You live in a mobile home.
- You live on the coastline, an off-shore island, or near a river or floodplain.
- You live in a high-rise.

If you're in a warning area:

- Closely monitor the NOAA weather radio or your local TV or radio for bulletins.
- Complete your preparations—put up shutters/plywood, store out-door objects, etc.
- Follow official instructions—if told to evacuate, do so.
- If evacuating, leave early; stay with friends or family, at a low-rise hotel/motel, or a shelter (pets are not allowed in shelters, so make other arrangements as noted in the disaster plan in Chapter 29).
- Leave mobile homes—they are unsafe in high winds.
- Notify family outside the warning area of your evacuation plans.

If you stay home because you have NOT been ordered to evacuate:

- Turn the refrigerator to maximum cold and open only when necessary.
- Turn off your utilities if told to do so by the authorities.
- Turn off propane tanks.
- Unplug small appliances.
- Fill tub and jugs with water in case water supply gets contaminated.

If winds strengthen:

- Stay away from windows and doors, even if they are covered; take refuge in a small interior room, closet, or hallway on first floor.
- Secure and brace exterior doors; close interior doors.
- In a multiplex, go to first or second floor and stay away from windows.
- Lie on floor under a sturdy object like a table.

Stay alert for:

- Tornadoes, which can be generated by hurricanes.
- The "eye" (calm) of the storm—after it passes, winds change direction and return to hurricane force.

After the storm:

- Keep listening to the radio or TV for updates.

- Wait until the area is declared safe to return or go outside.
- If you come to a closed road or barricade, turn around.
- Stay on firm ground as moving water can sweep you away and electrically charged water can kill you.
- Avoid washed-out roads and weakened bridges.
- Don't drive in flooded areas.
- Use your phone for life-threatening emergencies only.
- Carefully check gas, water, and electrical lines and appliances for damage.
- Don't use tap water until you're sure it has not been contaminated.
- Use flashlights instead of candles and other open flame objects.
- Be very cautious when using a chainsaw when cutting trees.

LIGHTNING AND THUNDERSTORMS

Although common and seemingly just noisy, severe thunderstorms can be life-threatening, causing serious injury and death. According to the National Weather Service, severe thunderstorms occur when wind speeds reach 58 mph or greater, and/or when hail reaches ¾ inches in diameter, and/or when a tornado is produced.

SEVERE THUNDERSTORM WATCH:

Conditions are favorable for severe thunderstorms in your area. Be prepared to seek shelter.

SEVERE THUNDERSTORM WARNING:

Severe thunderstorm is indicated by radar or reported by a reliable source. Immediately move to a safe place and stay away from windows.

Lightning ranks second only to floods as a top-killing natural disaster, killing approximately 100 people per year. Injuries and fatalities tend to occur because some people behave inappropriately during thunderstorms, and because many active people are outdoors in the late afternoons and evenings from late spring to early fall, when most thunderstorms occur. The seemingly random nature of a thunderstorm disallows any guarantees of complete safety from lightning strikes; however, simple precautions can often be the difference between life and death.

Lightning results from an accumulation of electrical charges inside a cloud due to friction from water droplets, dust, and ice. The bottom of the cloud then becomes negatively charged, discharging a lightning strike once enough charge has built up.

Lightning injury can occur five different ways:

1. A direct strike usually hits the head. These injuries can also injure the eyes and ears, since the lightning enters through the orifices.
2. A contact injury occurs when a person touches an object that is in the path of a lightning current.
3. Side flash injury occurs when lightning strikes an object near a person and ricochets to the person.
4. Ground current or step voltage injury happens when lightning current flowing in the ground radiates outward. Standing with one foot closer to the strike than the other creates a step voltage.
5. Blunt injury creates violent muscular contractions that throw victims several feet from the strike point.

While lightning causes about 100 deaths due to cardiac arrest per year, it also causes significant prolonged suffering in its survivors. Persons not rapidly resuscitated after their heart stops can suffer permanent brain damage. Even without heart stoppage, people can suffer brain injury symptoms, including short-term memory and new-information processing deficits, hyperirritability, sleep problems, severe ongoing headaches, and distractibility. Other victims may experience chronic pain or seizures, and some never return to normal functioning.

Most lightning fatalities occur in open fields, golf courses, ballparks, and playgrounds—near trees and close to water. All fatalities have one thing in common—the victim was the highest object or was near the highest object in the area. Thus, minimizing vertical height is critical to decreasing your child's chance of being struck by lightning.

OTHER SAFETY MEASURES TO REDUCE THE RISK OF LIGHTNING STRIKES:

Before the storm strikes:

- Listen to your NOAA or local radio station or TV station for weather forecasts.
- Keep an eye out for signs of sudden thunderstorms—darkening skies, flashes of light, increased wind, and sounds of thunder.

- If you do hear thunder, you're close enough to be struck by lightning; get to a safe place in a building or car (not a convertible), and keep the windows closed.

When the storm approaches:

- Get to a safe shelter (as above).
- Unplug appliances.
- Avoid using the telephone or any electrical appliances. Their lines conduct electricity.
- Turn off the air conditioner.
- Close windows and draw shades or blinds. If the windows break, the shades will prevent glass from shattering into your home.
- If you're outside, get to a low-lying, open place away from trees, poles, or metal objects, and make sure it's a place that does not flood. Squat low to the ground, placing your hands on your knees with your head between them with your ears covered. DO NOT lie flat—this only makes you a bigger target.
- If boating, get to land immediately.

After the storm:

- Stay away from damaged areas.
- Listen to your radio for further information.

The number of lightning fatalities from sports and recreational activities has experienced an alarming increase in recent decades. Three-fourths of lightning casualties happen between May and September, and nearly four-fifths between 10 A.M. and 7 P.M., which coincides with outdoor athletic and recreational events—the results, about one-half of the casualties were persons involved in outdoor recreational-related activities. Thus, the National Athletic Trainers Association recommends a proactive approach to lightning safety for athletics and recreation. If your child is involved in organized outdoor sports or recreation from May through September, ask the organizer if they utilize the association's recommendations, which are:

1. Formulate and implement a policy or emergent action plan specific to lightning safety that includes:
   a. a chain of command that establishes who should make the decision to remove everyone from the field or activity.

    b. a designated weather watcher who actively looks for signs of bad weather and notifies the chain of command if dangerous weather occurs.

    c. a way to monitor local weather forecasts and warnings.

    d. a list of specific safe locations from lightning strikes —one for each site or field.

    e. specific criteria for suspension and resumption of activities.

    f. the use of recommended strategies for lightning safety.

2. The first choice of a safe location should be a substantial, frequently inhabited building. Children should stay away from telephones and plumbing, as the pathways of these conduct electricity.

3. The second choice for a safer location is a fully enclosed vehicle with closed windows and a metal roof. No one should touch any part of the vehicle's metal framework during thunderstorms. Golf carts, convertibles and baseball dugouts don't provide protection from lightning dangers.

4. Seeking safe shelter at the first sign of a severe storm is highly recommended.

5. Activity should be postponed or suspended if a thunderstorm appears imminent before or during the activity—whether or not lightning is seen or thunder heard—until the danger has passed.

6. A waiting period of at least 30 minutes after the last lightning flash or thunderclap is recommended once activities have been suspended. Lightning safety tips should be placed in game programs and messages read over public-address systems to alert both spectators and competitors as to what to do and where to go to find a safe place in the event of a severe thunderstorm.

7. Extremely large events present a particular concern regarding lightning safety. A multidisciplinary approach (integrating weather forecasts, a weather watcher, real time thunderstorm data, and a flash-to-bang count to note the closeness between thunder and lightning) aids in decision making.

8. People should avoid contact with, or proximity to, open water or the highest point in the field. No one should take shelter under or near bleachers (metal or wood), metal fences, trees, flagpoles, or light poles.

9. No one should take showers or use plumbing facilities, including outdoor and indoor pools. No one should use land-line phones. Cellular and cordless phones are safer in emergencies.

10. Anyone feeling their hair stand on end or skin tingle, or hearing crackling noises should assume the lightning-safe

position—squatting with feet together, head lowered and ears covered. No one should lie flat on the ground.

11. First aid procedures to manage victims of a lightning strike should be initiated when needed:
    a. Surveillance of the scene for safety
    b. Initiation of call to activate the emergency medical system
    c. Careful moving of the victim to a safer location, if needed
    d. Evaluation for stopped breathing and heart rate, and administer CPR
    e. Evaluation and treat for hypothermia and shock
    f. Evaluation and treat for fractures
    g. Evaluation and treat for burns

12. Everyone should maintain current CPR and first aid certification.

13. People should have the right to leave the activity without fear of penalty to seek a safe structure or location if they feel that they are in danger from impending lightning.

Despite all precautions, there is no guarantee that your child will be totally safe from a lightning strike.

IF YOUR CHILD IS STRUCK BY LIGHTNING:

Call 911 or whatever you need to do to activate your emergency medical service.

If he has stopped breathing and his heart stopped beating, begin CPR.

Check him for burns where the lightning entered AND exited his body.

Give first aid as needed.

MUDSLIDES AND LANDSLIDES

Mudslides and landslides are serious and common hazards that occur in almost every state. They cause about $2 billion in damages and from 25 to 50 deaths per year in the United States; globally, they cause thousands of deaths and injuries.

While some landslides move slowly, others move so rapidly that they take lives suddenly and unexpectedly. Gravity drives their movement with help from water saturation, slope steepening by construction or erosion, alternate freezing and thawing, earthquake shaking, and volcanic eruptions. Most landslides develop after heavy rain or rapid snow melt, and tend to worsen the effects of the flooding that usually accompany these events. Lower thresholds of precipitation can initiate landslides in areas burned by brush and forest fires.

Mudslides, or debris flow, move quickly during periods of intense rain or snow melt. They tend to begin on steep hills as shallow landslides that liquefy and accelerate to a speed of about 10 to 35 mph or greater. Mudslide consistency ranges from watery to thick, rocky mud that can carry large items, including trees and cars. If the debris flows from several channels, they can combine to increase their devastation. As a mudslide rolls downhill, it grows in volume, gathering water, dirt, mud, boulders, trees, and other materials.

TO PROTECT YOUR FAMILY AND HOME FROM MUDSLIDES AND LANDSLIDES, CONSIDER THE FOLLOWING RECOMMENDATIONS:

Plan ahead:

- Develop a disaster plan.
- Find out about the risk in your area and ask if any corrective measures can be takes to prevent landslides and mudslides.
- Install flexible pipe fittings to avoid water and gas leaks.
- Check your insurance policy for coverage.
- Create an evacuation plan and know where to go in the event of a mudslide/landslide.
- Discuss mudslides/landslides with your children so that they know what to do if one occurs.

Before intense storms:

- You and your family should become familiar with the land around you.
- Watch patterns of storm-water drainage on the slopes near your home, especially those areas where water runoff converges.
- Watch the hillsides for any signs of land movement—small landslides or debris flow or progressively tilting trees. Small changes can alert you for a greater landslide threat.

During severe storms:

- Remain alert and awake. Most mudslide fatalities occur when people are asleep. Listen to your NOAA weather radio or local radio or TV stations for storm warnings, and realize that a short burst of rain can be devastating, especially after heavy rainfall and damp weather.

- If your area is susceptible to mudslides/landslides, consider leaving it if is safe to do so. Driving during severe storms can be hazardous. If you stay home, stay in the second story, if possible, and stay out of the path of land and mudslides.
- Listen for sounds that can indicate moving debris, such as boulders smashing together or trees cracking.
- If you live near a channel or stream, watch for a sudden rise or fall in the water flow or a change from clear to muddy water. Both indicate a landslide upstream. Act immediately.
- Be alert when driving because embankments are very susceptible to landslides. Watch for collapsed pavement, fallen rocks, mud, and other signs of debris.

If you suspect a land or mudslide:

- Contact authorities.
- Alert your neighbors.
- Evacuate.

During a land or mudslide:

- Get out of its path and move to a stable area.
- If you can't escape, curl up into a ball to protect your head and body.

After a land or mudslide:

- Stay away from the area because it may be unstable..
- Without directly entering the site, look for people trapped in the slide, but don't attempt rescue—alert rescuers to their location.
- Assist people with special needs—people with disabilities, the elderly.
- Listen to the radio or TV for the updates on the emergency.
- Watch for flooding.
- Beware of broken utility lines and report them to authorities.
- Check your foundation, chimney, and surrounding land for damage.
- Replant damaged ground because the erosion can lead to flash flooding.

- Seek the advice of a geotechnical expert to advise you of the best ways to prevent or reduce your risk from future land or mudslides without creating further hazard.

TORNADOES

Few weather phenomena create fear like tornadoes. In an average year, 800 rage through the United States, resulting in 80 deaths and more than 1,500 injuries. They can occur anywhere, but happen most frequently east of the Rocky Mountains during the spring and summer months. Although most tornadoes are weak, they can still cause substantial damage. Violent tornadoes can create tremendous destruction, with wind speeds greater than 205 mph or more and damage paths in excess of one mile wide and 50 miles long.

Defined as violently rotating columns of air in contact with the ground, tornadoes come in different sizes, many as rope-like swirls, others like wide funnels. When they don't touch the ground, they are referred to as "funnel clouds." Tornadoes can be seen for miles across the Plains, but may be masked in hail and rain in the East and Deep South, making them even more dangerous.

Two key atmospheric conditions create tornado potential—wind shear (change in wind speed and direction with height) and instability (warm, moist air near the ground, cool, dry air aloft). Unstable air mass promotes strong updraft development, and wind shear both increases strength and promotes storm rotation, spawning tornadoes. All thunderstorms hold the potential to produce tornadoes, but the storm that most commonly turns tornadic is the Supercell, a very severe and long-lived storm.

According to the National Weather Service, tornadoes come in many shapes and sizes:

Weak Tornadoes: 69% of all tornadoes; less than 5% of all tornado deaths; lifetime 1 to 10 minutes; winds of less than 110 mph.

Strong Tornadoes: 29% of all tornadoes; nearly 30% of all tornado deaths; can last 20 minutes or more; winds of 110 to 205 mph.

Violent Tornadoes: Only 25% of all tornadoes; 70% of all tornado deaths; can last more than an hour; winds greater than 205 mph.

TO PROTECT YOUR FAMILY FROM A TORNADO'S WRATH:

Prepare a home tornado plan:

- Choose a place for family members to meet if a tornado heads your way: basement, center hallway, bathroom, or closet on the lowest floor. Make sure the location remains uncluttered.
- If you live in a high-rise, pick a place in the center of the building. You may not have enough time to get to the lowest floor.
- Create your disaster kit.

Listen to your weather radio for warnings:

TORNADO WATCH: Tornado is possible in your area.

TORNADO WARNING: Tornado has been sighted and may be headed for your area.

If Watch is issued:

Listen to the radio or TV for updates.

Be alert for changing weather conditions—darkening, often greenish sky; blowing debris; wall cloud; large hail; and a loud roar, similar to a freight train.

If Warning is issued:

If you're inside, go to your safe place and protect yourself and your children from flying objects.

If you're outside, rush to the basement of a nearby sturdy building or lie flat in a ditch or low-lying area and cover your body and head.

If you're in a car, get out and head for safety (see above).

You can't out drive a tornado. Get out of the car and head for safety: the basement of a nearby sturdy building, or lying flat in a ditch or low-lying area.

After the tornado:

Listen to the radio or TV for updates and instructions.

Stay out of damaged areas and watch for fallen power lines.

Use a flashlight to check your home for damage.

Don't use candles.

TSUNAMIS

No, I never heard of them either until I started researching weather extremes for this book. But then, I'm an east coaster. Since 1946, six Tsunamis have caused billions of dollars in damage and killed more than 350 people in Alaska, Hawaii, and the west coast. Tsunami waves can rise several feet, sometimes tens of feet, to cause great loss of life when they come ashore, and they can travel upstream into rivers to extend their damage further inland.

A Japanese word for harbor waves, tsunamis (tsoo na meez) are ocean waves created by earthquakes and underwater landslides. They are frequently but incorrectly referred to as tidal waves. Tsunamis are actually a series of waves that travel at speeds of 450 to 600 mph.

The Pacific Tsunami Warning Center (PTWC) and the West Coast/Alaska Tsunami Warning Center send tsunami bulletins, and all tsunamis are potentially dangerous:

ADVISORY: An earthquake has occurred in the Pacific, which may generate a tsunami. Hourly bulletins will be issued–stay tuned.

INFORMATION: Message about an earthquake that isn't expected to generate a tsunami. Typically, only one bulletin is issued.

WATCH: A tsunami was or may have been generated, but is at least 2 hours away. You should prepare for possible evacuation if a warning is issued.

WARNING: A tsunami was or may have been generated and can cause damage. You're strongly advised to evacuate.

TO PROTECT YOUR FAMILY FROM TSUNAMIS:

Get familiar with the warning signs:

Strong earthquakes near the coast line
Noticeable rapid rise or fall in coastal waters
Plan ahead:

- Find out about tsunamis in your area by contacting your local American Red Cross chapter. Know the distance of your street from the coast or other high-risk water and the level of your street above sea level, because authorities may base evacuation orders on these numbers.

- Ask about your favorite vacation spot. Ask the resort/hotel/motel/campground personnel about their tsunami warning and evacuation procedure. Learn the designated escape routes before a warning is issued.
- Plan evacuation routes from your home and practice them before a warning is issued. Try to choose a safe place 100 feet above sea level or go up two miles inland, away from the coastline. If you can't go that high, go as far as you can.
- You should be able to reach your safe place on foot in 15 minutes. Footpaths usually lead uphill and inland, and roads may be impassable or blocked after a disaster. Follow posted tsunami routes whenever possible.
- Listen to your NOAA weather radio to keep informed of updates.
- Check your insurance—homeowner's policies don't cover flooding from a tsunami.
- Teach your children what to do if a tsunami warning is issued, and review flood safety suggestions with them.

After a tsunami:

- Continue to listen to the radio or TV for updates.
- Help neighbors who need assistance.
- Only use the telephone for emergencies.
- Stay out of your home if there is still water around it. The walls may collapse.

When re-entering your home, be very careful:

- Wear sturdy shoes.
- Use flashlights—no candles.
- Examine walls, doors, floors, windows, and staircases for signs of collapse.
- Inspect the foundation for cracks.
- Check for fire hazards (broken or leaking gas lines; flooded electrical circuits, submerged appliances or furnace).
- Check for gas leaks. If you smell gas or hear hissing, get out immediately. Turn off the gas supply from the outside if possible, and contact your gas company. Don't turn the gas back on.
- Inspect for electrical damage. If you see frayed or broken wires or sparks, turn off the main circuit breaker or fuse box—unless you have to step in water to do so. Call an electrician or the electric company.

- Look for water and sewage line damage. If you suspect damage, don't use the toilet. Call the plumber. If water pipes are broken, turn off the main water valve, don't use the tap water, and call the plumber or water company.
- Don't drink tap water until you know it's safe.
- Be observant for animals, particularly snakes that may have entered the house with the water.
- Open windows and doors to air out the house to prevent mold build-up.
- Shovel mud while it's moist to let floors dry.
- Get rid of any contaminated food.

VOLCANOES

Volcanoes lie dormant until they erupt, spewing hot solid and molten rock fragments and gases into the air. Ashflows can develop on all sides of a volcano, flowing hundreds of miles downwind. Valleys can then give way to dangerous flooding and mudflows (rivers of mud that move 20–40 mph). Even if you live near a volcano that has been dormant for ages, you and your family should be prepared for the worst.

Despite their devastating effects, volcanoes are simply vents in the earth's surface through which molten rock (magma) and associated ashes erupt periodically when pressure on the magma chamber forces the magma up and out of the volcano. Their cones develop from effusive and explosive eruptions.

IF YOU LIVE IN A VOLCANIC AREA, PLAN AHEAD:

- Make evacuation plans with a back-up route in mind.
- Have your disaster kit ready.
- Get goggles and a throwaway breathing mask for all family members
- Contact your local emergency management office for more information on volcanoes.
- Learn about your community warning systems.
- Be prepared for these disasters that can be spawned by volcanoes:
  —Earthquakes
  —Flash floods
  —Landslides and mudflows
  —Thunderstorms
  —Tsunamis

During a volcanic eruption:

- Evacuate as ordered, using your plan. Staying home can prove deadly.
- Stay away from areas downwind and river valleys downstream of the volcano.

If you get caught indoors:

- Bring all animals and livestock into enclosed shelters.
- Close all doors, windows, and dampers.
- Put all machinery inside the garage or barn.

If you get trapped outdoors:

- Seek indoor shelter.
- If caught in a rock fall, squat in a ball and protect your head.
- If caught near a stream, beware of mudflows. Move upslope.

During an ashfall:

- Wear long-sleeved shirts and long-legged pants.
- Wear your goggles.
- Use your dust mask. If you don't have one, cover your face with a damp cloth to help breathing.
- Keep vehicle engines off. Driving during ashfall will clog your engine.
- Stay out of restricted areas.
- Listen to your radio for updates.

After a volcanic eruption:

- Stay indoors if you have a respiratory ailment; keep your children inside if they have respiratory problems, such as asthma.
- Clear your roof of ashfall because it can cause collapse, but be very careful.

WINTER STORMS

Blizzards and Northeasters look like winter wonderlands, but winter white can be as dangerous as it's beautiful. The National Weather Service calls winter storms the "deceptive killers" because fatalities result not from the storms themselves, but from related automobile accidents and hypothermia. Whether home or on the road, you need to be prepared for the dangers of winter storms: cold, snow, ice, and winds.

WIND

Some winter storms arrive with very strong winds, creating blizzard conditions with blinding wind-driven snow, severe drifting, and dangerous windchill. Strong winds with these intense storms and cold fronts can knock down trees, utility poles, and power lines. Storms near the coast can cause coastal flooding and beach erosion, as well as sink ships at sea. In the west and Alaska, winds descending off the mountains can gust to 100 mph or more, damaging roofs and other structures.

COLD

Extreme cold frequently accompanies winter storms or remains in their wake. Prolonged exposure to the cold can cause frost-bite or hypothermia, which can become life-threatening. Infants and elderly people are most susceptible. What constitutes extreme cold and its effect varies across different areas of the United States. In areas unaccustomed to winter weather, near-freezing temperatures are con-sidered "extreme cold." Pipes may freeze and burst in homes that are poorly insulated or without heat. In the north, below zero temperatures may be considered as "extreme cold." Long cold spells can cause rivers to freeze. Ice jams may form and lead to flooding.

FROSTBITE is damage to body tissue caused by that tissue being frozen. It causes a loss of feeling and a white or pale appearance in extremities, such as fingers, toes, ear lobes, or the tip of the nose.

HYPOTHERMIA is low body temperature. The warning signs include: uncontrollable shivering, memory loss, disorientation, incoherence, slurred speech, drowsiness, and apparent exhaustion. Hypothermia can prove fatal!

INFANT HYPOTHERMIA has a different appearance. Your baby's skin may be bright red and cold, and he may have a lack of energy.

ICE

Heavy accumulations of ice can bring down trees, electrical wires, telephone poles and lines, and communication towers. Communications and power can be disrupted for days while utility companies work to repair the extensive damage. Even small accumulations of ice may cause extreme hazards to motorists and pedestrians.

SNOW

Heavy snow can immobilize a region and paralyze a city, stranding commuters, stopping the flow of supplies, and disrupting emergency and medical services. Accumulations of snow can collapse buildings and knock down trees and power lines. In rural areas, homes and farms may be isolated for days, and unprotected livestock may be lost. In the mountains, heavy snow can lead to avalanches. The cost of snow removal, repairing damages, and loss of business can have large economic impacts on cities and towns.

Types of Winter Precipitation :

FLURRIES: Light snow falling for short durations. No accumulation or light dusting is all that is expected.

SHOWERS: Snow falling at varying intensities for brief periods of time. Some accumulation is possible.

SQUALLS: Brief, intense snow showers accompanied by strong, gusty winds. Accumulation may be significant. Snow squalls are best known in the Great Lakes region.

BLOWING SNOW: Wind-driven snow that reduces visibility and causes significant drifting. Blowing snow may be snow that is falling and/or loose snow on the ground picked up by the wind.

BLIZZARD: Winds over 35 mph with snow and blowing snow reducing visibility to near zero.

SLEET: Raindrops that freeze into ice pellets before reaching the ground. Sleet usually bounces when hitting a surface and doesn't stick to objects. However, it can accumulate like snow and cause a hazard to motorists.

FREEZING RAIN: Rain that falls onto a surface with a temperature below freezing. This causes it to freeze to surfaces, such as trees, cars, and roads, forming a coating or glaze of ice. Even small accumulations of ice can cause a significant hazard.

Keep your family safe from the dangers of winter by dressing properly, preparing for winter storms, and knowing what to do if caught in a winter storm.

MAKE SURE YOU AND YOUR FAMILY DRESS PROPERLY FOR WINTER:

- Wear loose-fitting, lightweight, warm clothing in several layers.
- Wear outer garments that are tightly woven, water-repellent, and hooded.
- Wear a hat. Half your body heat loss can be from the head.
- Cover your mouth to protect your lungs from extreme cold.
- Mittens, snug at the wrist, are better than gloves.
- Try to stay dry.

TO PREPARE FOR A WINTER STORM:

- Have a NOAA or other portable radio
- Make sure your home is well-heated and that you have a back-up heating source that will operate if the power goes out.
- Keep extra blankets and batteries on hand.
- Have extra medicines, baby formula/food, pet food.
- Store canned food and bottled water.
- Have flashlights ready in case the power goes out.

Winterize your car before it gets cold, and make sure you have emergency supplies in the car:

- Extra clothes, blankets, hats, and gloves
- Booster cables
- Snow brush and ice scraper
- Shovel
- Bag of sand or kitty litter
- Snow chains
- Car emergency kit
- Emergency high-calorie food and water supply
- Carry your cell phone when in the car
- Keep your gas tank full
- Try not to drive alone or alone with the kids

Listen to your NOAA or local radio or TV for weather reports:

WINTER STORM WATCH: Severe winter conditions, such as heavy snow and/or ice, are possible within the next day or two. Prepare now!

WINTER STORM WARNING: Severe winter conditions have begun or are about to begin in your area. Stay indoors!

BLIZZARD WARNING: Snow and strong winds will combine to produce a blinding snow (near zero visibility), deep drifts, and life-threatening windchill. Seek refuge immediately!

WINTER WEATHER ADVISORY: Winter weather conditions are expected to cause significant inconveniences and may be hazardous. If caution is exercised, these situations should not become life-threatening. The greatest hazard is often to motorists.

FROST/FREEZE WARNING: Below freezing temperatures are expected and may cause significant damage to plants, crops, or fruit trees. In areas unaccustomed to freezing temperatures, people who have homes without heat need to take added precautions.

IF YOU AND YOUR FAMILY ARE CAUGHT OUTSIDE IN A WINTER STORM:

- Find shelter.
- Try to stay dry .
- Cover all exposed parts of the body.

If there is no shelter:

- Prepare a lean-to, windbreak, or snow cave for protection from the wind.
- Build a fire for heat and to attract attention.
- Place rocks around the fire to absorb and reflect heat.
- Don't eat snow: It lowers your body temperature. Melt it first.

IN A CAR OR TRUCK:

- Stay in your car or truck. Disorientation occurs quickly in wind-driven snow and cold.
- Run the motor about ten minutes each hour for heat.
- Open the window a little for fresh air to avoid carbon monoxide poisoning.
- Make sure the exhaust pipe isn't blocked.

Make yourself visible to rescuers:

- Turn on the dome light at night when running engine.
- Tie a colored cloth (preferably red) to your antenna or door.
- Raise the hood indicating trouble after snow stops falling.
- Exercise from time to time by vigorously moving arms, legs, fingers, and toes to keep blood circulating and to keep warm.

AT HOME OR IN A BUILDING:

- Stay inside. When using ALTERNATIVE HEAT from a fire place, woodstove, space heater, etc.:
- Use fire safeguards.
- Properly ventilate.

If you have no heat:

- Close off unneeded rooms.
- Stuff towels or rags in cracks under doors.
- Cover windows at night.
- Eat and drink. Food provides the body with energy for producing its own heat. Keep the body replenished with fluids to prevent dehydration.
- Wear layers of loose-fitting, lightweight, warm clothing.
- Remove layers to avoid overheating, perspiration, and subsequent chill.

ON THE FARM:

- Move animals to sheltered areas.
- Shelter belts, properly laid out and oriented, are better protection for cattle than confining shelters, such as sheds.
- Have a water supply available. Most animal deaths in winter storms are from dehydration.

We may be experiencing an increase in extreme weather and its consequences, but with careful preparation, you and your family can safely weather any storm—or other natural disaster.

4

FAT: TOO MUCH
OR
TOO LITTLE

FLORIDA, 2003:
Baltimore Oriole pitcher dies of multiple organ failure, due to a heat-stroke after taking the diet drug ephedra and severely limiting his food intake for several days.

SOME STATS

- Obesity is associated with type 2 diabetes, heart disease, lung dysfunction, arthritis, stroke, and some forms of cancer.
- Between 16 and 33% of children and teens are obese.
- The incidence of type 2 diabetes (obesity-related diabetes) is on the rise in children.
- Children who are obese between the ages of 11 and 13 have an 80% chance of becoming an obese adult.
- 5 to 10 million girls and women suffer from eating disorders (anorexia, bulimia, and binge-eating disorder).
- 1 million men have eating disorders.
- 81% of 10-year-olds are afraid of getting fat.
- 42% of first to third grade girls wish they were thinner.
- Most models are thinner than 98% of American women.
- Americans spend over $40 billion on diet-related products each year.

With obesity now a national epidemic, and anorexia and bulimia well out of the closet, it's easy to see how fat made the list of 21 Threats. Some of our kids are eating too much fast food, others are just fasting. How healthy is your child?

TOO MUCH FAT

As kids spend more time in front of the TV and computer munching chips and less time outside playing, their body weights keep rising.

Obesity is the most common childhood nutritional disorder in the United States. Its incidence rose an estimated 30% in the last 25 years. Obesity can result in a number of problems for children. They are more likely to acquire breathing problems, coronary artery disease, arthritis, and stroke as adults. During childhood, they are more likely to develop type 2 diabetes, high blood pressure, asthma, liver disease, orthopedic problems, sleep apnea, and self-esteem problems. Some experts believe that psychological and social problems are the most serious consequences of obesity in children.

Obesity is one of easiest conditions to diagnose, but one of the most difficult to treat. Along with sedentary lifestyle, obesity causes over 300,000 deaths per year and costs society nearly $100 million annually. Overweight children are more likely to become overweight adults unless they change their patterns of eating and exercise.

Obesity is defined as an excessive amount of body fat—total body weight greater than 25% on boys and 32% in girls. Another way to ascertain body fat is the body mass index or BMI, which is derived from someone's weight and height. A BMI that exceeds the 95 percentile for age and sex is diagnostic for obesity.

The BMI was just recently recommended as an additional measure of growth for children and as an indicator of body "fatness" and potential weight problems. Charts for BMI are becoming more common, and you may soon see your child's BMI measured and charted right along with her height and ·veight.

You can calculate your child's BMI by dividing her weight in kilograms by her height in meters squared, or by using this formula:

$$BMI = \frac{\text{Weight in pounds} \times 703}{\text{Height in inches}^2}$$

Or:

$$BMI = \frac{\text{Weight in kilograms}}{\text{Height in meters}^2}$$

You can also go to the Centers for Disease Control and Prevention's page on Body Mass Index for Children at: http://www. cdcgov/nccdphp/dnpa/bmi/bmi-for-age.htm, and click on the BMI calculator. Type in your child's information, submit it, and get her BMI automatically. Also, you can access the Child and Adolescent BMI charts to see where your child fits in.

PROBLEMS RELATED TO OBESITY

Childhood obesity has been associated with numerous health problems. Obese children have higher blood pressures, heart rates, and cholesterol levels than non-obese kids, and these can lead to heart disease. The excess weight increases their chances for orthopedic problems such as bowlegs, slipped hip, and weight stress on their leg joints, and it makes them more prone to skin disorders, especially heat rash. A fungal infection can develop in their skin folds, creating the suspicion of type 2 diabetes. Many obese children and adolescents have impaired glucose tolerance, a condition that often appears before the development of type 2 diabetes.

Obesity unleashes the potential for poor self-esteem, negative self-image, withdrawal from peers, and depression. Children learn at a very early age to stigmatize obese people as stupid, lazy, slow, and self-indulgent. Research shows that children prefer a playmate who is disabled or wheelchair bound to one who is obese. Psychological stress from obesity can be especially difficult during adolescence, when peer acceptance is a crucial component of development and identity.

CAUSES OF OBESITY

The causes of obesity are more complex than they seem, and include genetic, biological, familial, and environmental factors. Less than 10% of childhood obesity is associated with a genetic or hormonal defect, such as Turner's syndrome, Prader-Willi syndrome, or hypothyroidism. Most children with these types of disorders exhibit other symptoms, such as short stature and mental impairment, and they rarely have a family history of obesity. These disorders can be diagnosed by your child's health care provider via a careful history, physical examination, and laboratory tests.

Most overweight children have idiopathic (undetermined cause) obesity. They gain weight because their energy input—food—exceeds their energy output—basal metabolic rate: the thermal effects of food and activity. It takes 3500 calories to gain one pound; therefore, an excess intake of only 50 to 100 calories per day can lead to a 5 to 10 pound weight gain in just over a year. A relatively small imbalance between energy input and output can lead to a significant weight gain over time. Most obese children gain their weight slowly over a period of years.

GENETIC FACTORS OF OBESITY

Heredity has been shown to influence response to overfeeding, regional fat distribution, and even fatness. Babies born to overweight mothers have been found to be less active and to gain more weight by age three months when compared to babies born to normal-weight mothers, suggesting a possible inborn drive to conserve energy. For children who are genetically predisposed to obesity, prevention may be the best course of action. But genes are not destiny, and there are other factors involved in obesity.

BIOLOGICAL FACTORS OF OBESITY

As already noted, some disorders, like hypothyroidism, can cause obesity, as can some medications, including steroids and antidepressants. Another important biological factor is the "set point." Everyone has a weight that their body will defend—the weight that your body keeps coming back to after dieting. That weight is called the set point.

FAMILIAL FACTORS OF OBESITY

Parents pass genes to their children, but they also pass down habits and set patterns associated with eating and activity. When parents demonstrate poor eating and exercise behavior, they indirectly affect their children's behavior—present and future. Most cultures place great value on food, not only for its nutritional value, but also for its role in social occasions and celebrations. However, when food symbolizes comfort or reward, it can lead to excessive dietary intake. Eating can become a response to anxiety, boredom, frustration, and depression. Family instability and other stressors can have a negative effect on your child's self-esteem, causing her to overeat and risk obesity. As your child gains weight, social pressures may mount as she gets teased and bullied, causing her to again use food for comfort.

ENVIRONMENTAL FACTORS OF OBESITY

Regardless of genetics, environmental factors play a significant role in childhood obesity. Most cases of obesity result from too much food and too little exercise. And bad habits can invade even the best of homes:

1. Food ads are everywhere—TV, movies, billboards, magazines, and newspapers. Your child is constantly inundated with them.
2. Supermarkets lure you to the higher-priced, frequently not-too-healthy foods. How often do you walk in and face a stack of yummy baked goods? Notice that the expensive, sugar-laden cereals are directly at your toddler's eye level as she sits in the shopping cart seat? Both supermarkets and discount chains have candy at almost every checkout. Try to shop the parameter of the store where the fresh produce and dairy products tend to be stored, and use the "no candy" checkouts.
3. Super-sized means just that—a huge amount, not an average serving. But we like to get more for our money, and since it costs only pennies more to get the giant-sized portion, we give in, over and over again, until our eyes forget what normal portion size is all about. Feel gypped because the cereal box claims to hold 16 servings and you always only get 4? If you said yes, you have super-sized eyes!
4. Sugar-laden fruit drinks that pass for juice and soft drinks contain little to no nutrients, yet kids down them regularly. Fruit juice can even add to obesity when consumed in large quantities—consumption of 12 ounces or more a day has been associated with obesity in preschoolers.
5. Sedentary lifestyle contributes to obesity, and studies show that 48% of girls and 26% of boys don't exercise vigorously on a regular basis.
6. The prevalence of obesity is higher in kids who watch four or more hours of television per day. Television slows the metabolism of mesmerized couch potatoes, and children are more likely to snack on high-calorie junk food while watching it. So get them off the couch and on their bikes!

RISK FACTORS

Some children are more prone to obesity than others. If your children have any of the following risk factors, make sure they get proper nutrition and exercise:

- Parent who is or was obese
- Spends a lot of time involved in sedentary activities
- Doesn't get enough exercise
- Watches TV or plays video games for more than two to four hours per day
- Consumes large amounts of calories at a time

- Has little parental supervision
- Gets bored easily

WHAT TO DO IF YOUR CHILD IS OBESE

Obesity should be treated like any other disorder. Therefore, your child needs a complete examination from her health care provider who will first make sure her weight gain isn't from a physical illness. In the absence of a disorder, obese children need a program that creates lasting weight loss through reduced calories and increased exercise, and their health care providers can make sure that they are able to handle dietary change and exercise without injury.

According to obesity specialist Rebecca Moran, MD, successful weight loss programs contain five main components: reasonable goals, dietary management, physical activity, behavior modification, and family involvement.

Reasonable goals: For weight loss goals to work, they need to be obtainable and allow for normal growth. Make both short and long-term goals. Short-term goals should start small, so that your child doesn't get discouraged: lose one pound per week or five per month. Her long-term goal can be the total amount of weight loss needed or the ability to reach a previously unattainable task, like walking up a flight of stairs without getting out of breath.

Dietary management: A nutritionist can develop a sensible dietary program that will allow for both weight loss and normal growth. One pound of weight equals 3,500 calories; thus, the diet will need to eliminate 500 calories per day to achieve a one pound per week weight loss. This diet should provide the recommended percentages of protein, carbohydrates, and fats that your child needs. Your child should also consume an adequate amount of fiber to increase her feeling of fullness and to displace fat in her diet.

Make sure she eats a healthy breakfast—cold cereal with fruit and milk, or whole wheat toast with peanut butter. Failure to do so can result in binge-eating, as well as her doing poorly in school. Keep healthy snacks handy, choosing from different food groups (apple with peanut butter, milk and graham crackers), and discouraging empty calories from cookies, chips, and candy. Kids don't have to give up fast foods, but they should be smart in both selecting their choices and making sure they fit in their daily calorie plan.

Physical activity: Your child needs physical activity to maintain weight and redistribute fat. After getting approval from your health care provider, start your child off slowly to avoid discouragement. Start with a five minute walk or bike ride and work up to 20 or 30 minutes of physical activity per day, in addition to the exercise your child gets in school.

Behavior modification: An essential for lifestyle changes, behavior modification for weight loss includes self-monitoring, stimulus control, modification of eating patterns, and positive reinforcement. Your child can self-monitor her eating and exercising patterns by keeping a diary that documents the time, the amount and type of food eaten, and the amount of exercise performed. This will force her to have more awareness of how much she actually eats and how little she exercises.

Stimulus control means limiting the things that encourage her to eat, including sitting in front of the TV. Limit TV time and disallow eating while watching. TV isn't the only stimulus to eating. Many children eat when stressed or bored. To identify your child's stimuli, have her document the circumstances that surround eating. For example:

My Diary

6:30	**woke up and got ready for school**
7:00	**ate breakfast: 1 bowl of Cheerios with milk and a glass of orange juice**
7:30	**got on school bus, sat in the back. Totally gross.**
8:00	**started school**
12:00	**lunch time. That mean kid picked on me again. She would not let me sit at my favorite table and made fun of me because I'm fat. I was so embarrassed that I could not eat my lunch**
3:00	**got home. Mom's still at work and I'm hungry! Ate 2 peanut butter and jelly sandwiches with chocolate milk and only about 8 cookies. But it's okay, right, I did not eat any lunch, right?**

Without the help of her diary as a visual clue, this girl might not have realized that her negative eating behaviors resulted from her being bullied at school.

Help your child modify her eating behavior by encouraging her to sit, take smaller bites, chew the food longer, and put her fork down between bites. Reward her for positive behavior, but don't use food as a reward. Give her ample praise for reaching her goals. Occasional tangible rewards, like a trip to the mall or sporting equipment, can give her an extra boost. Avoid negative reinforcement. Telling your child that she's "fat" and depriving her of food when she's hungry can only destroy her self-esteem and cause rebound weight gain.

Family involvement: Long-term weight loss requires active family involvement and support. Without nagging, actively work with your child on her weight loss plan. And remember, children learn by watching what you do. If your diet and exercise patterns lead you to weight gain, your child will follow suit, regardless of the intensity of her weight loss program.

Weight loss medications are not recommended for children. Neither are surgical procedures such as gastric bypass. However, some programs, including Weight Watchers and Jenny Craig, accept children with parental and medical permission. Check the white pages of your phone book for centers near you.

Losing weight is never easy, and maintaining weight loss can be an even bigger challenge. But the consequences of obesity remain severe, and the benefits of weight loss are worth the challenge.

TOO LITTLE FAT

Eating disorders, particularly anorexia nervosa and bulimia nervosa, are serious, complex, chronic disorders, which can be life-threatening. They usually begin during adolescence and disproportionately affect females. About 3% of young women have an eating disorder, and 10% of people with eating disorders are male. Although cases have been reported in prepubertal children, statistical data remains unreliable.

ANOREXIA NERVOSA has been called the relentless pursuit of thinness. Affected individuals refuse to maintain a body weight at or above a minimally normal weight for their height and age. They weigh less than one-fifth their normal weight for their height, build, and age, yet they firmly believe that they are overweight. Anorectics have an intense fear of gaining weight or becoming fat—even when underweight—as well as a disturbance in the way in which their body weight or shape is experienced, have lost at least three consecutive menstrual cycles.

Anorectic individuals believe they are obese even when extremely emaciated. This body image disturbance can range from a mild distortion to a severe delusion and isn't related to the degree of weight loss. These teens may be preoccupied with their entire body or a specific body area, such as the abdomen, thighs, and buttocks.

BULIMIA NERVOSA signifies the chaotic eating patterns that characterize this disorder. Bulimic individuals have recurrent binge-eating episodes during which they eat a relatively large amount of food in a short period of time, feeling out of control during the binge. These episodes are accompanied by repeated compensatory mechanisms to prevent weight gain including self-induced vomiting, laxative and/or diuretic abuse, ipecac (medication to induce vomiting) abuse, fasting, and excessive exercise. Like anorectics, bulimics are constantly concerned with their body shape and weight.

Bulimic teens develop an intense preoccupation with food that progressively interferes with their educational, vocational, and/or social activities. Shame follows their binging, and they are usually quite distressed by their symptoms. Bulimic teens are also at risk for impulsive behaviors such as substance abuse, shoplifting, and promiscuity, increasing their chances for chemical dependency and sexually transmitted diseases, including HIV/AIDS.

In both disorders, thinking is concrete and somewhat superstitious, causing many eating-disordered teens to see things in an all-or-none/black-or-white fashion—"If I eat one cookie, I will have to eat the whole bag." "If I don't get an A in this course, I might as well fail it." Eating-disordered teens also have a high incidence of associated psychological problems, including substance abuse, obsessive-compulsive disorder, personality disorders, depression, and suicidal thoughts. Death from eating disorders usually is due to suicide, electrolyte (body salt) imbalance, or starvation.

Binge-eating disorder is a recently recognized problem that features episodic uncontrolled consumption, without compensatory activities such as vomiting or laxative abuse, to avert weight gain.

Eating disorders can cause a host of physical complications. Children with anorexia can develop heart, liver, and kidney damage from malnutrition. Their pulse and blood pressure drop, occasionally causing dizziness and fainting. They lose their periods (or don't start them if prepubertal) because of decreased body fat and low estrogen, which, along with low calcium intake, can lead to osteoporosis long before they reach middle age. They can't concentrate and may be moody and withdrawn.

Although extreme binging can lead to stomach rupture, most bulimic complications come from purging. The combination of the two causes "chipmunk cheeks" enlarged saliva glands caused by overuse from binging and irritation from the stomach acid bath of vomiting. At the least, self-induced vomiting can cause dental decay, but it can also lead to erosion of the esophagus and serious electrolyte imbalance, particularly potassium depletion, which can produce fatal heart problems. Some bulimics resort to using ipecac to induce vomiting. You may be familiar with this drug because your health care provider may have had you keep it on hand in case of accidental poisoning in your toddlers. Bulimics, however, tend to take massive dosages which can prove fatal because ipecac is toxic to the heart. Some bulimics resort to other purgative measures to lose weight, including laxative or diuretic (water pill) abuse, diet pills, and even enemas. All of this can lead to various problems, including dehydration and electrolyte imbalance.

The cause of eating disorders remains unknown, but is considered to be multifactorial—with individual, familial, and sociocultural factors. Eating disorders tend to be noted more often in girls with poor self-esteem, in families where other family members have eating disorders, and in cultures that stress thinness. Eating disorders are not contagious, but susceptible teens can be easily influenced by friends who think that being thin is the most important thing in the world.

As mentioned, culture plays an important role in the development of eating disorders, which have flourished in industrialized nations since Twiggy made her debut in the 1960s. Unfortunately, things have not gotten much better. The media still projects an image that equates success with thinness. The thin woman—be she actress or supermodel—gets the job, the guy, the car, the house, and the bucks. Add to this the multi-billion-dollar dieting industry, which advertises heavily, and teens are constantly bombarded with a distorted version of reality–the reality that 98% of women are larger than supermodels and that inner beauty is more important than outer.

HOW DO YOU KNOW IF YOUR CHILD IS AT RISK FOR DEVELOPING AN EATING DISORDER?

Your child has a higher risk than average if she fits any of the following:

- Has low self-esteem and is easily influenced by others
- Is interested in being a dancer, cheerleader, model, actress, or other thin-oriented profession
- Is an athlete, particularly a runner
- Is a perfectionist who is eager to please
- Has trouble controlling her impulses
- Has few friends
- Thinks that dieting will make her feel better about herself
- Has been physically or sexually abused
- Someone else in the family has an eating disorder
- Males are also at greater risk if they are gay, wrestlers, or jockeys

Eating disorders are not as obvious as obesity. The following are signs that your child may have an eating disorder. SHOULD YOU SUSPECT THAT SHE HAS A PROBLEM, contact your health care provider.

- recent weight loss or weight fluctuations of more than five pounds (bulimia)
- a fear of gaining weight or of being fat
- preoccupation with being fat or a specific body part
- signs of purging behaviors: going into the bathroom right after meals (to vomit); scrape or scar on her knuckles (sticking her fingers down her throat to induce vomiting); laxatives or diuretics found in room
- having a distorted image of her body's size or shape (for example, believing that she's overweight even though she is at a healthy weight)
- a preoccupation with thoughts of food, calories, and her weight
- restrictive eating patterns, such as skipping meals, fasting, or eliminating entire food groups
- preference for eating alone
- preoccupied with food and food-related items, like cookbooks
- telling family what to eat and commenting on calorie content of family members' food

- loss of periods or delayed onset of puberty and menarche (first period)
- being underweight
- exercising compulsively (gets stressed if exercise ritual is broken)
- shows extreme denial about her weight loss and eating disorder
- withdraws from friends and family, or very superficial friendships
- wearing bulky clothing to hide weight loss
- shoplifting
- large quantities of household food missing frequently; stealing to buy food
- recent or past event in her life that was very stressful

WHAT TO DO IF YOUR CHILD HAS AN EATING DISORDER

Eating disorders require professional treatment. If you suspect that your child has an eating disorder, contact your health care provider. She will first need a complete examination and some laboratory tests to make sure her weight loss or fluctuation isn't from a physical ailment and to see if she has developed any problems due to her eating disorder. Your health care provider should then see your child at regular intervals to keep her health at an optimal level. The frequency depends on the severity of her disorder.

Your health care provider will recommend that you and your child see a counselor and a nutritionist. The counselor will evaluate your child and the family for underlying stressors. Eating disorders can result from family dysfunction, but can also develop in functioning families. However, even in the best of families, eating disordered children can be difficult, so if your family was not chaotic before the eating disorder started, it will be afterward.

Rapid weight gain can be as physically harmful as it's psychologically harmful, causing potential liver problems and heart failure. Slow, healthy weight gain is preferred, under the guidance of a nutritionist who can best tailor an eating program to fit your child's needs. The nutritionist can also help your child learn how to eat according to healthy portion size instead of calorie counting.

Psychiatric mediation may be warranted, particularly if your child has a coexisting disorder, such as depression or obsessive-compulsive disorder. If a medication is ordered, give it time to work. Many of these drugs take a few weeks to see results.

Additional treatment will be needed for children who develop complications, such as dehydration, constipation, and menstrual irregularities. Treatment of eating disorders can be long and difficult, so hang in there, and make sure you have support, too.

PREVENTING OBESITY AND EATING DISORDERS

Obesity and eating disorder treatments can be long, stressful processes. The best approach is to try to avoid them altogether. Body image, self-esteem, eating patterns, and activity patterns develop early in life, all modeled on the adults children see every day—their parents. You need to realize that beliefs and habits formed at an early age can become lifelong practices. You choose the foods they eat, decide on the amount of TV they can watch, and foster their exercise routines, and you help them learn how to feel about their bodies and themselves.

PREVENTION: THE BALANCE BETWEEN TOO MUCH AND NOT ENOUGH

Obesity and eating disorders are very difficult to treat. The best thing that parents can do for their children is to prevent them to begin with. Prevention is a balancing act, and it starts early. Both bottle-fed and breast-fed babies can develop obesity when overfed, so respect your infant's appetite and realize that it's not necessary for her to finish every meal. As your child grows:

- Replace whole milk with skim after age 2.
- Never use food as a reward or insist that your child clean her plate to get dessert.
- Don't insist on her cleaning her plate—clean plates in America won't feed starving children in China.
- Provide a health diet, including breakfast.
- Minimize your use of processed and sugary foods. Plan ahead, cook larger quantities, and freeze some for a later meal.
- Limit trips to fast food places. When you do use them, choose the healthy alternatives: sandwiches, veggie burgers, salads, and yogurts, but allow the occasional burgers and fries.
- Encourage water and milk; discourage soda, sweetened drinks, and excessive amounts of juice.
- Keep healthy snacks on hand.

- Disallow eating in front of the TV.
- Eat as a family at least once a day, and make this a happy time. Don't use the dinner table as a boxing ring.
- Limit TV watching to about 2 hours per day.
- Encourage physical exercise.
- Never emphasize body shape as a measurement of worth to your child.
- Realize that certain sports and activities—wrestling, swimming, gymnastics, track, acting, and modeling—require weight restrictions, putting your child at risk for eating disorders. If your child doesn't have the natural physique to maintain the required weight in a healthy manner, help her find an alternative activity.
- Help your child feel comfortable and confident in her body.
- Talk to your children about what it means to be feminine or masculine, and help them realize that there are expanding ideas on these roles. Masculine can mean caring and nurturing, and men can enjoy activities like cooking and shopping.
- Don't be overprotective. Validate your child's striving for independence, and encourage her to develop all aspects of her personality.
- Show respect for gay men who display traits that stretch the traditional bounds of masculinity.
- Explain the paradox of the media's presentation of perfect body shapes.

In an age when looks carry far too much importance, it's difficult not to focus on body shape. But instead, help your child achieve and maintain a weight that is healthy, and to eat and exercise for health and enjoyment.

OBESITY RESOURCES

American Obesity Association
www.obesity.org

Weight Control Information Network
www.niddk.nih.gov/health/nutrit/win.htm

Weight Watchers
www.weightwatchers.com

USDA Weight Control Page
ww.nal.usda.gov/fnic/etext/000060.html

EATING DISORDER RESOURCES

Renfrew Foundation
www.renfrew.org/getting.htm

National Association Of Anorexia Nervosa And Associated Disorders
www.anad.org

National Eating Disorders Organization
www.kidsource.com/nedo/index.html

Anorexia Nervosa And Related Eating Disorders, Inc.
www.anred.com

American Anorexia And Bulimia Association
www.aaba.org

Eating Disorder Awareness & Prevention, Inc.
www.edap.org

Eating Disorder Referral & Information Center
www.edreferral.com

5

FEAR

CALIFORNIA, 1999:
9-year-old boy washes his hands every five minutes. His anxiety level is so high that his mother has to remove him from school.

SOME STATS

- Almost half of all 6- to 12-year-olds have seven or more fears.
- About 10 to 13% of children suffer from one of the anxiety disorders.
- According to a paper by the National Institute of Mental Health and the Anxiety Disorders Association of America, childhood anxiety disorders are vastly under-diagnosed, undertreated, and understudied despite their prevalence.
- Children with anxiety disorders commonly suffer from other problems such as depression, behavior problems, and substance abuse.
- Most adult anxiety disorders have their roots in childhood or adolescence and affect millions of people:

—Panic disorder	2.4 million
—Obsessive-compulsive disorder	3.3 million
—Post-traumatic stress disorder	5.2 million
—General anxiety disorder	4.0 million
—Social phobia	5.3 million
—Specific phobias	3.2 million

Abductions, terrorism, school shootings, SARS, product recalls, war . . .
The monsters have moved out of the closet.
Or have they?

As a parent, you worry about and for your child. You worry about his tackling illnesses, his first day of school, and his first kiss.

But now that danger seems to lurk behind every corner, you worry also about his facing abductors, biochemical weapons, and irate classmates.

Yet, we are living longer in the safety of modern life. That safety, accompanied by the increase in news reporting, may be amplifying our fears. The calm of our everyday existence shatters when we confront stories of new diseases and meaningless homicides. Dying prematurely today can mean dying 40 years ahead of time instead of 10. And while science has bettered our nutrition and environment, unpredictable events, such as September 11 and SARS, leave us feeling helpless, at least initially. Much of this book is dedicated to help you deal with today's threats, and fear makes the list.

Fear is a state of apprehension or response to a specific threatening situation. Fear turns into phobia when it become persistent, extreme, and irrational. But some fear is necessary for survival. The normal "fight or flight" fear response sends an adrenaline surge through our bodies that allows us to run away from a dangerous situation or face it head on.

Anxiety, fear's other half, is a diffuse uneasiness in response to less specific stimuli. Mild anxiety motivates us in today's world by preparing us to face challenges and take action when needed. Mild anxiety prepares you for that important job interview or final exam. However, should that anxiety escalate, your ability to prepare and take action disintegrates, falling totally apart when your anxiety level peaks.

Excessive fear can be destructive and contagious. Once gripped by fear, you can become paralyzed, unable to perform simple tasks like cooking. Anxiety takes its toll, causing problems with sleeping, eating, and concentrating—leaving you with headaches and stomach knots. Since children learn by watching their parents, fearful, anxious parents often have fearful, anxious children. Be careful not to overreact to your fears. Instead, confront them and deal with them so that your children learn that, while fears are normal, they can be managed.

Abductions, school shootings, and disasters remain rare, yet their horror places them firmly in our minds. That concern makes us want to shelter our children from these unspeakable terrors. However, when shelter turns to prison, we create "bubble children," who see the world as a scary place. Bubble children live in fear and don't learn how to cope when things go wrong. And despite how much we try, things always go wrong sooner or later. Don't make changes in your life to accommodate fear; this only reinforces it. Instead, keep life as normal as possible, and confront fear whenever it occurs.

NORMAL CHILDHOOD FEARS

All children experience fear and anxiety at some time or another. Some fears are part of growing up, and experiencing and dealing with fear and anxiety prepares your children to handle unsettling experiences and challenging situations throughout life. Remember, these fears are very real to your child, so take them seriously.

INFANTS

Even tiny babies feel fear. They cry, look away, arch their backs, and startle when frightened. Babies experience stranger anxiety and get clingy to their parents when confronted by someone they don't know. It's not unusual for parents to become alarmed when their usually easygoing infant starts screaming when grandma tries to pick him up. As they get a bit older, infants fear separating from their parents and falling.

Some babies, about 10% of all infants, are born with an inclination toward fearfulness, according to Dr. Kathryn Barnard, a professor at the University of Washington. These infants startle more easily and react intensely to anything out-of-the-ordinary.

Keep your baby on a schedule to help him feel more secure. Calm him with a soothing voice, letting him know that everything's okay. Touch is as important as voice, so make sure to cradle and rock him to ease his fears. To ward off stranger anxiety, gradually expose your baby to new people for short periods of time. Let him see the person from a comfortable distance before that person attempts to pick him up. Then make sure you stay in his sight so that he relaxes.

TODDLERS

By age 1 your child fears separation from you, noises, Santa Claus, large animals, bathtime, and his health care provider. As he reaches 2, toilet training and bedtime jump on the list. Separation anxiety peaks around age 18 months. Your child may get so upset when you leave that he becomes inconsolable. To diminish these fears, leave your child with "a part of you"—a photo, keys, a scarf—when you have to leave him, and let him know when you'll return—when it gets dark, when it's dinner time, when SpongeBob comes on TV. He can't tell time, so use something concrete that he can relate to. When he cries at the site of a big dog or Santa Claus, acknowledge his fears and tell him why he's safe. Don't mock him by belittling his concerns.

Make bathtime more pleasurable by using a small basin (big tubs are scary) and filling it with favorite bath toys. Don't force the issue of toilet training. He will be ready when he's ready. I guarantee that all healthy children will be fully toilet trained by their twenty-first birthday. Make sure his feet touch the ground when he sits on the potty, and use caution when flushing. Some toddlers see their waste products as body parts and fear getting flushed down the drain with them!

Bedtime brings out his separation anxiety. Make it easier by creating a ritual—having his bath, reading a book, getting a glass of water, then going to bed. Keep him on schedule and make sure his room isn't overstimulating. A favorite toy or blankie helps soothe separation fears.

PRESCHOOLERS

The preschool years, ages 3 to 6, are the peak time for childhood fears, thanks to the magical thinking that occurs during this stage. This magical thinking is responsible for the wonders of this stage, when children firmly believe in fairies and make-believe. But it's also has a dark side. His growing imagination turns his familiar room into a scary place with monsters lurking in his closets and under his bed. Common fears of preschoolers include: the dark; being left alone, especially at bedtime; animals, particularly large dogs; ghosts and other supernatural beings; body mutilation and pain, as well as objects and people associated with painful experiences.

Your preschooler is prone to parent-induced fears stemming from your remarks and actions, even though you're unaware that your behavior is instilling fear in your child. Allow your child to have a night-light, and encourage him to play out fears with dolls or other toys to give him a sense of control over the fear. Exposing him to a feared object in a controlled setting can provide an opportunity for desensitization and reduction of a specific fear.

Preschool curiosity can outweigh fear, so watch for impulsive reactions. A fear of heights may not keep him from jumping off the back deck when playing Spiderman. Make sure you discuss safety issues with him.

SCHOOL-AGE CHILDREN

During the school-age years, many fears of earlier childhood resolve or decrease. Older children can differentiate between fantasy and reality, and many of their fears center around school and friends. Common fears during this age may include failure at school, bullies, intimidating teachers, supernatural beings, storms, staying alone, scary things in TV and movies, consequences related to unattractive appearance, and death. You can help reduce your child's fears by communicating empathy and concern without being overprotective.

School-age kids don't usually state their fears directly. Instead, they may react in the opposite direction—"I ain't afraid of no stinkin' bullies. I'm the toughest kid in school." Translation: I'm petrified of the bullies, but too embarrassed to admit I'm scared.

Older children can easily become upset by recent news events. Even if you disallow your child to watch the news at home, he's likely to hear about it in school when other kids or teachers talk about frightening events, such as school shootings and terrorism. You can't shield your child from reality, but you can monitor what he sees at home and talk to him about his fears. You can also help by showing him that he's not powerless. Help him do something constructive, like write letters to servicemen or families of shooting victims.

Realize that children this age now know that death is irreversible and fear it. They may fear their own mortality and yours. Dr. Robert Brooks, a psychology professor at Harvard, recommends that you answer your child's questions honestly in a reassuring manner: "All people die, but most people live until they're very old."

ADOLESCENTS

Common fears of adolescents include: burglars, war, parental divorce, relationships with persons of the opposite sex, homosexual tendencies, ability to assume adult roles, drugs, HIV/AIDS, cancer, gossip, public speaking, plane and car crashes, and death. Listening to your adolescent's concerns and encouraging open communication helps him develop increased confidence in his ability to cope with fearful situations.

FEAR IS PART OF CHILDHOOD, BUT YOU CAN EASE YOUR CHILD'S WORRIES AND HELP HIM TO COPE BY TRYING THE FOLLOWING:

- Take care of yourself first. Kids detect parental anxiety in a heartbeat, and it becomes contagious.
- Realize that fears don't go away overnight.
- Don't belittle his fears, but don't cater to them either.
- Be matter-of-fact when you talk to them about their fears to avoid increasing their anxiety. But don't force your child to face his fears. This can make the situation worse and frighten your child even more. Let him face them at his own pace.
- Let him know it's okay to be afraid so that he doesn't feel guilty or embarrassed by his fears.
- Don't tell him that he's a big boy when he overcomes his fears. This places too much pressure on him.
- Sit down and talk with older kids and teens, but do so while assuring them that you're there for them and that they are safe. Younger children may do better with puppet play, coloring, painting, or play-acting.
- Help him understand his fears: play shadow puppets to help him with his fear of the dark; dogs bark because that is how they talk.
- Take time to point out what is RIGHT with the world, including school. Yes, there are a lot of drugs and bullies, but there are a lot of positive people and role models, too. Use positive talk about one's self and situation.
- Minimize the amount of time your kids spend watching the news on TV and the Internet. Kids under 6 should not watch the news at all.
- Encourage your kids to talk about what is bothering them as well as what they are happy with. If they are hesitant, ask them to draw their feelings.
- Let you kids be kids. Childhood should be a journey, not a race. Don't push them to grow up too fast. Instead, allow them to tackle developmentally-appropriate challenges on their own, even if they stumble, so that they can become independent and self-assured.
- Get them a pet (as long as they are old enough and responsible). There is nothing better than cuddling up with a bundle of unconditional love to decrease anxiety.

WHEN FEAR & ANXIETY GET OUT OF CONTROL

For many children, fear becomes phobia, and anxiety turns to another anxiety disorder. Youngsters with anxiety disorders are usually so afraid, worried, or uneasy that they can't function normally. These disorders can last a long time and interfere greatly with your child's life if left untreated.

Although very common, anxiety disorders in children are often overlooked or misjudged. Since a certain level of anxiety is normal, it becomes important to distinguish between normal levels and pathological levels of anxiety. The experience of anxiety often has two components: physical components, such as headache, stomach ache, and sweating; and emotional components, which include nervousness and fear. Anxiety disorders, on the other hand, often affect your child's thinking, decision-making ability, and perceptions of the environment. They can raise his blood pressure and cause a number of physical ailments, including diarrhea, shortness of breath, and palpitations, and they are frequently accompanied by other disorders, such as depression and substance abuse.

Anxiety disorders are true illnesses, not figments of your child's imagination. The ones commonly seen during childhood are: generalized anxiety disorder, adjustment disorder with anxiety, separation anxiety disorder, obsessive-compulsive disorder, specific phobias, social phobia, panic disorder, acute stress disorder, and post-traumatic stress disorder.

GENERAL ANXIETY DISORDER (GAD)

GAD is defined as excessive worry, anxiety, and apprehension occurring on most days for a period of six months or more. The worries are diffuse, covering a number of topics and events. The child has difficulty controlling his anxiety, which is associated with some of the following: feeling on the edge or pent up, restlessness, getting easily fatigued, trouble concentrating or feeling like his mind goes blank, irritability, muscle tension, and sleep disturbances. His anxiety causes serious distress or problems functioning.

ADJUSTMENT DISORDER WITH ANXIETY

This disorder occurs within three months of a specific stressor, such as a move, change of school, or parental divorce. The child experiences feelings of anxiety, nervousness, and worry that cause marked distress in excess of what would be expected from the situation, and that could seriously impair his social or academic performance. The problem usually dissipates six months after the initiating stressor ceases.

SEPARATION ANXIETY DISORDER

These children experience intense anxiety, sometimes to the point of panic, when separated from a parent or other loved one. It typically appears suddenly in a child who had no previous signs of a problem. The anxiety is so severe that the child can't perform his daily activities. When separated, he becomes preoccupied with morbid fears of harm that will come to them or fears that they won't return. Separation anxiety can give way to school phobia, whereby the child will refuse to go to school because they fear separation from their parent.

OBSESSIVE-COMPULSIVE DISORDER (OCD)

Once thought to occur only in adults (think Melvin Udall in *As Good as it Gets* or *Monk*), this disorder is now more frequently diagnosed in children. OCD is characterized by persistent obsessions (intrusive, unwanted thoughts, images or urges) and compulsions (intensive, uncontrollable, and repetitive behaviors or mental acts related to the obsessions). These obsessions and compulsions cause distress and consume a huge amount of the child's time. The most common obsessions involve dirtiness and contamination, repeated doubts, and the need to have things a specific way. Others include fearful aggressive or murderous impulses and disturbing sexual images. Frequent compulsions include repetitive handwashing, using tissues or gloved hands to touch things, touching and counting things, checking locks, counting rituals, repeating actions, and requesting reassurance.

Children with OCD become trapped in the cycle of repetitive thoughts and actions. Even though they realize that their thoughts and behaviors appear senseless and distressing, the behaviors are very hard to stop.

SPECIFIC PHOBIA

This is an excessive, persistent fear that is recognized as unreasonable, and that is triggered by a specific object: snakes, spiders, computers, close spaces, heights, flying and getting injured. Exposure to the object immediately provokes anxiety. The distress is so severe that it interferes with the child's functioning or routine.

SOCIAL PHOBIA

A very common phobia, social phobia is the persistent and substantial fear of one or more social situations in which the child is exposed to unfamiliar people or scrutiny by others. During these situations, he feels that he will behave in a manner that will be embarrassing or humiliating. Exposure to these situations causes significant anxiety and possible panic, despite knowing that the fear is unreasonable. This fear can lead your child to avoid such situations, leading to marked interference in his life.

PANIC DISORDER

Panic disorder consists of recurrent panic attacks: sudden, discrete episodes of intense fear that are usually accompanied by a desire to escape and a feeling of doom or impending danger. These usually peak in 10 minutes, subside in 20 to 30, minutes and are accompanied by at least four of the following: palpitations, sweating, shortness of breath or feeling smothered, trembling or shaking, sweating, nausea and abdominal pain, dizziness, lightheadedness, feeling faint, sense of unreality or being detached from one's self, fear of losing control or going crazy, numbness and tingling, and chills or hot flashes.

ACUTE STRESS DISORDER & POSTTRAUMATIC STRESS DISORDER

In both these disorders, the child is exposed to a traumatic event in which he experiences, witnesses, or is confronted by a situation (abuse, violence, natural or man-made disaster) that involves an actual or perceived threat of serious injury or death. His response involves intense fear, helplessness, or horror, and he relives the event in the following ways: recurrent images, thoughts, or dreams. He may also believe that the event is recurring or feel intense anxiety in situations that resemble the event. The child can also experience some of the following: inability to remember details of the event, marked participation in activities, feelings of detachment, restricted emotional range, difficulty making decisions, irritability, agitation, anger, resentment, numbness, spontaneous crying, and a sense of despair. Acute stress disorder occurs within two days of the event and lasts less than one month, while post-traumatic stress disorder has a delayed onset and lasts more than a month.

WHAT CAUSES ANXIETY DISORDERS?

Like most psychiatric disorders, the exact cause is unknown. However, several factors have been implicated:

1. Anxiety disorders can be the result of a combination of overwhelming internal and external stresses that surpass the child's coping abilities.
2. About 50% of people with panic disorders have at least one relative who has an anxiety disorder, and there is an increased chance of developing an anxiety disorder if a child's parents or siblings have one.
3. Certain brain chemicals and abnormal brain functions have been implicated in the development of anxiety disorders. Evidence support the involvement of norepinephrine, GABA, and serotonin, which helps to explain the success of certain medications to treat many of these disorders.
4. Certain illnesses, such as lung and endocrine disorders, can cause anxiety disorders. Therefore, all children with anxiety symptoms should be checked for underlying medical problems, such as hyperthyroidism. Some medications, including some that treat asthma, can also cause anxiety symptoms.

IS YOUR CHILD AT RISK FOR DEVELOPING AN ANXIETY DISORDER?

Researchers found that a child's basic temperament may play a role in his developing an anxiety disorder. Children who tend to be very shy and restrained in unfamiliar situations may be at risk. Researcher also suggest monitoring for signs of anxiety between the ages of 6 and 8, when imaginary fears should diminish and the child may be excessively anxious about school performance or social relationships. Your child may also be at risk if you or your spouse suffer from an anxiety disorder.

WHAT SYMPTOMS SHOULD YOU LOOK FOR?

Everyone gets anxious from time to time, and we all have our fears. However, signs of excessive anxiety mean that your child should be evaluated by a professional. Talk to your health care provider if your child exhibits any of the following:

- Shows difficulty concentrating
- Becomes more or less active than usual
- Eats a lot more or less than usual
- Regresses back to earlier behavior (starts sucking his thumb again)
- Has trouble sleeping
- Complains of stomach or headaches
- Wets or soils his pants

HOW ARE ANXIETY DISORDERS TREATED?

Anxiety disorders require professional treatment, which may include individual and/or family psychotherapy, medications, and environmental treatment. Some treatments work better with certain disorders, while other treatments work best with other disorders.

PSYCHOTHERAPY: Your child may benefit from a number of different therapies. Cognitive-behavioral therapy addresses underlying thoughts and feelings, as well as specific techniques to reduce or replace maladaptive behaviors. Psychotherapy aims at resolving conflicts or stresses, and behavioral therapy focuses on techniques such as imagery, relaxation techniques, and desensitization to reduce or eliminate phobias.

MEDICATIONS: Several medications benefit various anxiety disorders, including antihistamines. Your health care provider or psychiatrist will choose the one most likely to work for your child's age and disorder. Antihistamines (Benadryl, Atarax) can help mild anxiety. Benzodiazepines (Valium, Ativan) quickly reduce anxiety symptoms, but can cause tolerance if used for a long period of time. Tricyclic antidepressants (Tofranil, Elavil) are older antidepressant drugs that, for the most part, have been replaced by newer agents. Serotonergic agents (Paxil, Prozac, Zoloft) are the newer antidepressant drugs that are also used for anxiety with excellent effectiveness and tolerability. Combination serotonin/norepinephrine agents

(Effexor, Serzone, Remeron) also have excellent effectiveness. Buspirone (Buspar) is a combination serotinergic agonist/antagonist that is effective and nonaddicting. Many of these medications take two to six weeks to create their full effect, so give them time to work.

ENVIRONMENTAL TREATMENT: Children with anxiety disorders benefit from good sleep patterns and avoidance of stimulants such as caffeine, which is found in several products, including chocolate. Reduction of stressors at home or school can also help.

RESOURCES

American Academy of Child and Adolescent Psychiatrists
www.aacap.org

Separation Anxiety Support
www.medhelp.org/HealthTopics/Separation.html

Child and Adolescent Anxiety Disorders
http://www.mccg.org/childrenshealth/mentalhealth/anxhub.asp

6

FIRE

OHIO, 2002:
Fire soars through a suburban home, killing four children.

SOME STATS

- In 1999, more than 600 children under age 14 died from fire-related injuries.
- More than 70% of all fire-related deaths result from smoke inhalation.
- In 2000, nearly 100,000 children under age 14 were treated in hospitals for burn-related injuries.
- In 2000, more than 5,000 children under age 14 were treated for fireworks-related injuries.
- Fireworks, curling irons and hot curlers, room heaters, ovens, irons, and gasoline cause the most product-related burns in children.
- Almost two-thirds of childhood electrical burn injuries come from household electrical cords and extension cords.

Death, burns, and smoke inhalation cause devastation from house fires. The rate of fire-related injury has declined since the seventies, but fire and burns remain the fourth leading cause of injury-related death in children age 14 and under. Children under five are particularly susceptible to fire-related death because they a have a less acute perception of their environment, and a limited ability to react promptly and properly. Rural children have a greater chance of dying in a home fire as death rates in rural areas are twice the rates of deaths in big cities and three times higher than small towns.

More than 43% of home fire-related deaths happen to children under nine when they are trying to escape. The child may become unable to act or act irrationally. An escape plan may reduce the number of these deaths, yet only 26% of households develop and practice escape plans.

BURNS IN CHILDREN

Burns have been recognized as some of the most painful and debilitating injuries a child can sustain. They can require long periods of rehabilitation, multiple skin grafts, and painful physical therapy, and they can leave your child physically and emotionally scarred for life.

Burn injuries to one or more layers of the skin and underlying structures causing varying types of damage based on the depth of the burn:

FIRST-DEGREE burns involve only the epidermis or outer layer of the skin. This skin becomes red, dry, and painful but doesn't blister, as in mild sunburn.

SECOND-DEGREE or partial-thickness burns cause more serious damage to the top layer of the dermis, the next layer of skin, resulting in blistering. The area turns red and painful, but moist, and the tissue remains viable.

THIRD-DEGREE or full-thickness burns extend to all skin layers, leaving the fatty tissue exposed. The area looks charred, white, leathery, and firm. Third-degree burns also destroy nerve endings, thus your child may not feel any pain in the burned area.

FOURTH-DEGREE burns extend to muscle and bone. Fortunately, these are rare.

Burns involving large body surfaces can vary in their degree of depth, and because burn injuries are dynamic, their total effect may not be readily apparent at first.

CHILDREN MOST AT RISK

Young children under age 4 and children with disabilities run the greatest risk of burn-related injury or death. Their risk is highest for scald and contact burns. Boys have greater risk than girls, particularly boys ages 10 to 14 from fireworks injuries (children under 4 are high risk for sparkler injuries). And all children in homes without smoke alarms are at the greatest risk for fire-related injury and death.

FIRE PREVENTION

How fire safe is your home? Does anyone smoke in bed? Are any of your outlets overloaded? Are electrical extension cords running under the carpet? Do you own a wood-burning stove? When did you last get the chimney cleaned and inspected? Do your kids know what to do in case of fire?

Burns originate from a number of thermal, electrical, or chemical sources: wood stoves, kerosene heaters, space heaters, grills, hot liquids, cooking equipment, irons, hair curling equipment, electrical cords, cigarettes, matches, fireworks, and the sun.

To keep your children safe from fire, follow these suggestions compiled from the United States Fire Administration, the National Safe Kids Campaign, the American Academy of Pediatrics, the Hearth, Patio, and Barbeque Association, the New York City Fire Department, and the United States Consumer Product Safety Commission.

GENERAL SAFETY

Install and maintain UL-listed SMOKE DETECTORS on each level of your home and outside every sleeping area—for extra safety, install one inside each sleeping area, too. Follow the manufacturer's directions, test them once a week, and change their batteries twice a year and if it "chirps" for a battery change. Don't "borrow" the smoke detector batteries to operate anything else.

Install CARBON MONOXIDE DETECTORS. Invisible, odorless, and tasteless, carbon monoxide is a silent killer. Purchase UL-listed alarms to reduce the incidence of nuisance noise, and read more on carbon monoxide in Chapter 13: Poisons.

Keep FIRE EXTINGUISHERS handy, and know how to use them. Even though they come in many shapes and sizes, all are similar to operate. The Hanford Fire Department, operated for the United States Department of Energy, suggests remembering the PASS acronym for fire extinguisher use:

P = PULL the pin at the top of the device that keeps the handle from being accidentally pressed.

A = AIM the nozzle at the base of the fire.

S = SQUEEZE the handle to discharge the extinguisher, standing 8 feet away from the fire. The discharge will stop when you release the handle.

S = SWEEP the nozzle back and forth at the base of the fire.

Once the fire appears to be out, monitor it carefully to make sure it doesn't reignite.

Fire extinguishers come in 4 different classes or types (A, B, C, and D). Older extinguishers are labeled with colored geometric designs that hold the letter designations, while newer models use a picture/labeling system to designate their type. Class A and B extinguishers also carry a numerical rating, which is based on tests conducted by Underwriter's Laboratory to determine the extinguishing potential for each size and type of extinguisher.

CLASS A extinguishers put out fires in ordinary combustibles, such as wood or paper. The numerical rating for this class refers to the amount of water the extinguisher holds and the amount of fire it will extinguish.

CLASS B extinguishers are used for flammable liquid fires created by grease, gas, oil, etc. The numerical rating for this class stands for the approximate number of square feet of a flammable liquid fire that a nonexpert can expect to extinguish.

CLASS C extinguishers work on electrical fires. They don't have numerical ratings, and the presence of a "C" indicates that the extinguishing agent is nonconductive.

CLASS D extinguishers work on flammable metals and are often specific for the type of metal in question. There is no picture designation or numerical rating for this class, and they are not given a multipurpose rating for use on other types of fires.

Many extinguishers are multi-rated for different types of fires and will be labeled with more than one designator picture/geometric shape and letter, such as A-B, B-C, or A-B-C. If you use a multi-rated extinguisher, make sure it's properly labeled for your use.

Fire extinguishers also come in different types:

DRY CHEMICAL extinguishers contain an extinguishing agent and use a compressed, nonflammable gas as a propellant. They are usually multi-rated.

HALON extinguishers hold a gas that interrupts the chemical reaction that takes place when fuel burns. They are typically used to protect valuable electrical devices since they leave no residue to clean up. These have a limited range of about 4 to 6 feet and should be aimed at the base of the fire, even after the flames have been extinguished.

WATER extinguishers should only be used on Class A fires because they contain water and compressed gas.

CARBON DIOXIDE (CO_2) extinguishers work best on Class B & C (liquid or electrical) fires. CO_2 cools the surrounding air and will often cause ice to form around the "horn" where the gas is expelled from the extinguisher. The gas disperses quickly, so these extinguishers are only effective from 3 to 8 feet.

Automatic home fire SPRINKLER SYSTEMS have become more affordable. According to the Tri-State Fire Protection District in Illinois, automatic sprinkler systems act early in the course of a fire. They reduce the heat and the flames, as well as the amount of smoke produced.

Develop and practice an ESCAPE PLAN in case of fire. Plan at least two ways out of the house (preferably two ways out of each room) and choose a meeting place outside where you all can gather. Practice the plan often to help your children, since they may become confused and frightened during a fire.

If your home has a second level, obtain a noncombustible fire escape ladder, and practice using it. Apartment buildings should have safe, functioning fire escapes. Create a specific plan if your child has disabilities. Consult your local fire department for help. If your child is deaf or nonverbal, teach your neighbors the sign language sign for "fire." And make sure the fire escape plan is taught to all your child caregivers, including babysitters.

In case of fire, crawl low on hands and knees under smoke to exit a room. Use stairs to exit a building. Never use elevators as they can stop on a burning floor. Instruct your child to STOP, DROP, ROLL, and COOL if her clothing catches on fire.

Teach all children ages 3 and older what to do in case of a fire. Tell them that the sound of a smoke alarm means to go outside to the meeting place.

HEATING EQUIPMENT SAFETY

The use of supplemental heating systems, such as wood-burning stoves, fireplaces, kerosene heaters, and space heaters has decreased. Yet about 12,000 residential fires occur annually from the use of these heaters, representing 22% of all house fires. These fires kill approximately 600 people per year and cause thousands of contact burn injuries and hundreds of carbon monoxide poisonings.

No longer just a rural home staple, WOOD-BURNING STOVES have found their way into some affluent houses. Some of these are ornamental in nature, but many are used as primary heat sources. Wood-burners create considerable amounts of heat that can ignite nearby combustibles, such as curtains and furniture. Creosote, an unavoidable by-product of wood burning, can build up in the chimney flue resulting in a chimney fire.

TO PREVENT A HOUSE FIRE:

- Keep a fire extinguisher nearby.
- Make sure that your stove, chimney, and stovepipe have been installed correctly according to the manufacturer's instructions and building codes. If unsure, contact the manufacturer and/or your local building inspector for assistance.
- Have your chimney and stove inspected and cleaned by a professional chimney sweep, certified by the Chimney Safety Institute of America (CSIA) at least twice a year. These professionals can detect problems, such as cracks, faults, and structural damage that may not be visible from the outside. They will also remove creosote, leaves, bird's nests, and branches, and look for other problems within your system.
- Install a cap on the chimney to avoid animals or debris from blocking it.
- Inspect your stovepipe and chimney regularly during the burning season for creosote buildup.
- Stand your stove on a code-specific or listed floor protector that extends at least 18 inches beyond the stove at all sides to reduce the possibility of the floor igniting.
- Follow the manufacturer's instructions regarding the distance the stove should be away from combustible walls.
- To prevent creosote buildup:
  Burn only natural, dry, seasoned wood.
  Maintain a brisk fire
  Keep the flue temperature above 250 degrees Fahrenheit
- Never use gasoline or other flammable liquids to start the fire. These will ignite and explode.
- Never burn trash or paper.
- Keep combustibles such as curtains, furniture, and firewood at least 3 feet away from the stove.

- Store your ashes in an approved metal container with a tight-fitting lid.
- Gate the stove area to keep small children away.

FIREPLACES, both elaborate and simple, can be as dangerous as they are beautiful.

All hearth products, including fireplaces, should be maintained and operated correctly to function safely and efficiently. Regardless of the type of hearth product, it must be installed properly according to the manufacturer's instructions, preferably by a qualified technician. To verify if your installer is certified, contact the National Fireplace Institute at www.nficertifed.org (Phone: 703-524-8030—Fax: 703-522-0548—E-mail: info@nficertified.org), or use the hearth product manufacturer directory at www.hpba.org (The Hearth, Patio, and Barbeque Association).

TO PREVENT FIREPLACE FIRES:

- Keep a fire extinguisher nearby.
- Use natural, seasoned logs. If you use artificial ones, follows the package directions.
- Keep your fireplace and chimney clean and in good repair (see above information on chimneys).
- Make sure the damper is set so the draft will remove smoke and gases when the fireplace is on. But remember that too much airflow can cause the fire to get out of control.
- Use a fireplace screen and install a fireplace guard or hearth gate to protect young children. Use a cushioned edge guard if you have an elevated fireplace edge to prevent injuries from falls onto the edge.
- Keep young children and pets away from the fireplace.
- Don't burn Christmas trees, garbage, plastic, rolled newspapers, or charcoal in the fireplace.
- Store ashes in a noncombustible container with a tight-fitting lid.
- Keep flammables (carpet, books, logs, furniture, drapes, etc.) away from the fireplace.
- Don't close the damper until the embers have completely burned out.
- Never leave the fire unattended. Make sure it's completely out before leaving the house or going to bed.

- If you own a gas fireplace:
  —Provide routine maintenance to ensure safe and reliable functioning.
  —Keep glow embers and logs clean.
  —Adjust the millivolt output.
  —Clean the glass or screen.
  —Ensure that the vents are unobstructed and operating.

KEROSENE HEATERS should be used only in a well-ventilated area, away from flames and other heat sources. Use only the type of kerosene specified by the manufacturer for that device (usually K1)–never substitute gasoline. Wait until it cools to refill it, and refuel the heater outdoors to prevent ignition of spilled kerosene. When purchasing kerosene, use a properly labeled container to reduce the likelihood of mixing it with gasoline. Make sure you have a qualified technician check it annually.

Be sure that local building and fire codes permit the use of kerosene heaters in your area, and only purchase units that have been tested and approved by an independent laboratory against national standards, typically the Underwriter's Laboratories. You may also want to check your insurance company to see if the use of a kerosene heater will affect your policy.

Unvented **GAS SPACE HEATERS** (manufactured after 1983) should be equipped with an oxygen depletion sensor (ODS). The ODS detects a reduced level of oxygen in the area where the heater is operating and shuts off the heater before a hazardous level of carbon monoxide accumulates. These heaters should also have labels that warn users about the hazards of carbon monoxide.

If your space heater is vented, be sure that the heater and flue are professionally installed according to local codes, and that they get regular maintenance and inspection. Many carbon monoxide poisoning deaths occur every year because this isn't done. A voluntary standard requirement provides that a thermal shutoff device be installed on vented heaters manufactured after June 1, 1984. This device interrupts heater operation if the appliance isn't venting properly.

Older gas-fired space heaters may not be equipped with the safety devices required by current voluntary standards, such as an ODS or a pilot safety valve that will turn off the gas to the heater if the pilot light should go out. If the pilot light on your heater should go out, the United States Consumer Product Safety Commission suggests that you use the following safety tips:

1. Light the match BEFORE you turn on the gas to the pilot. This avoids the risk of a flashback and injury, which could occur if you allow gas to accumulate before you're ready to light the pilot.
2. IF YOU SMELL GAS, DON'T ATTEMPT TO LIGHT THE APPLIANCE. Turn off all controls, open a window or door, and leave the area immediately. Then call a gas service person from a neighbor's phone. Don't touch any electrical switches.
3. Remember that LP-gas (propane), unlike natural gas supplied from the gas utility distribution pipes, is heavier than air. If you believe a leak has occurred, go to a neighbor's phone to call your gas distributor or fire department. Don't operate any electrical switches or telephones in the building where the leak has occurred, because a spark could cause an explosion.

ELECTRICAL SPACE HEATERS manufactured after 1991 have many new performance requirements to enhance their safety. Heaters that may present a fire hazard when tipped over have a tip-over switch that turns the heater off until the device is turned upright again. New heaters also have indicator lights to let users know that the heater is plugged in or is turned on. Some manufacturers have installed technically innovative safety controls, such as infrared or proximity sensors, which can turn a heater off when objects come too close, or when children or pets come near it. These kinds of controls may prevent burn injuries to children who might play too near a heater, or reduce the risk of ignition of combustible materials that may contact the heater.

Unless certified for that purpose, don't use heaters in wet or damp places, such as bathrooms. Corrosion or other damage to parts in the heater may lead to a fire or shock hazard. Don't hide cords under rugs or carpets. This can cause overheating and fire. Avoid using an extension cord unless absolutely necessary. If you must use an extension cord, use one marked #14 or #12 AWG. (The number tells you the thickness or gauge of the wire in the cord. The smaller the number, the greater the thickness of the wire.) Don't use a cord marked #16 or #18 AWG. Using a light-duty, household extension cord with high-wattage appliances can start a fire. Only use extension cords bearing the label of an independent testing laboratory such a UL or ETL.

Be sure the heater's plug fits snugly in the outlet. Loose plugs can overheat, so have a qualified repairman replace the worn-out plugs or outlets. If the plug feels hot, unplug the heater and have a qualified repairman check for problems. If the heater and its plug are found to be working properly, have the outlet replaced—using a heater with a hot cord or plug could start a fire.

If you use your heater on an outlet protected by a ground fault circuit interrupter (GFCI) and the GFCI trips, don't assume the GFCI is broken. GFCIs protect the location where leakage currents can cause a severe shock; therefore, stop using the heater and have it checked, even it if seems to be working properly. Don't attempt to repair, adjust, or replace parts in the heater yourself.

All space heaters need space. **TO FURTHER PREVENT FIRES CAUSED BY ANY TYPE OF SPACE HEATER** (kerosene, gas, or electric):

- Select a heater with a guard around the heating element to keep children and pets away from the heat source.
- Choose the correct size heater for the area that you wish to warm. Too large a unit wastes energy and money, and it builds up extra pollutants in your environment.
- Use only electric or vented fuel-fired heaters in mobile homes.
- Read the owner's manual before use and follow its directions.
- Maintain the heater regularly according to the manufacturer's directions.
- Don't place heater in walkways.
- Keep heater at least 3 feet away from combustible materials.
- Don't use flammable aerosol sprays, lacquers, or solvents near the heater.
- Keep children and pets away from the heater. Some heaters can exceed temperatures of 500 degrees.
- Don't use the heater in the same room as flammable liquids.
- Don't place heater on furniture; it may tip over.
- Don't use heater to dry clothing or shoes.
- Never leave heater on when you go to bed or leave the house.

COOKING BURNS

Most childhood burns, especially those involving children ages 6 months to 2 years, result from hot foods and liquids spilled in the kitchen or wherever people prepare food. Nine children die each year from scald burns, and children under four account for nearly all of these deaths.

COOKING EQUIPMENT causes more than 100,000 fires each year, and almost 400 deaths. In fact, home cooking equipment, particularly when left unattended, is the leading cause of residential fires and fire-related injuries. Other human blunders such as falling sleep, poor control of the open flame, failure to turn off equipment, and placing combustibles too close to the stove contribute to these fires.

According to the National Fire Protection Association, equipment-related malfunction plays a lesser role, but still an important one. Electric stoves have a higher risk of fire-related injuries and property damage (but not deaths) than gas stoves. On the other hand, gas stoves have more than twice the risk of death due to fire as electric stoves.

Stove fires dominate the home cooking fire problem, far ahead of other cooking equipment like microwave ovens or toasters.

TO KEEP YOUR KITCHEN SAFE:

- Don't use the kitchen stove to heat the house.
- Turn off oven and burners when not in use.
- Carefully supervise all cooking; never leave it unattended.
- Keep small children and pets stay away from the cooking area; enforce a 3 foot kid/pet-free zone.
- Never leave children under 3 alone in the kitchen when food is cooking.
- Don't place cookies, candy, and other goodies over the top of the stove.
- Keep equipment clean to avoid grease fires.
- Move combustibles such as towels, potholders, plastic utensils, aprons, and curtains away from cooking surfaces.
- Make sure the area above cooking surfaces is free of flammable and combustible items.
- Don't wear loose clothing that can catch fire when cooking.
- Use the back burners and keep handles turned inward.
- Don't leave a hot oven door open.
- Remove pot lids carefully to avoid steam burns.
- Carefully place wet foods in frying pan or deep fryer containing grease since hot oil and water can cause splatter.
- Don't use wet potholders; they can cause steam burns.
- Use only appropriate containers for microwave ovens.
- Test microwaved foods for steam and heat before giving them to your child.

- Never heat up baby bottles in the microwave because they can develop hot spots.

Summertime brings outdoor cooking for many of us, and today more Americans are lighting their **BARBEQUE GRILLS** than ever before. Anytime you work with fire there is a chance of getting burned, and curious little eyes may want to peek inside to see what you're cooking, causing your child severe burn injury. Therefore, to ensure a safe barbeque, follow these suggestions from the Hearth, Patio, and Barbeque Association. These tips are general safety practices and are not intended to be exhaustive:

- Read the owner's manual before assembling and using your grill, and follow recommended safety measures. Call the manufacturer if you have questions.
- Unless you have one of the newer indoor/outdoor grills, use your grill outdoors only. Used in an enclosed area, your grill can create carbon monoxide gas that can prove fatal.
- Use the grill away from your house and combustible material and avoid high traffic areas.
- Make sure all parts are firmly in place and that the grill is stable.
- Once the grill is lit, don't leave it unattended.
- Never move a hot grill.
- Ensure that electrical accessories (rotisseries, etc.) are grounded.
- Don't wear loose clothing that can catch fire, and do wear long flame-retardant mitts.
- Keep a fire extinguisher or the garden hose handy and use baking soda to control grease fires.

EXTRA SAFETY TIPS FOR CHARCOAL OR WOOD CHUNK GRILLS:

- Form a pyramid with the charcoal or wood chunks, and then douse them with lighter fluid. Wait for the fluid to soak in before lighting.
- Cap the lighter fluid container immediately after pouring and before lighting the grill.
- Keep lighter fluid, matches, coal, and wood chunks out of your child's reach.
- Don't use gasoline, kerosene, or other volatile fluids as a starter—they can explode.

- You can use an electric, solid metal chimney or other starter made specifically for lighting charcoal or wood chunks as an alternative to lighter fluid. Use caution when removing the starter and wait until it cools to store it.
- Never use an electric starter when standing on wet ground or in the rain.
- If using instant-light briquettes, don't use starter fluid or chimney-style starters, and don't add more instant-light briquettes once the fire is lit. Use regular charcoal if more is required.
- Once lit, don't touch the charcoal or wood chunks to see if they are hot.
- Keep grill uncovered until ready to cook.
- Make sure the vents stay open while cooking, since the fire needs oxygen to burn.
- Allow fire to burn out completely and wait 48 hours before disposing coals/wood chunks in heavy-duty aluminum or a noncombustible container. If you must dispose the ashes before they cool, remove them to heavy-duty foil and soak them completely with water before placing in the noncombustible container.

EXTRA SAFETY TIPS FOR GAS GRILLS

- Don't overfill your LP cylinder with propane. Most hold 20 pounds of propane to allow room for the liquid to expand.
- After storage or disuse, check your grill for gas leaks, signs of deterioration, proper assembly, and burner obstruction before using.
- Don't use a propane grill indoors or in an enclosed area. Once the cylinder is connected, store the grill in a well-ventilated location.
- Keep the LP cylinder valve in the OFF position when not in use.
- Always check for gas leaks each time you connect or disconnect the regulator to the LP tank.
- Never disconnect or attach an LP cylinder or alter gas fittings when the grill is hot.
- Don't use your LP cylinder if it has dents, gouges, bulges, fire damage, corrosion, leakage, excessive rust, or other visible external damage. Have it checked by your propane dealer.
- Don't store spare LP tanks near the grill or other appliance. Store them upright in an area where the temperature won't exceed 120 degrees Fahrenheit.

- Perform general maintenance according to the manufacturer's directions and clean your grill at least twice a year.
- Check the regulator, hoses, burner parts, air shutter, and venture/valve section carefully. Make sure to turn off the gas source before checking the parts.
- Inspect hoses for abrasions and leaks before each use. Use soapy water to check for leaks (it will bubble if a leak is present). NEVER use a flame to check for gas leaks.
- Keep the lid open when lighting the grill to prevent a flash from gas buildup.
- Don't lean over grill when igniting or cooking.
- If grill doesn't light, turn off the gas. Leave the lid open and wait at least 5 minutes before trying to light it again.
- If the burners go out during cooking, turn off the gas and wait 5 minutes before trying to light it again.

EXTRA SAFETY TIPS FOR ELECTRIC GRILLS

- Don't use the electric grill in the rain or on a wet surface.
- Don't immerse or expose cords, plug, or heating elements in water or other liquid.
- Inspect cord, plug, and all connections for wear and damage before using the grill. Repair or replace damaged parts before use.
- Make sure knobs are in OFF position before plugging in grill.
- Unplug grill when not in use.
- Keep electrical cords secured during operation.
- Connect grill to a ground fault interrupter (GFI) outlet in accordance to your local codes to ensure protection against shock.

HOT WATER

Scald burns, which are caused by hot liquids or steam, are the most common type of burn-related injury among young children. Burns can easily result from spilled coffee, and third-degree burns can develop on a child who is exposed to hot tap water at 140 degrees Fahrenheit for only three seconds. Hot tap water accounts for nearly one-fourth of scald burn injuries, and is associated with more hospitalizations and deaths than any other hot liquid burns. More than 75% of scald burns among children 2 and under can be prevented by simple environmental and behavioral modifications.

TO PROTECT YOUR CHILDREN FROM SCALD BURNS:

- Set your water heater to 120 degrees Fahrenheit or below.
- Install anti-scald devices in water faucets and shower-heads:
    1. For approximately $15, you can purchase a valve that shuts the water off if the temperature gets too high. You can install these easily into your showerhead.
    2. For about $75, you can buy a valve that senses changes in water pressure and adjusts the mix of hot and cold water. A plumber must install these.
    3. You can also purchase an electric anti-scald device that remembers the temperature of your last shower. These start at $150.
- When using tap water, turn on the cold water first, and then add hot. When done, turn off hot water first.
- Test your child's bathwater with the back of your hand before placing your baby in the water.
- Never leave young children alone in the bathroom—not even to answer the phone. They can get burns or drown quickly.
- Keep hot liquids and foods away from table and counter edges.
- Don't leave hot liquids and food where children can reach them or pull them on themselves by pulling or hanging on the table cloth.
- Never carry hot liquids or foods and children at the same time.

ELECTRICAL APPLIANCES & CORDS

Electric current can cause serious burns, disrupt the electrical activity of the brain and heart, and injure other organs. Most infant injuries occur when they chew or suck on electrical cords. Toddlers can get seriously injured when they stick metal objects into electrical outlets.

Electrical home fires claim the lives of 700 people each year and injure 3,000 more. Some fires are caused by system failures and appliance defects, but more are caused by the misuse and improper maintenance of electrical appliances, incorrectly installed wiring, and overloaded circuits and extension cords. Most electrical fires occur in the winter months, particularly December, due to increased use of heating, lighting, and appliances.

TO PREVENT ELECTRICAL BURNS AND FIRES:

- Cover your outlets with plastic protective covers if you have small children.
- Use the correct fuse or circuit (size and amperage) for each socket in your fuse/circuit box.
- If a breaker trips or a fuse blows out, investigate why it happened. Remove excess appliances from breaker circuits that trip frequently.
- Electrical outlets near kitchen and bathroom sinks and basins should be protected by a Ground Fault Circuit Interrupter (GFCI). You can easily recognize these because they have the "test" and "retest" buttons. Older homes may not have these installed, since the GFCI building codes are fairly recent (1980s). If your home isn't protected, call your electrician.
- Keep electrical appliances away from the bathtub and swimming pool.
- When buying appliances, look for ones that meet the UL standard for safety.
- Routinely check your wiring and electrical appliances.
- Make sure that your TV is well-ventilated to prevent overheating and fire.
- Keep electrical appliances away from wet countertops and floors.
- Make sure your hands are dry when using electrical appliances.
- Don't allow children and pets to play around or with electrical appliances, including hair dryers.
- Replace all frayed, old, warm, or worn cords and plugs immediately.
- Disconnect any appliance that gives you a tingle when you touch it, if it emits a burning smell, or if it blows a fuse or trips a breaker. Don't use it again until you have had it examined by a qualified professional.
- Never overload outlets or extension cords.
- If your appliance has a three-pronged plug, use it only in a three-slot outlet. Never force it into a two-slot outlet or remove the third prong.
- Turn off and immediately have replaced light switches that are hot to touch or are connected to lights that flicker.
- Keep children and pets from chewing on electrical cords.
- Use extension cords wisely. Try to avoid their use as much as possible.

MICROWAVE OVENS

With more latchkey (home alone) kids fending for themselves, more children are injured by microwave oven accidents.
Children may not know which containers are microwave-safe. Eggs
left in shells may explode. Reheated foods may not be heated suffi-
ciently to kill bacteria. And food may heat unevenly, causing hot spots.

Thus, children under age 7 must be carefully supervised when
using a microwave. Children over 7 should be supervised and should
be taught MICROWAVE SAFETY:

- Follow the manufacturer's directions.
- Use only microwave-safe containers, since others may overheat
  and catch fire.
- Use oven mitts when removing containers from the microwave,
  since they are usually very hot.
- Don't cook eggs in their shells.
- Some foods heat unevenly—jelly-filled pastries may be scald
  ing hot in the middle while the outside is only warm.
- Use caution when cooking popcorn. The vapor made by the bag
  can exceed 180 degrees Fahrenheit.
- Hot liquids can cause scald burns.

CHEMICALS

Caustic chemicals (acids and alkalis), can cause burn injuries
in children. Chemicals tend to cause splash burns, and thus, your
child's eyes can be affected. These burns can result in blindness and
loss of the eye itself. Household cleaning agents cause most chemical
burns in children, but battery acid can be just as harmful.

TO PREVENT CHEMICAL BURNS:

- Keep all household cleaners and other harsh chemicals secure
  ly covered and away from children.
- Keep batteries away from small children.
- Don't try to recharge batteries not intended to be recharged.
  They could overheat and rupture.
- Don't use a car battery recharger to recharge flashlight batter-
  ies.
- Children may put batteries backward in their toys. Since this
  can also cause overheating and rupture, warn your children

about removing and replacing batteries, and install them yourself.

CIGARETTE LIGHTERS AND MATCHES

Lighters and matches cause more than 200 deaths each year.
Almost 66% of these result from children playing with lighters or
matches, and most of the victims are under 5 years old.

TO KEEP YOUR CHILD SAFE:

- If you smoke, stop. That will decrease the need for lighters in
  your household!
- Keep lighters and matches out of the reach of children.
- Don't use lighters as entertainment for children. They are not
  toys.
- Make sure cigarettes are extinguished before emptying ash
  trays.
- DON'T SMOKE IN BED.
- Check furniture where smokers were sitting for ashes and burn
  marks.
- Don't leave ashtrays on chair arms where they can be knocked
  off or cause burns.
- Purchase flame resistant sleepwear for your children.
- Use fabrics such as 100% polyester, nylon, wool, and silk that
  are more difficult to ignite and tend to self-extinguish. Cotton,
  cotton-polyester blends, rayon, and acrylic ignite and burn easily.

WILDFIRE

As people make their homes in woodland setting near forests
or remote mountain sites, they both enjoy the scenic beauty of their
environment and risk the great danger of wild fire. Most wild fires
begin unnoticed. They then spread quickly, igniting brush, trees, and
homes.

Most wildfires are started by humans. Do your part to pro-
mote and practice wildfire safety, by following the Outdoor Fire
Safety Tips from the United States Department of Agriculture-Forest
Service and the National Association of State Foresters.

CAMPFIRES

- Build campfires away from overhanging branches, steep slopes, rotten stumps, logs, dry grass, and leaves. Pile any extra wood away from the fires.
- Keep plenty of water handy and have a shovel for throwing dirt on the fire if it gets out of control.
- Start with dry twigs and small sticks.
- Add larger sticks as the fire builds up.
- Put the largest pieces of wood on last, pointing them toward the center of the fire, and gradually push them into the flames.
- Keep the campfire small. A good bed of coals or a small fire surrounded by rocks gives plenty of heat. Scrape away litter, duff, and any burnable material within a 10-foot-diameter circle. This will keep a small campfire from spreading.
- Be sure your match is out. Hold it until it's cold. Break it so that you can feel the charred portion before discarding it. Make sure it's cold. Conserve matches—carry a candle as a firestarter.
- Never leave a campfire unattended. Even a small breeze could quickly cause the fire to spread.
- Drown the fire with water. Make sure all embers, coals, and ticks are wet. Move rocks—there may be burning embers underneath.
- Stir the remains, add more water, and stir again. Be sure all burned material has been extinguished and cooled. If you don't have water, use dirt. Mix enough soil or sand with the embers. Continue adding and stirring until all material is cooled.
- Feel all materials with your bare hand. Make sure that no roots are burning. Don't bury your coals—they can smolder and break out.

CHARCOAL BRIQUETTES

After burning charcoal briquettes, "dunk 'em!" Don't sprinkle. Soak the coals with lots of water, stir them, and soak again. Be sure they are out—cold! Carefully feel the coals with your bare hands to be sure.

SMOKING

When smoking is permitted outdoors, safe practices require at least a 3-foot clearing around the smoker. Grind out your cigarette, cigar, or pipe tobacco in the dirt. Never grind it on a stump or log. It's unsafe to smoke while walking or riding a horse or trail bike. Use your ashtray while in your car.

LANTERNS, STOVES, AND HEATERS

Cool all lanterns, stoves, and heaters before refueling. Place them on the ground in a cleared area and fill them. If fuel spills, move the appliance to a new clearing before lighting it. Recap and store flammable liquid containers in a safe place. Never light lanterns and stoves inside a tent, trailer, or camper. If you use a lantern or stove inside a tent or trailer, be sure to have adequate ventilation. Always read and follow instructions provided by the manufacturer.

HOUSEHOLD TRASH

If you must burn trash, don't pile it on the ground. It won't burn completely and will be easily blown around. Local fire officials can recommend a safe receptacle for burning trash. It should be placed in a cleared area, away from overhead branches and wires.

Never attempt to burn aerosol cans; heated cans will explode. Flying metal from an exploding can might cause an injury. Burning trash scattered by such an explosion has caused the spread of many fires.

DEBRIS

Check local laws on burning. Some communities allow burning only during specified hours. Others forbid it entirely. Check the weather; don't burn on dry, windy days. Consider the alternatives to burning. Some types of debris—such as leaves, grass, and stubble—may be of more value if used for compost. Household items such as plastics, glass, paper, and aluminum cans can be recycled or hauled to a local sanitary landfill.

If you must burn debris, do it safely.

SPARK ARRESTERS

All types of equipment and vehicles are required to have spark arresters. Chain saws, portable generators, cross-country vehicles, and trail bikes—to name a few—require spark arresters if used in or near grass, brush, or a wooded area. To make sure that the spark arrester is functioning properly, check with the dealer or contact your local Forest Service or state forestry office.s

AGRICULTURAL RESIDUE AND FOREST LITTER

Be sure you're fully prepared before burning off your field or garden spot. To control the fire, you will need a source of water, a bucket, and a shovel for tossing dirt on the fire. If possible, plow a fire line around the area to be burned. Large fields should be separated into small plots for burning one at a time. Be sure to stay with your fire until it's out. Before doing any burning in a wooded area, contact your local forester. The forester will weigh all factors, explain them to you, and offer technical advice.

PROTECT YOUR FAMILY AND YOUR HOME FROM WILD-FIRE:

- Post fire emergency numbers by the phone.
- Teach your children fire safety to avoid wildfires.
- Report hazardous conditions that may cause wildfire.
- Plan several escape routes.
- Keep your gutters clear of debris which could catch fire.
- Use ½-inch mesh screen beneath porches, decks, floors, and the home itself, and screen openings to floors, roofs, and attics.
- Keep a ladder that will reach a roof.
- Install heavy fire-resistant drapes and protective shutters.
- Keep household items that can be used as fire tools: axe, rake, handsaw or chainsaw, bucket, and shovel.
- Plan your water needs:
  —Maintain an adequate outside water source, such as a pond or pool.
  —Have a garden hose long enough to reach all parts of the house, or multiples that reach each part of the house, one for each exterior water outlet.
  —Install freeze-proof exterior water outlets on at least two sides of the house and near other property structures.
  —Install additional water outlets at least 50 feet from your home.
  —Consider getting a portable gas-powered pump in case the electrical power goes out.

Create a 30 to 100 foot safety zone around your house. If you live in a pine forest, your zone should be at least 100 feet. However, if your home sits on a steep slope, standard protective measures may not help. Contact your local fire department or department of forestry for assistance.

- Rake all leaves and dead brush. Clear out all flammable vegetation.
- Remove leaves and debris from under structures and dispose of them properly.
- Thin a 15-foot space between tree crowns and remove limbs within 15 feet of the ground.
- Remove dead branches that hang over the roof.
- Prune vegetation away from within 15 feet of chimney and stovepipe outlets.
- Remove vines from outer walls.
- Regularly mow the lawn.

WHEN WILD FIRE THREATENS:

- Listen to your radio or TV for reports and evacuation orders.
- Park your car facing the direction of your escape.
- Close garage doors and windows, but keep them unlocked.
- Disconnect automatic garage door openers.
- Confine pets to one room, so that they are easier to catch should you need to evacuate—remember that human shelters don't accept pets, so make alternate arrangements for them. Don't leave them behind.
- If advised to evacuate, do so.
- Wear protective clothing, including a cloth to protect your face.
- Take your disaster kit.
- Lock your home.
- As you evacuate, observe changes in the speed and direction of fire and smoke.
- If you have time, take steps to protect your home:
  —Seal off attic and ground vents with commercial seals or plywood.
  —Turn off propane tanks.
  —Place outdoor combustible furniture inside.
  —Connect garden hose to outdoor water outlets
  —Place lawn sprinklers on the roof and near above-ground fuel tanks. Wet the roof.
  —Wet shrubs.
  —Close all doors, windows, and noncombustible window coverings; remove lightweight window coverings.

—Shut off the water and gas.

—Turn off your pilot lights.

—Close fireplace screens and open the damper.

—Move flammable furniture into the center of the home, away from windows.

—Turn a light on in every room to increase your home's visibility in heavy smoke.

7

FIREARMS

MICHIGAN, 2000:
First grader fatally shoots a 6-year-old classmate with a .32 caliber gun he brought to school from his home.

SOME STATS

- There are approximately 60 million guns in U.S. households with 2 to 3 million guns sold each year.
- Nationwide, 17.4% of high school students carried a weapon to school; 5.7% carried a gun.
- Firearm death rates for teenagers are higher in the U.S. than those in Canada, Israel, New Zealand, Australia, and England; rates are 16% higher than other industrialized nations.
- The majority of gun deaths among children and teens are homicides.
- Accidental gunshots account for 27% of all firearm deaths among children under 12.
- 40% of gun deaths in teens ages 12 to 16 are from suicide–teenagers are twice as likely to commit suicide if a gun is in the household.

The Second Amendment of the United States Constitution reads:

"A well-regulated Militia, being necessary to the security of a free State, the right of the people to keep and bear Arms, shall not be infringed."

A child as young as three can pull the trigger of many handgun models. Regardless of whether or not you believe owning firearms is your constitutional right, your priority is to protect your children by practicing and teaching them about gun safety.

Every day in America, 10 children are killed in handgun suicides, homicides, and accidents, and for every child killed, four are wounded. The firearm death rate for 15- to 19-year-olds increased 222% from 1984 to 1994, whereas the non-firearm homicide rate actually decreased almost 13%. With over 200 million guns, the

United States is the most heavily armed country in the world, and the only industrialized country in which handguns are widespread and easily available. In just one year, guns killed zero children in Japan, 19 in Great Britain, 57 in Germany, 109 in France, 153 in Canada, and 5,285 in the United States.

Almost 66% of firearm-owning parents with school-age children believe they keep their weapon safely away from their children. But one study found that 75 to 80% of 6- and 7-year-olds knew where the gun was kept. Too many parents are dead wrong—86 kids died from gunshot accidents in 2000 alone.

Many criminologists believe that handgun availability is related to the high rate of homicide in this country. Most victims of assault by other weapons don't die, but the death rate from assault by handguns is extremely high—85% of all homicides for adolescents aged 15 through 19 were committed with firearms. Research indicates that of all firearms, handguns are the murder weapon of choice, and that the people at greatest risk of being murdered by handguns are teens and young adults.

Firearm injuries are already the second leading cause of death in young people 10 to 24 years of age. By the year 2003, firearm related death may become the leading cause of accidental deaths, out ranking motor vehicle accidents. It already ranks as the leading cause in the District of Columbia and five states (Alaska, Louisiana, Maryland, Nevada, and Virginia). And firearm injury is costly in dollars and cents, costing U.S. taxpayers about $1.1 billion in 1995 alone. An estimated 20,000 people a year are paralyzed by a handgun bullet, creating lifetime medical costs that parallel the polio epidemic of the 1950s.

The American media glamorizes guns in a way that endangers the public health of children and adults. Guns rank as one of the leading causes of death among children and adolescents, yet gunplay and references to guns are still prevalent on prime-time television, in the movies, in video games, and in music lyrics. Programs that make instruments of killing more attractive or desirable are unhealthy and dangerous.

The media isn't the only source of exposure to guns for your child. Shows and programs dedicated to gun safety may actually be his introduction. He may learn about guns on the street, see them displayed in store windows, at a friend's house, or even in your own home. You can't gun-proof your child, but you can protect him from being a victim or perpetrator of gun violence.

KID AND GUNS

Guns pose a potential risk to ALL children, regardless of whether there are guns in their homes. Nearly all childhood accidental shootings occur around the home; half at the home of the victim and nearly 40% at a relative or friend's house. The majority of these deaths occur when children play with a gun that has been kept loaded and accessible.

Parents tend to have unrealistic perceptions of their children's abilities and behaviors that factor into these accidents–they misperceive their child's ability to gain access to the weapon, to distinguish between real and toy guns, to make good judgments about handling guns, and to consistently follow gun safety rules.

Accidental firearm-related injuries are more prevalent in rural areas where people are more likely to own guns. Rural accidents occur more frequently outdoors with a rifle or shotgun, while city shootings happen more commonly indoors with a handgun.

Statistics compiled by organizations such as the Center for Disease Control (CDC) and the Center to Prevent Handgun Violence demonstrate frightening results:

- Every day in America, 100,000 children take guns to school and 17.3% of high school students carry a weapon. About 35% of high school students in high crime areas carry firearms to school regularly.
- More than 6,000 students were expelled in one year alone for bringing handguns to school.
- Over 1.2 million latchkey kids have access to guns when they get home from school alone.
- Approximately 90% of accidental shootings involving children have been linked to an easy-to-find, loaded handgun in the house.
- Guns in the home increase the likelihood of homicide almost threefold—and of suicide, fivefold.

Despite these startling statistics, few laws exist to govern children's access to guns. Even though the Brady Law disallows children under 21 to purchase handguns from licensed dealer, a loophole still allows 18- to 21-year-olds to purchase handguns from private or unlicensed individuals, such as dealers at gun shows. Most states allow teenagers to possess long guns (e.g., rifles) without adult supervision. However, some states passed Child Assess Prevention (CAP) laws that hold gun owners criminally liable if a child accesses their loaded weapons to injure themselves or others. Accidental deaths of children from guns have decreased in states that passed CAP laws.

CAP laws, also called "Safe Storage" or "Gun Owner Responsibility" laws, generally require adults to either store loaded guns in a place that is reasonably inaccessible to children or use a device to lock the gun. If a child obtains an improperly stored and loaded gun, the adult owner is criminally liable. Not all states have CAP laws, and the content of these laws varies from state to state. Contact your state police or the Center to Prevent Handgun Violence (www.handguncontrol.org) for further information or to see if your state has CAP laws and what they mean for your children.

Your child is naturally playful and active. Experts don't agree on how much he actually understands about guns when he plays pretend gunfire or fantasizes about guns. Your toddler may point his finger and make shooting noises to convey a sense of anger or gain a sense of control, but he most likely won't understand that this behavior, when carried out with real gun, can result in injury or death. As he gets older, your child learns that guns can kill.

You may be wondering whether toy guns blur the line between fantasy and reality. The answer remains unclear. Interestingly, some gun control advocates believe occasional toy gunplay by young children isn't a problem, while some gun owners believe that toy guns should be off limits because guns themselves are not toys. Toy guns for older children may create danger because they can be difficult to distinguish from the real thing. Thus, older kids playing with toy guns or paintball guns may be at risk for being shot by someone with a real gun who believes he's firing in self-defense.

Does playing with a toy gun as a child necessarily mean that he will grow up to like real guns? No more than having an Easy Bake Oven will make him a chef.

According to the American Academy of Pediatrics, your teenager is especially at risk for firearm death and injury because of his unique developmental issues, easy access to guns, and the difficulties in educating him about gun safety. The political and social contexts of firearms are complex. Teens are influenced by the overall violence in American society and the glorification of violence in the media, as well as poverty, urbanization, family disruption, and the erosion of basic law and order.

Several developmental issues that surround your child's adolescent years and guns:

    Curiosity: Young adolescents have an irresistible curiosity about guns. They search for and find them in their allegedly safe places, handle them, and show them off to their friends.

    Immaturity: Everyone learns a great deal about safety through experience. When your teenager lacks experience, and subsequently judgment and self-control, dangerous experimentation may result.

    Identity issues and rite of passage: American tradition has long held gun ownership as an initiation into manhood. When carrying a gun, a teen may feel brave or manly, giving him a feeling of adult identity.

    Independence: Your teen has increasing amounts of freedom, privacy, and unsupervised time, added to a desire to challenge your and other adults' rules, leading her to the possibility of unsafe gun practices.

    Infallibility: To deal with emerging feelings of inadequacy, your teenager may react with reckless bravura, or defiant, daredevil behaviors that result in unsafe gun practices.

    Peer pressure: Friends who struggle with their own identity issues may prompt your teenager to carry, show off, or use a gun.

    Impulsiveness: Homicidal and suicidal behaviors relate directly to impulsive, ambivalent behavior. Thus, access to a gun creates potentially lethal consequences for a vulnerable adolescent.

    Substance use: Drug and alcohol use increases the chance of risk-taking behavior, as well as the risk for injury, including suicide and violence.

    Perceived need for protection: Reinforced by media news, teenagers increasingly view their world as a dangerous place. Given their limited coping and conflict resolution skills, your teen may respond by carrying a weapon.

    People believe that adolescent homicides relate mostly to crime, gangs, or premeditated assaults. However, the majority of shootings are committed by friends or relatives, typically after a heated argument over something trivial. These shootings are impulsive, unplanned, and immediately regretted. Although frequently propelled by alcohol, the lethal factor in teenage homicide is immediate access to a gun.

OTHER FACTORS THAT MAY PUT YOUR CHILD AT RISK FOR FIREARM INJURY

Some children are at greater risk for firearm injury and death than others. The Future of Children's "Children, Youth and Guns," presents risk factors and estimates the risk that children born in 1998 will die from a firearm injury before they reach age 20:

1. Older teens, ages 17 though 19, are more likely than younger ones to die from a firearm-related injury, with homicide accounting for most of these deaths.
2. Males have a greater chance of dying from a gunshot than females.
3. Black and Hispanic youths are more likely than white youths to die from gun homicides and unintentional gun injury, and white youths are more likely to die from gun suicides than Black and Hispanic youths.
4. Youths who live in core metropolitan counties are at greater risk for firearm homicide but lower risk for firearm suicide than those living in areas with populations less than 10,000.
5. Living in the northeast drastically lowers the risk for firearm death by homicide, suicide, and unintentional injury.

Although media coverage indicates otherwise, school shootings are relatively rare. From 1993 to 1998, less than 1% of all firearm-related deaths among children ages 5 to 19 occurred in schools. Your child is more likely to die as the result of a gun accident in your home than from a shooting in school.

GUN SAFETY

One of the best ways to keep your child away from guns is to keep them out of your home. However, many children are raised in homes with guns, particularly if family members engage in hunting or target shooting. Almost half of all American households with children contain a gun, and unfortunately, there is a gun left hidden but unlocked in one of every eight family homes.

Many people feel the need to own handguns for protection against crime. However, despite claims that you need a gun in your home to protect you and your family from outside invaders, public health research demonstrates that the person most likely to shoot you or a family member is already in the house. In other words, guns kept in homes for self-defense are more often used to kill friends or relatives than intruders. Guns are used as protection in less than 2% of home invasion crimes. According to the FBI, there were only 176 justifiable homicides in 1996, compared to 9,390 handgun murders.

Remember:

- Guns in the home increase the risk of homicide three times.
- Guns in the home increase the risk of suicide five times.
- Accidental shootings from household guns are all too common.

If these statistics don't convince you to not keep a gun for self-defense, ask yourself these questions:

1. Do you have the strength to face off with an unknown, armed intruder?
2. How fast can you get to your locked gun and separately locked ammunition, and then put the two together to confront the intruder?
3. Are you a good enough shot to hit the intruder faster than he can shoot you?
4. What are your chances of hitting a family member instead?
5. Wouldn't you rather invest in a security system that would discourage the intruder from entering your house in the first place?

If you do have a gun in your home, please follow safety guidelines to protect your child from harm. Unfortunately, even though most parents realize that guns endanger their children, many parents still leave guns within their children's reach. According to a Center to Prevent Handgun Violence survey of 806 parents: 43% of households have guns, 23% keep the guns loaded, and 28% keep a gun hidden and unlocked. More than half of these parents, 54%, stated that they would be highly concerned if they knew there was a gun in the home of their child's friend. Yet, despite parental concern, many parents fail to take the necessary steps to ensure their children's safety.

Young children die or are badly injured because their parents or other gun owners don't store their firearms properly. Children find loaded guns and use them unintentionally on themselves or other children. Older children may horseplay with accessible guns, and teen-agers may use them impulsively for suicide or crime.

Your child's safety rests solely on you. Even the National Rifle Association (NRA) advises that you accept the responsibility to learn, practice, and teach gun safety rules, and realize that your responsibility doesn't end when your child leaves your home.

If you don't own a gun, understand that your child probably knows someone whose parents do own one. He could come into contact with a gun at a neighbor's house, when playing with a friend, or other circumstances.

When you make a decision to own a gun, don't make it lightly. Be fully aware of the risks gun ownership creates for you and your family. Learn the dangers of firearms, teach your children about these dangers, as well as nonviolent ways to deal with anger and conflict, and practice firearm safety measures. Always remember that the child's life that you save may be your own.

Realize that kids typically know where you keep the guns in your home. You may think your child doesn't know, but kids have a knack for finding them.

Keep all firearms—handguns, sporting guns, antique guns, BB guns, pellet guns, and others—unloaded and safely locked up in a guns safe, fire safe, or lockbox. Loaded guns don't belong inside bedroom drawers where far too many people keep them. The manner in which you store your gun can be a matter of life and death. A variety of devices exist for securing your gun. Safes seem to provide the most security, but many people prefer locks which you can obtain for free or at low cost. Look for the gun lock distribution program in your area:

1. Call your local or state police.
2. Contact your local SAFE KIDS Coalition; call 202-662-0600 for the one nearest you.
3. Check with Project HomeSafe, a national gun lock distribution program; call 800-726-6444 for the program nearest you or click on www.projecthomesafe.org.

You will also find a variety of safes, cases, and other security devices at gun shops. Once you lock the gun, hide the keys where your child is unable to find them.

Your child should never have access to a gun without your supervision.

Store and lock ammunition in a separate location where your child can't access them.

Keep the keys for both the gun and the ammunition in a place different from where you store your other household keys, and keep these keys out of your child's reach.

Talk to your child about guns and gun safety. Nail guns, BB guns, air guns, handguns—all are easy for your child to obtain, and all are dangerous. At some point, your child will come into contact with some type of gun, so talk to him and teach him about gun safety. Be open, honest, and clear. Avoid statements such as, "stay away from guns," and "don't even think about going near the gun cabinet," without explaining your reasoning and giving her the opportunity to ask questions.

YOUNG CHILDREN: Rely on your intuition to decide when your child is ready to introduce the subject. Your child may be ready as early as 3 or as late as 6 or 8. Typically, you can introduce the subject when your child expresses interest in guns, even toy ones. Differentiate fantasy violence (TV, movies, games, toy guns) from real violence. Remember that a preschooler can't differentiate fantasy from reality, so he gets confused when he sees a character shot dead one week on TV and then sees the same actor alive and well the next week. Tell him that fantasy violence isn't real, and that real guns cause real injuries. He probably still thinks that death is reversible (clearly demonstrated when a child cries at a newly deceased pet's grave one minute, then tries to dig it up to play with it the next). Make sure you reinforce this concept frequently. Emphasize to him that he should never touch a gun, and that he should always tell an adult if he comes across one.

Teach him the following NRA safety steps from their Eddie Eagle Gun Safety Program:

STOP!

Don't touch.

Leave the area.

Tell an adult parent, neighbor, teacher, relative, or other trustworthy adult.

PRETEENS: Discuss the consequences of violence and the dangers of mishandling guns. Talk about ways to solve problems without violence. Begin to teach anger and conflict management as well as problem solving. Stress to him that he should never touch a gun without adult supervision. Despite all your child seems to know about guns, chances are he doesn't know how to handle one safely. Thus you need to talk to him about gun safety. Teach or reinforce the NRA safety steps, and tell him to call 911 (or your alternate emergency number) if there is no adult in the immediate area.

Stress the first two points (Stop, Don't touch) to counteract your child's natural impulse to touch a gun. Since your child may be at a friend's house after school, stress leaving the area when adult supervision isn't always possible. He should at least leave the room if he can't physically leave the house or apartment. Stress leaving the area because a child as young as age 3 can squeeze a trigger.

TEENS: At this point, it's easier to keep guns away from teens than it's to keep teens from guns. Continue to stress to him that he should never touch a gun without adult supervision. But keep the lines of communications open, no matter how difficult it becomes. Watch for changes in behavior that may indicate suicidal thinking or a tendency toward violence.

If your teen will use a firearm for hunting, make sure he knows how to use it, preferably through a formal training program. For all teens, continue to teach gun safety. There is no industry standard for gun safety. One handgun may have a pin, similar to the type that pops out of the turkey when it's cooked, to show that there is a bullet in the chamber. Your teen may see the pin but not know what it means. He may also know how to release a gun cartridge but not know that there is often a shell left in the chamber. Accidents can easily happen if your child believes a gun is empty.

Some experts recommend that you consider talking to your neighbors and your child's friends' parents about guns. With nearly half of all homes having guns, chances are your child has already or will be playing inside a home with a gun. Before your child goes over to a friend's house to play, ask the parents if they own a gun, and if so, how they store it and the ammunition. Verify that the gun is locked and unloaded, safely away from child access. Ask these questions along with the other questions you would normally ask before sending your child to someone else's home. Be factual, rather than emotional, explaining that nearly half of all homes have guns and that many are left loaded and unlocked. Explain that you just want your child to be safe, and that you would welcome the same questions from them about your home. If the parents store a gun in an unsafe manner, or if they refuse to talk to you about it, you can choose to not allow your child to play at that home, and invite the other child to your house instead.

Other experts feel that these conversations can be unreliable and that they can strain friendly relationships. Someone may honestly believe that they lock their guns safely away from their children and see no need to tell you about their guns, while others may not know that a gun is stored in their home. Therefore, it may be better to rely on teaching your child what he should do if he encounters a gun, instead of relying on what other adults tell you.

Realize your responsibilities if you own a gun. Seek professional guidance on the use and care of firearms, and follow these selected NRA guidelines:

1. Know your state gun laws on purchase, ownership, storage, transport, etc. Contact your state or local police for information if you're unsure about your state laws.

2. Know how to use your gun properly. Learn how to use it before you attempt to operate it. Know its parts, how to safely open and close the action and remove any ammunition from the gun or magazine.

3. Use the correct ammunition. BBs, pellets, cartridges, and shells are designed for particular guns, and most guns have the ammunition type stamped on the barrel. You may also find information printed on the ammunition box and/or stamped on the cartridge.

4. NEVER use alcohol or other drugs before or while using a gun. Substances impair normal mental and physical function, resulting in potentially dangerous consequences when mixed with gun use.

5. Wear protective ear and eye protection when needed. The loud noise from gunshots can damage hearing. Hot debris and gas emitted from guns can cause eye injury. Thus, shooters and spectators should wear shooting glasses and hearing protectors.

6. Keep your finger off the trigger until ready to shoot.

7. Know your target as well as what is beyond it. Be certain without any doubt that you have identified your target before you shoot. Far too many accidents occur when shooters lack that

certainty. Be aware of the area beyond your target, meaning you must observe the prospective area before you shoot. Never fire in the direction of other people, homes, play areas, or any other location of a potential mishap. Always think first before you fire.

8. Keep your gun clean, and know how to clean it so that you can operate it safely. Clean it after every use and after it has been in prolonged storage. Dirt, solidified oil and grease, and accumulated moisture can cause unsafe operation. ALWAYS make absolutely sure it's unloaded before cleaning. Be certain that no ammunition is present, and keep the action open during the cleaning process. Make sure you lock up gun cleaning supplies as they are often poisonous.

9. Keep the gun pointed in a safe direction so that if it were to go off accidentally, it doesn't cause injury or damage.

10. Know that some guns and many shooting activities require additional safety precautions.

If you find a gun or wish to dispose of yours, contact your local or state police, but don't use their emergency line or 911. State ordinances vary, but generally the police will check the gun to ensure that it's not part of a criminal investigation and then destroy it. You could also choose community buy-back or amnesty day as a disposal option. These programs allow you to bring your unwanted firearms to a designated location where the firearm will be rendered unusable. In exchange, you receive a gift certificate or other reward. Contact the police to find out if your community hosts such a program, but don't wait until one becomes available to dispose of an unwanted firearm.

Follow these guidelines, and encourage your teen to do likewise if she will be operating a gun under your supervision. However, DON'T rely on these guidelines as your sole source of information for safe gun use. Consult a professional.

8

HUMAN PREDATORS

CALIFORNIA, 2003:
Neighbor is sentenced to death for the abduction and murder of a 7-year-old girl.

SOME STATS

- The majority of missing children cases in the United States are runaways and parental abductions.
- Nearly 2,000 children were reported missing per day in 2001. Most of these cases were resolved quickly.
- 3,000 to 5,000 nonfamily abductions occur each year, most of which are short-term sexually motivated cases.
- About 203,900 children were victims of family abductions in 1999.
- 44% of family abductions are of children under 6.
- Modest estimates approximate that there are 300,000 reported cases of child sexual abuse each year. HOW-EVER, the number of unreported cases is probably greater.
- Most child and adolescent victims of sexual abuse are victimized by male members of their families.
- About 25% of girls and 13% of boys have nonconsensual sex before age 18, but only 6% of these children report these crimes.
- About 80% of sexually abused children and adolescents know their victims.

Scout leaders, teachers, clergy, friendly neighbors, babysitters, dads—most enrich children's lives. Some destroy them.

The rates of youth victimization run extremely high in this country. Stranger abductions, including high profile cases such as Adam Walsh, Danielle Van Dam, Elizabeth Smart, Polly Klass, and Samantha Runnion are much less common than family member abductions, but you should be prepared to prevent both. One-eighth of all boys and one-fourth of all girls are sexually abused before age 18, and you need to know how to keep your child safe.

- **What is your child's height, weight, and eye color? Can you accurately describe her?**
- **Do you have a recent photo?**
- **How do you keep your child safe from sexual abuse?**

Every year between 1.3 and 1.8 million children are reported missing in the United States. These children may be lost, runaways, or kidnapped. Some are taken by their noncustodial parent and some by strangers, while others disappear leaving few clues as to why.

Unfortunately, a recent survey by the National Center for Missing and Exploited Children showed that not enough parents know vital information, particularly their child's vital statistics. And knowing them could determine whether or not you see them again if they are ever abducted.

Recent scandals and cover-ups exposed the prevalence and consequences of sexual abuse. Otherwise respected, adult authority-figures justifiably face prison sentences, while their victims face emotional scars. If you think your child is immune from sexual abuse, think again. Your child, toddler through teen, needs tools to be safe, and she needs to receive those tools from you.

NONFAMILY ABDUCTIONS

The abduction and murder of both Samantha Runnion and Danielle Van Dam continue to cause many parents' anxiety levels to run high worrying about their child's safety. Yet, nonfamily abductions, especially those of preschool-age children, remain rare. The majority of missing children are preteens and teens. Statistics tend to be meaningless when our own children are concerned, but you can lower your anxiety level with a little knowledge and a bit of preparation.

The National Incidence Studies of Missing, Abducted, Runaway, and Throwaway Children (NISMART) describes a nonfamily abduction as an episode in which a nonfamily member takes a child by the use of physical force or threat of bodily harm, or detains the child for at least an hour without parental authority or lawful permission; or an episode in which a child younger than 15 or mentally

incompetent is detained or voluntarily accompanies a nonfamily perpetrator who takes the child unlawfully or without parental permission, and who conceals the child's whereabouts, demands ransom, or
expresses the intent to keep the child permanently.

A stereotypical nonfamily abduction occurs when a child is
detained overnight, transported at least 50 miles, held for ransom,
abducted with intent to keep the child permanently, or killed by a
stranger or slight acquaintance. A stranger is a perpetrator who is
unknown to the family or who has an unknown identity, and a slight
acquaintance is a perpetrator whose name is unknown to the child or
family prior to the abduction, and whom the child or family did not
know well enough to speak to; or a recent acquaintance who the child
or family has known for less than 6 months, or known for longer than
6 months but seen less than once a month.

In one study of 58,200 nonfamily abductions, 115 were
stereotypical kidnappings. Forty percent of these children were killed
and another four percent were never recovered.

Most high profile cases are stereotypical abductions—children
abducted, frequently sexually assaulted, and killed. However, not all
nonfamily abductions are stereotypical. Most children are abducted by
people they know: babysitters, boyfriends/ex-boyfriends (teen's or
parent's), classmates, and neighbors. Some are detained for short periods of time, as when one child confines another in the school bathroom to sexually assault her, or when a babysitter refuses to let the
children go home to their parents because she was not paid for prior
babysitting duties.

The majority of stranger abductions take place in streets,
parks, wooded areas, highways, and other public, generally accessible
places. Acquaintance abductions typically occur in the home, but 25%
of these kidnappings take place in public places. Both strangers and
acquaintances rarely abduct from schools or school grounds.

BE PREPARED

If your child were missing, could you accurately describe her?
The FBI counts 2,100 new missing children reports every day, which
can be more easily solved when parents provide descriptive information. Too many parents lack the vital information needed to find their
children in those crucial first hours. Don't be one of them.

Be prepared for the unthinkable.

1. Keep a complete description of your child, including her date of birth, height, weight, hair and eye color, and other identifying characteristics (birthmarks, braces, glasses, body piercings, tattoos).

2. Take an ID photo of your child every six months—every three months for children under two. ID-type, head and shoulder photos, taken from different angles are preferable to school and family pictures.

3. Know where her medical records are located and know how to access them. Make sure they contain information that can help identify your child.

4. Make sure your child has up-to-date dental records and know how to access them.

5. Have your child fingerprinted by your local police department and keep the fingerprint card they give you in a safe place. The police will NOT keep her record themselves.

6. Consider having your child's DNA tested. Fingerprints provide accurate identification, but DNA is far more accurate. For more information on DNA testing and how to get your child tested, go to www.dnafiler.com or www.kids-dna.com. Both sites offer at-home testing kits.

PREVENTING NONFAMILY ABDUCTIONS

Being prepared isn't enough. Both you and your child need strategies to prevent abductions:

General Safety:

•   Make sure your child knows her full name, address, and phone number. Older children should also know parent's names, work addresses, and work phone numbers.

•   Keep communication lines open. Don't belittle your child's fears or concerns.

•   Talk to your child. Kids who talk regularly with their parents have higher levels of self-esteem and assuredness, making them less vulnerable to predators.

•   Be sensitive to changes in her behavior.

•   Don't let her wear clothing with her name on it. The perpetrator will use her name to gain her confidence.

•   Set boundaries as to where your child can go. Young children should not leave the yard unsupervised, older children should ask permission. Teens should phone home to tell you where they are.

- Establish a parental back-up system so your child has somewhere to go in an emergency.
- Instruct her to tell you if an adult asks her to "keep a secret" or if someone offers her money, gifts, or drugs, or asks to take her picture.
- Tell her that adults don't usually ask children for directions or help finding their puppy or kitten.
- Instruct her to not go near the car of a person who tries to talk to her. Your child should learn which cars she may ride in. Share a code word with your child known only to family members.
- Tell her to go for help—police station, neighbor's house, store—if someone is following her on foot or in a car.
- Carefully choose babysitters, nannies, day care providers, preschools, and after-school programs. Check their references and, if possible, see if you can have access to their background information. Several states will allow you to access criminal and sex abuse registries. (Read more on babysitters, schools, and day cares in their appropriate chapters.)
- Know your child's friends and their parents.
- Know your neighbors.
- If someone demonstrates a great deal of interest in your child, find out why.
- Beware of gadgets that promise to keep your child safe.
- Don't rely on martial arts or self-defense training to keep your child safe. It may, however, build up her confidence.
- Teach online safety—see Chapter 10.
- If home alone, your child should not answer the door or tell anyone that they are home alone—see the home alone chapter for more.
- Tell her to say "NO" to anyone who tries to take her somewhere, touches her, or makes her feel uncomfortable in any way.
- Inform her to not go into anyone's home without your permission.
- Have a plan should you and your child become separated while away from home.
- Tell her not to look for you if you become separated while in a public place or shopping area. She should go to the nearest checkout counter, security office, or lost and found, and tell

them she's lost. She should never go to the parking lot without you.

- Instruct her to scream, "You're not my parent!" if someone tries to take her away.

AGE SPECIFIC SAFETY

PRESCHOOL-AGE CHILDREN:

- Never leave your child unattended and never leave her alone in a car, carriage, stroller, or yard.
- Make sure she knows how to dial 911 or another emergency number.
- Teach her to go to safe people—police officers, firefighters, teachers—to ask for help when needed.
- Play the license number and state reading game so that she will be able to recognize license plates.

Talk to her about "strangers." Preschoolers possess magical thinking, so they picture strangers as unusual-looking men with trench coats, sunglasses, and a moustache. And have you ever tried to get a 4 year old to NOT talk! Yikes. How can you get them not to talk to strangers? Teach them:

1. to be on the lookout for unusual situations and actions, rather than unusual people.
2. to be polite, but also let them know it's okay to be suspicious of any adult asking for help or directions.
3. it's okay to say "no" to adults if they feel uncomfortable, scared, or confused in any way.
4. to not let anyone touch them in areas where their bathing suit touches their body and to not touch anyone one else on those areas if that person asks them to do so.

You can also have her listen to Barney's "Stranger Danger" song, which is on the video, *Barney's Favorites, Vol. 1.* Stay calm, and let her know that she's safe and that she has adults to go to if needed.

SCHOOL-AGE CHILDREN:

- Have your child use the buddy system whenever away from you, including walking to school.
- Make sure she checks in with you when going from one site to another.

- Tell her to follow her gut—if she feels uncomfortable, get out of there.
- Teach her how to find a pay phone and call from it. Make sure she knows how to call long-distance.
- Instruct her to never hitchhike.
- Tell her to avoid dark or abandoned places and to come home before dark.
- Tell her to avoid adults who hang around playgrounds.

TEENAGERS:

- Continue to use the buddy system.
- Tell her that nothing she owns is worth risking her life for. If someone threatens her for an item, the safest thing to do is to give it up. And encourage her to tell you if such an incident occurs.
- As tough as she thinks she is, it's not tough enough when it comes to perpetrators. Make sure she practices safety.

FAMILY ABDUCTIONS

Hundreds of thousands of children are abducted by noncustodial parents every year, many of whom are motivated by revenge. Abducted children are faced with emotional, and sometimes physical, harm, and the custodial parent faces emotional and financial distress.

The Office of Juvenile Justice and Delinquency Prevention presents specific characteristics of abducting parents, as well as six specific profiles. Characteristics include:

- The abductor denies or dismisses the other parent's value to the child. They believe that they know what is best for their child and can't see how or why they should share parenting with the other parent.
- The abductor most likely has very young children. Young children are easier to conceal and transport and are unlikely to verbally protest. They may also be unable to tell others identifying information. When older children are abducted by noncustodial parents, they usually are vulnerable or in collusion with the abductor.
- The abductor (unless a paranoid-delusional) has a support network that provides practical (food, shelter, money) and emotional assistance with the abduction.

- The abductor doesn't consider his/her actions illegal or morally wrong, even after the district attorney is involved.
- Both mothers and fathers are equally likely to abduct their children—fathers when there is no child custody order in place, and mothers after the court has issued a formal custody decree.

The six profiles are listed below. Please bear in mind that the presence of one or more of these profiles in a parent doesn't mean that abduction is inevitable, nor does the absence mean that abduction isn't possible.

Profile 1: The parent who has committed a prior credible threat or abduction. This profile is usually combined with one or more of the others, as it's important to understand why the parent abducted the child. Other risk factors of flight include: the parent is homeless, unemployed, and without ties to the area; the parent has divulged plans to abduct and has the resources to do so; and the parent has liquidated assets and maxed-out credit cards or borrowed from other sources.

Profile 2: The parent who suspects or believes that abuse has occurred. Many parents abduct their children because they truly believe that the other parent is abusing, molesting, or neglecting their child. They feel the authorities have not taken their allegations seriously and have not properly investigated their concerns. These parents "rescue" the child with help from supporters who concur with their beliefs, including underground networks that help them obtain new identities and safe locations.

Profile 3: The parent who is paranoid delusional. These parents demonstrate paranoid, irrational, and sometimes psychotic beliefs and behaviors toward the other parent. They may claim that the other parent exercises mind control over the child or that the other parent harmed the child. This disorder is rare, but these parents are often dangerous, especially if they have a history of domestic violence, substance abuse, or hospitalization for mental illness. The psychotic parent doesn't see the child as a separate person. Instead they perceive the child as fused with themselves as a victim, or as part of the hated parent—which may cause them to abandon or kill the child. Marital dissolution and custody investigation can result in the psychotic parent committing murder-suicide.

Profile 4: The parent who is severely sociopathic (antisocial). These parents have contempt for authority, including the legal system, and often have flagrantly violated it. They are self-serving, manipulative, and exploitive. They hold exaggerated beliefs about their own superiority and entitlement, and are highly gratified by their ability to exert power and control over others. They typically have a history of domestic violence, and like paranoid abductors, they don't see the child as having separate rights and needs. Thus, they use their children as instruments of revenge and punishment, or as trophies in their fight with their ex-partner. This profile is also rare.

Profile 5: The parent who is a citizen of another country. These parents have strong ties with their country of origin and have long been recognized as potential abductors. The risk is very high at the time of separation, when these parents feel cast adrift in a foreign land and desire to reconnect with their ethnic or religious roots. Parents at greatest risk are those who idealize their own family, homeland, and culture, and deprecate the American culture. If their country has not ratified the Hague Convention on the Civil Aspects of International Child Abduction, the stakes are extremely high, as the recovery of the child can be difficult, if not impossible. (The Hague Convention establishes administrative and judicial mechanisms to bring about prompt return of the abducted child. See www.missingkids.com/Internation-al/international_division.html for current signatories.)

Profile 6: The parent who feels alienated from the legal system and who has support in another community. Several subgroups feel alienated and rely on their own networks of kin, who may live in another geographical community, to resolve family problems. These subgroups are:

1. parents who are indigent and poorly educated about custody laws, and who can't afford legal representation or counseling that would help them solve their dispute appropriately.
2. parents who have prior negative experience with criminal or civil courts, and who thus don't expect the family courts to be responsive to their plight. Many of these parents have a police record.

3. parents who belong to certain ethnic, religious, or cultural groups that hold child-rearing beliefs contrary to prevailing custody laws.

4. the mother who has a transient, unmarried relationship with her child's father, and who often views her child as her exclusive property.

5. parents who are victims of domestic violence, especially when the courts have failed to take the steps necessary to protect them and hold the abuser accountable.

PREVENTING FAMILY ABDUCTIONS

If you recently separated from your spouse/partner, and if he or she fits into any of the risk categories or profiles, you need to take appropriate steps to prevent your child from being abducted by his noncustodial parent.

GENERAL STRATEGIES

Most custodial parents benefit from these steps:

- Keep a friendly, at least civil relationship with your ex. This helps reduce the anger and frustration that often leads to abduction.

- Communicate openly with your child, reinforcing that you love her and always want her, no matter what anyone else says. Let her know she has the right to reach you, and make sure she knows how to make a long-distance phone call to you.

- Have certified copies of your custody agreement readily available and make sure the agreement gives the police the right to recover your child.

- Speak to your attorney immediately so that he can take the legal steps necessary to thwart abduction.

- Keep a discrete list of your ex's information: social security number, driver's license number, car registration number, and checking and savings account numbers. Use caution when obtaining them so as not to set off an abduction.

- Don't ignore abduction threats. Get advice from the police, a counselor, and your attorney.

- Notify your child's school or day care that your child isn't to be released to anyone, including your ex, without your permission.

- If you're not married, get a custody agreement anyway, because state laws vary as to whether the mother automatically gets custody in these cases.
- Find out if your state has an agreement with the Office of Child Support Enforcement of the United States Department of Health and Human Services, allowing state officials to use the Federal Parent Locator Service (FPLS). The FPLS is a national network that can help find an abducting parent in child custody, visitation, or criminal custodial interference cases. They are most effective when the abductor is receiving federal benefits or when the child has been missing for six months or more.

STRATEGIES FOR SPECIFIC PROFILES

The strategies for the specific profiles were released by the Office of Juvenile Justice and Delinquency Prevention and resulted from a series of research studies.

Profile 1: Previous threat or abduction. A court order should be obtained that specifies which parent has custody, defines arrangements for the child's contact with the noncustodial parent, designates which court has jurisdiction, and requires written consent of the custodial parent or the court before the noncustodial parent can take the child out of the area. If visitation is unsupervised, the plan should include dates, times, places of exchange, etc. The courts should also specify consequences for failure to observe the custody provisions.

The child's passport can be marked with the requirement that she not travel without authorization. School and day care officials, as well as medical personnel, should be presented with a copy of the custody agreement and can be told not to release any information on the child to the noncustodial parent.

Supervised visitation is a stringent way of preventing abductions, and is typically used to prevent recidivism in serious cases. It's usually difficult to convince a judge to curtail a parent's visitation unless there is substantial proof that the parent has committed a crime.

Profile 2: The parent who suspects abuse. The priority strategy is to ensure that a careful and thorough investigation take place. Accusing parents tend to calm down when they feel investigators are taking their concerns seriously. During the investigation, authorities must ensure that there is no ongoing abuse and protect the accused parent, who may be innocent, from further allegations. Precautions include supervised visitation, or even suspended visitation if the child demonstrates emotional or behavioral disturbances to the parent's visits. Counseling is beneficial for both parents and the child, and a legal representative may be appointed for the child in the event of further legal action.

Profile 3: The paranoid delusional parent. Courts need to have procedures in place to protect children from severely delusional parents. If the noncustodial parent is psychotic, visitation may be supervised in a high security facility, and the parent assisted with maintaining the child's safety at other times. However, the psychotic parent's visitation may be suspended if he: repeatedly violates the visitation order; highly distresses the child with his visits; or uses his time with the child to malign the custodial parent, obtain information on the custodial parent's whereabouts, or transmit threats of harm or abduction.

If the custodial parent is psychotic, extreme care must be taken during litigation and evaluation to prevent abduction or violence. The family court may need to obtain emergency psychiatric screening and use *ex parte* (without notice to the psychotic parent) hearings to effect temporary placement of the child with the other parent or third party, while investigators undertake a more comprehensive evaluation.

Profile 4: The sociopathic parent. When a parent is diagnosed as having a sociopathic personality, counseling and therapeutic mediation are inappropriate and potentially dangerous. They lack the capacity to develop a working relationship with a counselor and may even hide behind professional confidentiality to manipulate and control the other parties to achieve their own ends. If the sociopathic parent blatantly violates visitation orders, supervised or suspended visitation is appropriate. Courts also need to respond quickly and decisively with fines and/or jail time to any overt disregard of the custody and access orders. Counseling may then be appropriate once control mechanisms are in place.

Profile 5: The parent who is a citizen of another country. The range of actions suggested for Profile 1 are appropriate, especially those regarding passport and travel. Problems occur when the child has dual citizenship, since foreign embassies are not under obligation to honor restrictions when the request is made by the United States citizen parent. The court may require the foreign national parent to request and obtain these assurances of passport control from his or her embassy before allowing unsupervised visitation. The foreign national parent can also post bond that would be released to the other parent in the event of abduction. During times of acute risk, authorities can monitor the airline schedules, so that an abducting parent and child can be intercepted at the airport before leaving the country.

Profile 6: The parent who feels alienated from the legal system. Alienated parents, particularly mothers, have the best prognosis for effective interventions to prevent abductions. These strategies include: access to affordable counseling and legal services, family advocates to bridge cultural, religious, and economic gaps, and the inclusion of important members of their informal social network into brief intervention services.

HOSPITAL ABDUCTIONS

Unfortunately, your child may be at risk for abduction as soon as she's born. Fortunately, studies on abductions of infants from hospitals have led to good information on the motivations and tactics of the abductors.

According to the National Center for Missing and Exploited Children, most infant abductors are females with no previous criminal record. Their motivation may be to replace a lost infant or fulfill her desire to give birth vicariously if she's unable to conceive. Though appearing normal, she's likely to be psychiatrically ill, but because of her desire to have a baby, she generally takes good care of the infant.

The abductor makes herself known and becomes familiar with the hospital personnel, procedures, and even the baby's parents. She will visit the nursery several times before the abduction, and often impersonates hospital personnel, complete with uniform. Many have a male companion who is considerably older or younger, and who is usually an unwitting accomplice to the crime.

PREVENTING HOSPITAL ABDUCTIONS

The National Center for Missing and Exploited Children recommends the following steps to prevent hospital abductions:

- Be a concerned and watchful parent. It's normal!

- Never leave your baby alone. If you need to go to the bathroom, call the nurse to take the baby back to the nursery.
- Don't give your baby to anyone who lacks proper hospital identification. Know the staff and the unit.
- If strangers enter your room or ask about your baby, call the nurse immediately.
- Know when and where your baby will be taken for tests or procedures and know who authorized them.

Should your infant be abducted:

- Immediately call the authorities and search the inside and outside of the hospital.
- The hospital authorities should monitor all exits for your child and the abductor.
- Have the baby's description ready for police.
- Inform the media. The abductor will most likely show off "her" new baby, and the media can encourage people to contact the police if they see the baby.
- Call the National Center for Missing and Exploited Children at 1-800-843-5678 for technical assistance.
- Ask to be moved to a private room to protect you from stress.
- Insist that the abductor be charged and convicted to deter future crimes.

Fortunately, one study showed that 90% of abducted infants were found and safely returned.

WHAT TO DO IF YOUR CHILD IS MISSING OR ABDUCTED

In the event that your child is missing or abducted, take steps provided by the National Center for Missing and Exploited Children, the Office of Juvenile Justice and Delinquency Prevention, and the National Crime Prevention Council:

- Act immediately. Search your house inside and out, especially places where children can get trapped, like old refrigerators and trunks.
- Check with your neighbors and your child's friends to see if she's with them.
- If you still have not found her, call the police immediately. Describe your child, including the clothes she was wearing

when last seen. If the case meets the following criteria, an AMBER alert is issued:

1. Law enforcement confirms the child has been abducted.
2. Law enforcement believes circumstances indicate that the child is in danger.
3. There is enough descriptive information about the child to broadcast.

(The AMBER Alert System was created in 1996 as a legacy to 9-year-old Amber Hagerman, who was kidnapped and murdered while riding her bike in Arlington, Texas. Once initiated, the child's descriptive information is transmitted to radio stations designated under the Emergency Alert System who in turn send it to area radio and TV stations for broadcasting. TV stations run a "crawl" on the screen along with the photo of the child. Some states, including Pennsylvania, incorporate the information into their electronic highway billboards to alert the public of an AMBER alert. These signs display pertinent descriptive information on the child, as well as the suspected abductor's vehicle information if available.)

- Contact the National Center for Missing and Exploited Children at 800–843–5678 (TDD Hotline 800–826–7653) to report your child missing.
- Check for clues that will help find your child: notes, letters, items you don't recognize.
- Examine your phone bill for unfamiliar calls that may indicate where she has gone.
- Check the neighborhood for clues, and don't forget to ask children if they have seen your child.
- Look for clues in all areas of your child's life: school, activities, friends, and clubs.
- Tell everyone you meet that your child is missing, ask for help, and communicate a sense of love for your child.
- In urban areas, check generally inaccessible areas like basements and roofs.
- In rural areas, check barns, mines, boats, and caves.
- Contact the media and provide interviews.
- Post "missing child" flyers with a recent photo and description as well as contact information. Post these anywhere and everywhere you can.
- If you can afford it, hire a reliable private investigator (check his references).

- Use the National Center for Missing and Exploited Children's web site for further information: www.missingchildren.com.
- Take care of yourself. You can't help your child if you're falling apart. Counseling can help ease both your pain and any guilt you may feel.

SEXUAL ABUSE AND EXPLOITATION OF CHILDREN

The legal definitions of sexual abuse, assault, and exploitation vary from state to state but most definitions include the abuse of power, sexual contact, and the nonconsent of the victim. Children, by nature of their age, are not able to give consent. INCEST is any form of sexual contact between a child and an immediate family member (parent, stepparent, sibling), extended family member (uncle, aunt, cousin, grandparent) or surrogate parent (adult whom child views as a family member). Children can be abused by nonfamily members, usually someone they know, as well as other children, typically adolescents who have been victimized themselves.

Child sex abuse can be either contact or noncontact. Contact forms include fondling the child's genitals, masturbation, oral-genital contact, digital penetration, and vaginal and anal penetration. Noncontact forms of abuse are exposure, voyeurism, and child pornography. Despite media coverage to the contrary, few molesters abduct, rape, and murder their victims.

Child molesters come in all shapes and sizes and from all socioeconomic groups. Some may be janitors; others, CEOs. It's virtually impossible to profile a child molester. But some characteristics are clear: sexual abuse is the perpetrator's exploitation of power and authority; most children are offended by someone they know; the majority of victims are female; the majority of abusers are male; and child pornography is strongly linked to child molestation.

Although molesters vary, they can be categorized as being either preferential molesters or situational molesters. Preferential molesters, or pedophiles, are sexually attracted either exclusively or in part toward prepubescent children. Even their fantasies revolve around children. Situational molesters engage in sex with children for a variety of reasons—some connected to stress and substance abuse—with some situational molesters committing the act only once, while others have a life-long pattern of child sexual abuse that makes them difficult to distinguish from pedophiles.

The abuse can occur in a wide range of settings and situations. Long-term abusers typically "court" the child with attention, affection, and presents, essentially seducing the child. Other abusers use fear or bribery. Abuse occurs by either coercion or force, and the child is told to keep it a secret or threatened with harm should he tell about the abuse. The child then may feel guilty or ashamed about the abuse, which can also hamper disclosure. When caught by the justice system, many pedophiles claim that the child initiated the sexual activity, that the child wanted it, and any other gross rationalization that they can come up with.

Sexually abused children can suffer from a range of emotional and behavioral problems that can be mild to severe, and either short or long-term. Typical problems include stress disorders, guilt, depression, anxiety, fear, withdrawal, acting-up, and sexual dysfunction. Revictimization is common, as sexually abused children are more likely to be victims of rape or involved in physically abusive relationships as adults.

WHO IS AT RISK?

Although all children can be potential victims, some are at higher risk than others. These include children who:

- are loners or runaways
- live in a home where other forms of family violence occur
- have a parent who has been abused
- live in a geographically isolated area
- have a family that has extreme mistrust of outsiders
- have an overly close family with secrets and poor communication skills

Many pedophiles date single mothers to get access to their children, while others hang around playgrounds. Pedophiles also tend to take jobs or volunteer in occupations that involve children.

HOW WOULD I KNOW MY CHILD WAS ABUSED?

Since coercion is more common than force, watch for emotional and behavioral signs, as well as physical ones:

PHYSICAL SIGNS FOR ALL CHILDREN:

- torn or stained underclothes
- pain in the genital or anal area
- genital irritation
- swollen genitals
- vaginal or rectal bleeding
- vaginal or rectal discharge
- sexually transmitted diseases

BEHAVIORAL SIGNS BY AGE GROUP

PRESCHOOL CHILDREN

- excessive crying, fearfulness, or agitation
- excessive clinging to adults
- regression to infantile behavior such as thumb-sucking
- excessive fears or nightmares
- inappropriate sex play
- excessive masturbation
- toileting difficulties
- sleep problems

SCHOOL-AGE CHILDREN

- refusal to go to school or to take part in previously enjoyed activity
- school failure
- withdrawal from peers
- eating or sleeping problems
- aggressive behavior
- overt sexual behavior
- violent themes in art or school work
- bed wetting
- mood swings

TEENAGE CHILDREN

- school problems, including truancy
- running away
- eating and sleeping problems
- withdrawal from peers
- drug or alcohol abuse

- depression and possible suicide attempts
- aggression
- sexual promiscuity

PREVENTING SEXUAL ABUSE

Many parents have difficulty talking about the norms of sex with their children, let alone sexual abuse. Yet ignorance can lead to disaster—if your child can't recognize it, how will she know if she's being sexually abused? Given that 25% of all girls and 13% of all boys are sexually abused before age 18, you should feel obligated to protect your child with knowledge. Children often feel that they caused the abuse, and thus they need to know ahead of time that there is nothing wrong with them, and that abuse is the problem of the perpetrator— not the victim.

Although you can never completely protect your child from sexual abuse, you can do your best to drastically minimize her chances of being abused:

PRESCHOOLERS

- Teach her the proper name for body parts, including genitals and breasts.
- Tell her that no one—strangers, friends or relatives—has the right to touch her private parts (parts covered by a bathing suit) or hurt her.
- Tell her it's okay to say "NO" to people who make her feel scared, uncomfortable, or embarrassed.
- Instruct her to tell you if adults ask her to keep secrets.

SCHOOL-AGE CHILDREN

- Give her straightforward information about sex.
- Reinforce that her body belongs to her and that no one has the right to touch her private parts.
- Explain that some grown-ups have problems and are confused about sex, and that these adults may try to do things that make her feel uncomfortable.
- Teach her personal safety and to get away from those adults who make her feel uncomfortable.
- Tell her to come to you immediately if such an adult bothers her.

TEENAGERS

- Explain that unwanted sex is an act of violence, not an act of love.
- Discuss rape, date/acquaintance rape (see Chapter 12).
- Reinforce her right to say "NO."

Be sure to teach your child the safety techniques discussed in the abduction section to increase her protection from child molesters. But remember, sexual abuse can occur under your own roof—family members, babysitters—so keep the lines of communication open at all times. Listen to your children, and be alert for unusual behaviors from them and others in your household.

WHAT TO DO SHOULD YOU SUSPECT ABUSE

Child sexual abuse is difficult for anyone to comprehend, particularly the child and her parents, and especially when a family member is the abuser. Your first response is one of denial—"this can't be happening to my child." A parent who learns that her spouse or other family member is abusing her child could feel shock, confusion, and a sense of paralysis. You may feel like your whole world has shattered. Even when the abuser is unknown to the family, parents still may feel a sense of guilt at not being able to protect their child from mistreatment.

However, if your child even hints about abuse, the American Academy of Child and Adolescent Psychiatry suggests that you encourage her to talk, and don't be judgmental. Show her that you understand and take her seriously. Children who are listened to do better than those who are not, and the response to the child's disclosure is critical to her healing.

Assure her that she did the right thing coming to you, as she may feel quite guilty about revealing her secret. She may also feel frightened if the abuser threatened to harm her for telling about the abuse. Tell her that the abuse isn't her fault, and promise to take steps to make sure the abuse stops.

Then take those steps. Report the abuse to the local child protective agency if the abuser was a family member, and to the police if the abuser is outside the family. The agency receiving the report will conduct the investigation and will take action to protect the child.

Contact your child's health care provider who may refer her to a specialist who evaluates and treats child sexual abuse. Your child will be examined and treated for any problem that may have occurred from the abuse, such as a sexually transmitted disease, or in the case of a postpubertal girl, pregnancy. You and your child will also be referred to a mental health therapist to assist you in dealing with the abuse.

Most childhood allegations of abuse are true; however, false allegations are possible, especially in custody disputes. The therapist or court will help determine if your child is telling the truth and whether it will be harmful for your child to speak in court. You need to be on her side while things are straightened out.

RESOURCES

Check the Blue Pages of your phone book for local resources.

National Center for Missing and Exploited Children
www.missingchildren.com
1–800–THE–LOST (843–5678)

National Child Abuse Hotline
www.childhelpusa.org
1–800–422–4453

Children's Advocacy Center Program
www.nca-online.org
1–800–239–9950

Parents Anonymous
www.parentsanonymous-natl.org
909–621–6184

INFECTIOUS DISEASES

MICHIGAN, 2000:
Three children from different schools die from bacterial meningitis in a span of two weeks.

SOME STATS

- In 2002, approximately 2,000 children under the age of 15 years, and 6,000 young people aged 15 to 24 years became infected with HIV every day worldwide.
- Since 1987, tuberculosis cases in children under 15 have increased by almost 40% in the United States.
- Influenza rates among healthy children in the United States are estimated at 10 to 40% each year.
- The incidence of Lyme disease in the United States is highest among children ages 5 to 9 and adults ages 45 to 54.
- Outbreaks of meningococcal meningitis have increased since 1991.
- Varicella (chicken pox) is the most common viral rash illness in childhood, with an estimated 3 million cases occurring annually.
- Thousands of children will develop serious infectious diseases this year that could have been prevented by immunizations.

New and fatal infectious diseases tend to cause concern to the point of panic in many parents. Although you need to be aware of the causes and preventive measures of these illnesses, you also should know how to keep your child safe from the more common infections such as chicken pox and the flu, which can range from mere annoyances to deadly problems.

A review of all the infectious diseases that can affect your child would be far beyond the scope of this book. Instead, this chapter will help you understand the principles of infections, how they infect your child, some common child and adolescent infections, and methods of infection control and prevention.

WHY YOUNG CHILDREN ARE MORE VULNERABLE TO INFECTIONS

Infants are particularly vulnerable to infectious diseases for three reasons: (1) their immune system is immature; (2) the antibodies they received from their mothers fade over their first year of life; and (3) disease protection from immunization has not yet been completed. Children develop immunity as they grow, through immunizations and exposure to natural diseases.

As children grow, they interact more with other children and adults, increasing their exposure to infectious organisms, allowing them to develop antibodies (germ-fighting proteins) naturally. However, this exposure, especially in day care settings and schools, also increases their chances of getting sick. Kids don't have the best hygiene practices. They don't wash their hands after toileting, and they wipe their noses on their sleeves. They put toys in their mouths and then rub their eyes. And child care staff may also not use proper hygiene techniques, such as washing their hands after caring for a sick child.

Some children, due to illness or medication, have a greater risk for developing infection than others because they have suppressed immune systems. Children with congenital immune-deficiency disorders, pediatric HIV disease, and cancer fall into this category, as do children receiving certain chemotherapeutic agents and large dose corticosteroids. If your child is immunosuppressed, speak to your health care provider for additional ways to keep your child less prone to infections.

UNDERSTANDING INFECTIONS

Microscopic organisms are everywhere—in the air, water, and ground; in your food; on your pets; and even in your mouth and gut. Some of these are actually beneficial, such as those in the gut that assist in the digestive process. Others cause disease. The immune system fights off most infections, but that system isn't fully developed in young children, and some children have immune disorders that disallow their body to fight off infections properly.

Infectious agents include:

BACTERIA are one-celled organisms, shaped like spheres, spirals, or rods. They are very self-sufficient little fellows that multiply by subdivision. Only about 1% of bacteria cause disease. These invade and multiply quickly, many producing toxins (chemicals that destroy body cells). *Neisseria meningitides*, the bacteria that cause meningococcal meningitis, and *Escherichia coli* (E. coli), the bacteria that can come from contaminated meat, are examples of harmful bacteria, as are the streptococcal bacteria that cause strep throat.

VIRUSES are even smaller than bacteria. They are essentially capsules that contain genetic material, whose sole purpose in life is to reproduce. Unlike bacteria, viruses are not self-sufficient. They need a host to reproduce. When they choose your child as their preferred host, viruses instruct your child's body cells to help with their reproduction, creating more viruses and destroying your child's cells. Polio, HIV/AIDS, the flu, and the common cold are all caused by various viruses. (ANTIBIOTICS DON'T WORK ON VIRUSES!)

FUNGI consist of molds, yeast, and mushrooms. Some mushrooms are poisonous, but none are infectious. However, mold and yeast can cause infections. Fungi live in the soil, water, air, and on plants. Some can live on your body without causing illness, while others cause infection, especially in children with impaired immune systems. Many cases of diaper rash are due to fungi (yeast), as are vaginal yeast infections.

Why does your son get sick while your daughter gets off scot-free, when they are both exposed to the same sniffling kid? Several factors play into developing infections. These include the strength (virulence) and amount of germs your child is exposed to and your child's general state of health. Infections actually follow a chain of events:

1. A causative organism exists (bacteria, virus, fungi, etc.).
2. This organism needs a reservoir: a human, animal, plant or substance that provides the causative organism with both nourishment and a mode for dispersal.
3. The causative organism requires a means of exit from the reservoir. Therefore, the host must shed the organism through the respiratory, gastrointestinal, or urinary tract.
4. Once the organism exits, it needs a route of transmission to connect to its new host. Transmission routes include: direct

skin-to-skin contact or exposure, sexual or intravenous
fluids, or infected particles in the air. Different organisms
require different routes.

5. The host must be susceptible for infection to occur. Young age,
    organism virulence, and impaired body defenses increase sus-
    ceptibility to infection. Vaccines and previous infection can
    render a potential host immune, thus not susceptible.

6. The organism must gain entry to the susceptible host through a
    portal of entry, such as the respiratory tract.

INFECTIOUS DISEASES

MENINGITIS

Meningitis is an inflammation of the meninges (membranes)
that cover the brain and spinal cord. It's usually caused by bacteria,
but can be caused by viruses. Several different bacteria can cause
meningitis, but the more common ones are *Haemophilus influenza*,
Neisseria meningitides, and *Streptococcus pneumoniae*. Most cases
occur between ages 1 month and 5 years, and infants under 12 months
are the most susceptible to bacterial meningitis. If left untreated, bacterial meningitis is fatal. Viral meningitis (due to Coxsackie,
echovirus, or mumps) is a self-limiting disease that typically lasts 7 to
10 days. Common signs of meningitis include fever, headache, and
stiff neck. Children under two years tend to be irritable, resistant to
being held, and have fever, vomiting, and diarrhea.

MONONUCLEOSIS

Caused by the Epstein-Barr virus, "mono" occurs most often
in children and young adults. Although called the "kissing disease,"
mono can be spread through any type of close contact, including living with an infected person or sharing his food utensils, and can be
found in small children as well as teens. Initial symptoms are similar
to the flu—generalized weakness, fever, headache, and sore throat.
These are followed by painful, swollen neck glands (lymph nodes),
and occasionally a rash and swollen spleen. There is no treatment for
mono, other than rest, fluids, and acetaminophen (Tylenol ®) for
aches and fever.

TUBERCULOSIS (TB)

Caused by *Mycobacterium tuberculosis*, tuberculosis is a leading cause of death worldwide. Improved living conditions and antibiotics have caused a decrease in the number of cases and deaths. Children most likely to become infected are those with HIV disease or other immunosuppressive disorder, diabetes mellitus, kidney disease, or malnutrition, or those who live in poor, overcrowded conditions. Infants and children tend to not have any symptoms. That is why regular TB testing is required for children who live in areas where TB is prevalent. Symptoms in adults and teenagers include chest pain, chronic cough, and shortness of breath. Since children are more likely to get TB from an adult than another child, it's important that adults be tested for TB when symptomatic.

INFLUENZA (THE FLU)

Most flu epidemics are caused by types A and B influenza virus, which are easily spread by direct or indirect (touching contaminated articles) contact. During flu outbreaks, school age children become infected and bring the virus home to their parents and siblings. Symptoms include fever, chills, runny nose, sore throat, cough, nausea, vomiting, and diarrhea. Infants and small children can develop dehydration, trouble breathing, and meningitis symptoms.

MEASLES (RUBEOLA)

Measles, a viral disease spread by close contact, has increased in incidence recently due to the failure to immunize preschool children, as well as outbreaks in adolescents and young adults who were vaccinated appropriately at the time, but did not receive the second vaccine according to current guidelines. Early symptoms include fever, nasal congestion, red eyes, and a mild cough. In a few days, the child develops white spots in his mouth, followed by high fever and a red rash. Infected children are contagious 3 to 5 days before the appearance of the rash.

GERMAN MEASLES (RUBELLA)

German Measles is a mild rubiviral illness in children, characterized by fatigue, fever, headache, and a rash. Complications are rare in children. However, pregnant women who are exposed to

German measles are at risk for fetal miscarriage, stillbirth, or birth defects that include heart defects, mental retardation, and blindness.

MUMPS (PARODITIS)

This infection of the saliva glands is caused by the paramyx-ovirus. It usually begins with fever, headache, and appetite loss, followed by earache. By the third day, the child develops swelling of the gland or glands. Although usually not a severe disease, mumps can lead to meningoencephalitis, orchitis and sterility in males, arthritis, and pneumonia.

CHICKEN POX (VARICELLA)

The most common rash illness in childhood, chicken pox is caused by the varicella-zoster virus. It's transmitted from child to child by direct contact or airborne droplets. After the primary infection, the virus remains in the body in a dormant form, and reactivation results in shingles. Chicken pox begins with cold-like symptoms, then progresses to a spot-and-blister rash that scabs and covers the whole body. The child is contagious until all the blisters have scabbed. Chicken pox is very dangerous to immunosuppressed children, who can develop a fatal form of the disease. If your child is immunosuppressed and exposed to chicken pox, contact your health care provider immediately.

FIFTH DISEASE (ERYTHEMA INFECTIOSUM)

Commonly referred to as the "slapped cheek disease," fifth disease is caused by the human parvovirus B19, spread by airborne droplets. The illness starts with headache, nausea, and body ache, followed by a bright red rash on the cheeks. The cheek rash fades and a pale pink rash appears on the body. Fifth disease is usually mild, but can cause severe anemia in children with immunosuppression, as well as sickle-cell anemia and other similar chronic anemias. Fifth disease can also cause severe fetal anemia or miscarriage in pregnant women. Fortunately, most women are immune because they had fifth disease as a child. However, if you come into contact with an infected child during pregnancy, consult your health care provider.

SCARLET FEVER

Scarlet fever is caused by group A beta-hemolytic streptococcus (GABHS), the same bacteria that caused strep throat. It usually has a sudden onset with tiredness, fever, chills, headache, sore throat, nausea, and vomiting. The red sandpaper rash appears in 12 to 48 hours, as does the "strawberry tongue." Scarlet fever should be treated with antibiotics to prevent rheumatic fever.

DIPHTHERIA

More common in crowded conditions, diphtheria is caused by *Cornyebacterium diphtheriae,* which can be present in discharge from the eye, nose, throat, and skin lesions. It's transmitted from person to person by close personal contact with a patient or a carrier. Diphtheria is classified according to groups: tonsillar, conjunctival (eye), respiratory, skin, and genital. Symptoms vary with location, but the classic tonsillar diphtheria causes a low fever, rapid heartbeat, severe sore throat, and enlarged lymph glands ("bull neck").

WHOOPING COUGH (PERTUSSIS)

Caused by *Bordatella pertussis*, whooping cough is characterized by repeated coughing without being able to take a breath. As soon as the child takes a breath, he makes a whooping sound. The coughing is accompanied by fever, vomiting, and weight loss.

POLIO

The polio viruses are transmitted via the fecal-oral (eating contaminated food) or respiratory route. If a susceptible child comes into contact with a poliovirus, one of three things can happen: (1) he can develop a mild illness with fever (most common), (2) he can develop a form of meningitis, or (3) he can get the paralytic type (least common). This infection is currently rare in the United States.

LYME DISEASE

Lyme disease is caused by *Borrelia burgdorferi*, which is most often transmitted by a deer tick. For more on Lyme disease and how it can be prevented, read about it in Chapter 1: Bites and Stings.

PREVENTING CHILDHOOD INFECTIOUS DISEASES

Most of these childhood infectious diseases can be prevented with as little as handwashing and proper immunizations.

HANDWASHING

The best defense against infection takes only 15 seconds and requires no special equipment or training. All you need is a little soap and water. Yet, despite all the evidence that demonstrates the effectiveness of handwashing, many people just don't do it. See all those reminders for employees to wash their hands when you're in a public restroom? Wouldn't you think all people would want to wash their hands after going to the bathroom? Unfortunately, many don't. Yuck!

Organisms accumulate on your hands—on doorknobs, on telephones, on toilet handles, on faucet handles, and on and on. Not washing your hands can result in a host of ailments, such as the ones already noted in this chapter, as well as pneumonia, diarrhea, and hepatitis. You can easily infect yourself when you touch something, then rub your eyes, nose, or mouth. The most common way of spreading the common cold is through touching contaminated surfaces and not washing your hands.

You can't keep your hands completely germ-free, but you should wash your hands:

- before eating
- before feeding the baby
- before, during, and after preparing food (raw meat, poultry, fish, eggs)
- after you use the bathroom
- after changing a diaper
- after touching animals or animal waste
- after handling money
- after handling garbage
- after coughing or sneezing
- after blowing your nose
- after gardening or other yard work
- before and after treating wounds
- when someone at home is ill (frequently)
- whenever your hands are dirty

Whisking your hands under the faucet isn't enough to kill germs. To properly wash your hands, follow these guidelines from the Centers for Disease Control and Prevention:

1. Wet your hands and apply soap.
2. Rub your hands vigorously as you wash all surfaces for 15 seconds.
3. Rinse well and leave the water running.
4. Dry hands (preferably with a single-use towel).
5. Turn the faucet off with a paper towel (so you don't recontaminate yourself).

As you well know, it's difficult, but not impossible, to get your kids to wash their hands. Start by being a good example, and then supervise them as they learn to wash properly. But make it fun:

- Give him a sticker each time he washes his hands.
- Have him create a "wash the germs away" poster and place it where it can remind him to wash his hands.
- Play the glitter game. Have him rub glitter that represents germs on his hands, and then have him wash the "germs" away. He will see how he has to really wash them to get that glitter off!

HAND SANITIZERS

Hand sanitizers, the cleaners that don't need water, are a good alternative when soap and water are not available, especially when you're on the road. When rubbed into the hands for 15 seconds, these sanitizers kill nearly 99.9% of germs. But don't use them too often. They are made with alcohol that can irritate and dry out sensitive skin, making it even more susceptible to infection. Hand sanitizers are also flammable and can be fatal if swallowed. Therefore, don't let small children use them without adult supervision, and keep the sanitizers out of their reach.

CLEANING AND DISINFECTING

Cleaning with soap and water works for most of the house as it removes dirt and most germs. But some areas require disinfecting to give you and your family a better safety margin. Disinfectants, including household bleach, have bacteria-destroying ingredients that kill infectious germs that lurk on supposedly clean surfaces—germs that would otherwise survive for hours, even days.

Bathrooms require extra attention to rid both germs and odor, but your kitchen can be the most dangerous room in your house. Infectious bacteria from raw food can lurk on your cutting boards and counter tops, waiting to contaminate other food products, you, and your children.

To disinfect your home, the Centers for Disease Control and Prevention suggest:

- Follow the directions on cleaning product labels and read safety precautions carefully.
- Clean and disinfect surfaces when a family member is ill.
- If cleaning up body fluids, such as blood, vomit, or feces, wear rubber gloves, especially if you have cuts on your hands or if a family member has HIV/AIDS, Hepatitis B,or another disease transmitted through body surfaces.
- Clean surfaces with soap and water before disinfecting.
- Apply disinfectant and let it stand for a few minutes or longer, depending on manufacturer's recommendations.
- Wipe surface with paper towels and throw towels away.
- Store cleaners and disinfectants out of the reach of your children.
- Wash your hands, even if you used gloves.

IMMUNIZE!!!!!!!!!!!!

In 1952, 20,000 people were disabled by polio, and measles and diphtheria once killed thousands of people each year. The best way you can protect you child from many of the childhood infectious diseases is to immunize him. Immunizations, or vaccines, introduce specific antigens (foreign substances that trigger immune response) into the body, allowing immunity to develop against a specific disease.

Despite the benefits of immunizations, more than 20% of 2-year-olds in the United States are missing one or more recommended immunizations. One reason may be the ongoing concern that many parents have about immunization safety. Many fear that immunizations may cause serious side effects or the disease itself, and much of this is due to media reports regarding severe reaction or illness that occurs after a child receives a vaccine.

Vaccines must meet strict Food and Drug Administration (FDA) safety standards and serious side effects are rare, occurring in 1 in thousands to 1 in millions of doses. However, like prescription medications, they are not completely free of side effects, most of which are mild and temporary, like a soreness; and some vaccines should not be given to children with certain allergies or immunodeficiency disorders.

Talk to your health care provider about your child's immunizations. Ask about their safety and side effects, and ask what you can do to alleviate the temporary discomfort that your child may feel after getting his "shots." To keep abreast of the latest immunization schedule, click on http://www.cispimmunize.org/pro/2002_main.html.

FOODBORNE ILLNESSES (FOOD POISONING)

Foodborne illnesses cause an estimated 76 million illnesses, 325,000 hospitalizations, and 5,200 deaths in the United States each year. Known organisms account for about 14 million illnesses, 60,000 hospitalizations, and 1,800 deaths annually. According to the Centers for Disease Control and Prevention, more than 250 foodborne diseases have been described. Their symptoms vary widely depending on causative organism, but diarrhea and vomiting are the most common. Many different bacteria (e.g., *Campylobacter, Salmonella, E. coli*), viruses (e.g., caliciviruses), parasites (e.g., *Giardia, Cyclospora*), and natural and man made chemicals (e.g., mushroom toxins and heavy metals) have been implicated in foodborne illnesses.

One group of bacteria most commonly found is called **Campylobacter**. These may be present in unpasteurized milk or raw poultry. *Salmonella* may be present in raw meat, poultry and eggs. *Staphylococcus Aureus, Clostridium Perfringens* and *Bacillus Cereus* produce toxins or poisons in food which may result in severe vomiting. *C. Perfringens* is usually associated with meat and *B. Cereus* with rice. *E. Coli 0157*, a variant of the normal E. coli found in the intestines, is present in some cattle and may contaminate raw meat. It can cause bloody diarrhea and kidney failure, particularly in young children.

FOOD SAFETY

Many of us have suffered through the stomach upset of mild food poisoning, but since this problem can be extremely dangerous to your child–and older adults—you should take steps recommended by the Centers for Disease Control and Prevention to assure food safety:

1. Be careful when you purchase food:
    —buy perishables (meat and dairy) last
    —avoid unpasteurized or raw milk
    —don't allow meat, poultry, fish, or egg juices to drip on other foods
    —don't allow food to spoil in the car
2. Store food properly:
    —refrigerate dairy products, eggs, raw meat, poultry, and seafood
    —keep them in containers that prevent contamination to other foods
    —keep refrigerator at 40 degrees F
    —keep freezer at 0 degrees F
    —clean and disinfect the refrigerator and freezer regularly
3. Use precautions when preparing food:
    —wash hands and preparation surfaces before, during, and after handling, cooking, and serving food
    —wash fruits and vegetables before eating them
    —defrost frozen food in the refrigerator or microwave, never on the counter
    —cook food immediately after defrosting
    —use different dishes and utensils for cooked and raw foods
4. Use proper cooking guidelines:
    —eggs should be firm and not runny; don't eat raw or partially cooked eggs
    —cook poultry to an internal temperature of 180 degrees F; juices should be clear and the meat white
    —cook fish until it's flaky and white
    —cook meat until brown, especially hamburger
5. Store leftovers quickly and properly:
    —don't leave perishable food out for more than 2 hours; store immediately during warm weather
    —refrigerate leftovers in shallow containers or wrap tightly in bags.

SEXUALLY TRANSMITTED DISEASES (STD)

When we were young, sexually transmitted diseases were something you did not talk about. Today, some of them can be life-long or life-threatening. Share this section with your teen.

CHLAMYDIA is the most common bacterial STD in the United States, and 50% of these cases have no symptoms. Untreated infections can cause pelvic inflammatory disease, ectopic pregnancy, epididymitis, and infertility.

GONORRHEA can also appear without symptoms and with Chlamydia. Both males and females may mistake its burning for a urinary tract infection.

TRICHOMONIASIS causes a foul, frothy vaginal discharge, pain on intercourse, and menstrual irregularities, and it can occur with other infections.

HUMAN PAPILLOMAVIRUS (HPV; venereal warts) is the most common female STD. The warts may be visible or not, and they increase the risk of cervical, penile, and anal cancers.

GENITAL HERPES has increased in incidence in the United States. Love may be fleeting, but herpes is forever. The ulcers are very painful, and the disease can spread even when the person has no symptoms.

SYPHILIS rates vary by geography in the United States. Its early painful ulcers can increase the risk for HIV, while left untreated, its late stage can cause heart and brain damage.

HUMAN IMMUNODEFICIENCY VIRUS (HIV) remains a problem in teenagers who engage in unsafe sex practices or intravenous drug abuse.

PREVENTING STDs

So far there are no vaccines for STDs, but there are still steps you can teach your teen to prevent STDs:

- Abstinence is the best form of prevention.
- Realize that alcohol and drugs can increase sexual risk-taking. Don't mix them with sex.
- Limit the number of sex partners and practice monogamy.
- Oral and anal sex are still sex and both can spread STDs.
- Always use a latex condom with a spermicidal gel for vaginal and anal intercourse.
- See your health care provider if you have any symptoms.
- Have an examination twice a year if sexually active.

10

INTERNET DANGERS

CONNECTICUT, 2002:
Internet predator lures 13-year-old cheerleader to her death.

SOME STATS

According to the Youth Internet Safety Survey by the Crimes Against Children Research Center:

- 1 in 5 youths received a sexual approach or solicitation over the Internet in the past year.
- 1 in 33 youths received an aggressive sexual solicitation in the past year, meaning a predator asked a youth to meet somewhere, called a youth on the phone, and/or sent the youth correspondence, money, or gifts through the United States Postal Service.
- 1 in 4 youths had an unwanted exposure to pictures of naked people or people having sex.
- 1 in 17 youths was threatened or harassed.
- Most youths who reported these incidents were not very disturbed about them, but a few found them distressing.
- Only a fraction of these episodes were reported to authorities such as the police, an Internet service provider, or a hotline.
- About 25% of the youths who encountered a sexual approach or solicitation told a parent.
- Almost 40% of those reporting an unwanted exposure to sexual material told a parent.

ASL

Do you know what that means? ASL stands for "age, sex, location" and is computer lingo used by Internet pedophiles to start up a chat with your child.

The Internet (the "Net") offers your children access to newspapers, libraries, and museums all over the globe. It provides seemingly endless information on school subjects, sports, hobbies, music, and more, making it as fun as it's educational. Your child can also chat with children in other nations and download their world in seconds.

Millions of wonders abound on the Internet, but so do thousands of predators waiting to lure your child into their universe of unspeakable horrors.

Pedophiles are not the only criminals roaming the Net. Others commit crimes such as fraud and theft by gaining access to your personal and credit information, or expose your child to gambling, harassment, or drug and alcohol information and access. Your child can innocently click on to a pornographic or hate site–easy to do—first click on www.whitehouse.gov, then hit www.whitehouse.com–one's government, the other adult entertainment. You need to protect your child and yourself, even if you don't own a computer, because your child can easily access the Internet at school, the local library, or a friend's house.

INTERNET PEDOPHILES

Internet pedophiles are quite sophisticated in computer technology, with some acting as entrepreneurs, selling products on their own home pages. Some predators gradually seduce children with attention, affection, kindness, and even gifts, sometimes devoting considerable amounts of time and money in the process. They listen to children, empathizing with their problems and learning their interests and hobbies, and then gradually lower the children's inhibitions by introducing sexual content and context into their conversations. They build long-term relationships with children in chat rooms, and even teach the children to manipulate their parents so that they "don't cause problems."

Others immediately engage in sexually explicit conversations with children. Some collect and trade child pornography, while others seek face-to-face contact with children through online contacts. Computer sex offenders can be any age or sex person, and most don't fit the stereotype of the dirty old man in a trench coat.

According to the United States Department of Justice Office for Victims of Crime, children and teenagers can and do become victims of Internet crimes. Predators can contact your children over the Internet and victimize them by:

- Tempting them through online contact for the purpose of engaging them in sexual acts.
- Using the Internet for the production, manufacture, and distribution of child pornography.
- Using the Internet to expose your children to child pornography and encourage them to exchange pornography.
- Enticing and exploiting your children for the purpose of sexual tourism (travel with the intent to engage in sexual behavior) for commercial gain and/or personal gratification.

The United States Department of Justice Office for Crime Victims also notes that several characteristics distinguish Internet crimes from other crimes committed against children:

1. Actual physical contact between the child and the perpetrator doesn't need to occur for a child to be a victim or for a crime to be committed. Innocent pictures can be digitally transformed into pornographic material and distributed across the Internet without the victim's knowledge.

2. The Internet provides a source for long-term victimization of a child that can last for years, often without the victim's knowledge. Once a pornographic photo of a child is displayed on the Internet, it can stay there forever without damage to the quality of the image.

3. Internet child abuse transcends jurisdictional boundaries, frequently involving multiple victims from different communities, states, and countries. The geographic location of a child isn't a major concern for perpetrators who target victims over the Internet. Pedophiles often travel hundreds of miles to engage in sexual acts with children they met over the Internet.

4. Many child victims of Internet crimes don't reveal their victimization or even realize that they have been victims of a crime. Many victims of Internet crimes remain anonymous until pictures or images are discovered by law enforcement during an investigation. The presumed anonymity of Internet activities often provides a false sense of security and secrecy for both the victim and the perpetrator.

Children, particularly teens, can be very curious about sex and sexually explicit material. They may be seeking more independence from their parents and looking to develop new relationships outside the family. The Internet acts as an easy tool for these children—they can search for pornographic material in the privacy of their computer for free without having to worry about nosy adults supervising them at the magazine stand. Pedophiles are well aware of this, and they use the children's curiosity to lure them in.

HOW PEDOPHILES CONTACT CHILDREN THOUGH THE INTERNET

Cyberspace is a big place, and there are many ways for people to contact each other. Pedophiles use four different avenues to attract children: websites, chat rooms, e-mails, and bulletin boards.

WEB SITES

Most web sites contain benign, often helpful, material. Others contain content that is violent, racist, hate-filled, demeaning, obscene, pornographic, or offensive in other ways. These sites can bother adults, let alone children. Sites may ask for your child's name, mailing address, e-mail address, and phone number before allowing access, making them more enticing to children. Some promise prizes for personal information. At the very least, your child's information will be added to a database so that companies can try to sell you things. At worst, a pedophile may try to harm your child. Anyone, including weirdos and criminals, can create their own web site.

If your child has her own web site, as many children do, make sure she doesn't post her personal information or any photos of herself. It's also best that children not post their e-mail addresses.

CHAT ROOMS

Chats allow people to engage in live conversations with each other—around the block and around the world. Everyone in the chat room can see what each person types. Some chats are just open conversations; others are moderated by someone who leads a discussion. Some chats have monitors who maintain order and rid the room of people who act inappropriately. But monitors can't prevent people from going off into private chats that are seen only by those directly involved. Instant messaging is also a form of chat room.

Chat rooms are most likely the most dangerous places on the Internet. Kids tend to see other chatters as friends, not realizing that some of these 'friends" are actually pedophiles posing as children. The pedophile then goes into the listening and empathetic mode, gaining the child's trust. The child may then inadvertently give the pedophile personal information or photos, or even arrange to meet him.

Kids using chat rooms tend to use chat vocabulary and emoticons to speed up their conversations. If you're not up on the latest lingo, use the charts at the end of this chapter, and keep them handy to decode your child's chats and e-mails.

E-MAILS

E-mails are generally one-to-one communications, although there are such things as group e-mails and Listservs where large numbers of people may be sharing information. Pedophiles may contact your child directly after obtaining her e-mail address, or indirectly by "spamming," a process by which e-mail is sent to thousands of people, prodding them to buy something, do something, or visit a web site.

E-mails have a return address. Some spammers use a sexually explicit address, while others use seemingly innocent, but catchy ones, such as: youwonit@bigprizes.com or importantmessage@read me.com. E-mails also contain a subject line that provides information about its content. This may also be explicit or outwardly innocent. The e-mail content may contain graphic information or pictures, or a link to a pornographic web site.

BULLETIN BOARDS

Also called newsgroups, forums, and B-boards, bulletin boards are places where your child can read and post messages or download or upload files. Bulletin boards are not live or "real time." Kids and adults post messages to be read at a later time. They can also post computer programs, photos, and illustrations. You have seen or used bulletin or discussion boards on parenting web sites.

Bulletin boards abound, and many are fun ways to share information on hobbies and interests. But some exist for the purpose of sharing sexually explicit and pornographic material. Posting on the latter can prove dangerous, because doing so causes your child to broadcast her e-mail address to everyone who visits that site.

KEEPING YOUR CHILD SAFE ON THE INTERNET

The Internet is an exciting and helpful tool, but it can also be very dangerous. Therefore, you need to take steps to keep your child safe. Don't assume that she will be protected by the supervision or regulation of the online services.

To keep her safe, try these general guidelines:

1. Keep the computer in a room that the whole family uses, and make the Internet a family activity. Don't leave it in her room. This way you can keep an eye on her. Tell her she can't do anything online unless you can see what she's doing.
2. Become computer literate so you can monitor her properly. Check with your local schools or colleges for classes.
3. Discuss sexual victimization and Internet dangers. Talk to her about the issues that concern you, such as violence, pornography, hate literature, and exploitation. This way she will know how to respond should she encounter these things.
4. Ask her to tell you about it.
5. Don't open e-mails from unknown senders.
6. Report and block obscene spam.
7. Turn off browser if an obscene web site appears.
8. Set up a master account with your service provider—AOL, MSN, cable company, or whatever provider you use. Don't give your child the password to the master account. Create a separate screen name for your child so that you can block access to inappropriate sites.
9. Use blocking or filtering software to allow you to control your child's access to certain areas on the Internet. Different products offer various levels of parental control, so investigate each one carefully to choose the one best for your family.
10. Be aware that your child can outsmart many of the parental controls and filtering services. Therefore, nothing can replace your supervision and involvement.
11. Limit the amount of time she spends online. You can print out a "Family Contract for Online Safety" for you and your child to sign at www.SafeKids.com.
12. Establish clear and concise rules for using the computer, and post them near the computer.
13. Help her find useful, positive web sites and bookmark them.
14. Let her take you for a trip through cyberspace. You will learn how she navigates the web, and she will get a chance to show you that she's smarter than you.
15. Keep tabs on her Internet usage. If she logs off when you enter the room, or you suspect that she may be doing something inappropriate, find her history trail. Sign on to your service provider. Right click on your Windows Start button and click

on Explore. Find your main hard drive (probably C), and look over the folders until you find History. Click it open to find out the sites your child has visited. The site names are usually obvious, but if you're not sure about the content of one, double-click it to go to the site.

You can purchase tracking software to track where she goes online. These programs allow you to monitor the length of time she spends on the Internet, time of day sites were visited, sites visited, and time spent offline but on the computer. School systems use these to track where students go online.

16. Randomly check her e-mail, but remember she may be contacted via the U.S. mail, too. Be honest about your access so as not to lose her trust.

17. Find out what Internet safeguards are used by her school, her friends, and the library. These are areas outside your supervision where your child may encounter an online predator.

The FBI suggests that you teach your child to:

- Never arrange a face-to-face meeting with a person she met online.
- Never post photos of herself on the Internet or e-mail them to people she doesn't personally know.
- Never give out her name, address, phone number, e-mail address, or any other identifying information.
- Never download anything from an unknown site or e-mail as it may contain sexually explicit or other objectionable information.
- Never respond to suggestive, obscene, harassing, or belligerent messages or postings.
- Realize that what she reads online may or may not be true.
- Always tell you when an online experience makes her uncomfortable.

HOW WOULD YOUR KNOW YOUR CHILD IS AT RISK?

There are warning signs for children who may be targeted by a pedophile:

- She turns off the computer or changes the screen suddenly when you enter the room.
- She spends large amounts of time online, especially at night. Most predators work during the day and prey in the evening or at night.

- Your child receives calls from men you don't know, or you find long distance charges to numbers you don't recognize.
- She receives money, gifts, or packages from someone you don't know.
- Your child uses an online account that belongs to someone else.
- You find pornography on your computer, disks, or writable CDs.
- She becomes withdrawn from the family.

WHAT TO DO IF YOU SUSPECT YOUR CHILD IS A VICTIM OF AN ONLINE PREDATOR

If you suspect your child has been targeted by an online perpetrator, talk to her about your suspicions. Be calm and nonjudgmental. Realize that even if your child is a willing participant in any type of sexual exploitation, she's not at fault and is the victim.

- Perform a computer history search as noted above.
- Use Caller-ID to determine who is contacting your child, and block incoming calls from that number. (The predator can always use another phone, so stay alert.) Ask your telephone company if they offer a service that allows your number to be blocked from appearing on someone else's ID.
- Monitor your child's online activity.
- Contact your state police, the FBI, and the National Center for Missing and Exploited Children (1–800–843–5678) for any of the following via the Internet:
  1. If anyone in your house receives child pornography.
  2. Someone sexually solicits your child, knowing she is under 18.
  3. Someone sends your child sexually explicit images, knowing she's under 18.
- Keep the computer turned off to preserve evidence for future law enforcement use.
- Don't attempt to copy images or text unless directed to do so by law enforcement.

CHAT AND E-MAIL VOCABULARY, SYMBOLS, AND EMOTICONS

VOCABULARY	MEANING
2U2	To you, too
AFAIK	As far as I know
AFK	Away from keyboard
ASAP	As soon as possible
ASL	Age, sex, location
AYOR	At your own risk
BAK	Back at keyboard
BBL	Be back later
BEG	Big evil grin
BRB	Be right back
BTW	By the way
CU	See you
CUL	See you later
CYA	See ya
DIY	Do it yourself
DTRT	Do the right thing
F2F	Face to face
FOAF	Friend of a friend
FOCL	Falling off chair laughing
GAL	Get a life
GTG	Got to go
H&K	Hugs and kisses
HAND	Have a nice day
IB	I'm back
IHQ	I have a question
IYKWIM	If you know what I mean
JIC	Just in case
J/K	Just kidding
LD	Later dude
LOL	Laughing out loud
LTNS	Long time no see
M or F	Male or female, or person who asks that question
MOTOS	Member of the opposite sex
MOTSS	Member of the same sex

ONNA	Oh no, not again
OLL	Online love
PLS	Please
PU	That stinks
REHI	Hello again
ROFL	Rolling on floor laughing
SO	Significant other
SOHF	Sense of humor failure
TANSTAAFL	There ain't no such thing as a free lunch
TNX	Thanks
TIA	Thanks in advance
TLK2UL8R	Talk to you later
TSWC	Tell someone who cares
URL	Web page address
w/b	Welcome back
w/o	Without
WRT	With regard to
WTGP	Want to go private?
WU?	What's up?
WWW	World Wide Web
WYSIWYG	What you see is what you get
YGWYPF	You get what you pay for
ZZZ	Sleeping

SYMBOLS FOR CHAT PROTOCOL

SYMBOLS	MEANING
/ga	Go ahead
/	Denotes end of message
?	Person is asking a question
!	Person has a comment

EMOTICONS/SMILEYS

EMOTICON	MEANING
0:) or 0-)	Angel
:ll or :-ll	Angry
:@ or :-@	Angry
;)=) or :-)=)	Big grin

:o or :-o	Bored
:c or :-c	Bummed out
:=(or :=-(	Sad or crying
};^)=	Devil
:> or :->	Devilish grin
>;->	Devilish wink, lewd remark
:-)..	Drooler
:*)	Drunk
}) or }-)	Evil
:] or :-]	Friendly
:(or :-(	Frowning
:/ or :-/	Frustrated
:-)	Girl flirting
:]	Gleep; gladly be your friend
8) or 8-)	Glasses
:D or :-D	Grinning
<3	Heart
:I	Hmmm...
{}	Hug
[]:*	Hugs and kisses
:*) or :-*)	Kiss
:x or :-x	Kissing
:X or :-X	Kiss, big wet
:-@	Kiss, French
:-9	Licking his/her lips
:-Q	Person who just had cyber-sex & is enjoying a ciga-rette
:[or :-[	Real downer
:< or :-<	Sad
B) or B-)	Shades (sunglasses)
=:) or =:-)	Shocked
:0 or :-)	Smiling
:O or :-O	Surprised
:() or :-()	Talking
:P or :-P	Tongue out
:^(	Unhappy
8:-)	User is a little girl
:-)~	User just drooled
:>	What?

:@	What?
:-@	Whistling
;) or ;-)	Winking
:} or :-}	Wry smile

11

MENACING MEDIA

KENTUCKY, 1997:
14-year-old kills three and wounds five others in a shooting spree inspired by a dream sequence in the film *Basketball Diaries*.

SOME STATS

- American media are the most violent and sexually suggestive media in the Western Hemisphere.
- The average child spends more than 38 hours each week using media (TV, videos, video games, computers, and music).
- By the time a person reaches 70, he will have spent the equivalent of 7 to 10 years of his life watching TV.
- American children view 10,000 murders, rapes, and aggravated assaults per year on TV.
- The average child sees 30,000 TV commercials each year.
- American children spend more time watching TV than they do in school.
- About 75% of concept (storytelling) music videos involve sexual imagery, while about 50% involve violence, usually against women.
- The average American teen views 14,000 sexual references per year, and only 165 of these deal with self-control, abstinence, birth control, or the risk of pregnancy or sexually transmitted diseases.

The average American child spends about 6 ½ hours per day using various media, time that displaces more important activities such as reading, exercising, and socializing with family and friends. Media can be informative and entertaining, but it can also have negative effects as children are exposed to violence, unsafe sex, racial and sexual stereotypes, drugs and alcohol, and commercials for toys and fast food, the latter increasing the childhood obesity rate.

VIOLENCE IN THE MEDIA

By the time a child reaches age 18 she will have seen 16,000 simulated murders and 200,000 acts of violence. Three to five acts of violence occur per hour during prime time, and 20 to 25 acts of violence happen per hour during Saturday morning children's programming. All of this doesn't take into account the amount of time spent watching movies, playing video/computer games or online interactive media, listening to music, and surfing the Internet—all of which contain violent content. American media is the most violent on earth.

Media violence can be hazardous to your child's health. The American Academy of Pediatrics, the American Medical Association, the American Academy of Child and Adolescent Psychiatry, and the American Psychological Association recently released a joint statement linking violent images on TV, in the movies, and in video games with an increase in violent behavior in children. Media violence can promote aggressive and antisocial behavior, desensitize viewers to future violence, and increase viewers' perceptions that they are living in a vicious and dangerous world.

SEX AND THE MEDIA

The United States has one of the highest rates of teen pregnancy and the highest rate of teen sexually transmitted diseases in the world. Several factors affect early sexual activity, but the media are believed to play a major role, especially since the media represent the most easily accessible and remediable influence on young people and their sexual attitudes and behaviors.

Studies show that messages in TV, movies, and music have become more explicit in their sexual dialogue, lyrics, and behavior. These messages frequently contain unrealistic, inaccurate, and misleading information that teenagers take as fact. Teens rank the media second only to school sex education programs as their leading source of sex information.

Sexual themes have increased in the lyrics of music and the images of music videos, and at least one study showed a relationship between risky adolescent behaviors and a preference for heavy metal music. Soap operas, a teen and preteen favorite, rank as an ideal venue for sexual portrayals, and one study of 50 hours of daytime soaps found 156 acts of intercourse with only 5 references to safe sex, and unmarried lovers outnumber married ones 3 to 1. Sexual themes, including bizarre ones, are common on talk shows, and even family hour shows contain an average of more than 8 sexual incidents, 4 times more than in 1976. Vulgar language is also increasing.

Sex sells, and commercials contain a tremendous amount of sexual imagery, including the inappropriate use of children in provocative poses. According to a report by adolescent expert, Victor Strasburger, MD, sex is used to sell common products from shampoo to hotel rooms; but when children respond to these cues and become sexually active too young, people blame the children, not the advertisers. Heavy exposure to media sex increases the perception of the frequency of sexual activity in the real world.

STEREOTYPES

Television personnel believe that stereotypes help to quickly establish character when time is an issue. But stereotypes present a skewed view of cultural diversity. They are less real, more perfect or imperfect, and more predictable than their real life counterparts. Although things have improved, a fair amount of gender and racial stereotyping persists. The typical stereotyped male is macho, masterful, adventurous, and unshakable, while stereotypical females are someone's apron-clad wife or barely-dressed girlfriend. Stereotyped children are frequently precocious. These portrayals can affect children's expectations, as well as their views of themselves.

Cultural stereotypes still roam the channels. Blacks are frequently shown as happy-go-lucky or dangerous, Italians as criminals, and Native Americans as wearing buckskins on the rare occasions they are even shown on TV. Mothers-in-law, police officers, nurses, gays, and the elderly are among others characterized as stereotypical. Stereotypes can give children false impressions of gender roles and various societal groups. One British survey even showed that stereotypes in advertising can reinforce racism and school bullying.

TOBACCO, DRUGS, AND ALCOHOL

The Federal Trade Commission (FTC) reviewed alcohol advertising practices in 1999 and issued a report that recommended several "best practices" for the alcohol industry aimed at reducing children's exposure to alcohol advertising. However, a study by the Center on Alcohol Marketing and Youth at Georgetown University revealed that alcohol companies have fallen short of following these "best practices" and continue to make underage youth a target. Marketers of beer and distilled spirits delivered more product advertising to youth than to adults in magazines.

The alcohol industry spends nearly 2 billion dollars each year to promote their products on TV, radio, magazines, newspapers, billboards, clothing, and sponsorship of community events such as sports, music, festivals, and fairs. Beer is the most heavily advertised—one study showed that teens see between 1000 and 2000 beer commercials carrying the message that "real men" drink beer—and children who report greater awareness of TV beer commercials have more favorable beliefs about drinking, greater knowledge of beer brands and slogans, and increased intention to drink as an adult.

Tobacco products are not directly advertised on TV; neither are illicit drugs. But both are commonly seen used by characters in both TV and film. The consequences of these behaviors are rarely shown, giving the wrong message to your children.

COMMERCIALS

The food industry links food with entertainment, especially movie and TV characters—notice who is in your child's fast-food kiddie meals? Aggressive marketing is one of the biggest contributors to the increased childhood obesity rate.

Marketing to children has only been acceptable since the past decade or so, but it's now a 12-billion-dollar industry. Children who are inundated with commercialism and materialism suffer not only from obesity, but also body-image and other emotional problems, eating disorders, and tendencies toward violence.

Young children don't understand sales pitches. They believe what they are told, and may even feel deprived if they don't get the advertised products. Considering most children see more than 30,000 commercials each year, that can become a huge problem.

TELEVISION PROGRAMMING

Americans have an ongoing love affair with their television sets. Almost 90% of American homes have two TV sets, and 66% watch TV while eating dinner. More than half of children aged 2 to 18 have TVs in their rooms, and the average 1-year-old watches six hours of TV per week, even though the American Academy of Pediatrics recommends that they watch none.

Despite the plethora of newer media, television remains the single most important medium in the lives of young people. Compared to other media, TV demands attention by activating the nervous system with rapid movements and loud music. It centers on brevity of sequences. The interactions between people and events are vivid and short, so its quick succession of material prevents children from mentally reflecting on new material to process or make sense of it. Because of its influence, TV has been a matter of concern since the 1960s. These concerns include how TV delivers information, the content of the information, and the parts of children's lives that TV displaces.

TV delivers information in short, fast-moving bits of imagery and talk to keep viewers' attention. Small children are fascinated by these images, but they don't have the thinking skills to understand them. Story techniques such as flashbacks, close-ups, lighting, and music work well on adults, but they are lost on even middle school children, who need help translating the story in fast-paced programming. Thus, the way that TV delivers information creates confusion for children. They miss quite a bit of what they see, often can't make connections, and are likely to focus on the more intense scenes—such as violent moments—not the most important: images and story components.

TV content creates concern in three areas: violence, values, and stereotypes. More than 80% of TV programs contain violence, and recent studies demonstrate a connection between viewing violence and committing it, whether or not the viewer is predisposed to violence. Television violence is graphic, realistic, and intensely involving, and shows inequity and domination, as most victims are women, children, and the elderly. The aggressive acts lead to a heightened arousal of the viewer's aggressive tendencies, bringing feelings, thoughts, and memories to consciousness, and causing outwardly aggressive behavior.

Many families find TV situations, relationships, and solutions at odds with their own values, especially on issues of attitudes on alcohol and drugs, sexual mores, and attitudes toward crime and law enforcement. Without explanations or alternative models on how to handle life's problems, children quickly pick up TV program ideas as solutions. As noted earlier, consequences are not depicted, and children assume that certain actions have no repercussions. Diversity remains a problem as TV exposes children to stereotypical images of dependent and less competent women, weak and foolish elderly, and comic minority figures—all of which do nothing to foster tolerance, the lack of which contributes to violence.

Research demonstrates that seeing violent, sexually explicit, or pornographic material on television has long-term effects on children, including the following violence-related adverse effects:

- TV encourages short attention spans and hyperactivity with its use of snappy attention-getting devices.
- TV causes a confusion of values.
- TV creates uncertainty about what is real and unreal in life.
- TV promotes use of products that may be unhealthy or dangerous.
- TV produces loss of interest in the less exciting but more necessary classroom or home activities.
- Heavy TV watching decreases school performance by interfering with studying, reading, and thinking time. If children lose sleep because of late night TV watching, they won't be alert enough to learn well the following day.
- TV increases aggressive behaviors with its use of violent program content, loud music, and camera tricks.
- TV increases passive acceptance of aggressive behavior as a way to deal with problems.
- TV escalates anxiety, fear, and suspicion of others.
- TV de-emphasizes the complexity of life, especially being consequenced for negative behavior.
- TV conveys stereotyped images.
- TV increases—not causes—emotional problems such as conduct disorders.
- Children who watch too much TV spend less time conversing with family members.
- Heavy TV viewers have difficulty developing their imaginations and a playful attitude, and they tend to be more restless and have more behavior problems in school.
- TV advertising encourages children to demand material possessions. Seeing materialism as the "American Way," children won't only pressure parents to make purchases, but they will also have an additional motivation for aggression by wanting what other children have and pressuring the others to give it to them.

Is television all bad? Absolutely not. Quality shows air all the time, and your involvement can significantly improve your child's gains. *Sesame Street* stimulates learning, and public TV has a host of wonderful shows. Cable channels, such as the Discovery Channel, Animal Planet, and others provide enormous amounts of educational material in an entertaining fashion. Steve Irwin, the Crocodile Hunter, and his wife, Terri, teach children and adults alike to respect animals —a great step in learning how to respect other humans. They are also terrific role models for children! Find the shows that have your child's needs in mind, such as educational, social, and wholesome fantasy programs.

Your child will be exposed to both good and bad things that she would otherwise not see at home. TV brings the language of cultures into your living room. But you still need to be involved. Be vigilant. Interact with your child and discuss what she watches to help her link what she sees on TV to her own life. Help her reflect by clarifying and emphasizing the main points.

How can you counteract the negative effects of television?

You can compete with TV and win:

1. Remove the TV set from her room—permanently.
2. Don't use the TV as a babysitter.
3. Don't use TV as a reward or punishment. Both make TV more important to your child.
4. Set limits on TV watching time. Programs are designed to be enticing and TV viewing is habit-forming. Know how much time your child spends in front of the TV, and don't hesitate to reduce that time. The American Academy of Pediatrics recommends limiting viewing time to 1 to 2 hours per day on school days and 2 to 3 hours a day on weekends and holidays. Allow additional time for educational programs. Limit preschoolers to no more than 1 hour of noneducational TV per day. Talk about the effects of watching too much television.
5. Turn the TV off during conversations and mealtime. Family time is minimal to begin with; don't decrease it further with the intrusion of television. Don't center your family/living room furniture around the TV, and don't put the TV in a prominent position in your home. Make family conversation time a priority.

6. Ban TV before homework completion. If this isn't possible, ban it during homework. If your child has academic difficulties, decrease his viewing time to 1 hour or less a day.

7. Plan viewing together, in advance, by using your TV Guide or newspaper. Use the Television/Motion Picture Association of America (TV/MPAA) rating system to determine which shows are appropriate. Discuss your reasons for both approving and disapproving shows. Turn the set on for these programs only, and discuss them when they are over. If schedules conflict, videotape the programs for future viewing.

8. Preview programs first whenever possible. Screen new shows intended for children. Help her choose shows that educate or stimulate discussions or activities. Learn about great white sharks. Share some hot cocoa while the two of you watch the Ice Capades.

9. Forbid shows with graphic violence. With the availability of cable and pay-per-view movies and other programs, children have easier access to violent programs. Realize that they cannot see R-rated films without adult supervision in the theater because these films may contain graphic violence as well as other material unsuitable for children.

10. Watch along with her so you can help interpret what she sees. Use the shows to express and discuss difficult topics, such as love, sex, work, and family life. Encourage interactive discussions and invite her to question and learn from what she views. Let her know that her comments are valued, and comfort her when something is sad or scary.

11. Observe her as she watches. What is her mood? Is she sad, confused, worried, happy, or bored? Talk about her reactions, and foster her critical thinking skills. Persuade her to turn the set off if the show is boring.

12. Play critics and review programs. Rate them on a scale of 1 to 10 on various themes, such as violent content and advertising messages. Have her look for stereotypes and lack of consequences, and then rewrite the script herself.

13. Clarify confusing issues. Explain frightening special effects, including makeup and sound effects. Differentiate fantasy from reality. Discuss how the characters are not injured in the story because they are just actors, and that real people would be severely injured or killed in similar real life circumstances.

14. Use V-chip technology to block your child from watching inappropriate material on TV. The V-chip reads the electronically coded ratings systems for the programs, then denies

access if the program meets the limitations you set. Be aware, however, that the V-chip may not block material from news and sports programs, unedited movies on premium cable channels (HBO, SHOWTIME, etc.), and Emergency Broadcasting Systems. Go to www.vchipeducation.org for further information and instructions, as well as frequently asked questions about V-chip technology.

15. Provide alternative activities for her free time, both indoor and outdoor:

- Participate in family fun night. Construct puzzles, play board games, bake cookies, refinish a piece of furniture.
- Learn a new hobby or craft, or learn how to play a musical instrument.
- Exercise or play a sport.
- Interact with friends. Have a sleepover, a homework party or a group activity night.
- Read, read, read—and read some more.
- Go on a trip to the museum, zoo, or other place of interest.
- Of course, there are always chores and homework to fill up time!

16. Set an example and practice what you preach. Your child won't learn self-discipline when it comes to TV if you do not show it yourself. Watch only acceptable programs, and spend your free time doing alternate activities.

17. When your child sees a violent event on TV:

- Ask her why she thinks the character acted in a violent manner.
- Ask if the character could have chosen another way to react.
- Make sure to point out that violence isn't the way to solve problems.
- Discuss the consequences of the violent act shown. If there are none, discuss what would happen in real life.
- Look for examples of nonviolent problem solving.

THE NEWS

Your child sees or hears news every day, not only through television, but also via newspapers, radio, magazines, and the Internet. This can be a positive educational experience for your child. However, the news covers stories on natural disasters, homicides, child abductions, and school violence, all of which can be stressful to your child, causing her to view the world as a confusing, threatening place to live.

Unlike entertainment programs, the news is real. By the time your child reaches age 7 or 8, television news can seem all too real. The vividness of a sensational news story may be internalized and transformed into a belief that it can happen to her. TV news sometimes promotes a "nasty world" picture by concentrating on violence, giving your child a false impression of what society is really like.

Several recent changes in the way the news is reported increase the potential for your child to experience negative effects:

1. News is reported 24 hours a day both on TV and on the Internet.
2. TV news teams broadcast news live as the events unfold.
3. News people have increased their reporting of the details of the private lives of public figures and role models.
4. Competition puts pressure on the industry to get the news to the public.
5. They run detailed and repetitive coverage of natural disasters and acts of violence.

The public debate over TV violence just recently caught up with news broadcasts, so thus far, the rating systems and other controls don't apply. Children are just as prone to imitating what they see in the news as they do in fictitious programs, resulting in what has been labeled as "copy cat" events.

Research has demonstrated that news reports don't always accurately reflect local or national trends. As an example, the incidence of crime has decreased. However, the incidence of reporting crime has increased 20%. Local news broadcasts frequently open with "the crime of the day," and devote as much as 30% of their air time to crime reporting.

Use your child's maturity level to guide the amount and type of news your child watches. You can lessen the potential negative effects of the news by watching it with your child and talking about what you see and hear. Put the stories in their proper perspective; explain that certain stories are isolated. Provide reassurance about her own safety, emphasizing that you're there to keep her safe. If you're concerned about your child watching the news, expose her to the news through newspapers or magazines, as these are usually less sensational than television. Finally, look for signs that the news may have triggered anxieties or fears, such as sleep disturbances, nightmares, bed wetting, and crying.

MOVIES

Much of the television discussion applies to movies. In addition, check your newspaper or movie Internet sites to investigate movie ratings and content before your child sees them. As a general rule of thumb, think twice before taking your young child to a film that carries a rating inappropriate for her age. Don't be one of those parents who drag their 8-year-old to an R-rated film matinee just because they don't want to go alone or pay for a sitter.

You can't police your teenager who may be dying to slip into a risqué, R-rated coming-of-age flick. However, you can have a heart-to-heart discussion with her about why you find such films objectionable. If, on the other hand, you find out that she has already attended one without your knowledge, discuss it with her. If she attends after being told not to, impose the consequences that you set up for this potential problem ahead of time.

VIDEO GAMES (NINTENDO, SEGA, PLAYSTATION, COMPUTER SOFTWARE)

Video games were introduced in the 1970s and rapidly became a preferred childhood leisure activity, causing adults to be concerned about their possible ill effects. Early research results were inconclusive; however, a resurgence in video game sales in the late 1980s has renewed the interest in examining their effects.

Video games may actually have some benefits for your child. Some advocates suggest that the games increase hand-eye coordination, while others propose that they have creative benefits. However, more recent accounts express negative effects. In 1990, the National Coalition on Television Violence (NCTV) conducted a research review and found that 9 out of 12 research studies on the impact of violent video game playing reported harmful effects.

A report of two research studies described in an April 2000 news release by the American Psychological Association (APA) states that playing violent video games like DOOM or MORTAL COMBAT can increase the player's aggressive feelings, thoughts, and behaviors, both in laboratory settings and in real life. The report also noted that violent video games may be more harmful than violent television and movies, because the games are interactive, very engrossing, and require the player to identify with the aggressor. In today's video games, that aggressor is a fully digitalized human image.

In one of the APA's referenced studies, the researchers found that college students who played more violent video games in junior and senior high school tended to engage in more aggressive behavior. They also found that the amount of time spent in playing video games in the past was associated with lower academic grades in college. Results of the second study demonstrated that students who played a violent video game (WOLFENSTEIN 3D) punished an opponent with a blast of noise for a longer period of time than students who played a nonviolent video game (MYST).

One researcher, Craig A. Anderson, Ph.D., of Iowa State University, commented that violent video games provide a forum for learning and practicing aggressive solutions to conflict situations. One of the major concerns is the interactive nature of violent video games, as they are potentially more dangerous than violent television or movies, both known to have significant effects on aggression and violence.

You can still protect your child from the negative effects of today's high tech, fast-paced, violent video and games:

1. Look for the ratings on the front of the video game package. Most North American video and computer game makers utilize the Entertainment Software Rating Board (ESRB) system that was implemented in 1994, which classifies games according to age-based categories. The Canadian Interactive Digital Software Association (CIDSA) assigns the ESRB ratings in Canada. A quick trip to a local Wal-Mart revealed easy-to-find ratings on their displayed games by Nintendo, Playstation, and Sega.

2. Evaluate games for their potential impact on your child before buying them. Don't give in to her, no matter how badly she wants it.

3. Examine the game's box carefully and read the description. A number of games packages are quite graphic and contain luring, promotional details about what the game has to offer. Look on the back of the package for the content descriptors

designated by the ESRB. They describe things such as sexual or violent content and vulgar language.

4. If you don't know the game's content, ask the dealer for a demonstration.

5. Ask the dealer if the store provides a 100% refund or exchange on the product should violent or sexually explicit material slip past you.

MUSIC AND MUSIC VIDEOS

Music plays an integral role in our lives. It wakes us in the morning, makes us want to sing and dance, and soothes us when we are sad. Music sums up a wide range of emotions, most of which are marvelous. But some music communicates potentially harmful messages, especially when it reaches the ears of vulnerable children and adolescents.

The thundering boom from your teen's room makes you painfully aware that she listens to music an average of 40 hours per week. Music acts as an important aspect of your teen's identity, because it helps her define important social and subcultural boundaries. Therefore, it's important that she listen to lyrics that are not violent, sex-filled, drug-oriented, sexist, or antisocial.

Most likely, your child interprets her favorite songs as being about love, growing up, life's struggles, fun, cars, and other typical teen topics. Music isn't typically a danger to teens whose lives are happy and healthy. However, there are a small number of teens whose strong preference for music with a seriously destructive theme may be a marker for alienation, depression, drug and alcohol abuse, and other risk-taking behaviors.

Music lyrics have changed drastically since we started to "rock around the clock" to rock music more than 40 years ago. Heavy metal and rap music have caused the greatest concerns, as music lyrics have become increasingly explicit, especially with reference to sex, drugs, and violence. Many not only condone but encourage violent acts, especially towards women, and glorify guns, rape, and murder.

The *Entertainment Monitor* noted that only 10 of the 40 popular CDs on sale during the 1995 holiday season were free of profanity or references to drugs, sex, or violence. One song by performer Marilyn Manson contains the phrase, "Who said date rape isn't kind." You may already be aware of this particular "artist," as well as others who receive media attention for their outrageous lyrics and performances. However, a recent survey by the Recording Industry of America found that many parents don't know the lyrics in the popular music that their children listen to.

Music videos hit the airwaves more recently, and since the majority of American households receive cable television, most teens have access to MTV and VH1, giving them round-the-clock music videos. Your child may not be able to understand the garbled words of the song—actually one study shows that only 30% of teenagers knew the lyrics from their favorite songs, and their comprehension varied. But she will certainly have no difficulty comprehending the disturbing images flashed in a number of music videos. When she again hears the song on the radio or her compact disc player, she will immediately flashback to the video scenes.

To protect your child from being inundated with inappropriate music and music videos:

1. Be aware of the drug-oriented, sexually explicit or violent lyrics on compact discs, tapes, music videos, and the Internet.
2. Take an active role in monitoring the music that your child purchases, as well as to what she's exposed to.
3. Monitor her watching MTV, VH1 and other music videochannels just as you would any other television broadcast.
4. Listen to the music with her and discuss lyrics as necessary—provided you both can understand them!
5. Treat violent music videos as you do any other violent program on television.

Clarify media messages for your children, and teach them your own values. Keep the lines of communications open, and know what your child is listening to and watching.

12

NEGATIVE PEERS

CALIFORNIA, 1997:
Two teens watch and help as their friend brutally murders a 16-year-old girl.

SOME STATS

- 30.7% of high school students ride with a driver who has been drinking alcohol.
- Kids start smoking because a friend, particularly a best friend, smokes.
- Peer pressure plays a significant role in the more than 1,400 alcohol-related deaths of college students.
- 9.5% of high school students have been hit, slapped, or physically hurt on purpose by their boyfriend or girlfriend.
- The prevalence of dating violence ranges from 6.9% to 18.1%.
- 7.7% of high school students, particularly females, have been forced to have intercourse.

Peer pressure can lead to a host of negative behaviors when your child associates with—or dates—peers who engage in high risk or problem behavior. This is especially true for your teenager if he feels the need to conform to the norms of the group. Children with low self-esteem are the most vulnerable to peer pressure.

Peer pressure can be destructive when it's negative, but it can also be very helpful when it's positive.

THE VALUE OF PEERS

A peer is a companion, a person with equal or near-equal status, often of the same sex and age, with whom your child can share mutual concerns. His peer group is a fairly informal association of children who share common experiences, with an emphasis on common rules and the understanding of the limits that the group places on the individual.

During the school years, the peer group provides your child with companionship, shared time, conversation, and activities with a widening group of children outside the home. The group becomes extremely important to your child who, between the ages of 7 and 9, probably forms close relationships with peers of the same gender and age.

The peer group serves several functions for your school-age child:

It delivers information about his world—school, the neighborhood, dress, games, and manners.

The group provides an audience for the development of self-concept, self-esteem, and unique personality traits.

It gives him an opportunity to compare himself to and compete with others his same age.

It teaches him rules and logical consequences, because most groups punish members who disobey their rules.

The group helps him develop values and goals, because group members expect conformity.

It gives him the opportunity to test his mastery in a world that parallels adult society with its organization, rules, and purposes.

The group delivers emotional support during the stressful times in his life.

The peer group protects him against other children who may bully, threaten, intimidate, or actually harm him.

Your child must earn membership in his peer group, and being accepted into the group is a major concern for him. Many factors determine his acceptance, including his appearance and friendliness. Rejection is always a risk, and being an outsider can be just as detrimental as belonging to a negative group. But the lack of a peer group at this age can be easily overcome through having a best friend or chum.

The gang (as in pack, not street gang) becomes important during preadolescence. A gang is a group of people who earned their membership on the basis of performance, usually of a physical activity. The stability of the gang is often communicated through symbols such as passwords, codes, and uniforms. The gang's code takes precedence to everything, and may range from an agreement to not snitch on each other to boycotting a school activity. Typically, gang codes are distinguished by joint action against the morals of the adult world. As a member of a gang, your child can learn healthy outlets to unload hostility and aggression against peers rather than adults and learn how to work out their own social patterns without adult, intervention and interference. Some gangs do take out their aggression in a negative manner on other children and adults, and when this occurs, the pattern is set for delinquent behavior.

Around age 9 or 10, your child enters the chum stage when affection moves from the peer group and gang to one special friend or chum. This is critical because it's his first "love" attachment outside the family. This chum becomes an extension of your child's own self as he shares his ideas and feelings, learning more about himself and his friend. He discovers how he's similar and how he's different, and he learns to accept himself for who he is. This self-acceptance enables him to better accept others, so that he can be sociable, generous, sympathetic, and liberal about the ideas of others. He learns that others can be different and still be all right. His loyalty to his chum may be greater than his loyalty to his own family, something that can put a strain on your relationship.

Teen peer groups differ from school-age groups. School-age groups typically contain friends or neighborhood acquaintances, and the groups are not usually as formalized as adolescent groups. Teen groups tend to have a broader array of members: in other words, teens other than friends and neighborhood acquaintances. They are more likely to include members from different ethnic groups. However, teens from ethnic minorities may have difficulty joining peer groups and clubs in predominately White schools. Minority teens may have two peer groups, one at school and one in the community.

The peer group reaches its peak influence once your child reaches adolescence. Now the group has greater influence than parents, teachers, popular heroes, religious leaders, and other significant adults. He will be intensely loyal to them, and social relationships take precedence over family interactions to counteract feelings of isolation and loneliness.

Your teen may belong to more than one peer group, and members may overlap between the groups. Membership is extremely important because the group becomes a way for him to develop his own identity—learning about who he is and where he fits in. Once in the group, he must conform to its norms, such as dressing like them. Boys tend to wear similar clothes, jackets of the same style and color,

or tee-shirts with the same inscription or insignia, like Nike® or
Tommy Hilfiger®. Girls spend a lot of time talking together or on the
phone planning hairstyles and outfits. Visit your nearest mall (without
your teen's knowledge!) and observe groups of teens. Not only do
they dress alike, they also act alike and talk alike, using group-specif-
ic slang.

**The peer group serves different functions now that your child is a
teenager:**

It gives him a sense of acceptance, belonging, and prestige.

It creates a sense of immediacy by concentrating on the here-
and-now—what happened last night, who is doing what today, what is
going on in class.

The group gives him a sense of importance; a sense of being
and identity.

The peer group provides role models and relationships to help
define his identity as he adapts to his changing body image, heightened sexual feelings, and more mature relationships.

It provides opportunities to try out a variety of behaviors within the safety of the group.

The group helps him to cope with social rejection and failure,
and to resolve interpersonal problems.

The peer group helps him incorporate new ideas into his self-
image. If he's rejected by his peers, he won't learn the high degree of
social skills or the ability needed to form relationships necessary for
adulthood.

POSITIVE PEER PRESSURE

Conformity pressures can benefit family values, school performance, and your child's overall well-being. Peers can teach compromise in a way that parents and siblings can't, for if he keeps insist-
ing on his own way, he won't have many friends. Peer pressure can
keep your child involved in religious activities, scouts, 4-H meetings,
and sports teams. Most peer groups encourage individual achieve-
ment, especially in sports or academics. They can encourage
your child to try out for the football team or the school play, study
harder for exams, and to win a track race. Some groups even raise
money for their clubs or community charities, and participate in community service activities.

The peer group provides a source of affection, sympathy, and understanding, and it serves as a supportive setting for two primary adolescent developmental tasks—identity: finding out who he is and where it fits in, and autonomy: separating from his parents and becoming independent. Peer pressure creates the desire for change and change itself. Most often that change is positive.

DEALING WITH PEER PRESSURE IN GENERAL

Start by surrendering your belief that all peer pressure is bad. Most groups encourage positive behaviors. They foster your child's self-esteem and abilities, and children with positive self-esteem are less likely to be swayed by negative peer influence.

Get to know your child's friends and their parents. Encourage all of the parents to get together as a group. Work together to develop ground rules, such as curfew. You and the other parents will have an easier job if you're all on the same moral ground.

Defer your judgment when your child confides in you about his friends, even when the conversation revolves around something that makes your jaw drop, like drinking. Instead, use this time as an opportunity to share experiences. That way he will know that he can turn to you when he's confused.

What should you do when your child insists on something you forbid because his friends have/do it? First, forget about the old standby, "If your friends all jumped off the Empire State Building, would you want to jump, too?" It did not work when your parents used it on you, and still won't work when you try to use it on your child.

Don't criticize him or make negative comments about his friends. He will only think that he doesn't fit in with his friends, or conclude that since he's just like his friends, you don't like him either. Try another tactic. Tell him that you understand how he feels (how much he wants to stay out later or get the newest pair of $100 sneakers), then see if the two of you can come up with an alternative in cases where that is possible.

Acknowledging his desire to be part of his group doesn't obligate you to give in to his every desire. But choose your battles wisely. Compromise on the minor issues, such as hairstyles and pierced ears. Hold firm on the major issues, such as shoplifting. Acknowledge that you know it's hard when his friends dare him, but firmly say that stealing is always wrong.

Avoid coming down hard on the really minor peer-influenced behaviors, such as wearing his pants backwards. Let him struggle with the obvious complication of that fashion trend. Give in on these issues so that you can save your influence and credibility for the things that really matter. Eventually, he will grow out of it, and no longer be swayed by his peers. And remember, even though it may not seem that way, he really does value your opinions and values.

NEGATIVE PEER PRESSURE

Peer groups become harmful when they lead your teen into delinquent behavior because of the pressure to conform and his need to fit in. He may participate in alcohol and drug abuse, sexual activity, and violent acts, not because he wants to or because he enjoys them, but because he wants to prove himself, vent aggression, or gain superior position on younger members of the group. Street gangs are the extreme example of negative peer pressure, and they tend to appeal to teens when other healthier groups are not available. If your child has low self-esteem, he may be exceptionally vulnerable to this negative influence.

DEALING WITH NEGATIVE PEER PRESSURE

When things go wrong, you have the right and obligation to be concerned about your teen's friends and guide him into wholesome activities and groups that will reinforce your values.

When should you worry? Worry if he engages in negative behaviors (cheating, stealing, fighting, vandalism, selling fireworks or drugs) or if you notice any of these three warning signs:

1. He's extremely secretive about his friends or his whereabouts, or he won't bring his friends home for you to meet them.
2. He consults his friends for even minute decisions or worries excessively about what they think of him or something he did or said.
3. He refuses to take responsibility for his own actions when he's in trouble, and he blames his friends or others.

If he falls victim to negative peer influence, consider the following:

Talk to him. Tell him what you know or suspect, then listen to his side. Encourage him to talk, but don't force a confession out of him. Always make sure that what you heard or suspected is true before acting on it.

Once you have verified that the behavior occurred, let him know that it's not acceptable. Contain your anger and focus on the behavior—don't condemn your child. For example, say something like, "Spraying graffiti on public property is wrong, and I don't approve of what you did." Avoid statements like, "I can't believe you were stupid enough to spray-paint graffiti on the school wall." Punishment alone just teaches him not to get caught next time. Your disappointment makes a greater impact.

Explain the consequences and enforce them. If your child receives an outside consequence, such as suspension from school, acknowledge that you agree with it and that you will go along with the sanction. If you think that the sanction is too harsh, tell him that the school may be a little stricter than you are, but that he still should not have done what he did. Behaviors have consequences, and your child needs to know that when he gets into trouble, you can't be there and should not be there to bail him out.

Once the incident is over, talk to him to get to the root of the problem. Find out why he prefers that particular peer group.

Help him develop and nurture positive friendships. You can't expect him to give up his peer group if he has nothing to substitute for it.

Should you deem his peer group inappropriate, help him find another. It will be easier for him to give up his group if there is another to be part of. Remember how important a group is to your teen.

DATING VIOLENCE AND DATE RAPE

The United States Department of Justice defines dating violence as "the perpetration or threat of an act of violence by at least one member of an unmarried couple on the other member within the context of dating or courtship." Dating violence crosses all socioeconomic groups, and most victims are female.

Insulting, bruising, isolating the partner from friends, forcing the partner to have sex—all constitute dating violence. Although nothing new, dating violence has developed some worrisome trends with possessive dating behavior extending into even younger ages, and some teens believing that dating violence is acceptable. The Centers for Disease Control (CDC) estimates that 22% of high school students, predominantly females, have been victims of dating violence.

Abusers act out of their need to control another person. Not only do they want to have power over the other person, they believe they are entitled to it, no matter the cost. Abuse includes behaviors that not only cause physical harm; it also includes behaviors that arouse fear, prevent a partner from doing things she wants to do, or forcing her to do things she doesn't want to do. Abusers use a variety of physical and psychological tactics to keep their partners tied to them, including: criticism, threats, moodiness, being overprotective and falsely caring, ignoring their partners needs, isolating the partner from other people, and using physical and/or sexual violence.

A person's tendency to control usually doesn't show early in the relationship. Talk to both your daughter and son about the WARNING SIGNS below, and if your teen displays any of these traits, talk to him/her, and seek professional help:

- Has a negative attitude toward women; doesn't treat his mother, sisters, or female colleagues with respect.
- Doesn't respect partner's work; puts it down or encourages partner to give it up.
- Is self-centered; doesn't listen to partner.
- Is jealous or possessive; wants to constantly be with partner and questions her every move when she's not with him.
- Has to always get his own way and explodes when he doesn't get it.
- Is frequently moody and critical; blames partner for his mistakes.
- Drinks too much or uses drugs.
- Refuses to take precautions for safe sex.

Rape isn't about sex; it's about violence. Date or acquaintance rape is the use of force to have sex with someone against that person's will by someone the victim knows or is dating. One factor in its occurrence appears to be the double standard about appropriate sexual behavior for men and women that causes a commonly held cultural myth: nice women don't say yes to sex, even when they want it, and real men don't take no for an answer.

TO HELP PREVENT DATE RAPE, counsel your teenage daughter to avoid going to parties alone, stay sober at parties, double date and/or use own transportation for new acquaintances, avoid going into their date's room unless they know them very well, and learn to say no assertively. Sons should be taught to be aware of social pressure and that it's permissible to not "score." They should learn to understand what "no" means, and not assume that sexy dress and flirtatious behavior are invitations to sexual activity. Both sons and daughters need to know that alcohol and drugs interfere with clear communications regarding sex.

GANGS

Gangs slip in when you're not looking. Keeping tabs on your teen—knowing where she is, what she's doing, and who she's doing it with are keys to protecting her from gangs.

Gangs that support antisocial values and behaviors, such as intimidation, vandalism, extortion, and other acts of violence, create fear. If your child affiliates herself with one of these groups, she's likely to adopt their values, imitate their behaviors, and behave in a violent manner. When teens become involved in gangs, they have higher incidences of violent and delinquent behaviors compared to when they are not active in a gang. Gang violence is intense, often resulting in injury and death.

Gang problems have escalated since the 1960s, with most gangs being comprised of males with similar ethnic and racial backgrounds. Ethnic conflict is associated with the emergence of gangs in certain communities, but most gang conflict occurs between gangs of the same ethnicity. Gang violence is no longer just an inner-city problem. Every day, more and more teens turn towards gangs to seek a "family." Many others are intimidated into joining gangs to avoid continued harassment, and still others join to get protection from other gangs. And gang members are getting more multiethnic, more youthful—children join gangs as young as 14, and sometimes even younger, and gangs are more likely to have female members.

Gangs tend to have a leader or group of leaders who give orders and enjoy the fruits of the gang's labors. Gangbangers (gang members) wear their "colors," certain types of clothing, tattoos, brands, or likewise imprint their gang's name, logo, or other identifying marks on their bodies. Many gangs adopt specific hairdos and communicate through hand signals and graffiti. Organized graffiti is one of the first ways to know that a gang is taking hold in your community. Experts use graffiti to track gang growth, affiliation, and membership information.

The "three R's" have a whole new meaning in gang mentality:

REPUTATION/REP is a critical concern to gangbangers. The rep extends to each individual and the gang as a whole. Gangbangers gain status by having the most "juice" (power), based largely on one's rep. The manner in which one gains juice is important, so many members embellish their past gang activities to impress the listener, freely admitting to crimes. To gain membership, a person must be "jumped in" by being "beaten down" until the leader calls for it to end. Afterwards, they all hug each other to further the "G thing," an action that bonds members together. Young members frequently talk of this fellowship as the reason they joined the gang.

RESPECT is something that they carry to the extreme for each member, the gang, their territory, and various other things, real or perceived. Some gangs require that members always show disrespect ("dis") for rival gangs through hand signals, graffiti, or a simple "mad dog" or stare down. If a member fails to dis a rival, causing a violation to her fellow posse (gang members), she will be "beaten down" by her own gang as punishment.

REVENGE/RETALIATION shows that no challenge goes unanswered in gang culture. Many drive-by shootings follow an event perceived as a dis. Typically, a confrontation takes place between a gang set and a single rival gangbanger. The gangbanger leaves, only to return with his "home boys" to complete the confrontation and keep his rep intact.

To keep your child from becoming a gang member:

- Spend quality time with your child and convey a strong sense of family.
- Supervise her activities, and know her whereabouts at all times.
- Teach her values, and let her know why you think gangs are dangerous.
- Get involved in her activities.
- Stress the importance of schooling and encourage good study habits.
- Create rules, set limits, and be consistent, firm, and fair.
- Respect her feelings and attitudes.
- Foster her healthy self-esteem.

- Help her develop self-control and deal effectively with problems.
- Tell her not to:
  —associate with gang members or wannabe members
  —communicate with gang members
  —hang out near or where gangs hang out
  —approach strangers in cars
  —wear gang-related clothing
  —wear gang initialed clothing (BK [British Knights] also stands for Blood Killer)
  —use words like "slob" where gang members may be, like malls
  attend parties sponsored by gangs
  hang out near graffiti or take part in graffiti activity
  use any type of hand signal in public
- Teach her what to do if approached by a gang member. Her best response is to walk away. Tell her not to respond with the same gesture, as a gang member could be "false flagging," using a sign of a rival gang, which could result in violence.
- Contact your school if any gang activity takes place there. If they are not helpful, contact the police.
- Look for signs of gang activity in your community, especially graffiti and young people hanging out on corners or near school property.

Look for following warning signs if you suspect that your child is involved in a gang, but realize that many of these can signal other problems, such as drug abuse.

- admits to being in a gang
- obsesses with one particular color or logo
- wears excessive distinct jewelry; wears it on one side of the body
- obsesses with "gangsta" music
- withdraws from family
- associates with undesirables
- develops a strong desire for privacy
- uses hand signals at home
- has physical signs of being beaten and lies about events surrounding the injuries
- wears peculiar drawings or language on books or hands
- has unexplained cash or goods
- uses drug and alcohol.

If you do suspect that your child has joined a gang, get professional help. You won't be able to deal with this alone. Contact your local police as many have a gang crimes unit. The unit may help you find counseling and tell you how to help your child.

13

POISONS

VERMONT, 2003:
Man, woman and child found unconscious in their home from carbon monoxide poisoning.

SOME STATS

- United States poison centers handle one poison exposure every 15 seconds–more than 2 million in 2000.
- Most calls are placed between 4:00P.M. and 10:00P.M.
- Children under 3 account for 40% of poisonings, while children under 6 account for 53%.
- Most poisonings occur via ingestion, followed by dermal (skin), inhalation, and ocular (eye) absorptions.
- 71% of poisonings are managed at home without need for an emergency room visit.
- 90% of poisonings occur at the home, most in the kitchen.
- About 9% of children have a potentially harmful lead level.
- Carbon monoxide causes 3,500 to 4,000 deaths per year, two/thirds from fires, one-third from accidental carbon monoxide poisoning.
- Environmental tobacco smoke (ETS) is linked to up to 2 million ear infections per year.

Pesticides, household cleaners, prescription medications. You realize that all these are potentially poisonous to your child. But how about alcohol, multivitamins, plants, paint, and even the air inside your home?

The National Capital Poison Center lists the most dangerous poisons for children as; medicines, iron pills, cleaning products, nail glue remover and primers, hydrocarbons, pesticides, antifreeze, wild mushrooms, and alcohol. And the Environmental Protection Agency notes that the air inside your home may be even more polluted than the air outdoors, even if you live in a major metropolis.

But you can keep your child safe by poison-proofing your home.

A poison is any substance a person eats, breathes, or gets into his eyes or on his skin, that causes unintended symptoms, sickness, or death. Poisons can be solids (pills, plants, powders, granules), liquids (lotions, polishes, syrups), sprays (paints, pesticides) and gases or vapors (carbon monoxide).

Children are at risk for poisoning because of their curiosity, and, in the case of young children, the desire to put everything in their mouths. When exposed to poisons, children are more likely to suffer more serious consequences than adults, because they have faster metabolic rates and less ability to handle toxins in their bodies. Pound for pound, children drink more water, eat more food, and breathe more air than adults, thus increasing the amount of potential toxins in their bodies.

COMMON HOUSEHOLD POISONS

More than 90% of poisonings occur in the home, usually in the kitchen during late afternoon or evening. Among children age 5 and under, nonpharmaceutical products, such as plants, cleaning substances, pesticides, art supplies, and cosmetics account for 57% of poisonings, with medications and drugs making up the other 43%. Most poisonings occur when parents don't closely supervise their children, typically around the hectic dinner hour, a time that poison control center personnel refer to as the "arsenic hour."

Poisonings also occur most often: when there are changes in the daily routine; during holidays; when a product is being used; when a product is carelessly or improperly stored; when adults fail to follow product directions; when the child is visiting a grandparent or friend; when children are hungry or thirsty; when teens or adults become depressed or angry; or when someone becomes confused.

According to pediatric nurse practitioner Theresa Eldridge, the most common ingested items are acetaminophen (Tylenol®), ibuprofen (Motrin®, Advil®), iron (found in most multivitamins with minerals), aspirin, soaps, detergents, cleaners, plants, vitamins, antihistamines and cold medications, disinfectants, deodorizers, miscellaneous medications, perfume, and toilet water.

Button batteries can easily be swallowed, causing burns in the esophagus or intestines. Tobacco and smoking cessation products contain nicotine, which can cause seizures and death. Other common poisons include: rat poison, camphor, pool chemicals, kerosene, gasoline, motor oil, lighter fluid, paint thinner, pesticides, antifreeze, several types of wild mushrooms and berries, and alcohol. Alcohol, which is also found in mouthwash, facial cleaners, and hair tonics, can cause seizures, coma, and death in children–including high school and college students who binge drink. Hydrocarbons (kerosene, gasoline, etc.) can cause choking when swallowed. If choking occurs, the child could breathe the poison into his lungs, making it hard to breathe and possibly causing pneumonia.

EXAMPLES OF POISONOUS AND POTENTIALLY HARMFUL HOUSEHOLD PLANTS

Arrowhead Vine (Syngonium podophyllum)
Asparagus Fern (Asparagus setaceus plumosus)
Azalea (Rhododendron occidentale)
Bird of Paradise (Strelitzia reginae)
Boston Ivy (Parthenocissus quinquefolia)
Caladium (Caladium spp.)
Chrysaaanthemum (Various spp.)
Creeping Charlie (Glecoma hederacea)
Creeping Fig (Ficus)
Crown of Thorns (Euphorbia milli)
Glacier Ivy (Hedera glacier)
Gold Tooth Aloe (Aloe nobilis)
Heartleaf (Philodendron cordatum)
Ivy (Hedra helix)
Majesty (Philodendron hastatum)
Poinsettia (Euphorbia pulcherrmia)
Pot Mum (Chrysanthemum mortifolium)
Spengeri Fern (Asparagus densiflorous 'sprengeri')
Umbrella Plant (Cyperus alternifolius)

PREVENTION

To minimize the chance of your child getting poisoned by household products:

- Keep the poison control phone number near the telephone. (National number: 1–800–222–1222) Call the ASPCA's

Animal Poison Control Center at 1–888–426–4435 if your pet is poisoned.
- Read labels and know which products are poisonous.
- Store products properly:
—Lock them out of the reach and site of children.
—Store them in their original containers.
—Buy child-resistant packages, but realize your child may still be able to open them.
—Keep your cosmetics away from your child's reach.
- Use products safely:
—Follow product directions carefully.
—Don't mix cleaning solutions.
—Never leave the product unattended when in use.
—Store it properly immediately after use.
- Never call medicine candy.
- Throw away old medications and other poisons.
- Teach your child to never put plant matter in his mouth.
- Keep syrup of ipecac on hand, but don't use it unless instructed to do so by your health care provider or poison control. Ipecac is an antiemetic; it causes vomiting.
- Ask grandparents, relatives, friends, and sitters to take the same precautions.

WHAT TO DO IF YOUR CHILD IS POISONED

Should your child come into contact with a household poison, don't wait for him to get sick. Call poison control immediately and follow these suggestions from the American Association of Poison Control Centers:

SWALLOWED POISONS:

Don't give him anything to eat or drink before calling poison control.
Don't give him ipecac or make him vomit unless instructed to do so by poison control or your health care provider.

INHALED POISONS:

Get him into fresh air immediately.

SKIN POISONS:

Rinse his clothing and skin with water for 10 minutes.

EYE POISON:

Flush his eyes for 15 minutes with lukewarm water held 2 to
4 inches from his eyes.

Have this information ready when you call poison control:
your child's age, weight, and condition; product containers or bottles;
the time the poisoning occurred; and your name and phone number.
Follow the instructions they give you carefully.

ENVIRONMENTAL TOBACCO SMOKE (ETS)

If you smoke, your child smokes too, by breathing in the poisons from your tobacco products. Plus, your example increases the
likelihood of his smoking.

Environmental tobacco smoke (ETS), also known as passive
smoking and secondhand smoke, comes from both smoke emitting
from the ends of burning cigarettes, cigars, and pipes, and the smoke
breathed out by smokers. It contains over 4,000 chemicals, including
200 poisons and 43 carcinogens (cancer-causing agents).

According to a study published by the American Academy of
Pediatrics, ETS accounts for 2 million ear infections, 530,000 doctor
visits for asthma, 436,000 episodes of bronchitis, and up to 190,000
cases of pneumonia each year. Children of smokers also cough,
wheeze, and have a tough time getting over colds, get more sore
throats, suffer from eye irritation, and become hoarse.

If you smoke during pregnancy, you expose your unborn child
to all the chemicals in tobacco. This can lead to miscarriage, prematu-
rity, low birth weight, Sudden Infant Death Syndrome (SIDS), and
some childhood cancers. Problems related to exposure from ETS may
not surface until adulthood, such as lung cancer, heart disease, and eye
disease.

PREVENTION

If you don't smoke, don't start. If you do smoke, quit.

Don't let anyone smoke in your home or car. Put up "no
smoking" signs and don't put out ashtrays to discourage people from
lighting up.

Use a child care provider who doesn't smoke and who does-n't allow smoking in the house.

Use the nonsmoking sections in public places.

LEAD POISONING

Lead poisoning, or plumbism, is a major health problem in the United States. The CDC (Centers for Disease Control and Prevention) estimates that 890,000 children ages 1 to 5 have elevated lead levels. Ingesting dust from deteriorating lead-based paint is the most common cause of lead poisoning. However, poisoning can come from other lead sources, such as tap water from lead pipes and unglazed ceram-ics.

Lead interferes with the development and functioning of most body organs. High lead levels can cause seizures, coma, and death, while moderate levels may result in mental retardation, impaired growth, anemia, and hearing loss. Even low levels can cause problems such as hyperactivity, distractibility, impulsivity, learning problems, and mild intellectual deficits. Without treatment, lead stays in the body for years; thus, even small amounts can cause trouble over time.

Lead poisoning can affect any child—or adult. But young chil-dren are most at risk, especially young children living in old, rundown houses, children in houses built before 1978 (renovations tend to release lead dust into the air), and children who exhibit pica (eating nonfood objects).

PREVENTION

To prevent lead poisoning, follow these suggestions from the CDC:

- Wash your child's hands frequently.
- Keep your child from gaining access to peeling paint or chew-able surfaces that are coated with lead-based paint: put furniture in front of peeling walls and cover other surfaces.
- Mop or damp dust all hard surfaces with a high (5 to 8%) phos-phate cleaner (read cleaning labels for phosphate content). Sweeping and dusting spread the lead dust around the house.
- Pick up loose paint chips with a paper towel wet in the high phosphate cleaner.

- When renovating, don't sand, scrape, or burn lead paint off surfaces because this forces the lead into the air where your child can inhale it. Contact a specialist for assistance in removal.
- Dispose of paint in a safe manner.
- Provide a diet high in calcium and iron, which may decrease pica.
- Use only cold tap water for consumption and cooking, and run it 2 to 3 minutes before using.
- Don't store food in opened cans.
- If your soil is contaminated, plant grass or other ground cover.
- If unsure, have your water and soil tested for lead.
- Don't use inadequately fired pottery or ceramics for food or drink.
- Don't store food, liquid, or baby formula in lead crystal.
- Avoid folk remedies that may contain lead.
- Avoid exposure to lead from adult hobbies or occupations.

CARBON MONOXIDE POISONING

An odorless, colorless gas, carbon monoxide is a product of the incomplete combustion of carbon-based fuels such as gasoline and wood, and one of the leading causes of poisoning deaths in the United States. Carbon monoxide usually exits our homes through vents, flues, or chimneys. But sometimes malfunctions or air pressure changes cause carbon monoxide gas to stay in the home.

Carbon monoxide interferes with the body's ability to carry oxygen to vital organs, including the brain. When inhaled, carbon monoxide binds to hemoglobin (part of the red blood cells) and displaces oxygen, which normally combines with the hemoglobin.

Carbon monoxide can cause temporary or permanent damage to the brain. Symptoms include headache, fatigue, nausea, and dizziness. How quickly these symptoms appear depends on the concentration of carbon monoxide in the air and the duration of exposure. The danger to infants and children is considerable, because their high metabolic rate causes them to accumulate the gas faster than adults. Unborn babies run the risk of defects, neurological damages, and death.

Common sources of carbon monoxide emissions include:

- Kerosene, oil and gas space heaters.
- Gas-run furnaces, clothes dryers, ovens, and other appliances that don't burn or vent properly.

- Improperly vented stoves and fireplaces.
- Gas grills that leak into open windows.
- Autos or gas run equipment (lawn mowers, snowblowers, leaf blowers) running in the garage or improperly exhausting.
- Boat exhaust.

PREVENTION

- To keep your child and the rest of your family safe from carbon monoxide poisoning:
- Install UL-listed carbon monoxide detectors in every sleeping area and on the ceiling about 15 feet from fuel-burning appliances.
- Keep your equipment in proper working order and properly vented.
- Have your chimney cleaned at least twice a year by a qualified professional.
- Don't use the oven to heat your home.
- Never leave the car or gas-powered equipment running in the garage.
- Avoid swimming or body surfing near the exhaust system while the boat or generator is running.
- If the CO detector alarms, get everyone out of the house.
- If your child shows any signs of carbon monoxide poisoning, get him to an emergency room immediately.

ARSENIC POISONING

A favorite in murder mysteries, arsenic is a naturally occurring element that, in higher than average doses, causes death. Organic arsenic is found in pesticides, while the inorganic form is used in compounds to preserve wood. Children can be exposed to arsenic by eating food, drinking water, or breathing air containing it. They can easily be exposed in the sawdust or smoke from burning wood treated with arsenic (pressure-treated wood, commonly used to make outdoor decks).

Breathing high levels of inorganic arsenic can cause sore throat or lung irritation; ingesting high levels can cause death. Lower levels can cause nausea and vomiting, decreased production of red and white blood cells, abnormal heart rhythm, blood vessel damage, and a "pins and needles" sensation in the hands and feet.

Inhaling or ingesting low levels of inorganic arsenic for a long period of time can cause skin darkening and small warts or corns on the palms, soles, and torso. Skin contact may result in redness and swelling. Organic arsenic compounds are less toxic, but high levels can cause similar effects as inorganic compounds.

PREVENTION

When using arsenic-treated wood at home, wear a dust mask, gloves, and protective clothing to decrease your exposure to the sawdust, and keep children away from the project. Don't store arsenic-treated wood indoors. If you live in an area with high arsenic levels, use cleaner sources of water and limit contact with the soil.

MERCURY POISONING

Mercury is a shiny, silver-white, odorless liquid metal that turns into a colorless gas when heated. It's commonly used in thermometers, dental fillings, and batteries, and occasionally used in skin-lightening creams and antiseptic ointments. Mercury enters the environment from mining ore deposits, burning coal and waste, and from manufacturing plants. It enters the soil or water through natural deposits, waste disposal, or volcanic activity, and builds up in the tissues of fish, with large, older ones having the highest levels.

Mercury harms the nervous system, and methylmercury and metallic mercury vapors are more harmful than other forms because more mercury can reach the brain. Mercury exposure can permanently damage the brain, kidneys, and the developing fetus. Brain damage can result in irritability, shyness, tremors, vision and hearing problems, and memory problems. Short-term exposure to metallic mercury vapors can increase blood pressure and heart rate, damage the lungs, and cause nausea, vomiting, diarrhea, eye irritation, and skin rashes.

Young children are more sensitive to mercury than adults, and mercury can build up in the fetus or transfer to your child during breast-feeding. Infants can develop brain damage, mental retardation, blindness, incoordination, seizures, and the inability to speak.

PREVENTION

Utilize nonmercury thermometers to take your child's temperature, and carefully dispose of your old mercury ones. Carefully handle products that contain mercury, such as weather thermometers and fluorescent lightbulbs. Don't vacuum spilled mercury, as it will vaporize and increase exposure. If a large amount spills, call your health department. And teach your children not to play with shiny, silver liquids—even if you did so growing up!

FOOD POISONING

Since food poisoning is caused by microorganisms, this topic is discussed in Chapter 9: Infectious Diseases.

THE AIR YOU BREATHE IN YOUR OWN HOME

The air in your home may be more polluted than the air outside. Modern insulation keeps us warmer, but it also can keep harmful substances right under our noses. According to the EPA, lead, ETS, and carbon monoxide are three potential pollutants. The others are radon, biologicals, nitrogen dioxide, organic gases, respirable particles, formaldehyde, pesticides, and asbestos.

RADON is found in the earth and rock beneath homes, well water, and building materials. It has no immediate symptoms, but contributes to between 7,000 and 30,000 lung cancer deaths each year.

To reduce exposure:

Test your home for radon.
Fix your home if radon levels are at or above 4 picocuries per liter (pCi/L).
Radons levels less than 4 pCi/L may still pose a risk and may be reduced.
For more information, contact your state radon office or call 1-800-SOS-RADON.

BIOLOGICALS (pollens, molds, dust mites) can lurk in: wet or moist walls, ceilings, carpets, and furniture; poorly maintained humidifiers, dehumidifiers, and air conditioners; bedding; and even your pets. They can cause dizziness, lethargy, fever, eye, nose and throat irritation, shortness of breath, digestive problems, and infectious diseases.

To reduce exposure:

Install and use fans in bathrooms and kitchens.

Vent clothes dryers to the outdoors.

Clean humidifiers in accordance to the manufacturer's instructions and refill with fresh water daily.

Empty water trays in air conditioners, dehumidifiers, and refrigerators.

Remove, or clean and dry water-damaged carpet.

Only use your basement as a living area if it's leak-proof with adequate ventilation.

Keep humidity levels between 30 and 50%. Purchase hygrometers to measure levels in each level of the house.

NITROGEN DIOXIDE emits from kerosene heaters, unvented gas stoves and heaters, and cigarette smoke. It causes eye, nose, and throat irritation.

To reduce exposure: Use the same safety measures as for carbon monoxide.

ORGANIC GASES come from several household products such as paint, paint strippers and other solvents, wood preservatives, aerosol sprays, air fresheners, hobby supplies, and dry-cleaned clothes. They can cause headaches, loss of coordination, eye, nose, and throat irritation, nausea, and damage to the liver, kidneys, and central nervous system. Some cause cancer.

To reduce exposure:

Use household products according to the manufacturer's directions.

Make sure you have fresh air when using the products.

Throw away unused or little-used containers safely.

Buy in quantities that you will use soon.

Keep locked safely away from children and plants.

Never mix household products unless directions say otherwise.

RESPIRABLE PARTICLES come from tobacco products, fireplaces, woodstoves, and kerosene heaters. They cause eye, nose and throat irritation, respiratory infections and bronchitis, and lung cancer.

To reduce exposure:

Change filters on central cooling and heating systems and air cleaners according to manufacturer's directions, and fol low the safety instructions for ETS in this chapter and heating systems in Chapter 6: Fire.

FORMALDEHYDE exists in pressed wood products (particleboard, hardwood plywood wall paneling, fiberboard) and furniture made from these products. It's also found in ETS, combustible sources, durable press drapes, and other textiles, and glues. Health effects include fatigue, eye, nose, and throat irritation, coughing and wheezing, skin rash, and severe allergic reactions. It can also cause cancer and the problems noted under organic gases.

To reduce exposure:

Use exterior grade pressed wood products, because they contain phenol resins as opposed to urea resins.
Use air conditioners and dehumidifiers to maintain moderate temperature and low humidity.
Increase ventilation, especially when bringing new sources of formaldehyde into the home.

PESTICIDES are used both indoors and out, and can cause eye, nose, and throat irritation, as well as nervous system and kidney damage and an increased risk of cancer.

To reduce exposure:

Use according to the manufacturer's directions.
Mix or dilute outdoors.
Use only in recommended quantities.
Increase ventilation when using indoors.
Use nonchemical controls whenever possible.
Don't store unneeded pesticides in the home.
Store clothes with moth repellent in separately ventilated areas, if possible.
Keep indoors clean to reduce pest problems.

ASBESTOS is found in deteriorating, damaged, or disturbed insulation, fireproofing, acoustical materials, and floor tiles. There are no immediate symptoms, but there is a risk of later chest and abdomen cancers.

To reduce exposure:

Leave undamaged material alone.
Use trained contractors for control measures.
Follow proper procedure when replacing woodstove door gaskets that may contain asbestos.

BASIC STRATEGIES FOR BETTER INDOOR AIR QUALITY

First, eliminate sources of pollution. Some sources, like ones containing asbestos, can be sealed or closed; others, such as stoves, can be adjusted to decrease emissions. Second, increase ventilation— open the windows and use bathroom and attic fans. Finally, consider purchasing air cleaners. There are numerous types that range from table-top models to whole house units. Air cleaners are helpful, depending on the model used, but none rid the house of all pollutants, and they are not recommended by the EPA to remove radon.

14

RECREATION PERILS

NORTH CAROLINA, 1999:
Four-year-old girl dies after being struck in the head by playground equipment.

SOME STATS

- More than 6,000 deaths each year are associated with recreational activities.
- Nearly 20 children die each year as a result of a playground injury.
- 70% of playground equipment injuries occur in public playgrounds.
- In 2000, more than 232,000 children ages 14 and under were treated in emergency rooms for playground injuries.
- 9 out of 10 trampoline injuries occur to children 14 and under.
- Since 1990, 11 people have died from trampoline injuries.
- At least 17 children under age 11 died from toy-related injuries in 2000.
- Amusement park injuries increased 87% from 1994 to 1998, even though attendance rose just 12%.

Playtime should be fun and carefree. But playtime can become dangerous when safety concerns fall by the wayside. Regardless of whether your child is tot or teen, keep her playtime safe.

TOY SAFETY

More than 3.3 billion toys and games were sold in the United States in 2000 to entertain and educate. Although the majority of these are safe, they can still become hazardous when misused or used by children too young to use them. Injuries frequently result from toys, with children ages 4 and under at especially high risk.

Choking remains the leading cause of toy-related death, and one-third of choking deaths result from latex balloons. Other toy-related deaths were caused by drownings, suffocation, and motor vehicle crashes. Tricycles and other riding toys can lead to fatalities when the child rides the toy into the road, a pool, a pond, or another body of water. Riding toys are also implicated with more injuries (mostly falls) than any other toy group.

Injuries and deaths have been documented from toy box lids falling onto children's heads and necks. Finger crushing incidents were also reported. If your child's toy box has a lid, keep it locked so that your child can't open it without supervision. But make sure the lock is easy to open from the inside. If the lid is heavy, remove it. If you're about to purchase a toy box, consider the following: (1) lidless plastic crates are safer; and (2) lids should be lightweight and completely removable, and fitted with rubber or other stoppers that allow a gap of 12 mm or more when the lid is closed.

GENERAL SUGGESTIONS

- Read and follow the manufacturer's recommendations, instructions, and warnings before buying any toy.
- Adhere to the age recommendations for overall safety. You claim that your child grows up too fast—don't speed up the process!
- Look for sturdy construction.
- Instruct your child on the proper use of the toy.
- Avoid projectile and high volume toys that can harm eyes and ears.
- Don't choose toys with straps, cords, or strings longer than seven inches that could cause strangulation.
- Periodically examine toys for breakage and potential hazards. Throw away or repair damaged ones.
- Contact the Consumer Product Safety Commission at 1-800-638-2772 or www.cpsc.gov with questions about toy safety or to check on recalls.

AGE-SPECIFIC SUGGESTIONS

YOUR INFANT:

Your baby's play reflects her development and awareness of the environment. It's basically solitary (noninteractive) play that helps her develop sensory and motor skills by manipulating toys and other objects.

WHEN BUYING TOYS:

Think big, as in big parts. Remember, children under 3 put everything in their mouths. Buy toys with parts bigger than your child's fist to prevent choking. They also pull, prod, and twist toys, so look for well-made toys with tightly secured eyes, noses, and other parts, and avoid toys with sharp edges and points. Age-appropriate toys for infants take into account her short attention span, with features that appeal to her sight, hearing, and touch.

Examples of age-appropriate infant toys are:

a.   Age 1 – 3 months: mobile, mirror, music box, stuffed animal without detachable parts, and a rattle

b.   Age 4 – 6 months: squeeze toys, busy boxes, play gym

c.   Age 7 – 9 months: various cloth-textured toys, splashing bath toys, large blocks, and large balls

d.   Age 10 – 12 months: durable books with large pictures, large building blocks, nesting cups, and push-pull toys

YOUR TODDLER

Toddlers engage in parallel play—playing alongside, not with others—and frequently change toys due to their short attention span. Imitation is one of their most common forms of play, and locomotion skills can be enhanced with push/pull toys.

WHEN BUYING TOYS:

Safety considerations still include no detachable or small parts. Avoid marbles, balls, and games with balls that have diameters less than 1¾ inches. Consider toys that encourage imitation, language development, and gross and fine motor skills.

Examples of age-appropriate toddler toys are:

a.   Appropriate rocking horses and rideable trucks
b.   Play phones
c.   Play dough, finger paints
d.   Large piece wooden or plastic puzzles
e.   Dolls, housekeeping toys
f.   Large blocks, cloth books

YOUR PRESCHOOLER

Typical play for this age is interactive and cooperative as she starts learning how to share; thus, she needs contact with age-mates. Imitative, imaginative, and dramatic play are important, and this is the typical age for imaginary friends. Activities should promote growth and motor skills—jumping, running, and climbing. TV and video games should only be a part of the her play, and you should monitor content and amount of time spent in use.

WHEN BUYING TOYS:

Avoid ones constructed with thin, brittle plastic that might easily break into small pieces or leave jagged edges. Look for the designation "ASTM D-4236" when purchasing household items such as crayons and paint sets, as these have been reviewed by a toxicologist and, if needed, labeled with cautionary information.

Examples of age-appropriate preschool toys are:

a. Toys/games that encourage gross and fine motor development include: tricycle, big wheels, gym sets; wading pools, sand boxes; large blocks, puzzles; crayons, paints, simple crafts; and age-appropriate electronic games
b. Toys/games that encourage imitative/imaginative play include: dress up clothes and dolls; housekeeping toys, play tents; and puppets, doctor and nurse kits
c. Curious and active preschoolers need to be adult supervised, especially near water and gym sets

YOUR SCHOOL-AGER

Play becomes more competitive and complex during the school-age period, and rules and rituals become important aspects of play and games. Characteristic activities include team sports, secret clubs, "gang" activities, scouting or other organizations, complex puzzles, collections, quiet board games, reading, and hero worship. Humor becomes important as children between the ages of 6 and 8 years have the ability to resolve incongruities and enjoy a joke. Older children enjoy more complex jokes, because these jokes allow them to show off their cognitive abilities.

WHEN BUYING TOYS:

If you buy a bicycle, get a helmet, too, and make sure she wears it. If buying a toy gun, buy one where the barrel or entire gun is brightly colored so it's not mistaken for a real one. Teach her to put her toys away properly so no one trips on them, and teach her to keep her toys away from younger siblings.

Examples of age-appropriate toys for school-age children are:

a. Increasingly complex board and card games
b. Books
c. Crafts
d. Music and art supplies
e. Athletic equipment
d. Video games (check the ratings and descriptors)
e. Microscopes and telescopes

YOUR TEEN

Friends become the focus for activity for your teen, and teens rarely think of their toys as toys.

When buying toys:

Buying for teens is a near impossible task. The essential guideline appears to be: if you love it, she will hate it and vice versa. However, choose items that are not saturated with sex and violence.

Examples of age-appropriate toys for teens are:

a. Sports, camping, fishing gear
b. Videos, video games, computer games
c. Radios, compact disc players
d. Personal telephones
e. Models and collectibles

PLAYGROUND SAFETY

Playgrounds provide your child with opportunities to develop her motor, thinking, and social skills. However, they are often sites of unintentional injuries. The majority of injuries take place in public playgrounds, including park, school, and childcare playgrounds. A

1998 survey graded United States playgrounds C- based on physical hazards and behavioral elements such as age-appropriate design and adult supervision.

Most fatal playground injuries result from strangulation due to entanglement or entrapment, and the majority of these occur on home playgrounds during evening hours, when kids are out of school and unsupervised. Nonfatal injuries result chiefly from falls when children tumble off or trip over equipment. Climbers account for the majority of injuries at public playgrounds, while swings are responsible for most injuries at home.

Playground safety responsibility lies in adult hands. Regular maintenance, limiting equipment height, maintaining adequate surfacing, and utilizing age-appropriate equipment, combined with adult supervision, greatly reduce the incidence and severity of playground injuries.

PREVENTION

- Make sure all equipment meets government safety standards.
- Ensure proper inspection and maintenance of playground equipment and grounds.
- Don't let your little ones play in areas designated for bigger kids.
- Avoid asphalt, concrete, grass, and soil surfaces. Instead use playgrounds with surfaces that reduce injuries—shredded rubber, wood chips, wood, sand,—at least 12 inches in depth and 6 feet around stationary equipment. Synthetic turf, rubber mats, and other artificial materials are also safe.
- Remove hoods and drawstrings from your child's clothing to prevent strangulation. Also disallow necklaces, scarves, and purses.
- Make sure slides are cool to prevent burns.
- Check for splinters and nails that stick out from playground surfaces.
- Make sure there are no pieces of glass, debris, or sharp rocks in the play area.
- Use fenced-in play areas for young children so that they don't wander off into the streets.
- Prevent pushing, shoving, fighting, crowding, and inappropriate use of the equipment.
- Provide constant supervision to prevent injuries AND abductions.

TRAMPOLINE SAFETY

Now that they are cheap and on the pages of every discount store's sale flyer, trampolines are more common than ever–and so are trampoline injuries. The injury rate was 140% higher in 1996 than 1990, which added up to 83,400 injuries in 1996 alone. Most of these injuries occurred at home. Since 1990, the Consumer Product Safety Commission has received reports of six deaths due to trampoline injury.

Trampolines are meant to be sporting or gymnastic equipment that require skill and supervision. Despite current safety measures, the potential for serious injury while using a trampoline remains, and the need for supervision and trained personnel at all times makes home use very undesirable. Thus, the American Academy of Pediatrics advises:

1. Parents not purchase trampolines for home use or allow their children to use a home trampoline.
2. Trampolines should never be part of routine school physical education classes.
3. Trampolines should not be used in outdoor playgrounds or considered play equipment.
4. Limited use of trampolines in supervised training programs should include: a safety pad that covers all portions of the steel frame and springs; impact-absorbing safety surface material on the surface around the trampoline; appropriately used safety harnesses and spotting belts; considering setting the trampoline in a pit so that the mat is at ground level; and not using access ladders, as they may provide unintended access to the trampoline by small children.

AMUSEMENT PARK SAFETY

Fortunately, serious safety problems are rare at amusement parks because they are designed and operated with children in mind. However, accidents happen, and the number of amusement park injuries increased 87% from 1994 to 1998, and only 5% to 10% of these injuries resulted from faulty equipment or mechanical failure. Most accidents resulted from rider or operator errors or a flaw in the design of the ride.

Roller-coasters can be dangerous, but so can whirling rides, Ferris wheels, bumper cars, and even merry-go-rounds. Children can easily get lost, or worse: abducted. To keep your child safe, follow the general and age-specific guidelines suggested by Safe Parks. If your child has a disability, follow those additional suggestions.

GENERAL SAFETY

Riding doesn't come naturally. Learn the rules and use common sense. If either the ride or the attendant looks unsafe, don't get on!

- Don't fall victim to "patron daze"—read and adhere to all posted health warnings. Some conditions can make certain rides deadly.
- Follow all age and height restrictions.
- Obey all instructions from the ride attendants.
- Don't overload a ride.
- Make sure your child is secured, especially since some attendants improperly secure children.
- Tell your child to stay seated and keep her hands and feet inside the ride at all times.
- If she has long hair, keep it tied back when riding.
- No goofing around when on the ride.
- Tell her to make sure the ride has completely stopped and she has been told to exit before doing so.
- No riding under the influence of alcohol or drugs—this goes for parents, too.
- Set a good example so your child knows how to behave.
- If something goes wrong, Don't panic. Follow the park employee's instructions.

AGE-SPECIFIC SAFETY

KIDS 6 AND UNDER

Should you let your tyke on the rides? That depends on her temperament. If she's calm and cooperative, chances are she will do okay. If she's shy and fearful, she will start crying the second you're out of reach. If she's impulsive and adventurous, she's apt to start climbing if left alone on a ride. You may want to note that Disney, owners of the most trusted parks in the world, requires adults to accompany children under 7 on all rides. Don't let cost determine whether or not you ride with your child—she's priceless. And don't let kids supervise younger kids.

Since there are no government rules regarding height limits and child safety equipment, some parks let diaper-wearing tots ride open-air vehicles without safety restraints. See past the sales pitch, and make safe choices for your child. Check out the ride, and ask the attendant what happens if your child gets frightened while the ride is operating. Don't put your child on the ride if she's afraid. Her first impulse will be to get away. Always use the safety equipment, but realize that many lap belts and bars are more psychological than physical barriers. Loose-fitting bars and belts also allow children to slide around when the ride is in progress.

Remember basic safety rules so that your child doesn't get lost or abducted. Dress her in bright-colored clothes, carry her photo with you, and keep a very close eye on her.

SCHOOL-AGE KIDS

Injuries for school-age kids take a sharp increase, accounting for 31% of all amusement ride accidents. They are more independent, thus more apt to ride by themselves, and they are beginning to ride bigger and faster rides. They respond to peer pressure, playing games of tricks and dares. Fortunately, they are also becoming more logical and more receptive to safety teaching.

Talk with her before you go to the park. Discuss the various rides and why it's important to follow safety rules. Let her search the Internet for information about the rides. She will love to learn how things work at this age. If she's going to the park with a school or other group, discuss peer pressure and what she should do if they call her "chicken" if she's afraid to go on a specific ride. Point out safety equipment and warning signs. Allow her to see how people get on and off the ride before she tries it.

TEENAGERS

Accidents decline in this age group, but some kids are out to prove themselves, and peer pressure, horseplay, and substance use become big risk factors. Young teens are most likely to remove safety belts and stand up during the ride just for the thrill of it.

Discuss the different rides and rules before she goes to the park. Share stories of amusement ride injuries, and try to find the lesson in the story. Stress the importance of good behavior around the rides, and the importance of not using drugs and alcohol. In 1994, a six-year-old was killed on a kiddie ride when a teenager decided to play a prank on the ride operator and turn the ride on. The little boy was crushed under the ride.

KIDS WITH DISABILITIES

If your child has a disability, find out which rides she can ride safely. Some parks and carnivals have brochures that discuss the abilities required on each ride. If still unsure, ask the ride operator or manager. But use careful judgment to make your decision, and don't try to force a ride operator into bending rules or ignoring safety restrictions intended to protect the safety of the riders.

Physically Challenged Patrons: Some amusement rides create strong forces that can be dangerous to a child who can't maintain her balance, hold her head steady, and/or hold onto the safety bars.

Mentally or Emotionally Challenged Patrons: Start with gentle rides and observe for signs of overstimulation. The thrill of many rides works on surprise, fear, and strong forces, and may be too much for your child. If she panics and tries to get off the ride, she could endanger herself or others. Most restraints won't prevent a rider determined to exit.

Seizure-Prone Patrons: Rapid flashing lights may trigger seizures in susceptible people.

If your child is disabled, supervise her carefully. Make sure she's seated properly with the restraint system in place before the ride starts. Ask the operator for assistance if needed.

15

SCHOOL AND
DAY CARE DANGERS

LOUISIANA, 2003:
Gunmen armed with an AK-47 assault rifle and a semi-automatic pistol kill one student and injure three others in a New Orleans high school gymnasium.

SOME STATS

- School shootings, though high profile, are rare.
- 17% of students carry a weapon to school.
- 33.2% of students have been in a physical fight.
- 6.6% of students missed at least one day of school because they felt unsafe.
- 8.9% of students have been threatened with a weapon on school property.
- Nearly 30% of kids report moderate or frequent involvement in bullying.
- 2.2 million children ages 14 and under sustain school-related injuries.
- 31,000 children under age 4 were injured in school or day care settings in 1997.
- At least 56 children died in day care settings in 1990.

Millions of children are injured in school accidents; others become victims of violence and bullying. Thousands more are hurt in day care. No matter how hard you try, you can't supervise your child while he's away at school or day care. But you can still take steps to help keep him safe.

SCHOOL INJURIES

More than 53 million kids spend 25% of their total waking hours in school or on school property. Ten to twenty-five percent of them will be injured on the playground, during sports, or on the school bus. This book discusses all three of these dangers in separate chapters.

257

However, the Centers for Disease Control and Prevention offer general guidelines to promote school safety. Contact your child's school to see if they are utilizing them.

- Create an environment that promotes safety and prevents unintentional and intentional injuries.
- Provide a physical environment, both inside and outside the buildings, that promotes safety and prevents injury.
- Implement curricula that help students develop the knowledge, attitudes, confidence, and behaviors needed to adopt and maintain safe lifestyles and to advocate for health and safety.
- Provide safe physical education programs and extracurricular activities.
- Provide services to meet the physical, emotional, mental, and social needs of the students.
- Establish short- and long-term responses to crises, disasters, and injuries.
- Integrate school, community, and family efforts to prevent unintentional and intentional injuries.
- Provide regular staff development opportunities that impart knowledge, skills, and confidence to effectively promote safety and prevent injury, and support their students to do the same.

SCHOOL VIOLENCE

School shootings may be rare, but violent incidents are not. One-third of students get into fights and nearly one-tenth have been threatened with a weapon. Schools can't do it alone. Get involved.

THE CENTER FOR THE PREVENTION OF SCHOOL VIOLENCE SUGGESTS THAT YOU:

- Know your child's school. Know what they are doing to establish and maintain a safe environment.
- Know your child. Know his normal behavior pattern so that you can recognize subtle changes when something goes wrong.
- Know how to connect with your child. Talk to him about his day at school.
- Explain the facts about school safety to him. Tell him what the school is doing to keep him safe.
- Know the odds and talk to your child about them. The United States Department of Education states that the chances of getting killed in school are less than one in a million.

- Explain to him that school safety is everyone's responsibility, including his, and that he should report negative behaviors, such as seeing a weapon in school.
- Tell him that violence isn't an acceptable solution to problems.
- Explain that you're always there for him and ready to listen.

YOU SHOULD ALSO BE AWARE OF THE WARNING SIGNS OF VIOLENCE:

- Cruelty to animals
- Gradual and eventually complete withdrawal from social contacts
- Expresses feelings of isolation and being alone
- Expresses feelings of being rejected
- Projects blame on others
- Irrational beliefs and ideas
- Fascination with weaponry or explosives
- Unreciprocated romantic obsession
- Drastic change in belief system
- Family or fellow students feel fear because of your child
- Violence toward inanimate objects
- Sabotages projects or equipment
- History of being a victim of violence, including physical and sexual abuse, at home, in school, or in the community
- Low interest in school
- Expresses violence in drawings or writings; listens to music with violent themes
- Displays "dark side" when doing school projects that show anger or frustration
- Demonstrates patterns of impulsive and chronic hitting, intimidating, and other bullying behaviors
- History of being bullied
- History of disciplinary problems
- Past history of violent or overt behavior, including fire setting, vandalism, lying, and cheating
- Intolerance to differences and prejudicial attitudes towards others based on race, ethnicity, religion, language, gender, sexual orientation, ability, and physical appearance
- Inappropriate access to firearms
- Brings weapon to school
- Increased risk-taking behaviors

BULLYING

Kip Kinkel, Dylan Klebold, and Eric Harris–all school shooters, all victims of bullying. Bullying may have been around since time began, but its consequences are certainly far more deadly today.

Bullying goes far beyond good-natured ribbing. It appears very similar to other forms of aggression, but with distinct features. Bullying behavior is purposeful, not accidental, with the goal of gaining control over another child, one who is physically or emotionally weaker, by using verbal or physical aggression. Bullies attack without any reason other than that the victim seems to be an easy target, and the result is intentional pain and distress for the victim. Bullies also tend to be more popular than kids who are simply aggressive.

Bullying usually consists of direct behaviors, such as taunting, threatening, hitting, and stealing that are initiated by one or more students against one or more victims. Bullying can also be indirect, such as spreading vicious rumors that cause the victim to be socially isolated by intentional exclusion. Boys tend to use the more direct methods, while girls seem to prefer the indirect. However, be it direct or indirect, bullying is intimidation that occurs repeatedly over a period of time to create an ongoing pattern of harassment and abuse.

Some bullies behave in an active, aggressive, outgoing manner. They use brute force or open harassment. They reject rules and need to rebel to feel superior and secure. Other bullies behave in a more reserved manner, and don't want to be recognized as harassers or tormentors. They control by soft-talking, saying the "right thing at the right time," and lying. They build their sense of power carefully through cunning, manipulation, and deception. These types may seem different, but they have the same underlying characteristics–concern with their own pleasure, desire for power over others, a willingness to use people to get what they want, and the inability to see things from another's perspective.

Kids who bully appear to derive satisfaction from inflicting injury and suffering on others. They appear to have little to no empathy for their victims, and often defend their actions by saying that their victims provoked them in some way. They seem to have little anxiety and strong self-esteem. Contrary to popular opinion, there is little evidence to support the belief that bullies victimize others because they feel bad about themselves.

Bullies don't always target children with physical characteristics that deviate from the norm, such as obesity, thinness, or wearing glasses, any more than children without those characteristics. They tend to target children who are shy, anxious, or insecure. These children lack the social graces and skills,—and friends. They tend to be close to their parents, and may have parents who are overprotective. Usually physically weaker and emotionally vulnerable, they become easy targets who don't fight back.

Another group of potential victims are children who tend to be restless and irritable, and who tease and provoke others. These kids fight back when attacked, but easily lose the fight. Some experts suspect that some children with Attention Deficit Hyperactivity Disorder (ADD/ADHD) fit into this category.

Girl victims are likely to be teased about their clothing or gossiped about in a malicious manner. They may find nasty notes in their desk or locker. Bullies may extort girl victims with the promise of inclusion in a peer group if they join in excluding someone else, or if they participate in a cruel or humiliating prank.

WHAT TO DO IF YOUR CHILD IS BEING BULLIED

The effects of bullying don't often appear as obvious as a black eye or bloody nose. Listen to your child talk about school, social events, the other kids in his class and school, and his route to and from school. Look for subtle signs, as well as the obvious ones (keep in mind that some of these signs can signify other problems, such as depression or substance abuse):

- He acts moody or sullen, or he withdraws from family interaction.
- He becomes depressed.
- He loses interest in schoolwork, causing his grades to drop.
- He invents stomachaches or a mysterious illness to avoid going to school or outright refuses to go to school (15% of absenteeism relates directly to fears of being bullied).
- His sleep or eating patterns change drastically.
- He waits to use the bathroom at home.
- He arrives home with torn clothes or unexplained bruises.
- His personal belongings disappear, or he asks for extra money or allowance for school lunch or supplies.
- He wants to carry protection, such as a knife or gun.

Sit down with your child in a safe, comfortable, and private location, and talk to him. Take his complaints seriously, since minor complaints may be covering a more severe grievance. He may be afraid or ashamed to tell you that he was bullied, so listen carefully to his complaints. You may want to ease him into the conversation of bullying by asking him what it's like to walk home from school or ride the bus. He may have suddenly changed routes to avoid contact with the bully. You could ask him if he knows any kids who were hurt by bullies. That way he doesn't have to start by talking about his own experiences, and it will help him see that he's not alone.

Once you find that he has been victimized, don't overreact. He's the victim. Don't add to his burden with an angry or blaming response. And don't let him see that you're upset. He may interpret that as your being disappointed with him. Reinforce the idea that it was not his fault. Tell him, "The bully has a problem, not you. He picked on you for no reason. You did not do anything to cause it."

Talking about the problem helps and comforts by letting your child know that you're on his side. But that doesn't change the fact that the bully will still be there at school the next day. You need to teach him how to handle the problem:

- Instruct him to try to avoid places where the bully hangs out. Staying out of harm's way is sensible, not cowardly.
- Tell him not to show anger or fight back. Anger and violence won't solve the problem; they actually can make matters worse. Fighting back gives the bully exactly what he wants, encouraging him to come back to taunt again. Fighting may also put him at greater risk for physical injury, since the bully is most likely stronger.
- Encourage him not to go along with everything the bully says or wants, and not to give his possessions to the bully. Your child needs to recapture his dignity and repair his self-esteem. Giving in won't accomplish that.
- Persuade him to act first by looking the bully in the eye and saying something like, "I don't like it when you tease me, and I want you to stop it, right now." Tell him to then walk away and ignore any further teasing.
- Discourage him from retaliating, as it just reinforces violence as a solution to problems.
- Tell him to find a teacher or other adult and report the incident.
- If the bullying seems to have affected your child's self-esteem, seek professional help.

You should notify the school whenever an incident occurs, and be persistent until they take some type of action. Ask school personnel to encourage class discussions about bullies, or ask that your child be moved into another class. Alert them to carefully monitor your child and assure his safety. If your school refuses to do anything about the bullying, transfer your child to another school. You can even consider more drastic responses, such as reporting the incident to the police or filing a civil suit against the bully's parents or the school.

Help your child develop social skills to make friends. He's less likely to be bullied in a peer group. Foster his healthy self-esteem and teach him problem-solving skills. Teach him how to be assertive rather than submissive. Involve him in a special activity, like karate or sports that will give him self-confidence and gain the respect of other children. Confident, resourceful children are less likely to be bullied or to bully others.

WHAT TO DO IF YOUR CHILD IS THE BULLY

It's more difficult to detect bullies than it's to detect victims. Bullies are adept at hiding their mistreatment of others because in their minds the victims deserved what they got. You may have no idea that your child is bullying until a teacher or another parent confronts you about it. Your child may act cocky, arrogant, and self-assured, and he may have difficulty accepting authority. If you ask him about bullying, he's apt to be condescending about responding to questions.

If you find out that your child is a bully, stay calm. Your first reaction may be disbelief, finding it impossible to believe that your child could do such a thing, but try to be objective—no matter how hard it's to do so. Don't become angry or defensive, because this could make a bad situation even worse. Since he most likely won't confess to his behavior, ask him to tell you exactly what he has been doing. Explain how his behavior constitutes bullying, and ask why he thinks he bullies and what might help him stop. Since bullying often stems from unhappiness, try to find out what is bothering him.

To help modify his bullying behavior:

- Take the problem very seriously. If your child is a bully now, he's at risk for more severe problems later in life.
- Supervise him more closely, and stay near by when he plays with other kids. If you can't watch him, such as times when he's

in school, arrange for adult supervision or ask that he only participate in supervised activities.

- Set limits. Tell him that bullying won't be tolerated, and make sure he understands you. Develop consequences and follow through on them when needed.
- Help him to understand the rights and feelings of others. Ask how he would feel if someone bullied him? Use examples from books, television, and movies.
- Stop any display of aggression immediately, and help him find nonviolent outlets for frustrations and to handle problems.
- Foster his participation in physical activities such as sports to give him healthy ways to feel powerful and strong.
- Praise him for appropriate behaviors.
- Teach him how to be assertive rather than aggressive.
- Talk to his school counselor and teacher and explain that he's trying to improve his behavior, and ask them for their assistance.
- If older siblings tease him, instruct them to stop and administer consequences as needed.
- Be a positive role model. Control your own aggression.
- Seek professional help. Bullying behavior often requires outside assistance. Take advantage of the counseling services offered at his school or your community.

DAY CARE

The United States Consumer Product Safety Commission (CPSC) conducted a study in 1998 to identify potential safety hazards in 220 licensed child care centers across the country. They investigated eight potentially hazardous product areas: cribs, soft bedding, playground surfacing maintenance, child safety gates, window blind cords, drawstrings in children's clothing, and recalled children's products. Two-thirds of the child care settings exhibited at least one safety hazard, which means that children in these settings may be at risk for injury or death.

Thirteen million children under six are in nonparental child care during some part of the day. About 29% of these children are in center-based care, such as Head Start, day care centers, and nursery schools. The other 71% are in non-center-based care, including family child care, in-home child care, and care by a relative. There are about 99,000 licensed child care centers and about 283,000 regulated or licensed family child care providers. In reviewing state licensing requirements for child care, the CPSC found that most of the hazards in their study were not addressed. For example, although cribs are covered by federal regulations, many states did not require day care centers to use cribs that met all standards, and none of the states had requirements for addressing nursery equipment recalls. Therefore, state licensing requirements don't adequately meet child safety needs, and many child care providers and parents may not even be aware that hazards exist.

To resolve this situation, the CPSC prepared an easy checklist for both parents and child care providers. Use this to check for these hazards at your child's day care setting, as well in your own home.

CONSUMER PRODUCT SAFETY COMMISSION'S CHILD CARE SAFETY CHECKLIST FOR PARENTS AND CHILD CARE PROVIDERS:

CRIBS: Make sure cribs meet current national safety standards and are in good condition. Look for a certification safety seal. Older cribs may not meet current standards. Crib slats should be no more than 2 3/8" apart, and mattresses should fit snugly.

This can prevent strangulation and suffocation associated with older cribs and mattresses that are too small.

SOFT BEDDING: Be sure that no pillows, soft bedding, or comforters are used when you put babies to sleep. Babies should be put to sleep on their backs in a crib with a firm, flat mattress.

This can help reduce Sudden Infant Death Syndrome (SIDS) and suffocation related to soft bedding.

PLAYGROUND SURFACING: Look for safe surfacing on outdoor playgrounds—at least 12 inches of wood chips, mulch, sand, or pea gravel, or mats made of safety-tested rubber or rubber-like materials.

This helps protect against injuries from falls, especially head injuries.

PLAYGROUND MAINTENANCE: Check playground surfacing and equipment regularly to make sure they are maintained in good condition.

This can help prevent injuries, especially from falls.

SAFETY GATES: Be sure that safety gates are used to keep children away from potentially dangerous areas, especially stairs.

Safety gates can protect against many hazards, especially falls.

WINDOW BLIND AND CURTAIN CORDS: Be sure mini-blinds and Venetian blinds don't have looped cords. Check that vertical blinds, continuous looped blinds, and drapery cords have tension or tie-down devices to hold the cords tight. Check that inner cord stops have been installed. See www.windowcoverings.org for the latest blind cord safety information.

These safety devices can prevent strangulation in the loops of window blind and curtain cords.

CLOTHING DRAWSTRINGS: Be sure there are no drawstrings around the hood and neck of children's outerwear clothing. Other types of clothing fasteners, like snaps, zippers, or hook and loop fasteners (such as Velcro), should be used.

Drawstrings can catch on playground and other equipment and can strangle young children.

RECALLED PRODUCTS: Check that no recalled products are being used and that a current list of recalled children's products is readily visible.

Recalled products pose a threat of injury or death. Displaying a list of recalled products will remind caretakers and parents to remove or repair potentially dangerous children's toys and products.

For more information, contact the CPSC at 800-638-2772 or www.cpsc.gov.

Choosing the right day care is one of the most difficult choices you have to make. If you have not made that decision yet, start considering your options early, at least 2 to 3 months ahead of time. This way you can compare choices and costs, and still have time to evaluate quality and safety.

Unfortunately, cost is an issue for most of us, and full-day child care can range from $4,000 to $30,000 per year, depending on your child's age, where you live, and the type of child care you choose. For one child, outside day care tends to be cheaper than in-home care, but some types of home care, such as au pair child care providers, can make the cost of home care more competitive with day care centers. Many companies and the government will subsidize child care cost, and you can find help with child care at the National Child Care Information Center (www.nccic.org/faqs/choosecare.html), so look into these options.

CHOOSING AND EVALUATING CHILD CARE

Essentially, there are three types of child care settings: child care centers, family child care home, and in-home care. Each has its advantages and disadvantages, and all need to be evaluated.

CHILD CARE CENTERS

These day care centers range from local churches to independent operators to nationally franchised centers. Their quality ranges just as widely, but all must be licensed. Location adds to their popularity, and many are cropping up in industrial parks and office complexes. Successful centers understand the needs of both parent and child, but some are better at promoting these concepts than implementing them.

Advantages: Child care centers provide structured programs in a licensed environment. They also are usually the least expensive option, expose your child to a diverse group of children and providers, schedule part-time care when needed, and are usually open even if one provider is absent.

Disadvantages: Centers can lead to more infectious illnesses for your child due to exposure to other kids. They also offer less individualized attention and may not offer a consistent, primary provider.

To best evaluate these settings, visit them and look around. Do you feel comfortable? Are people friendly or frenzied? Do the staff and children look healthy and happy? Is the environment safe and child-proof? Are there emergency exits? Do the staff wash their hands frequently, especially before handling food and after changing? Do the children wash their hands before eating and when they use the bathroom? Are the toys clean? Does each infant have its own crib? Is there a quiet place for nap time?

What should you look for and ask?

1. **A license**. All day care centers must have a license. Check with your state day care licensing agency to learn about your state regulations and to get a list of licensed day cares. Go to nrc.uchsc.edu/states.html to look up your state.
2. **Child-to-staff ratio**. Regulations vary per state, but the fewer children per staff member, the better. Here is the child-to-staff ratio for Pennsylvania as an example:

When children are grouped in similar age levels, the following maximum child group sizes and ratios of staff persons apply:

Similar Age Levels	Staff	Children	Maximum Group Size	Total Number of Staff Required for the Maximum Group Size
Infant	1	4	8	2
Young toddler	1	5	10	2
Older toddler	1	6	12	2
Preschool	1	10	20	2
Young school-age	1	12	24	2
Older school-age	1	15	30	2

3. **Staff training**. What type of training did the staff receive? Are they trained in: child development, basic first aid, CPR, preventing illness and injury, handwashing, and child abuse recognition? Look for child care providers who are certified by the National Association for the Education of Young Children.
4. **Staff background checks**. Many states require criminal background and child abuse checks of all day care workers. Check the state licensing site to see if this applies in your state.
5. **Policies and programs.** Find out about their policies on discipline, child progress evaluation, parental visits, staff health check-ups and TB tests, smoking, fire safety and other important issues. Are the policies in writing? Don't use centers that have no written policies, allow corporal punishment or smoking, don't require regular staff check-ups and TB tests, have no specific fire safety plan, or that don't have open door policies for visiting.
6. **Building and playground safety.** Are emergency numbers clearly posted? Are children protected from strangers? Are there smoke detectors throughout the building? Does the playground have impact-absorbing surfaces, such as wood chips, under the equipment?

7. **How they care for sick children.** Is a check-up required before admission? When should children stay home because of illness? Is a doctor or nurse available? How would you be told if there was an illness or problem circulating among the children? Is there a sick room for kids with minor illnesses, such as colds? Do they keep records of health-related problems?

8. **References.** Talk to other parents about: caregiver reliability, discipline, how their children enjoyed the experience, how caregivers respond to parents, and respectfulness of center toward cultures and values. Ask if they recommend the center. If their child is no longer there, ask the parent for the reason.

9. **Resource information.** Check with the licensing office to see if there is a record of complaints against the center your considering.

FAMILY CHILD CARE HOME

This setting is typically a home in or near your neighborhood or workplace in which a mother takes care of three to five children. These may be certified or licensed, depending on individual state laws. Some areas require that family day cares meet basic safety requirements, such as basic child-proofing and fire extinguishers, but there may be little or no screening of the facility. However, this may be a less expensive and more home-like alternative for your child, and you usually have a closer relationship with your child's caregiver.

Advantages: Family care centers provide a home-like atmosphere and less exposure to illness because of the smaller number of children. Many offer more individualized care and flexible hours.

Disadvantages: Since many are not licensed, it's difficult to monitor the quality of care. And you will need a back-up plan if the provider becomes ill.

Visit the home to observe the environment. What is the atmosphere like? Are you comfortable? What areas of the house are accessible to the children? Are they child-proof? Are they clean and orderly? Are there smoke alarms and a fire safety plan?

What should you look for and ask?

1. **Child-to-caregiver ratio.** Find out the maximum number of children cared for, and don't forget to inquire about her own children. Fewer children for each staff is still preferable.

2. **Emergencies.** Ask what she would do if there is a serious injury or fire. Does she have emergency and parent numbers posted near her phone?
3. **Play area.** Is the outside play area contained and safe? The playground should have impact-absorbing surfaces under the equipment. Is the play area well-constructed and maintained?
4. **Provider absence.** Inquire as to what she does to cover her vacations and illnesses.
5. Look over the day care center list, and utilize appropriate questions and observations.

IN-HOME CARE

In-home can be costly, especially if you have only one child. You will pay salary, taxes, and increased food and utility bills. The operating costs can run from $50 to $150 per month in addition to salaries. However, the comfort benefits to your child may outweigh the costs. If strapped for cash, consider sharing the in-home care with a neighbor or friend. Several types of in-home care exist, including: au pair, full-time babysitter, housekeeper, nanny, and grandma.

AU PAIR: Typically a college-age European woman (or man), the au pair lives with you and takes care of your children in order to have the opportunity to live in the United States. Wages are low, but you hire the au pair sight unseen, and you lose the cost of her travel if the arrangement doesn't work out. And many parents feel as if they have taken on the responsibilities of another teen. However, there are advantages: most are from big families and have lots of experience working with children; your child will be exposed to another culture; the cost is fairly reasonable, but you may have to pay up to $6,000 up front to cover airfare, insurance, tuition, and program fees. Before hiring an au pair, check the credentials of the au pair company and check with at least two parents who have used their services. For further information and a list of au pair organizations, contact the International Au Pair Association at www.iapa.org.

FULL-TIME BABYSITTER: Full-time sitters provide child care but do not reside in your home. Those without early childhood education receive a $12 per hour minimum. Contact religious, senior citizen, or community groups for potential sitters. Ask for and check at least three references.

HOUSEKEEPER: This person cares for your children, cleans house, and cooks, and can be live-in or not. Although this sounds like a dream come true, a housekeeper will be more costly than a babysitter, ranging up to $2,800 per month.

NANNY: Professional nannies receive varying amounts of education in basic child care and development. Some are young women who work as nannies short-term; others are mature women who have already raised their own families. This is the most expensive option, costing as much as $4,000 per month, plus room and board if she's a live-in. To find a nanny or learn more, contact the International Nannies Association at www.nanny.org.

GRANDMA: The benefits of having grandma babysit are obvious. Your child will have optimal love and attention. Do consider the biggest potential disadvantage: grandmas live to spoil the grandkids. Full-time babysitting means assuming some of the parental role, including discipline. Make sure she's comfortable with that before considering this option.

Advantages: In-home care can provide more nurturing one-to-one care. He stays in a comfortable environment, exposed to fewer illnesses, and you don't have to worry about his transportation.

Disadvantages: Beside the cost, disadvantages include less socializing for your child, difficulty monitoring quality, and the need for a back-up plan when the provider is ill.

Since you can't usually observe the in-home sitter at another site, have her spend time with your children under your supervision. If possible, pay her to spend the entire day, so that you can see how well she does with your children, and how well your children do with her. How comfortable is she with them? How well do they respond to her? Explain the job in detail, discuss your philosophy on parenting, discipline, limit setting, etc., and see how she reacts.

You can't tag along with him to school or day care, but you can make sure that he's as safe as possible when he's there.

16

SPORTS HAZARDS

GEORGIA, 2002:
Boy dies after being struck in the chest with a baseball.

SOME STATS

- More than 30 million children play in organized sports.
- About 3.5 million children get hurt each year in sports or recreation incidents.
- Children between ages 5 and 14 account for almost half of all sports-related injuries for all age groups.
- More than 75,000 children are treated in hospital emergency rooms for sports injuries, and 25% of these injuries are serious.
- Most injuries result from falls, being struck by an object, collisions, and overexertion.
- The highest rates of sports injury involve contact and collisions.
- Girls experience more injuries before puberty, while boys suffer more during puberty.
- Head injury is the leading cause of death in sports injuries.

Sports promote fitness, but they can also foster injury. Each year, hundreds of thousands of children require emergency treatment for sports-related problems that include accidents (sprains, fractures, eye injuries, spinal injuries, etc.) and overuse injures (shin splints, tennis elbow, etc.), most of which are preventable.

Here are more uninteresting but important statistics on sports injuries, listed by sport, for children ages 5 to 14 per year:

Basketball	-	194,000 injuries
Base/softball	-	99,000 injuries and 3 to 4 deaths
Bicycling	-	340,000 injuries and 203 deaths
Football	-	172,000 injuries

Gymnastics	-	22,500 injuries
Ice skating	-	16,000 injuries
In-line and roller skating	-	58,600 and 27,000 injuries respectively
Skateboarding	-	32,000 injuries
Sledding	-	14,000 injuries
Snow skiing/Snowboarding	-	16,300 and 19,000 injuries respectively
Soccer	-	81,000 injuries

Organized sports provide a number of physical and social benefits for your child. However, the younger your child, the greater the safety concern. Reports of ballet dancers with late menstrual onset and gymnasts with short stature have added to these concerns, but it's unclear whether these problems were the results of intensive training or other factors such as dietary practices, emotional stress, or selection bias for the sport.

The effects of immaturity stand out. When the demand of the sport exceed the child's thinking and physical development, that child may develop feelings of frustration and failure. Young children may not be capable of understanding the rules of a sport or performing the skills. And coaches may not be capable of dealing with the issues of children, resulting in their blaming failures on the child. Expecting children to perform before they are capable results in dissatisfaction, not long-term success in the sport.

Parental supervision and participation is usually a good thing. But overzealous and inappropriate parental and other adult interference can have vast negative effects. Sports should be for the children —to develop fitness, skills, and team spirit, and to have fun. They should not be for the parents—to line the den with trophies, to brag to the buddies, or to live vicariously through their children. Don't ridicule or demean your or any other child; don't insist on your child being in the spotlight; be respectful, and watch your behavior. People have already been injured and even killed by inappropriate parents at sporting events. Your child models your every behavior. Think about what she will learn if she hears you cursing the umpire as you throw a full-blown temper tantrum.

On the positive side, organized sports provide a greater opportunity to develop rules specifically designed for health and safety than does free play. According to the American Academy of Pediatrics, organizers can develop sound criteria to determine readiness to play, and can allow for a fairness process in choosing teams, matching competitors, and enforcing rules. Rules made specific for young athletes can decrease injury. Organizers can limit dangerous practices such as sliding headfirst into home base and body checking, and they can suggest smaller playing fields, shorter contest times, pitch counts adjusted for Little Leaguers, softer baseballs, matching opponents by weight in youth football, and adjusting play for extreme climactic conditions. Finally, organizers should hire qualified coaches, a key factor in providing safety and a positive experience.

Keep your child safe by letting him be himself and not pushing him into something he can't do, and learning more about sports, their potential hazards, and ways to keep your child safe.

CLASSIFICATION OF SPORTS BY CONTACT AND STRENUOUSNESS

Collision and contact sports result in the most serious injuries. However, limited contact sports such as gymnastics, softball, and downhill skiing, and noncontact sports, including power lifting and swimming, can still be dangerous. Not sure which sports are contact and which are not? Here is a list:

1. **Contact/Collision:** basketball, boxing (participation not recommended for any child/adolescent), diving, field hockey, tackle football, ice hockey, lacrosse, martial arts, rodeo, rugby, ski jumping, soccer, team handball, water polo, and wrestling
2. **Limited contact:** baseball, bicycling, cheerleading, canoeing/kayaking (whitewater), fencing, field, high jump, pole vault, floor hockey, flag football, gymnastics, handball, horseback riding, racquetball, skating, skiing (cross-country, downhill, and water), softball, squash, ultimate Frisbee, volleyball, windsurfing and surfing
3. **Noncontact:** archery, badminton, bodybuilding, bowling, canoeing/kayaking (flatwater), crew/rowing, curling, dancing ballet, modern, jazz), field (discus, javelin, shot put), golf, orienteering, powerlifting, race walking, riflery, rope jumping, running, sailing, scuba diving, strength training, swimming, table tennis, tennis, track, and weight lifting

Sports can also be classified by Strenuousness:

1. **High to moderate dynamic and static demands:** boxing (not recommended), crew/rowing, cross-country skiing, cycling,

downhill skiing, fencing, football, ice hockey, rugby, running, speed skating, water polo, and wrestling

2. **High to moderate dynamic and low static demands:** badminton, baseball, basketball, field hockey, lacrosse, orienteering, ping-pong, race walking, racquetball, soccer, squash, swimming, tennis, and volleyball

3. **High to moderate static and low dynamic demands:** archery, diving, equestrian, field events (jumping and throwing), gymnastics, karate and judo, motorcycling, rodeo, sailing, ski jumping, water skiing, and weight lifting

4. **Low intensity (Low dynamic and low static demands):** bowling, cricket, curling, golf, and riflery

MEDICAL CONDITIONS AND SPORTS

Certain conditions may disallow or limit participation in various sports. Should your child have any of these conditions, sports participation may create an increased risk of injury, or adversely affect that medical condition. Children should have a preparticipation sports examination before participating in any sport; however, if your child has a medical condition, you should be aware of her limitations. According to the American Academy of Pediatrics, the following conditions disallow or limit participation:

- Atlantoaxial instability
- Bleeding disorder
- Carditis
- Congenital heart disease (CHD)
- Hypertension
- Dysrhythmia
- Heart murmur
- Mitral valve prolapse
- Cerebral palsy
- Diabetes mellitus
- Diarrhea
- Eating disorders (anorexia nervosa and bulimia nervosa)
- Eye problems (functional use of only one eye, eye loss, detached retina, previous eye surgery or injury)
- Fever
- Heat illness in the past
- ** **HIV infection:** Since there is minimal risk to others, full participation is allowed. Skin lesions should be covered, and

athletic personnel should follow universal precautions on all athletes when handling blood and other bodily fluids.

- Kidney, absence of one
- Enlarged liver
- Cancer
- Musculoskeletal disorders
- History of serious head or spinal trauma, severe or repeated concussion, or craniotomy
- Convulsive disorder
- Obesity
- Organ transplant recipient
- Ovary, absence of one
- Lung disease, including cystic fibrosis (CF)
- Asthma (Only children with the most severe asthma need to modify participation.)
- Acute upper respiratory infection
- Sickle cell disease
- Sickle cell trait (Sudden death or other medical problems during athletic participation is unlikely, except in the most extreme conditions of heat, humidity, and possibly increased altitude. These children should be acclimatized and hydrated to reduce risks
- Contagious skin rash
- Enlarged spleen
- Undescended or absent testicle

WHY ARE KIDS MORE AT RISK FOR INJURY?

Children are more susceptible to sports injuries than adults for several reasons. Some due to their own development, others due to external factors:

Developmental reasons:

1. Physically immature bones injure easily possibly, causing premature cessation of growth or abnormal calcification.
2. Rapid bone growth outpaces muscle length, increasing injury risk and causing growing pains.
3. Injuries can occur if there is size/weight/maturation mismatching.
4. Other potential factors include the use of steroids, excessive dieting or obesity, lack of flexibility, and a past history of injury.

External factors include:

1. Injuries are more likely to occur during organized competitions and practices of sports clubs than physical education classes.
2. High school students over 14 years have nearly twice the injury risk of elementary school children.
3. The severity of injuries increases with the chances of contact.
4. The more a teen participates in sports, the greater the risk of injury.
5. Unsafe playing fields and equipment can easily result in injury, as can not wearing safety equipment.
6. The sports with the most injuries also have the more serious, and possibly disabling injuries: football, gymnastics, wrestling, and ice hockey.
7. More serious consequences can occur if coaches are not certified in CPR and first aid.

WHAT YOU SHOULD DO TO PREVENT ACUTE SPORTS INJURIES

Acute injuries occur suddenly, usually from trauma. They include minor bruises, sprains, and strains, as well as more serious injuries such as broken bones and torn ligaments. Most occur because of the lack of proper equipment or the use of improper equipment. Experts estimate that half of children's sports injuries can be prevented by following general guidelines, as well as suggestions for specific injury prevention.

GENERAL GUIDELINES

Wait until your child is ready. Readiness is relative to the demands of the sport, so you may want to talk to your child's health care provider to help determine your child's readiness. You can do this when you bring your child in for a complete physical to make sure there are no reasons to prohibit or limit participation.

Use the proper equipment, which should be the correct size for your child. For example, she should wear a shatterproof polycarbonate helmet for baseball, softball, bicycling, and hockey. Protective eyewear should be worn during racket sports and basketball. Ask the coach about other items such as shoes, mouth guards, padding, and athletic cups and supporters.

Make sure the equipment is approved by an appropriate certifying organization. Sports goggles should be approved by the American Society of Testing and Materials (ASTM) or pass the racket sports test of the Canadian Standards Association (CSA); hockey face masks by the Hockey Equipment Certification Council (HECC) or the CSA; and bicycle helmets by the Snell Memorial Foundation or the Consumer Product Safety Commission (CPSC). Equipment should also be safety-oriented and maintained on a regular basis.

The playing surface is an important piece of equipment. It should be safe and free from holes, ruts, and debris.

Make sure your child knows how to play before you put him "out there." She needs proper training and warm-up sessions before practices begin. Proper preparation decreases the chance of injury and bolsters her self-esteem.

See that the sport is supervised by qualified adults who are committed to safety and injury prevention. The coach should promote the player's well-being and sportsmanship over winning, and should know first aid and CPR. Coaches with a win-at-all-costs attitude can lead their team straight to the emergency room. Coaches should also make sure that safety rules are enforced, and that the children are equally matched for size, skill, and maturity.

SUGGESTIONS FOR SPECIFIC INJURY PREVENTION

SPRAINS AND STRAINS

Sprains involve injuries to the ligaments, while strains involve muscles or tendons.

To prevent these injuries:

1. Perform preseason stretching.
2. Warm up body temperature before stretching.
3. Tape sites of previous injuries.
4. Maintain playing surfaces.
5. Use proper footwear.
6. Limit practice time.

FRACTURES

Fractures are broken bones.

To prevent these injuries:

1. Perform strength conditioning exercises.
2. Use proper skill techniques for each sport.
3. Use protective gear that fits.

HEAD AND NECK INJURIES

Head injuries can be anything from a slight bump on the head to severe brain damage. Neck injuries range from simple strains to severed spinal cords, which can cause paralysis. Both head and neck injuries can be fatal.

To prevent these injuries:

1. Have appropriate supervision, such as when using a trampoline.
2. Adhere to safety rules.
3. Assess for potential dangers, such as investigating water depth before diving.
4. Use proper equipment

EYE INJURIES

Eye injuries can range from a good old-fashioned black eye to vision loss.

To prevent these injuries use head gear and protective eyewear.

WAYS TO PREVENT OVERUSE INJURIES

Overuse injuries occur over time due to prolonged, repeated motion or impact, and range from tiny muscle strains to stress fractures. As more children and teens participate in sports, more develop overuse injuries, particularly those who play all year or train too intensely. Poor training and conditioning, and insufficient rest can also lead to overuse injuries. Injured children too frequently "play through the pain" and resume activity before the appropriate time.

These injures occur more frequently in competitive sports, chiefly baseball, basketball, running, gymnastics, and swimming. But any activity with repetitive motion can result in overuse, especially if kids try too hard. Throwing can lead to shoulder and elbow injuries, whereas jumping and running strains the shins and feet. Hands and forearms fall victims to overuse from sports that require gripping, including golf, tennis, and gymnastics.

According to the Orthopaedic Department of the Lucile Packard Children's Hospital, the most common overuse injuries are:

JUMPER'S KNEE (PATELLAR TENDONITIS), which causes tenderness right below the knee or the upper shin area.
LITTLE LEAGUE ELBOW OR SHOULDER results in pain in the elbow or shoulder area, especially after activity.
OSTEOCHONDRITIS DISSECANS leads to knee pain and swelling.
SEVER'S DISEASE causes heel pain with limping, especially after running.
SHIN SPLINTS lead to pain and tenderness over the shin area.
SINDING-LARSEN-JOHANSSON DISEASE results in knee pain, especially after jumping.
SPONDYLOLYSIS and SPONDYLOLISTHESIS cause back pain.
STRESS FRACTURES cause pain and tenderness, but no swelling.

Like acute injuries, overuse injuries can be prevented. General prevention strategies include: using warm-up and cooldown exercise; stopping the activity when pain is felt; using proper technique and equipment, including athletic shoes; staying well-hydrated; and seeing your child's health care provider when an injury occurs.

Some specific tips:

Stress fractures:
1. Use soft running and playing surfaces
2. Proper foot gear
3. Strengthening exercises
4. Stop activity when pain occurs

Little League Elbow and Shoulder:
1. Engage in thorough conditioning and strengthening
2. Use large handle racket
3. Limit curveballs and pitching time

Shin splints:
1. Stretch before and after exercise
2. Pronate and supinate feet while standing
3. Use soft playing surface
4. Wear proper foot gear
5. Avoid sudden increase in activity
6. Limit forceful, extensive use of foot flexors

WHAT SCHOOLS CAN DO TO PREVENT INJURY

Health, growth, and safety must take precedence over winning. Schools should first set reasonable goals and appropriate strategies to attain those goals. The American Academy of Pediatrics list reasonable goals as acquiring basic motor skills, increasing motor skills, learning the social skills needed to work as a team, learning good sportsmanship, and having fun. See how that fun thing keeps coming up.

Sports activities should be tailored to match the developmental level of the players. Factors such as success, variety, freedom, family participation, peer support, enthusiastic leadership, and FUN encourage and maintain participation; while dynamics such as embarrassment, failure, competition, boredom, regimentation, and injuries discourage participation.

17

STRESS

MARYLAND, 2000:
A 15-year-old girl kills herself as part of a suicide pact with her boyfriend.

SOME STATS

- Suicide is the third leading cause of death in children ages 10 to 19.
- In 1999, more teenagers and young adults died from suicide than from cancer, heart disease, AIDS, birth defects, stroke, and chronic lung disease combined.
- From 1980 to 1997, firearm-related suicides accounted for more than 6% of the increase in the overall rate of suicide among youths ages 15 to 19.
- The dramatic increase in the rate among persons aged 10 to 14 years underscores the urgent need for intensifying efforts to prevent suicide among persons in this age group.
- The prevalence of depression among adolescents ranges from 4.7% to 8.3%.
- As many as 1 in 10 children ages 6 through 12 experience depressive symptoms. Three to six million children suffer from depression.

Stress overload can cause your child to be withdrawn, depressed, and suicidal, and it can give him a number of physical ailments. It can also make him irritable, disobedient, and uncooperative. He can become aggressive and get into fights, and stress overload can propel him into drugs, alcohol, and delinquent behaviors such as truancy, stealing, and fire setting.

Adverse, harsh, or stressful living cause heightened nervous system activity, and can even alter the structure of the brain, especially for the young child. Brain chemicals can be affected for the long-term. A steady flow of stress chemicals in the brain changes the brain's system of response, leading to problems such as emotional shutdown, depression, intermittent impulsiveness, and acting out.

Stress is a part of everyday life for both you and your child. Some people love stress and are very productive under pressure. Others dread it and fall apart. Strange as it sounds, but it's a necessary part of life. Without the stress of everyday things, life would get pretty boring. You and your child would not have to deal with the everyday events that make you think, respond to problems, and grow. Too little stress can be as bad as too much stress, because constant boredom can make you feel sad and even depressed. The key to the balancing act is stress management.

WHAT IS STRESS?

Stress refers to both the situations that trigger physical and emotional reactions (STRESSORS), and the reactions themselves (STRESS RESPONSES). Stress also describes the physical and emotional state that accompanies the stress response.

Stress is a natural bodily function in response to a real or perceived threat, leading to quick reaction—fight or flight. Any disrupting activity or event can be stressful—traffic jams, waiting in lines, juggling career and family, even positive events such as graduations, weddings, and the birth of a child. Whatever the trigger, a cascade of physical and emotional responses follows.

The nervous and endocrine systems are responsible for the body's physical response to stress. The autonomic nervous system contains two parts, the parasympathetic and sympathetic divisions. The parasympathetic division is in charge while you're relaxed, controlling digestion, breathing, heart rate, blood pressure, and hundreds of other activities. The sympathetic division activates during emergencies, and targets several organs including blood vessels, muscles, and sweat glands. The sympathetic system commands your body to stop storing energy and to start using it in response to stressors. Thus, digestion stops, hearing increases, the bladder empties to release excess weight, the pupils dilate for better vision, the heart accelerates to increase blood flow to where it's needed, voluntary muscles contract to get ready for action, and the adrenal glands stimulate secretion of adrenaline (the "fear hormone") and noradrenaline (the "anger hormone") to create changes that boost energy.

Emotional responses to stress vary from person to person. Some people respond well to stressors by talking, laughing, exercising, meditating, or problem solving. Others respond poorly by developing physical symptoms, or by reacting inappropriately and using such behaviors as aggressively acting out or using substances.

RESILIENT CHILDREN

Some children withstand an onslaught of stressors. No matter what happens, they bounce back in the face of stressful events and situations. These children tend to have specific characteristics:

- They have a loving relationship with at least one adult, and connections with adults outside the family.
- They believe in their own effectiveness, and that they are lovable and worthwhile.
- They can solve problems effectively.
- They believe that they have the ability to make things better for themselves.
- They have spiritual resources.

SIGNS OF STRESS

Chronic stress leads to feelings of being "stressed out" or "burned out." Stress may not be easy to recognize because it often affects the body, leading you to believe that your child is ill rather than stressed-out.

Signs of chronic stress include:

- headaches, backaches, chest pain, stomachaches, indigestion, nausea, or diarrhea
- rashes
- overeating or undereating
- sleep disturbances (too much sleep, restless sleep, difficulty falling asleep, difficulty staying asleep, waking up early)
- twitching
- having trouble concentrating or with schoolwork
- feeling anxious or worried
- feeling inadequate, frustrated, helpless, or overwhelmed
- feeling bored or dissatisfied
- feeling pressured, tense, irritable, angry, or hostile
- aggressive behavior
- substance abuse
- excessive or inappropriate crying
- avoiding others

CHILDREN'S STRESSORS

Childhood is full of stressors, including developmental stressors such as toilet training, the first day of school, and puberty; and situational stressors, such as moving and going to a new school. The way your child copes with these stressors can affect his development and the way he handles subsequent life events. Coping mechanisms vary, depending on your child's developmental level, helpful resources, situation, style, and previous experience with stressful events.

Stress affects children as it does adults. Children have a variety of innate and acquired coping skills or strategies, including positive ones such as questioning, talking to a friend, crying, using humor and playing; and not-so-positive ones such as yelling and throwing a tantrum. Children must learn to cope with fear, a normal emotional reaction to a specific real or perceived danger. Children perceive this hazard to be larger than themselves and thus a threat. Most childhood fears are limited and outgrown. Some fears are realistic and persist into adulthood, such as fear of physical danger and bodily harm.

Some stressors are universal to all children; others are age-specific. Illness and hospitalization are stressful to all children, regardless of age. Exposure to violence—in the family, in the community, or in the media—places significant stress on children of all ages. Discover the stressors that can affect your child so that you can minimize their effect.

TODDLERS

It's hard to believe that young children experience stress. But the normal demands of growing up, together with the pressures most families experience disallow a stress-free existence for most young children. Little stressors are beneficial because they teach toddlers to cope, but excessive stress is harmful, and your toddler is especially vulnerable because of his limited coping abilities.

Sources of stress for your toddler:

- Fear of losing his newly-developed skills
- Having his rituals taken away; change in daily structure or disruption of family routines
- Separation from parents or parental loss (divorce, death, jail)
- New sibling

- Strangers
- Bedtime (can be viewed as separation from parents)
- Loss of security object (favorite blanket, doll)
- Overstimulation (too much commotion at once, such as a family reunion)

Your toddler may cope with stress by using infantile motor activities (rocking, restlessness, changing positions to move away from stressor) until he begins to use other strategies, such as play. Play serves as a stress relief method for toddlers. He can get out his frustrations and anxieties by banging on drums, working with a play hammer and nails, or molding clay dough. Your toddler will also hug his favorite toy, throw tantrums, suck his thumb, and even withdraw and become quiet.

PRESCHOOLERS

Due to the magical thinking during this stage, your preschooler faces many unique stressors. Some are due to his own distinctive understanding of the world, such as his fears; others are imposed, including preschool.

Preschool stressors include:

- Separation from parents creates less stress than it did when he was a toddler, but it still persists, and seems to increase for a while around age 6.
- Being mocked or insulted by others. Despite the fact that he may like to insult others to boost his own self-image, your preschooler doesn't like to be on the receiving end of such comments.
- Having his questions go unanswered. Your enterprising preschooler asks constant questions, especially, "why?" and he easily becomes upset if you don't respond or know the answer.
- Decreased attention. Your preschooler likes to talk, and he can become frustrated if ignored or put off.
- Your preschooler may attempt to handle stress in a variety of ways, including occasionally lapsing into babyish behaviors such as thumb-sucking or bed-wetting. He may also develop unsightly nervous habits such as nail-biting, hair-pulling, nose-picking, or masturbation.

SCHOOL-AGE CHILDREN

Today's school-age child has more stressors than ever, and your child is no exception. He's pressured by friends to be like them and do what they do, and by you to excel in school and extracurricular activities. Extracurricular activities (sports, clubs, scouts, dance classes, karate) themselves can be stressful, especially if they take up much of his free time. Being out in the world more than when he was younger exposes him to more violence. The school environment creates stress to his self-image as he competes for grades and teacher recognition, and he's probably worried about being asked to smoke cigarettes, drink alcohol, take drugs, or steal.

Your child may be pressured to think, feel, and behave at a level of maturity far beyond what should be expected of him. He may have adult responsibilities, like watching young siblings or cooking meals, or he may be making decisions that he's not really capable of making. Your child may even have little time for being a child and enjoying the spontaneous activities of childhood.

General sources of stress for school-aged children are:

Starting school. This may be his first experience with being away from home all day. He may be fearful of getting lost or making an embarrassing social mistake. Help him cope by being there that first day, and showing him the ropes.

Long vacations mean extended time away from peers. Friends are important at this age, and your child may fear losing them by his absence. Minimize this by allowing him to keep in touch with postcards or e-mail.

Moving signifies changes in both school and peer group, both very stressful. He will need to adjust to both losing old friends and making new ones.

Change in family structure (divorce, remarriage) is an all too common stressor. Your child's ability to cope depends on a number of factors.

Christmas. Believe it or not, Christmas is just as much a stressor for children as it's for you.

Puberty. Preteens, especially girls, may become self-conscious regarding obvious signs of sexual development.

Your school-age child uses a number of coping mechanisms to deal with stress. Some of these are unconscious, such as denial and reaction formation. Denial temporarily allows your child to deny that the stressor occurred in the first place. Reaction formation allows him to act or say the opposite of how he actually feels. For example, if your child is afraid, he may say something like, "I'm not afraid of anything. I'm the bravest one in this whole room." These mechanisms are healthy and normal, but help your child learn more age-appropriate coping mechanisms, such as communication and problem solving when he's ready.

ADOLESCENTS

Adolescence itself is stressful because of all its physical and psychological changes. Add the stresses of relationships, school, competition, and the uncertainty of what lies ahead. Your teen also needs to become less dependent on you and learn to make his own decisions.

Sources of adolescent stress:

- Pregnancy
- Peer loss
- Breakup with boy/girl friend
- Parental loss (divorce, death, jail), or death of other loved one
- School demands or frustrations
- Changes in his body and/or negative thoughts or feelings about himself
- Having too many activities or having too high expectations

Adolescents have a variety of coping mechanisms. One is cognitive mastery, whereby the teenager attempts to learn as much as possible about the situation. They can then use their problem-solving skills to work through the situation. By using conformity, your teen attempts to mirror the actions and appearance of his friends. Controlling behavior allows him to be in charge of some aspects of his life, and he won't accept parental or school rules without questioning them. Young teens use fantasy, and teens of all ages rely on motor activities, such as sports, dancing, or other high-energy activities—all very effective tension-relieving strategies.

Adolescents may react negatively to stress by acting out, blaming others for their mistakes or problems, or by using drugs and alcohol. Therefore, it's helpful to teach your teens healthy stress management techniques before they feel overwhelmed by stress.

SIGNS OF STRESS IN KIDS

ALL AGES

Sleep problems
Changes in eating habits
Frequent colds

AGES 1 TO 5

Excessive clinging or crying
Regressed behavior (goes back to wanting his bottle)
Severe sensitivity to loud noises
Irritability
Trembling

AGES 5 TO 12

Vague physical complaints
Refusal to go to school
Easily distractible
Poor school performance

AGES 12 TO 14

Isolates from family and friends
Feels sad or depressed
Aggression

AGES 14 TO 18

Same as ages 12 to 14
Antisocial behavior (fights, stealing)
Night fears

STRESS MANAGEMENT TECHNIQUES

HEALTHY LIFE STYLE

Your child can deal better with stress when he has proper nutrition, plenty of exercise, and adequate sleep and rest. A healthy diet gives your child the energy he needs to draw on when he's stressed. It also enhances feelings of self-control and self-esteem. Make sure he stays away from caffeine, which can make him jittery, irritable, and unable to sleep. You say your 10-year-old doesn't drink coffee or tea? Great, but caffeine is also found in chocolate, cola, and other soft drinks, and more than a thousand over-the-counter medications, including cough syrups.

The following daily food choices are recommended for healthy nutrition:

6 grain products (breads, cereals, rice, pasta, bagels)
3 vegetables
2 fruits
3 dairy products (milk, cheese, yogurt)
2-3 proteins (meats, legumes)
Limited number of fats and sweets; sweets are not to be eaten every day.

Exercise eases anxiety and leaves your child feeling more relaxed and energetic. Active children react less to stress and have a greater sense of wellness. So if your child is a couch potato, get him up and moving. Let him walk or bike safe distances; don't drive him. Encourage outdoor activities instead of TV watching or Internet surfing. Plan family bike outings or hikes.

The lack of sleep can be both the cause and the effect of stress. If your child doesn't get adequate sleep, his mental and physical processes deteriorate, leaving him with headaches, forgetfulness, the inability to concentrate, and irritability. Ample sleep improves his mood, fosters his feeling of competence, and provides him with optimal mental and physical functioning. To prevent or stop sleep problems, set regular bedtimes and provide a consistent, soothing bedtime routine such as reading. If he's still sleepy, make his bedtime earlier.

Teens need more sleep than school-age children. During this period, rapid growth, overexertion in activities, and a tendency to stay up late commonly interfere with sleep and rest requirements. In an attempt to "catch up" on missed sleep, your teenager may sleep late at every opportunity. Help your teen develop a steady sleep schedule that includes brief afternoon naps if necessary. Discourage sleeping more than two extra hours over the weekend. Staying in bed until the afternoon is equivalent to jet lag, leaving him even more sluggish and more likely to not be able to fall asleep the next night.

SUPPORT

Your child needs to share his joys, fears, and frustrations. It's crucial for him to experience a secure parent-child relationship. This, along with a sense of worth and lovableness, serves as a foundation for effective coping. Talk with him and provide the support he needs. Despite all his protests, he still needs and wants your love, attention, and support.

Encourage him to develop a strong friendship network, especially in his teens. Friends are vital to your teenager, who needs friends who he can count on for emotional support, feedback, and caring. Doing something with people he enjoys is a great way to help him refocus, and he will realize that his friends have many of the same stressors that he has. Together they can come up with a variety of ways to beat stress.

TIME MANAGEMENT

Time crunches create stress for almost everyone, including children whose lives are busier than ever. Your child may feel that he never has enough time to do all the things he has to do, causing him to feel overwhelmed. Learning time management is critical to managing day-to-day stress:

Set priorities. If your child is over-booked with schoolwork, clubs, sports, family responsibilities, and other time consumers, have him prioritize them into three groups: essential, important, and trivial. Then have him focus on the first two groups and ignore the third.

Break up long-term goals into short ones, and write them down. Have your child break up large homework assignments, such as papers, reports, and projects, into small, manageable chunks, then write down what he has to do.

Keep a calendar. Using a pocket or wall calendar, have your child keep track of all his assignments, extracurricular activities, family responsibilities, and social activities. Use different color inks for each category of activity for easier tracking. Once you create the calendar, study it to see if it's realistic. Can all these activities be done in their allotted time-frames, and still allow for personal time, relaxation, and "the-unexpected-and-time-consuming-stuff-that-just-happens"? If not, you both may need to rethink the schedule or discontinue some activities.

Allow time each day for all that unexpected-and-time-consuming-stuff-that-just-happens. Mistakes, interruptions, and unanticipated events always happens at the worst possible moment. Plan extra time so that your child will have time to deal with the unexpected.

Encourage your child to visualize his goals. Have him "see" the finished paper or project in his mind. Mental rehearsals enable children to reach their goals more smoothly.

Discourage procrastination. Have him do unpleasant tasks first and get them out of the way. Then let him work on the project he enjoys. It helps to analyze why your child procrastinates. If he hates tidying up his room, help him find ways to make it more pleasant. Perhaps he and his friends can join together to have cleaning parties at each others' homes to help clean each others' rooms.

Tell him it's okay to say "no". Some children find it difficult to turn down opportunities or friends. Let him know that he doesn't have to please everybody or do everything. And be a good role model by learning to say "no" yourself.

Encourage him to take breaks. Let him have a breather in between tasks and every 20 minutes when doing homework.

HUMOR

Laughter is the best medicine, even for children. Laughter defuses anger, increases alertness, decreases depression, improves mental health, and may even prevent disease. A hearty chuckle elevates the heart rate, aids digestion, eases pain, and releases endorphins, the pain-inhibiting brain hormones. Once a good laugh is over, your muscles relax and your pulse and blood pressure dip below normal. You're relaxed.

Humor is a great way to cope with stress—it's hard to hurt when you smile. But today's children are so busy growing up that they have little time for laughter. Foster play for the sake of playing and having fun, not competition. Play with them, and be silly. Wear clown noses or crazy hats; watch a funny movie together. Cartoons really can be therapeutic. Let Bugs Bunny or the Muppet Babies take his mind off hurting. Have a funny-face-making contest so he can win a tempting treat. Share jokes. Blow magic bubbles and let the aches sail away. Smile when you feel tense or down, and encourage your children to do the same.

HOBBIES AND EXTRACURRICULAR ACTIVITIES

Hobbies, clubs, sports, scouts, and other activities are great stress-busters. When your child is busy and feeling a sense of accomplishment, he's on his way to dealing with stress. Activities can be done solo, with friends, or with a large group of people, just as long as the goal is to be involved in something he likes that will relieve tension. Remember, the activity should relieve stress, not cause it.

Need ideas? How about after-school clubs, Girl or Boy Scouts, 4H Clubs, and school or local sports clubs. Older children and teens enjoy hobbies and collections, such as the traditional stamp, doll, card, and coin collecting, or the more unique Pez dispenser, bottle cap, or rock collections. Check to see if your church or synagogue has youth activities. Encourage volunteering to both relieve stress and help others. Last but not least, foster old-fashioned activities such as knitting, needlework, woodwork, and pet care.

EXERCISE

Regular exercise not only prevents stress, it also helps manage it. Exercise helps your body to release endorphins, giving you a feeling of calmness and well-being. The body releases endorphins both during and after exercise, helping to relieve stress for a while. Vigorous activity helps release muscle tension, making it a natural outlet when your child's body is in a "fight or flight" state of response.

Encourage moderate, low-intensity, and aerobic exercises. Aerobic exercise involves sustained large muscle group activity and requires deep breathing, which in itself can reduce stress. Examples include running, swimming, bicycling, brisk walking, and cross-country skiing. Moderate, low activity exercises are less vigorous than aerobic ones, but they still relieve stress while adding to strength and flexibility. Low-intensity exercises may be best as starters if your child has been a couch potato.

RELAXATION TECHNIQUES

Useful in reducing the endocrine effects of chronic stress, relaxation techniques can decrease the stress response and elicit the relaxation response. Identified by Herbert Benson of the Harvard Medical School, the relaxation response is a state characterized by a feeling of warmth and quiet mental alertness. Relaxation techniques slow the heart rate and blood pressure, slow metabolism, and increase the blood flow to the brain and skin. They need to be practiced regularly, until your child feels comfortable with them. He should feel relaxed and refreshed after each session. If one technique doesn't work after he's used it for a reasonable period, try another.

Relaxation requires cooperation, so set the mood with easy listening music. Small children can cuddle a favorite soft toy while being rocked gently. Older children can use deep breathing and muscle relaxation techniques.

For deep breathing, have your child close his eyes or look at an appealing item such as a toy or poster. Then have him take slow deep breaths in and out in a rhythmic manner. You may want to count out loud to keep him focused on the breaths instead of the stress.

Your child can learn progressive muscle relaxation if you treat it as a game. He could become the Amazing Shrinking Hero, who shrinks his body bit by bit to squeeze into tiny places to save the world. Your hero gets to rest after his hard work by letting his muscles relax back to normal size. Any game will do as long as it uses the techniques that result in relaxation:

- Start with a comforting environment—quiet, or soft music.
- Have your child lie on his back. Tell him to feel relaxed.
- Ask him to tighten one specific group of muscles (a hand, his face, a foot, etc.) for about five seconds.
- Now tell him to relax that muscle group and think about how it feels.
- Continue this process until all muscle groups have been relaxed.
- Make sure that he's in a well-supported, comfortable position. He may prefer to keep his eyes open through the whole process. He probably doesn't want to miss anything.
- Guided imagery uses your child's natural imagination and experiences to allow him to concentrate on one or more mental images instead of the pain. It works best when incorporating as many of the five sense as possible, and can even be used for imaginative tots.
- Imagery should be fun. Allow your child to dream up his own images, real or imagined. He can be the center of attention as everyone stops to admire his sand castle on the beach. Or he

could be the brave scientist who destroys the bad germs that make people sick. If your child can't come up with any images, help him by talking about his favorite things–hero, TV show, story, sport, vacation, pet, holiday, or season. You can also ask him to make three wishes and then guide him through one or all of them.

OTHER STRESS BUSTERS

Encourage him to cuddle with a pet. Pets offer unconditional love and companionship. They can lift and soothe your child's spirits, and they can lower his stress response.

Tell him to listen to music.

Let him draw.

Inspire him to write.

Allow him to talk it out. Don't force him, but give him the opportunity.

Discourage the use of tobacco, alcohol, or drugs.

Help him to replace negative thoughts with positive ones. Instead of saying, "I'm stupid," say, "We all make mistakes."

MOOD DISORDERS

The most common mood disorders found in children and adolescents are major depressive disorder, reactive depression, dysthymic disorder, and bipolar disorder. Mood disorders such as depression increase the risk for suicide, which reaches its peak during the adolescent years. About two-thirds of children and adolescents with depression also have another mental health disorder, such as an anxiety disorder, a disruptive or antisocial disorder, an eating disorder, or a substance abuse disorder.

MAJOR DEPRESSIVE DISORDER

Major depression is a serious condition that is characterized by one or more major depressive episodes, that last an average of 7 to 9 months, and that has many features similar to adults. These kids become sad, losing interest in the activities that please them most. They criticize themselves and believe that others criticize them. They feel pessimistic, helpless, and unloved. They experience difficulty making decisions, have trouble concentrating, and may neglect their appearance and hygiene. Feelings of hopelessness can arise and evolve into thoughts or actions of suicide.

Depressed children and teens often act irritable and some-times become aggressive. Some teens feel a surge of energy, occupying every minute of their day with activity to avoid their depression. Depressed youths may become anxious and have separation fears, and they may have somatic complaints, like headaches, stomachaches, and other aches and pains.

REACTIVE DEPRESSION

Also know as adjustment disorder with depressed mood, this is the most common form of depression in children and teens. Their depression is usually short-lived and results as a response to an adverse experience, such as rejection, a slight, a letdown, or a loss. Thus, children can develop reactive depression to divorce, moving, a death, or changing schools.

DYSTHYMIC DISORDER

Dysthymia is similar to major depression with fewer symptoms and a more chronic course. Because of its persistent nature, dysthymia tends to interfere with normal development. The child feels depressed for most of the day, on most days, and for several years, with an average duration of four years. Some are depressed for so long, they don't recognize their state as abnormal, and thus don't complain of being depressed.

Characteristics of dysthymia include low energy or fatigue, changes in eating and/or sleeping patterns (too much or too little of either), poor concentration, and hopelessness. About 70% of dysthymic children eventually experience an episode of major depression.

BIPOLAR DISORDER

Also called manic-depressive disorder, bipolar disorder demonstrates episodes of depression and mania, with depression usually occurring first. The manic stage may not appear for months or years after a symptom-free period. Mania may be expressed with unusual energy, poor judgment, euphoria, and feelings of grandiosity, or it my appear with irritability and aggression. They are overconfident, and they talk rapidly, loudly, and a lot. They can't sleep, rarely eat, feel like their thoughts are racing, and do things quickly in a creative but chaotic, disorganized manner. Some may experience delusions of great self-importance, engaging in risky behavior, such as careless sex or fast driving.

SUICIDE

Although somewhat unusual in younger children, suicide isn't uncommon in teenagers. As a matter of fact, it's the third leading cause of death in people ages 15 to 24, and rates for younger teens are rising. Females attempt suicide more often than males, but males are more successful in actually committing suicide, because they use more lethal weapons.

Most victims of suicide have a psychiatric illness, particularly major depression or bipolar disorder. Other victims frequently have severe anxiety, exhibited violent and impulsive behavior, have no plans for the future, or are deficient in social skills. Most attempted suicides and completed suicides are preceded by a precipitant, such as a relationship break-up, family or school violence, rejection, sexual abuse, pregnancy, or a sexually transmitted disease. Drugs and alcohol play a key role in suicide, as do exposure to suicide in family or friends and availability of weapons. "Copycat" suicides remain common among teenagers, especially vulnerable ones.

Your child is at increased risk for suicide if he fits any of the following risk factors. If any of these apply to your child, talk to your child's health care provider:

- Previous suicide attempts (risk is greater if happened in past 3 months)
- Psychiatric disorder
- Family member with mood disorder or suicide attempt or success
- Child or family member has substance abuse problem
- Family discord
- Impulsiveness
- Hostility
- Poor social skills
- School problems, including truancy
- Romantic break-up
- Homosexual or bisexual preference

Bring him to an emergency facility immediately for any of these:

Stating he wants to hurt or kill himself
Any suicide plan

Irrational speech
Sudden alienation from family
Sudden interest or loss of interest in religion
Taking unnecessary risks
Hears voices or sees visions
Drug and alcohol abuse
Giving away his possessions
Writing notes or poems about death
Preoccupation with death-themed music, movies, art, or video
    games
Feelings of hopelessness
Statements like, "You won't have to worry about me any
    more."

Mood disorders can be successfully treated with therapy or medication. If you suspect that your child may have a mood disorder, call your health care provider or contact a mental health service near you. You should be able to locate one in the blue pages of your phone book.

18

TERRORISM

SEPTEMBER 11, 2001:
More than 3,000 people died in the terrorist attacks on New York, Washington, and Pennsylvania.

SOME STATS

- April 19, 1995: 168 men, women, and children were killed in the bombing of the Murrah Federal Building in downtown Oklahoma City.
- January 17, 2003: 5 children were attacked in their home in Bremerton, WA.
- October, 2002: A 13-year-old boy is shot by the DC sniper in Bowie, MD.
- 1995: The FBI uncovers a terrorist effort to release a chlorine gas bomb in the Disneyland theme park in California. That same year, the nerve agent sarin injures 5,000 people in Tokyo, killing 12.

The events of September 11, 2001 left us with a painful sense of vulnerability about our homeland security. Efforts continue to lessen this vulnerability to future assaults, but our country very well may not be able to completely eliminate the possibility of another terrorist attack. Therefore, you need to take steps to minimize the impact of potential disaster on your children, particularly if you're a military family—get prepared, arm yourself with the facts, minimize what your kids see on TV, and help your children feel safe. Military parents also need to deal with separation issues, and possibly parental loss.

GET PREPARED

Create a family disaster plan and kit as suggested in Chapter 29.

Pay attention to the Homeland Security Advisory System. This system contains five threat conditions, each identified by a description and corresponding color:

SEVERE (RED)
Severe risk of terrorist attack
HIGH (ORANGE)
High risk of terrorist attack
ELEVATED (YELLOW)
Significant risk of terrorist attack
GUARDED (BLUE)
General risk of terrorist attack
LOW (GREEN)
Low risk of terrorist attack

The higher the threat condition, the greater the risk of a terrorist attack. Risk includes both the probability of an attack occurring and its potential gravity. Threat conditions are assigned by the Attorney General in consultation with the Assistant to the President for Homeland Security. Threat conditions may be assigned for the entire nation, or they may be set for a particular geographic area or industrial sector. Assigned threat conditions are reviewed at regular intervals to determine whether adjustments are warranted.

UNDERSTAND THE POTENTIAL AGENTS OF MASS DESTRUCTION

It seems that for every wonder of science there is an equal measure of destruction. Millions of years, millions of battles, yet we never learn. We have gone from fists, to swords, to guns, to bombs, to weapons of mass destruction–biological, chemical, nuclear, and radiological devices. Yet, chemical and biological agents are nothing new. The Chinese used arsenic smoke as early as 1000 B.C., and in 1495 A.D., the Spanish offered wine spiked with the blood of leprosy patients to the French near Naples.

According to the Centers for Disease Control and Prevention (CDC), one of the most imminent terrorist threats is the use of biological or chemical weapons. Agents that were produced for war are increasingly being sought by civilian groups who seek revenge, publicity, reaction, and chaos.

BIOLOGICAL AGENTS

Biological weapons can be aerosolized so that they can be easily spread into the air and inhaled by humans. They can also be put into water or food, where they would be ingested. Many can also cause harm if they contact human skin.

The Centers for Disease Control and Prevention (CDC) divides biological agents into categories according to their threat to national security. This information is current as of April, 2003. To update the information, go to http://www.bt.cdc.gov/Agent/agent list.asp.

The present categories are:

Category A agents (Anthrax, Smallpox, Botulism, Plague, Tularemia, Viral hemorrhagic fevers). High-priority agents include organisms that pose a risk to national security because they:
Are easily spread or transmitted from person to person
Result in high death rates and have the potential for major public health impact
Might cause public panic and social disruption
Require special action for public health preparedness

Category B agents (Food poisoning, Brucellosis, Ricin, Viral encephalitis). Second highest priority agents include those that:
Are moderately easy to spread or transmit from person to per son
Result in moderate public health impact and low death rates
Require enhancements of the CDC's diagnostic and disease surveillance abilities

Category C agents (emerging infectious disease threats). Third highest priority agents that include emerging pathogens that could be engineered for mass distribution in the future because of:
Availability
Ease of production and distribution
Potential for high death and illness rates and major health impact.

CATEGORY A

ANTHRAX is an acute infectious disease caused by the bacterium *Bacillus anthracis*, which is naturally found in soil. The anthrax bacteria can form a protective coat around themselves called spores, and they can release poisonous substances into the bodies of infected people.

You and your children can't catch anthrax from each other or from another person. If someone were to put the bacteria that cause anthrax in your workplace on purpose, it's highly unlikely that you would carry the bacteria home to your children on your clothes or hair.

You and your children could come into contact with anthrax bacteria three ways. You can be exposed and infected by breathing in (inhaling) the bacteria, by coming into contact with the bacteria through cuts or abrasions in the skin, or by eating something that contains the bacteria (usually undercooked meat from an infected animal). The chance of coming into contact with the bacteria in any of these ways is very low. Also, our bodies have defenses against bacteria, so not everyone who comes into contact with the bacteria will become ill with anthrax.

There are three kinds of anthrax, all of which are treatable with antibiotics:

1. Skin (cutaneous) anthrax is the least serious form of the disease. The first symptom is a small, painless sore that develops into a blister. One or two days later, the blister develops a black scab in the center.
2. Gastrointestinal anthrax is more serious than skin anthrax, but is also the least common form. The initial symptoms are nausea, loss of appetite, and fever, followed by severe abdominal pain.
3. Inhalational anthrax is the most serious form of the disease. It begins with symptoms similar to those for a cold or the flu. If caught early, inhalation anthrax can be treated successfully with antibiotics. If it's not caught early, and more serious symptoms develop, inhalation anthrax usually results in death. Almost all cold and flu symptoms are not anthrax.

The signs and symptoms of anthrax infection in children older than 2 months of age are similar to those in adults. The illness affects children and adults in much the same way, though children may be more likely to suffer side effects from some of the antibiotics used to prevent or treat the disease.

You may be tempted to ask your doctor for a supply of antibiotics to keep on hand, but neither the CDC nor the American Academy of Pediatrics recommends doing so. You should not obtain antibiotics for your children unless public health authorities have confirmed that it's likely that your children have come into contact with the bacteria that cause anthrax. Giving your children antibiotics when the antibiotics are not needed may do more harm than good. Many antibiotics have serious side effects in children, and using antibiotics when not needed may lead to drug-resistant forms of bacteria that won't respond to antibiotics when your child develops the ear, sinus, or other infections that children frequently develop.

Currently, there is no anthrax vaccine for children. The anthrax vaccine used for adults has not been studied in children, and isn't recommended for people younger than 18. It's presently available only for the military, although public health officials are considering its use for people in other high-risk professions.

The chances of your children coming into contact with anthrax bacteria are extremely low. However, if public health officials confirm or suspect that you or your children have come into contact with anthrax, your health care provider will prescribe antibiotics to keep you and your children from developing anthrax.

Early treatment of anthrax in children is critical, so call your health care provider immediately with any questions or concerns.

SMALLPOX is a serious, contagious, and sometimes fatal infectious disease that comes in two forms: major and minor. The major form is the severe and most common form of smallpox, with a more extensive rash and higher fever. Historically, the major form has an overall fatality rate of about 30%. The minor form is a less common presentation of smallpox, and a much less severe disease, with death rates of 1% or less.

Symptoms usually don't begin until about 12 days after exposure to the virus. At first, it's like the flu—causing an under-the-weather feeling of fever, nausea, vomiting, headache, and backache. Then, severe abdominal pain and disorientation can set in, as small, round sores erupt all over the skin. About 30% of people who become infected will die, and survivors can be left with permanent scars.

Vaccination can prevent smallpox infection. However, in January of 2003 the American Academy of Pediatrics (AAP) testified before Congress that, given the information currently available, the general public, particularly children, should not receive the vaccine prior to an outbreak. The AAP also called for further testing to ensure that the smallpox vaccine is tested for use in children, similar to the testing used for other childhood vaccines.

BOTULISM is a rare, muscle-paralyzing disease caused by a toxin made by a bacterium called *Clostridium botulinum*. It's not spread from one person to another. Three types of botulism have been identified:

1. Foodborne botulism occurs when someone ingests preformed toxin that leads to illness within a few hours to days. Foodborne botulism is a public health emergency because the contaminated food may still be available to other people besides the patient. Food botulism is the reason you need to be very careful when home-canning foods.
2. Infant botulism, the most common form in the U.S., occurs in a small number of susceptible infants each year who harbor *C. botulinum* in their intestinal tract. This is why you should not give honey to babies.
3. Wound botulism occurs when wounds are infected with *C. botulinum* that secretes the toxin.

Symptoms of botulism include blurred vision, drooping eyelids, slurred speech, difficulty swallowing, dry mouth, and muscle weakness that always descends through the body, starting at the shoulders and working down to the legs. Paralysis of breathing muscles can cause a person to stop breathing and die, unless assisted with mechanical ventilation (breathing). Infants with botulism appear sluggish, feed poorly, become constipated, and have a weak cry and poor muscle tone.

The CDC maintains a supply of botulism antitoxin, which is effective in reducing the severity of symptoms if administered early in the course of the disease. Most patients eventually recover after weeks to months of supportive care.

PLAGUE is a disease caused by the bacterium *Yersinia pestis,* which is found in rodents and their fleas in many areas around the world. Used in an aerosol attack, this bacterium could cause the pneumonic form of plague, which is contagious from person to person via close contact. Because there is a delay between the time of exposure to the bacteria and becoming sick, people could travel over a large area before becoming contagious and possibly infecting others, making disease control more difficult. Unfortunately, the making of biological weapons with this bacteria is possible because it occurs in nature, and can be grown in a laboratory by people with advanced knowledge and technology.

Pneumonic plague differs from bubonic plague, even though both are caused by *Yersinia pestis*, because they have different modes of transmission and symptoms.

Pneumonic plague can transmit from person to person; bubonic plague can't. Pneumonic plague affects the lungs and is transmitted when a person breathes the organism in the air. Bubonic plague is transmitted through the bite of an infected flea or through exposure to infected material in a break in the skin. Symptoms of bubonic plague include swollen, tender lymph glands called buboes. These buboes are not present in pneumonic plague. However, if bubonic plague goes untreated, the bacteria can infect the lungs, causing a secondary case of pneumonic plague.

People with pneumonic plague usually become ill within 1 to 6 days with fever, weakness, and rapidly developing pneumonia with shortness of breath, chest pain, cough, and occasionally bloody or watery sputum. Nausea, vomiting, and abdominal pain may occur. Without early treatment, pneumonic plague can lead to respiratory failure, shock, and rapid death.

To prevent a high risk of death, an infected person needs to receive antibiotics within 24 hours of the first symptoms. Several types of antibiotics are effective for curing the disease and for preventing pneumonic plague. People who experience close contact with an infected person can greatly reduce their chance of becoming sick by beginning treatment within seven days of their exposure. Treatment consists of taking antibiotics for at least seven days.

TULAREMIA is caused by the bacterium, *Francisella tularensis*, found in animals, especially rodents, rabbits, and hares. Humans can contract tularemia different ways: through the bite of an infected insect, handling infected animal carcasses, eating or drinking contaminated food or water, or breathing in the bacteria.

Symptoms of tularemia usually appear 3 to 5 days after exposure and include sudden fever, chills, headaches, muscle aches, joint pain, dry cough, progressive weakness, and pneumonia. Persons with pneumonia can develop chest pain and bloody spit, and can have trouble breathing or even sometimes stop breathing. Other symptoms of tularemia depend on how a person was exposed and can include ulcers on the skin or mouth, swollen and painful lymph glands, swollen and painful eyes, and a sore throat.

Tularemia doesn't spread from person to person. However, people who have been exposed to the bacteria should be treated as soon as possible, because the disease can be fatal if it's not treated with the appropriate antibiotics. There is no vaccine currently available in the U.S. for tularemia, but the FDA is reviewing one.

VIRAL HEMORRHAGIC FEVERS (VHFs) refer to a group of illnesses that are caused by several distinct families of viruses, such as the *Ebola* and *Marburg* viruses. The term "viral hemorrhagic fever" is used to describe a severe multisystem syndrome (multisystem in that multiple organ systems in the body are affected). Characteristically, the overall vascular (blood) system is damaged, and the body's ability to regulate itself is impaired. These symptoms are often accompanied by bleeding, which by itself is rarely life-threatening. While some types of hemorrhagic fever viruses can cause relatively mild illnesses, many of these viruses cause severe, life-threatening disease. Some of these viruses, including *Ebola* and *Marburg*, can be spread from person to person.

For the most part, no specific treatment exists for these viruses. Affected persons are treated symptomatically. Vaccines exist for yellow and Argentine hemorrhagic fevers, but not for the others as of yet.

CATEGORY B

FOOD POISONING occurs when a person eats foods contaminated by harmful organisms, such as bacteria, parasites, or viruses. Symptoms of food poisoning typically include nausea, vomiting, and diarrhea. Botulism can be a type of food poisoning, but most people are more aware of poisonings by the bacteria *E. coli* and *Salmonella*. Other organisms include *Shigella, Campylobacter* and *Staphylococcus*. Most cases of food poisoning are mild, but salmonella can be severe enough to warrant hospitalization, and both botulism and E. coli can be life-threatening.

Treatment usually consists of treating the complications, primarily dehydration, which requires replacement of fluids and electrolytes (body salts). Young children can become dehydrated very quickly, and they may require intravenous fluids. Antidiarrheal medication isn't usually recommended, because it may make the illness worse by trapping the toxins in the body. Similarly, antibiotics are not recommended unless the illness is severe. Food poisoning from *Campylobacter* is an exception, and the American Academy of Pediatrics recommends that this be treated with an antibiotic to decrease the duration of illness.

Food poisoning occurs regularly in the U.S. due to the improper handling of food. To minimize the chance of your family developing food poisoning, the United States Department of Agriculture recommends the following:

- Wash your hands and food surfaces frequently.
- When shopping, preparing, and storing foods, separate raw, cooked, and ready-to-eat items.
- Refrigerate perishables promptly.
- Carefully follow directions on food labels.
- Cook foods to a safe temperature.
- Serve safely.
- When in doubt, throw it out!

BRUCELLOSIS affects livestock but may be transmitted to humans. Caused by one of four different species of the bacteria that belong to the genus *Brucella*, Brucellosis is rare in the United States but common elsewhere in the world. Early infection may result in flu-like symptoms including fever, headache, loss of appetite, muscle pain, and severe night sweats. The illness may occur suddenly, or gradually over a period of months. If left untreated, the disease may take months to resolve once appropriate therapy is begun.

Brucellosis may be restricted to a certain area of the body, or have serious widespread complications that affect the central nervous system, spine, and other body organs. The disease can be prevented if people drink only pasteurized milk, because pasteurization kills the bacteria that cause the disease. However, farmers and butchers may also be affected by brucellosis.

RICIN, which can also be considered a chemical weapon, is a poison made from the waste left over from processing castor beans, the beans used to make castor oil. A stable substance not very affect-ed by extreme heat or cold, ricin can be in the form of a powder, mist, or a pellet, or it can be dissolved in water or weak acid.

Accidental exposure to ricin is highly unlikely, as it would take a deliberate act to make ricin and use it to poison people. Poisoning can occur by breathing in ricin mist or powder, or by eating or drinking tainted food or water. Regardless of route, ricin poisoning isn't contagious and can't be spread from person to person.

Death from ricin poisoning can take place in 36 to 48 hours, regardless of exposure route. However, if a person survives longer than 5 days, she probably will not die. The symptoms and signs of ricin poisoning depend on the route:

1. Inhalation: within a few hours of inhaling significant amounts of ricin, a person would experience coughing, tightness in the chest, difficulty breathing, nausea, and aching muscles. Within the next few hours, the airways would become severely inflamed, excess fluid would build up in the lungs, breathing would become even more difficult, and the skin might turn blue.
2. Ingestion: if someone swallows a significant amount of ricin, she would have internal bleeding of the stomach and intestines that would result in vomiting and bloody diarrhea. Eventually, the person's liver, spleen, and kidneys might stop working, and the person could die.
3. Injection: injection of a lethal amount of ricin at first would cause the muscles and lymph nodes near the injection site to die. Eventually, the liver, kidneys, and spleen would stop working, and the person would have massive bleeding from the stomach and intestines. The person would die from multiple organ failure.

No antidote exists for ricin, and treatment consists solely of supportive care to minimize the effects of the poisoning.

VIRAL ENCEPHALITIS is a viral inflammation of the brain tissue that can be caused by a number of viruses, including measles, mumps, mono (Epstein-Barr) and herpes viruses. Other cases are caused by arboviruses and can be transmitted via mosquito and tick bites. Cases caused by mosquito bites usually occur during the summer and early fall when the insects are most active. Rabies can also cause an encephalitis that is almost always fatal if not treated before symptoms develop.

Encephalitis is serious and sometimes fatal. People tend to recover fully from the illness within a couple of weeks, but others, especially children and the elderly, may have permanent problems including seizures, memory loss, personality changes, or brain damage. The chance of death or permanent problems depend on a number of factors, such as the person's general condition, treatment, and the causative organism (e.g., herpes encephalitis is fatal 70 to 80% of the time if not treated promptly).

Symptoms of encephalitis include drowsiness, lack of energy, personality changes, trouble learning and understanding, memory loss, restlessness, confused speech, hallucinations, stiff neck and back, nausea and vomiting, photosensitivity (abnormal sensitivity to light in the eyes), seizures, tremors, and coma.

Encephalitis from the herpes or chicken pox viruses can be treated with intravenous acyclovir and antiviral medication. Early treatment is critical, as it can drop the chance of fatality to less than 30%. Arboviruses can't be destroyed with antivirals; therefore, treatment is symptomatic.

CHEMICAL AGENTS

Unfortunately, many chemical agents are easy to produce and don't need sophisticated missiles or delivery devices for dispersion. Unlike biological agents, these are capable of producing illness rapidly. Chemical agents caused over 1 million casualties in World War I; 90,000 of these were fatal. The recent wave of terrorism has made these weapons more known to the public.

Chemical agents are classified as follows: nerve agents, vesicants/blister agents, blood agents, choking agents, and caustics.

NERVE AGENTS

Nerve agents are absorbed through the skin or lungs via vapor or liquid exposure. They block a key enzyme, which allows a chemical buildup at key places in the nervous system, causing hyperactivity of muscles and organs, and can affect the eyes, nose, airways, gastrointestinal tract, muscles, and central nervous system (brain and spinal cord). Nerve agents act very quickly in vapor form; more slowly in liquid form.

SARIN (GB), **SOMAN** (GD), **TABUN** (GA) and **VX** are manufactured compounds. The G compounds are clear, colorless, and essentially tasteless, while VX is clear and amber-colored. GA has a slightly fruity odor, and GD has a slight camphor-like odor.

Nerve agents are highly toxic, even in small amounts, when ingested, inhaled, or absorbed through the skin or eyes. The initial effects vary according to the route of exposure and may not be present for up to 18 hours when these poisons are absorbed though the skin. Regardless of the exposure route, the signs of nerve agent exposure include runny nose, chest tightness, tiny pupils, trouble breathing, drooling and sweating, nausea and vomiting, abdominal cramps, involuntary bowel movement and urination, muscle twitching, confusion, convulsions, paralysis, coma, and death. Devastating effects occur within 1 to 10 minutes, and fatal effects can occur within 1 to 10 minutes for GA, GB, and GD, and within 4 to 18 hours for VX. Fatigue, irritability, nervousness, and memory defects may persist for as long as 6 weeks after recovery from an exposure episode. These agents are not listed as carcinogens, but it's unknown at this time if exposure to them can result in reproductive problems.

Antidotes, including atropine, are available for all of these gases.

VESICANTS/BLISTER AGENTS

Blister agents are either inhaled or absorbed through contact with skin. They affect the eyes, airways, skin, and gastrointestinal tract, and they cause large, often life-threatening blisters of the skin and mucous membranes that resemble burns.

MUSTARD AGENTS, the most common vesicants, cause injuries that heal much more slowly and are more susceptible to infection than other chemical burns. Mustard damages eyes and airways after contact, and the gastrointestinal tract and bone marrow (where immune system cells are produced) after high doses are absorbed. The effects are delayed, because it causes no pain on contact. There is no antidote to mustard poisoning. The victim's eyes should be flushed with water immediately. Bleach can decontaminate skin, and oxygen should be given if mustard was inhaled.

LIQUID LEWISITE smells like geraniums and is amber to dark brown in color. As a vesicant, it causes blisters but also can be toxic to the lungs and the whole body. When inhaled in high concentrations, it can kill in 10 minutes. The vapor form of Lewisite is also dangerous but less effective in humid conditions. Lewisite poisoning can be treated with an antidote (British Anti-Lewisite), if it's administered early after inhalation.

BLOOD AGENTS

Blood agents act by causing the victim to essentially suffocate, because they cause reactions in the bloodstream that result in a lack of oxygen. They are generally inhaled and distributed through the blood.

ARSINE is a flammable, colorless, and highly toxic gas that is nonirritating and produces no immediate symptoms. Thus, a person may be exposed to high levels without being aware of its presence. Inhalation is the major route of absorption and there is little known about absorption though the skin, although exposure to liquid arsine can cause frostbite. Initial symptoms of arsine exposure include not feeling well, headache, thirst, shivering, trouble breathing, and abdominal pain. These symptoms can be delayed up to 24 hours. Arsine combines with the blood's hemoglobin, causing the red blood cells to break down, resulting in severe anemia.

CYANIDE, probably the best known poison gas, is colorless and has a sharp, pepper-like odor. It interferes with the body's use of oxygen. Liquid forms of cyanide burn skin and eyes. Cyanide acts quickly, but is only deadly in large amounts, and it can be treated.

CHOKING AGENTS

Choking agents are inhaled and absorbed through lungs, creating irritation to the respiratory tract. This irritation causes fluid to build up in the lungs, effectively "drowning" the victim.

CHLORINE kills bacteria in public water systems and swimming pools, and it can kill people in high concentrations. Green-yellow in color with a bleach-like odor, chlorine was the first chemical weapon used effectively in war—during World War I. It irritates the eyes, nose, and respiratory tract, causing runny nose, coughing, choking, and chest pain. Fluid buildup in the lungs occurs several hours after exposure, which can lead to pneumonia.

AMMONIA is a colorless gas with a strong odor that is familiar to most people as a cleaning agent. This odor is a good thing, because you will probably be well aware of its presence before being exposed to a concentration that could harm you. However, low levels can harm people with asthma and other sensitivities. Slight exposure, similar to what happens when you spill ammonia on the floor, causes eye irritation and cough. Significant exposure, such as walking through a dense cloud of ammonia, would cause serious burns to the skin, eyes, mouth, throat, and lungs, that could result in permanent blindness, lung disease, and death.

PHOSGENE initially looks like fog, but then becomes colorless as it spreads. It may smell like newly-mown hay but with a poisonous, suffocating odor. Like other choking agents, phosgene causes fluid buildup in the lungs, but not until up to 48 hours after exposure. Inhalation can lead to irreversible lung damage such as scarring and emphysema. Phosgene can burn the eyes and cause severe damage to nose and throat. Victims need oxygen and eye flushing after exposure.

RADIATION

Radiation is a form of energy that comes from the sun, man-made sources such as X-ray machines, and from some radioactive materials such as uranium in soil. Small amounts of radioactive materials occur naturally in the air, water, and food we use, and in our own bodies.

The negative health effects of radiation exposure may not be seen for many years. These adverse health effects can range from mild effects, such as skin reddening, to serious effects such as cancer and death, depending on the amount of radiation absorbed by the body (the dose), the type of radiation, the route of exposure, and the length of time a person is exposed. Exposure to very large doses of radiation may cause death within a few days or months. Exposure to lower doses of radiation may lead to an increased risk of developing cancer or other adverse health effects.

"Dirty bombs," also called radiological dispersion devices, combine conventional explosives, such as dynamite, with radioactive materials. The goal of a dirty bomb is to blast radioactive material into the area around the explosion, possibly causing buildings and people to be exposed to radioactive material; however, the main purpose of a dirty bomb is to scare people and make buildings or land unusable for a long period of time. If low-level radioactive sources are used, the main danger from a dirty bomb is the blast itself. At the levels created by most probable sources, not enough radiation would be present in a dirty bomb to cause severe illness from exposure to radiation.

Should a nuclear attack occur, people may experience two types of exposure to radioactive material: external and internal. External exposure happens when radioactive material contacts a person's body, while internal exposure occurs when a person eats contaminated food or breathes contaminated air. Exposure to massive doses of external radiation can cause death within a few days or months. External exposure to lower doses and internal exposure may lead to health problems that range from mild skin reddening to severe effects such as cancer and death, depending on the amount of radiation absorbed by the body, the type of radiation, the route of exposure, and the length of time of the exposure.

Radiation sickness, or acute radiation sickness (ARS), occurs when the body receives a high dose of radiation, usually over a short period of time. Many survivors of the Hiroshima and Nagasaki atomic bombs of World War II, and many of the firefighters who first responded to the 1986 Chernobyl nuclear power plant disaster became ill with ARS. ARS occurs only if: the radiation dose is high; the radiation penetrates to internal organs; the entire body or most of it receives the dose of radiation; and the radiation is received in a short time, typically minutes. The chance of survival decreases with increasing radiation dose.

Initial symptoms of ARS are nausea, vomiting, and diarrhea that occur within minutes to days after the exposure, last for minutes to several days, and may come and go. The victim then may look and feel healthy for a short time, only to again become ill with fatigue, fever, loss of appetite, nausea, vomiting, diarrhea, and possibly even convulsions and coma. This stage can last from a few hours up to several months.

People with ARS usually also have hair loss and some skin damage (redness, swelling, and itching) that can develop within a few hours after exposure. As with the other symptoms, the skin symptoms may heal for a short time, only to return days or weeks later. Complete healing of the skin may take from several weeks up to a few years, depending on the radiation dose received.

EFFECTS OF MAN-MADE DISASTERS ON CHILDREN

Due to their developing minds and bodies, children are far more vulnerable to the effects of terrorism than adults. According to the American Academy of Pediatrics Policy on Chemical and Biological Terrorism and its Children, Terrorism and Disasters Toolkit:

1. Children are very vulnerable to aerosol agents because they breathe more times per minute than adults do, thus inhaling larger doses of the aerosolized chemical or biological agent.
2. Due to their size, children are closer to the ground where agents such as chlorine and sarin accumulate because they are heavier than air.
3. Children's skin is thinner than adults, and they have a larger surface-to-mass ratio, making them more susceptible to absorbing agents through their skin.
4. This larger body surface area also makes children more susceptible to heat loss when showered, thus skin decontamination with water can result in hypothermia (low body temperature) unless warming equipment it used.
5. Children have less fluid reserve than adults and dehydrate more quickly when they develop vomiting or diarrhea, effects of many biological and chemical agents, as well as radiation.
6. Children have smaller blood volumes than adults, making them quickly susceptible to shock from blood loss.
7. Children don't have the thinking or motor skills to escape the site of a terrorist incident.
8. Vesicants can cause greater injury to children because of their poor keratinization (skin thickening).
9. Children's reactions to terrorist attacks vary based on their developmental level and experience, and they are highly influenced by the emotional state of their caretakers. If the caretakers are emotionally devastated by the events around them, their children will likely be affected.
10. Children require different medication dosages and different sized equipment, which may create a problem in times of emergency.

HELPING YOUR CHILDREN TO FEEL SAFE

According to the National Center for Post-Traumatic Stress Disorder and studies on the effects of the Oklahoma City bombing by Pfefferbaum and Associates, children may display a wide range of emotional and physical reactions after a disaster. The more severe reactions are associated with: higher degrees of exposure, such as life threat, physical injury, witnessing injury or death; closer proximity to the disaster; a history of earlier traumas; poor parental response and parental psychological problems; knowing the person injured or killed; and viewing bomb-related media.

To help your children through these tough times of terrorism and war, try these suggestions from the National Association of Pediatric Nurse Practitioners' KySS Campaign, the American Academy of Pediatrics, and the National Center for Post-Traumatic Stress Disorder:

- First, take care of yourself. Your child depends on you to feel safe. If you're nervous or angry, she will pick up on your emotions and be affected by them.
- Help your child feel safe. Whenever possible, keep her in a familiar environment with people she's close to. Keep her routine as regular as possible. Let her know what the government if doing to keep the family safe.
- Ensure her that you're safe. Children fear losing their parents during wars and terrorist strikes. If you're a military parent, see the section below.
- Watch for signs of stress: irritable moods, sleep problems, nightmares and night terrors, appetite changes, withdrawal, repetitive acting out of traumatic event that interferes with normal activity, separation fears, headaches, stomachaches and other somatic complaints, aggression, school avoidance, accident-proneness, rebellion, or depression.
- Minimize her exposure to news reports of terrorism and war, especially for young children. It only reinforces the belief that the world is a very unsafe place. If your child does watch TV, watch it with her. If you can't watch with her, talk to her about what she sees.
- Be honest. Provide explanations that she can understand. Don't overwhelm young children with too much detail. It may be easier to talk to them through their dolls or stuffed toys.
- Giver her extra emotional support and reassurance. Allow her to talk about what happened, and encourage her to ask questions. Encourage her to draw her feelings with art work.
- Reassure young children that they did nothing wrong to cause the event—a common feeling of children under 6 when something bad happens.
- Let her know that her emotions are normal and that others feel the same way.
- Help her release anxiety through exercise and diversional activities. Ensure that she eats and sleeps properly. Healthy living is key to stress management.
- Use the situation as an opportunity to help her develop coping skills (prayer, listening to music, writing, drawing, etc.).

- Contact your health care provider if she exhibits signs of stress or has difficulty maintaining her routines.

CHILDREN OF MILITARY PARENTS

Military families face the challenges of frequent moves, changing schools, making new friends, and leaving old friends behind. Military parents need to deal with additional issues due to the possibility of deployment. Deployment causes separation, and having to explain this to a child is difficult. Families have to deal with not knowing if or when a parent will be sent overseas, where the parent will go, or if the parent will return. Returning home itself can be an additional stressor.

To help your child:

1. Assure her that she did nothing wrong to cause you to leave. Explain that it's part of your job to defend your country.
2. Maintain communication for as long as possible.
3. Leave something behind that your child can keep for you until you return, and make sure your child has lots of photos.
4. Use a calendar to help her understand when you're coming back home.
5. Use a map to show your child where you're going.
6. Make sure the family has support systems in place to cope during your absence.
7. In times of war, be prepared for the worst. Make sure your family will be cared for should you not return.

19

VEHICLES

TEXAS, 1999:
Six-year-old boy killed as he stood waiting for the school bus.

SOME STATS

- 75% of motor vehicle crashes occur within 25 miles of home. 60% occur on roads with posted speed limits of 40 mph or less.
- In 2000, 7,497 children under age 19 died in motor vehicle accidents. 5,125 of these were ages 15 to 19. An estimated 248,000 children ages 14 and under were injured as occupants in motor vehicle-related accidents.
- Rural areas have higher incidences of motor vehicle accidents with higher death rates.
- Nearly one-half of children killed in alcohol-related crashes were passengers in vehicles with drunk drivers.
- In 1999, 733 children ages 14 and under died from pedestrian injuries.
- In 1998, 48% of deaths in passengers riding in the cargo area of pickup trucks were children.
- 9,160 nonfatal and 78 fatal injuries occurred to children under age 14 years who were left unattended in or around motor vehicles that were not in traffic, such as in the driveway.
- An estimated 50,000 emergency room visits and 1,500 hospitalizations occur each year due to skateboard injuries.
- Nonpowered scooters resulted in 9,400 trips to the emergency room just between January and August 2000.
- 130 children were hospitalized as a result of ATV injuries between 1992 and 1996; 25% of these children died.
- In 1999, 173 children ages 14 and under died in bicycle-related crashes. In 2000, 373,000 were treated in the emergency room.
- Since 1985, five children have died from shopping cart-related injuries.

319

Although motor vehicle accidents remain the leading cause of fatal accidents in children ages 1 to 19, other vehicles add to the fatality statistics, resulting in more than 8,000 childhood transportation fatalities in the year 2000 alone. Bicycles, skateboards, scooters, and all-terrain vehicles (ATVs) contribute to the death and injury toll. Children can be killed in their own driveway or while walking on the sidewalk, and they can even be injured by shopping carts.

MOTOR VEHICLE ACCIDENTS

Motor vehicle safety starts with you. If looking for a new car, consider a model with a wider wheelbase, as these provide greater protection for passengers in the event of an accident. Drive with caution at all times. Heed the speed limit, and don't drink and drive. Drive defensively, not aggressively—your children depend on you and they watch and model your every move:

- Keep your car maintained, and make sure your tires are properly inflated.
- Plan ahead, so you don't have to rush.
- Remain alert; if tired, don't drive.
- Keep your eyes on the road.
- Use your seat belt and lock the car doors.
- Strap or stow objects that could become missiles.
- Don't speed.
- Don't weave in and out of traffic.
- Keep your distance and don't follow too closely.
- Don't cut other drivers off.
- Slow down and turn on your lights in work zones—workers are some kid's parents, too.
- Don't make gestures at other drivers—especially obscene ones.
- Don't run red lights or stop signs, and look before you leap.
- Use your turn signals when turning or changing lanes.
- Yield the right-of-way.
- Don't pass on the shoulder or on unpaved portions of the road.
- Avoid developing road rage: take a deep breath, count to ten, and remember your kids are with you.
- Carry a cell phone (but DON'T use it while driving); pay phones are rapidly becoming an endangered species.
- Keep a first aid kit and emergency equipment handy.

Cars present a danger to all children, including infants. Unfortunately, many parents have been led to believe that it's safer to hold their baby in the front seat than to have the baby restrained in the back. Some parents may even think that it's safer to be thrown clear of an accident than it's to be restrained. However, both of these practices increase the probability of fatality. A mobile child isn't only a distraction to the driver; she's also more vulnerable to be thrown.

SAFETY SEATS

Riding unrestrained is the greatest risk factor for injury and death. 56% of the children killed in crashes in the year 2000 were not using restraints at the time of the collision. Thus, the risk for injury or death is twice as high for your child if she doesn't use a safety restraint.

All fifty states, as well as the District of Columbia and United States territories, have child occupant protection laws, which vary in their exemptions, age requirements, enforcement procedures, and penalties. As of September 2002, all new cars (except convertibles) are required to have a LATCH (Lower Anchors and Tethers for Children) system. This systems compliments matching features on newer child safety seats (hooks, buckles, or other connectors). The connection devices help to better stabilize car seats, reduce the potential for head injuries, and reduce the number of seats installed incorrectly.

Safety seats are extremely effective when correctly installed and used in passenger cars, reducing the chance of death by 71% for infants, 54% for children ages 1 to 4, and reducing the need for hospitalization 69% for children age 4 and under. Children ages 4 to 8 (about 40 to 80 pounds in weight) benefit by the use of booster seats, because adult seat belts don't adequately protect them. There is no "safest" seat on the market. The best seat is the one that fits your child's weight and size, can be installed correctly in your car, and can be used every time you travel with your child.

Safety seats come in several styles and sizes:

INFANT-ONLY: These seats best fit newborns and must be used facing the rear of the car.

CONVERTIBLE SEATS: These are used rear-facing for infants and forward-facing for toddlers. Rear-facing seats should never be placed in the front seat of a vehicle equipped with an air bag.

COMBINATION SEATS: These are used with a harness for toddlers and later convert to boosters for children who weigh over 40 pounds.

BOOSTER SEATS: These are designed for children who are too big for a car safety seat but too small to fit well in an adult seat belt.

BUILT-IN SEATS: Many new vehicles come equipped with built-in safety seats designed for forward-facing children who are older than 1 year and weigh more than 20 pounds. Younger and lighter infants should face the rear of the vehicle in a separate safety seat until they meet the age and weight requirement for the built-in seat.

The American Academy of Pediatrics recommends the following on selecting and installing safety seats:

- Always use child safety seats, booster seats, and seat belts correctly every time you drive.
- Call the National Highway Traffic Safety Administration's Auto Safety Hotline (888–327–4236), to check on possible recalls or safety notices on your child's safety seat.
- Never place rear-facing safety seats in the front passenger side of any vehicle that has an air bag on that side.
- Experience with side air bags and safety seats is limited, but laboratory tests indicate that unrestrained and out-of-position children are at risk for serious injury. So, place children and safety seats away from air bags, choose a vehicle with side or rear air bags, or deactivate side and rear air bags if children are transported in adjacent positions.
- Read the vehicle instruction manual and the safety seat instructions carefully.
- Once the seat is installed, test it for a snug fit and any compatibility problems with the vehicle seat or seat belt.
- For rear-facing seats, place your infant's shoulder harness in the slots at or below the shoulders. Make sure the harness is snug and that the retainer clip is positioned at the level of the baby's armpit, not the abdomen or neck area.
- For forward-facing seats, the shoulder strap should be at or above your child's shoulders. The harness should be snug and the retainer clip should be positioned level with the child's armpits.
- Forward-facing seats, combination seats, or a belt-positioning booster seat should be used for children who have

outgrown convertible seats but are still too small for the vehicle's safety belt.

- Booster seats should be used until children are able sit against the back of the seat with their feet hanging down and their legs bent at the knees.
- Shield boosters have not been certified by manufacturers for children weighing more than 40 pounds. Shields can be removed from current models, and the restraint can be used with a lap and shoulder belt as a belt-positioning booster seat for children too big for a full harness. Children weighing 40 pounds or less are best protected in a seat with a full harness.
- Avoid using aftermarket add-on devices for adjusting poorly fitted seat belts until performance standards are developed for them.
- Special needs children should have appropriate restraint systems. Be sure to check with your health care provider to get the seat that works best for your child.
- Small or premature babies should not be placed in safety seats with shields, abdominal pads, or armrests that could have contact with the infant's face or neck during impact.
- Infants who weigh more than 12 pounds at four months of age should use a convertible safety seat that allows for heavier weights. They should still face the rear of the car. Place convertible safety seats in a semireclined position, facing the rear of the car for children younger than one year and weighing less than 20 pounds.
- Never leave your child unattended in a safety seat in or out of the car.

ADDITIONAL RECOMMENDATIONS BY AGE AND WEIGHT

(From the National Safe Kids Campaign)

Age: Infant to 1 year
Weight: Up to 20 pounds

Your baby should ride rear-facing to reduce risk of cervical spine injury in the event of a crash.

The top of your infant's head should be at least one inch (1") from the top of the child safety seat's shell to protect the head from injury.

Age: 1 year to 4 years of age
Weight: 20 to 40 pounds

Use forward facing seat with a harness

Place the seat in an upright position, according to the manufacturer's instructions.

Harnesses must be routed through slots that are reinforced for that purpose. The only reinforced slots in most seats are the top sets. Check the manufacturer's instructions to determine if other slots are appropriate for forward use.

Be careful about thick clothing or padding between your child and the safety seat or harness. This material could compress in a crash, creating slack and affecting the safety seat's protection.

Age: Between 4 and 8 years
Weight: 40 to 80 pounds

Adult seat belts usually don't fit these children properly.

Use a belt-positioning booster.

Some manufacturers have designed forward-facing safety seats with harnesses or shields that are rated for weights over 40 pounds, as an alternative to booster seats. For example, the Fisher-Price Futura 20/60 is rated to 60 pounds.

Your child must sit all the way back against the seat.

Use both lap and shoulder belts with belt-positioning boosters.

Never let your child put a shoulder belt under her arm or behind her neck. This can result in serious injuries.

If your child is over 40 pounds and you only have lap belts in your back seat:

> Buy a forward–facing safety seat with harnesses or a crushable shield rated for weights higher than 40 pounds.

> Buy a special harness that is anchored to your vehicle (E-Z On Vest or E-Z On Universal 86-Y Harness at www.ezon-pro.com).

> Contact your dealership about installing shoulder belts. If the dealer is unfamiliar with retrofit shoulder belts, contact the vehicle manufacturer directly.

Age: Over 8 years old
Weight: Greater than 80 pounds

Vehicle lap and shoulder belts should fit correctly.

Your child should be able to sit with his back against the back of the seat with her knees bent comfortably over the edge of the seat cushion.

The lap belt should fit snug and flat against her upper thighs.

The shoulder belt should fit snug and flat against the chest and collarbone.

If your child doesn't meet the above guidelines, consider getting a belt-positioning booster seat.

Never let your child put a shoulder belt under her arm or behind her neck. This can result in serious injuries.

If you only have lap belts in the back seat, follow the directions above.

CARS ARE NOT TOYS

Unfortunately, many parents believe that they can leave their child in the car while running a "quick" errand. Quick is never quick enough, and a delay of just a few minutes can prove tragic. Heat rises rapidly inside a car—even when the windows are slightly open. The temperature can rise from 93° to 125° in twenty minutes, and 140° in 40 minutes. And heat is more dangerous to a child than to an adult because it rapidly overwhelms the child's ability to regulate temperature. A young child's temperature can increase three to five times faster than an adult. The child can go into shock, causing vital organs to fail.

Never, never leave your child or pet in a parked car when the weather is warm.

Kid's also think that cars, especially trunks, are great hiding places. Yet young children don't have the developmental ability to get out of a car once they have crawled in. Many die when trapped in the sweltering heat.

The National Safe Kids Campaign suggests the following precautions to prevent your child from becoming entrapped or overheated in the car:

- Never leave your child unattended in the car, not even for a few minutes with the windows down.
- Teach your child not to play near or in cars.
- Always lock the car—doors and trunk—and keep the keys out of your child's reach.

- Keep rear-fold seats closed to prevent your child from getting into the trunk from inside the car.
- Ask your dealership about retrofitting your vehicle with a trunk release mechanism if you don't already have one.
- Teach older children how to disable child-resistant locks in case they become entrapped in a motor vehicle.
- Make sure all your children—including sleeping infants—leave the car when you reach your destination.
- Watch your kids carefully around the car, especially when loading and unloading things.
- Check the temperature of the car seat and belt buckles before restraining your child to avoid burns.
- Use windshield and window shades and a light cover over the seat when parking on a hot day.
- Should your child get locked in the car, get him out, and call 911 or your local emergency number immediately, if needed.

AAA SUGGESTIONS FOR AN AUTO EMERGENCY KIT

Flashlight
Flares or reflective triangle
Distress sign
First aid supplies
Basic tools
Fully charged cell phone and phone change
These items are recommended:
Boots
Hats
Gloves
Coat
Jumper cables
Kitty litter, piece of carpet or sand for traction
Ice scraper and snow brush
Food and water supply (chocolate does help!)

PICKUP TRUCKS

Pickups have become increasingly popular for passenger transportation, especially in rural areas. Pickup registrations numbered 36.2 million in 1998, and data in 1992 showed that 92% of pickups were used for personal transportation.

Passengers who ride in the cargo area of a pickup are three times more likely to die than the occupants of the cab in crashes involving fatalities. And a disproportionate number of cargo riders are youths. Since the cargo area isn't designed for passengers—or pets—it's neither required nor designed to meet occupant safety standards applicable to passenger locations. Forty-eight percent of cargo rider deaths were children; 9% of these children were under age 5.

Children who ride in the cargo area are more likely to sustain multiple and more severe injuries and have a greater likelihood of death. The most significant hazard is ejection, even without a crash, as a child can be ejected due to a sudden stop, swerve, turn, or loss of balance. Children can also be injured by unintentional or intentional jumps and falls from the area. Nearly one-third of cargo passenger deaths were the result of non-crash events.

Enclosed cargo areas, including camper shells, don't provide adequate protection. Children still have sustained deaths from injuries when riding in covered cargos, and some have succumbed to carbon monoxide poisoning from the exhaust.

Fewer than 50% of the states restrict passenger transport in the cargo area, and no two states have identical laws. Restrictions vary according to age group, conditions of travel, and the presence of an enclosed cargo area. Many Native American nations have adopted restraint laws for pickups, as well as passenger cars; other nations use the laws of the state.

Manufacturers have created pickups with extended cabs that have additional seating capacity, such as a rear bench seat, side-facing back seats, a full back seat with lap/shoulder belts, and/or a middle front seat position with a lap belt. Crash data for occupants of these seats is limited; however, compatibility issues exist between vehicle seats and child safety seats, including boosters. Car seats only fit properly secured in a full-sized rear or front seat. Many rear-facing car seats don't fit in pickups with limited space in front of them. This limited space may not provide adequate head movement distance for children in untethered forward-facing safety seats. Booster seats must be used with lap/shoulder belts, which may not be available in the rear seat of many pickups.

The American Academy of Pediatrics recommends the following for parents who own pickup trucks:

- Never transport passengers or pets in the cargo area.
- Plan trips in advance to ensure that the proper restraint device and seat position can be used.
- Check the compatibility between the pickup seat (front and back) and the car safety seat before the safety seat or vehicle is purchased.
- Infants in rear-facing safety seats should never be placed in the front seat of pickups with air bags, unless an air bag on/off switch is installed and activated.
- Safety seats should fit completely on the rear seat and should be properly secured facing the rear for infants younger than one year and weighing less than 20 pounds. They should face forward for older children. The addition of a tether may improve the security of a safety seat.
- Always use a top tether in addition to the vehicle belt when installing forward-facing safety seats.
- Teach your children, especially your teens, to agree that they will never ride or transport others in the cargo area of a pickup truck.

DRIVEWAY INJURIES

Off-the-road injuries are most likely to happen to children under age 3 because they can easily get into the road environment but don't yet know they need to get out of the way of a moving vehicle. Off-the-road accidents can occur in car parks, private roads, on farms, and even in driveways. Most children are injured in their own driveways, and studies in the U.S., Canada, and New Zealand show that vans, light trucks and SUVs are involved in 40 to 76% of driveway back-up injuries. The blind spot behind a minivan, SUV, or light truck can be twice as long as that of the typical sedan.

According to Kids and Traffic, most injuries occur from everyday events:

- when the child is playing in an unfenced play area or the street
- when a relative or family friend is driving off or returning home
- when the car is reversing
- when the driver has no idea that a child is behind
- when the adult who is supervising the child is unaware that the child has slipped away

TO KEEP YOUR CHILDREN SAFE:

- If possible, fence in your child's play area.
- Monitor small children at all times.
- Keep toys and sports equipment off the driveway.
- Walk around and behind your vehicle prior to moving it, and know if another adult is properly supervising the children before moving your vehicle.
- Be aware that steep inclines, large SUVs, vans, and trucks add to the difficulty of seeing behind your vehicle.
- Make sure all children passengers have left the vehicle after it's parked.
- Consider installing convex or cross-view mirrors, and/or a back-up detection device in your vehicle.
- Equip your vehicle with sensors that alarm when your vehicle gets close to any object.
- Purchase driveway safety devices: the Kidcatcher Driveway Protector ($119.95) is a 25' L x 36" H net that installs between two posts to form a barrier between your child's play area and the driveway. The Curbside Safety Sign is a bright yellow sandwich board that reads: Caution: Kids at Play ($13.95). Both can be found at www.safebeginnings.com or 1-800-598-8911.
- When a child is missing, check vehicles and trunks right away.

PEDESTRIAN SAFETY

Numerous state and local laws exist to protect children from pedestrian injuries. These include: low speed limits in residential areas, protecting pedestrians in crosswalks, providing for pedestrian walkways, prohibiting vehicles from passing school buses while loading and unloading children, providing crossing guards, and requiring that pedestrians not cross streets at locations other than designated crosswalks. Yet, pedestrian injury is the second leading cause of injury-related death in children ages 5 to 14. While most of these are traffic-related, children under age 2 are most likely to suffer from non-traffic-related injuries, including those occurring in driveways, parking lots, and sidewalks. Children are at high risk for pedestrian-related injuries because they are exposed to traffic threats that exceed their thinking, behavioral, physical, and sensory skills.

Parents also tend to overestimate their children's pedestrian skills. Children are impulsive, and they have trouble judging speed, distance, velocity, and spatial relations. Your child's auditory and visual acuity, depth perception, and proper scanning ability develop gradually and don't fully mature until she's 10 years old.

TO DECREASE YOUR CHILD'S RISK OF PEDESTRIAN INJURY:

Always model and teach proper pedestrian behavior:

- Cross streets at the corner.
- Obey traffic signals.
- Use crosswalks where available.
- Make eye contact with drivers prior to crossing in front of them. Don't assume that they can see you.
- Don't let your child cross the street alone if she's under 10 years old. She needs adult supervision until she develops traffic and judgment skills.
- Educate your child that red means stop, and that she should never cross on a red light, even when there is no traffic.
- Teach your child to look left, right, then left again before crossing the street, and to continue looking as she crosses.
- Tell them to walk, not run when they cross.
- Teach your child to walk facing traffic, as far to the left as possible, if there are no sidewalks.
- Require that your child wear bright, reflective clothing and carry a flashlight at dawn and dusk.
- If you use a stroller or carriage during dawn or dusk, add a reflective strip or stickers to it.
- Prohibit play in driveways, streets, and parking lots, as well as unfenced lots adjacent to streets.
- Forbid the use of headphones when walking or jogging.
- Tell you child to never dart or play between parked cars.
- Advocate for better traffic laws, pedestrian walkways, and reduced traffic and lower speed limits in residential areas.

MORE THAN A FEW WORDS ON TEEN DRIVERS

Motor vehicle accidents (MVAs) remain a leading cause of death in adolescents—2 out 5 deaths among United States teens result from a motor vehicle crash. Results from the 2001 Youth Risk Behavior Surveillance (YRBSS) indicated 14.1% of high school students had rarely or never worn seat belts. The survey also revealed that during the 30 days prior to the survey, 13.3% drove a car or other vehicle after drinking alcohol and 30.7% had ridden with a driver who had been drinking alcohol.

A driver's license is a major milestone for your teen, and a major anxiety producer for you. Many adolescents view a license as a right of passage and/or a passport to freedom rather than a tremendous responsibility in assuring safe transportation. They are also more likely to engage in risk-taking behavior, and they lack driving experience. All of these increase their risk of crashing and sustaining injuries or worse.

Several factors impact on teen risk-taking, including egocentrism. Adolescents magnify the importance of their own ideas, displaying a form of cognitive arrogance. This causes them to frequently refuse to listen to parental advice. Their self-consciousness creates an "imaginary fable," that places them on permanent display for all to see, especially their peers. Conformity is critical, and risk-taking occurs because "everyone else does it." Their thoughts become so special to them that they develop their own "personal fable," complete with feelings of uniqueness and infallibility. This can result in careless attitudes about driving since "nothing bad will ever happen to them."

Risk-taking behavior combines with youth to form a lethal combination behind the wheel. The Committee on Injury and Poison Prevention, and the Committee on Adolescence, both of the American Academy of Pediatrics (AAP), list five principle reasons why teens are at greater risk for vehicle crashes:

1. Adolescents' overall judgment and decision-making processes may not yet be fully developed. As novice drivers, they lack the experience and ability to perform several complex driving tasks, such as detecting and responding to hazards, controlling the vehicle, and integrating speed. These deficits disappear with years of experience, implying that the brevity of drivers' education programs doesn't constitute sufficient training and can't replace supervised driving by parents and other adults.

2. Adolescents' driving habits may be highly influenced by emotions, peer pressures, and other stressors, predisposing them to take more risks. More teen accidents occur when teen passengers are involved, than when teens drive alone.

3. Night driving is more difficult for all new drivers. Relatively speaking, adolescents drive fewer hours than adults overall, but they drive disproportionately more at night and have a significantly higher crash fatality rate. Adolescents are four times

more likely to be killed while driving at night than during the day.

4. Alcohol and drug use put adolescents at risk. Alcohol is involved in about 30% of all fatal teen-involved crashes; drugs are involved in about 10% to 15% of teen fatalities. The combination of alcohol and marijuana is common and deadly.

5. The risk of injury is higher in adolescents due to their low rate of seat belt use. Air bags alone are not adequate, as they don't provide enough restraint, and are thus not protective, especially in rollover, rear impact, or side impact crashes.

The seat belt usage problem is intensified in rural areas where pickup truck usage increases the rollover risk factor, roads are not as well maintained, and where medical assistance may be a great distance away.

PROTECT YOUR TEEN BY DOING THE FOLLOWING:

- Treat driving as a privilege with responsibilities, not as a birthright.
- You control the car keys—not your teen.
- Ensure the mechanical safety of your car(s) and have your teen participate in its maintenance, even if that just means accompanying you to the mechanic's garage.
- Set a good driving example and follow traffic rules, as well as your own rules.
- Require that she maintain good grades to keep her driving privileges. Ask your auto insurance company if they have a "good student" discount.
- Remind her how easy it's to get distracted on the road and that she must stay focused when driving. No using cellular phones when driving.
- Enforce household restrictions, such as disallowing certain passengers from the family car, and always returning the car with a full tank of gas.
- Create a reward system for a safe driving record (increased drive time; free tank of gas), as well as consequences for unsafe driving (decreased drive time, loss of all driving privileges).
- Don't tolerate drinking and driving. Let your teen know that you will pick her up if she does drink.
- Be alert to any signs that indicate that she's drinking or using drugs.

- Support programs that make driving safer for teens:
  —Graduated license laws
  —Minimum drinking age laws
  —Safety belt laws
  —Curfews
  —Educational efforts to teach teens about safe driving habits
  —Safe ride programs so teens won't drive after drinking at parties

Teen drivers have fewer crashes in states with graduated driver licensing. The crash rates declined sharply for all levels of severity among 16-year-olds in North Carolina and Michigan since graduated license laws were enacted. However, not all states have such laws, and those that do vary in their requirements. Experts from the American Medical Association note that these laws should include provisions for the teen driving with a responsible adult supervisor for at least six months, followed by prohibitions on unsupervised nighttime driving and transporting of passengers, until the teen has accumulated at least six months of additional driving experience without adult supervision.

If your state doesn't have a graduated licensing program, you can create your own, using a staging system recommended by the American Academy of Pediatrics, using the recommendations that work best for your teen:

STAGE ONE

- your teen must be at least 15 ½ years old or have a learner's permit
- she must drive with a responsible licensed adult at all times
- teen and all passengers must wear seat belts (I suggest disallowing other teen passengers until Stage 3 due to the increased incidence of crashes when there is more than one teen in the car.)
- no night driving (after sunset and before sunrise)
- no tobacco, alcohol, or other drugs
- your teen must remain ticket and crash-free for 6 months before moving up to the next stage

STAGE TWO

- your teen must be at least 16 years old or have a learner's permit for at least 6 months
- your teen may drive unsupervised during the day

- your teen must drive with a licensed adult during night-time hours
- teen and all passengers must use seat belts (I suggest dis-allowing other teen passengers until Stage 3 due to the increased incidence of crashes when there is more than one teen in the car.)
- no tobacco, alcohol, or other drugs
- your teen must remain ticket and crash-free for 12 months before moving up to the next stage

STAGE THREE

- your teen must be at least 18 years old or have driven at least 2 years in the previous stage
- no restrictions as long as she remains ticket and crash-free driver and passengers must use seat belts
- no tobacco, alcohol, or other drugs

Questions to consider asking your teen about driving to test her skill, level of accountability and safety knowledge:

How often do you use your seat belt?

What would you do if a passenger refused to wear a seat belt?

Do you ever ride with someone who has been drinking?

How would you get home if you and your friends use alcohol and you have the family car?

What would you do if an exciting new boyfriend offered you a joint at a red light?

Who is at fault if you crashed the car after your best friend gave you a couple of beers?

How would she respond in emergency situations: tire blow-out, skidding on ice or wet road?

Who would she contact in an emergency, and how would she contact them?

How often does she intend to drive at night? What is the pur-pose of the night driving?

SCHOOL BUS SAFETY

Riding the school bus is an extremely safe method of trans-portation. However, each year children are injured or even killed in school bus-related accidents. To keep your child safe, follow these guidelines from the National Safety Council:

- Find a safe and sheltered place for your child to wait for the bus.
- No playing in or near the street or on private property while waiting for the bus.
- No pushing or shoving.
- Don't go near the bus until it comes to a full stop and the driver says it's okay to board.
- Stay in your seat while the bus is in motion.
- Use seat belts if provided.
- Don't stick head, arms, legs, or objects out the window.
- Don't talk to the driver while the bus is moving—unless it's an emergency.
- Speak softly. No shouting.
- No pushing, shoving, fighting, name-calling, hitting, or weapons on the bus.
- Learn where the emergency exits are on the bus and how to get out in an emergency.
- Take at least 10 giant steps away from the bus when you get off, so that the driver can see you get to a safe place.
- Never walk in front of the bus until the driver signals that it's okay.
- Never walk behind the bus.
- Make sure that all the cars are stopped before crossing the street, and look both ways before crossing.

ALL-TERRAIN VEHICLES (ATVs)

Members of the kidney transplant team at a major medical center in Pennsylvania refer to ATVs as "donor-mobiles." That should be enough said.

Initially sold as "toys" in the early 1980s, ATVs are 3- or 4-wheeled motorized vehicles with large, low-pressure tires designed to be ridden in off-road conditions. It quickly became evident that ATVs posed a serious health hazard, resulting in an estimated 106,000 emergency room-treated injuries and 347 deaths in 1986—40% of these were children under age 16. Because of these statistics, the United States Consumer Product Safety Commission and the major ATV manufacturers signed a decree that went into effect in 1988. The decree included the agreement to stop making 3-wheel ATVs, to develop nationwide training and safety education programs, and to make ATVs safer. The distributors also agreed to prohibit the use of ATVs with engines larger than 90mL to children under 16, and to prohibit the use of ATVs with engines larger than 70mL to children younger than 12. However, follow-up analysis revealed no decrease in the proportion of children who were injured in ATV crashes—children under age 16 still sustained 40% to 50% of all ATV-related injuries and accounted for more than 35% of all ATV-related deaths.

Although consent decrees were sponsored by the federal government, each state legislates ATV use, and thus may not necessarily implement age restrictions or passenger limitations as specified in the decrees. The following is an example, using the regulations from the Pennsylvania Department of Conservation and Natural Resources– Forestry ATV rules and safety code:

PENNSYLVANIA DEPARTMENT OF CONSERVATION AND NATURAL RESOURCES–FORESTRY–ATV RULES

1. Operators of all-terrain vehicles must abide by state forest rules and regulations and the ATV law.
2. All all-terrain vehicles (ATVs) used in Pennsylvania, except those used for farming or business purposes, must be registered with the Department of Conservation and Natural Resources' Snowmobile/ATV unit.
3. The Department of Conservation and Natural Resources' local District Forester will regulate trail use.
4. The designated ATV trails will be open from the Friday before Memorial Day through the last full weekend in September.
5. Some ATV trails reopen for winter use in conjunction with the snowmobile season from the day following the last day of the regular or extended antlerless deer season as established by the Game Commission through the following April 1, conditions permitting. Check with the District Forester to be sure that winter use is permitted. The trail may also be open to snowmobiles.
6. The operation of a vehicle in a reckless or negligent manner is not permitted.
7. Place all litter in waste containers, where provided; otherwise practice the "carry-in, carry-out" procedure.
8. Don't disturb, drive, or pursue wildlife with your vehicle.
9. Don't carry loaded firearms on your ATV.
10. ATVs are **NOT** permitted on state forest roads open to licensed motor vehicles.
11. Persons under 10 years of age may not operate an ATV on state-owned lands.

12. Persons 10 through 15 years of age must possess an ATV Safety Course Certificate to legally operate an ATV anywhere except on their parent's property.
13. It's illegal to operate an ATV without a securely fastened helmet on the head of the operator.

PENNSYLVANIA DEPARTMENT OF CONSERVATION AND NATURAL RESOURCES–FORESTRY–ATV SAFETY CODE

Learn all the mechanical controls and safety devices of your ATV before you ride. Read your owner's manual.

Wear a helmet and eye protection at all times and other protective clothing suitable to the environment when you ride.

Don't carry passengers on your ATV.

Don't let young or inexperienced riders operate ATVs without supervision.

Don't use alcohol or other drugs when you ride.

Learn proper riding skills from an instructor or qualified rider and practice such skills before riding any ATV Trails.

Use the "buddy" system and ride with others.

Obey the laws.

Don't modify the exhaust system.

Protect the environment. Don't litter, harass wildlife, or damage plant life.

Respect the rights of others who use state forest land. Stay on trails designated for ATVs.

THINK SAFELY

ACT SAFELY

REGARDLESS OF LOWER AGE RESTRICTIONS BY STATE LAW, CHILDREN UNDER AGE 16 SHOULD NEVER RIDE ADULT-SIZED ATVs.

ATVs are unstable. They are difficult to ride and require constant attention to avoid crash or tip over. Most accidents occur when an ATV overturns after hitting an obstacle or irregularity in the terrain, or while turning or traversing a slope. ATVs are designed for one driver, and the presence of a passenger seriously impairs the driver's ability to shift weight to steer and control the vehicle. Since children lack the physical size and strength, as well as the fine motor and thinking skills required to operate an ATV properly, their risk for harm is greater than that of an adult.

Most child safety experts–including this one–recommend that children not ride ATVs. But if you choose to allow your child to do so, follow these guidelines:

- Don't allow your child to drive any ATV if she's under age 12.
- Don't allow your child to operate an adult-sized ATV if she's between 12 and 15.
- Place flags, reflectors, and lights on the ATVs to make them more visible.
- Have her wear appropriate gear: helmet, eye protection, gloves, heavy boots, and elbow pads.
- Have her take a hands-on training course.
- Always read the manufacturer's instructions before she uses the ATV.
- Follow the manufacturer's guidelines for use, maintenance, and pre-use checks.
- Observe local laws and regulations for use of ATVs.
- Don't allow her to ride double.
- Instruct her that ATVs should not be operated on paved roads.
- Enforce that ATVs should never be operated under the influence of alcohol or other drugs.
- Encourage her to always drive carefully and to use good judgment.
- Check with the Consumer Product Safety Commission for recall information on ATVs: 1-800-638-2772.

SNOWMOBILE SAFETY

The popularity of snowmobiles has increased, but these still pose a significant risk to children, with head injuries causing the most serious problems and death from snowmobiles colliding, falling, or overturning during operation. Children are also injured while being towed by snowmobiles. Head injuries are the leading cause of death, and near-drowning events are infrequent. Only one child died due to drowning after falling through thin ice. Frostbite and hypothermia were also infrequent.

The American Academy of Pediatrics recommends the following:

- Don't allow children under age 16 to operate snowmobiles.
- Don't allow children under age 6 to ride on snowmobiles; they don't have the strength or stamina to be transported as passengers on snowmobiles.

- Check the weather forecast before snowmobiling.
- Know the signs of frostbite (see weather chapter), and check regularly for frostbite.
- Travel at safe speeds, especially on unfamiliar or rugged terrain.
- Avoid the use of alcohol or other drugs.
- Wear helmets approved by Snell or another standards organization.
- Wear well-insulated, protective clothing, including goggles and waterproof snowmobile suits, gloves, and rubber-lined boots.
- Carry a first aid kit, a survival kit with flares, and a cellular phone.
- Travel in groups of 2 or more and only on designated, marked trails away from roads, waterways, railroads, and pedestrian traffic.
- Avoid snowmobiling on ice if uncertain about the its thickness or condition.
- Keep headlights and taillights on at all times to improve visibility of the snowmobile to other operators.
- Don't pull anything behind the snowmobile. This includes tubes, saucers, tires, sleds, and skis.
- Keep the snowmobile well-maintained. Take precautions when fueling the snowmobile to avoid burns.

TWO-WHEELED VEHICLES

Miniature motorcycles are intended for off-road use. **Minibikes**, which are the smallest and most primitive of the 2-wheelers, are motorized bicycle-style frames that weigh less than 100 pounds and are powered by <4 horsepower engines. **Minicycles** are more sophisticated and higher-powered. They are constructed with suspension systems and transmissions that resemble miniature motorcycles. **Trailbikes or trailcycles** are larger and have design and power characteristics that make them suitable for rough terrain. **Mopeds** are bicycles with small, unenclosed motors that travel at a maximum speed of 30 mph. Mopeds are intended for street use, but many states don't require licensing for either the moped or the driver. All two-wheeled vehicles typically have short and relatively unstable wheelbases, small tires, slow acceleration, borderline brakes, and poor visibility in traffic.

Twenty-six percent of the 40,000 injuries related to 2-wheeled vehicles in the years 1994-1996 were children. Injuries usually resulted from loss of control of the cycle on rocks, bumps, or holes, or from illegal on-road use. Shoulder, knee, and leg injuries account for more than one-third of the injuries; head injuries account for most of the deaths. Deaths are also more likely to be related to racing and jumping.

If your child (16 or older) uses a two-wheeled vehicle, follow these suggestions:

- Use flags, reflectors, and lights to make the vehicle visible to other drivers.
- No passengers
- Wear a helmet, eye protection, and protective reflective clothing. Helmets should be those used for motorcycles, not bicycles.
- Never permit street use for off-road vehicles.
- No nighttime riding.
- No use of alcohol or other drugs when operating the vehicle.

BICYCLE SAFETY

More than 70% of children ages 5 to 14 ride bicycles, accounting for approximately 27.7 million children. And bicycles are related to more childhood injuries than any other consumer product except the automobile. Bicycle-related head injuries account for 153,000 emergency department visits per year and 500 deaths.

Most bike accidents occur at non-intersection locations during the months of May through September and between the hours of 3 P.M. and 7 P.M. Almost 60% of all childhood bike-related deaths occur on minor roads, usually within one mile of the child's home. More than 80% of bicycle-related fatalities are associated with the bicyclist's behavior, such as riding into a street without stopping, running a stop sign/light, turning left or swerving into traffic that is coming from behind, and riding against the flow of traffic.

The single most effective safety device to reduce the incidence of head injuries from bicycle crashes is a helmet. Helmets reduce the risk of death and the severity of injury when an accident occurs. However, national estimates show that only 15 to 25% of children use their helmets when riding their bikes. Helmet use is lowest in children ages 11 to 14. If your child resists wearing a helmet, point out how athletes wear them. If she still refuses, don't let her ride the bike. If she still refuses, consequence her, and dismantle the bike so that it can't be used.

To keep your child safe on her bike, make sure she:

- Uses the correct-sized bicycle because she can't control a bike that is too large. She should be able to straddle the bike and stand with both feet flat on the ground.
- Has safety reflectors on her bike on the front, rear, and wheel spokes.
- Wears her helmet at all times when riding her bike! Buy one that meets or exceeds the safety standards developed by the United States Consumer Product Safety Commission. It should be approved by the American National Standards Institute (ANSI), the Snell Foundation, or the American Society for Testing and Materials (ASTM). The helmet should have a chin strap and buckle to keep it in place, and it should be made out of a hard outer shell and an absorbing liner at least one-half inch thick.
- Wears her helmet correctly. It should fit snugly and comfortably, but not too tightly. It should sit on the top of her head in a level position, and it should not rock forward and backward or side to side.
- Keeps her helmet straps buckled all the time.
- Rides in a straight line near the curb and is alert for car doors opening into traffic.
- Learns the rules of the road and obeys all traffic laws:
  —Ride on the right side of the road, with traffic, not against it
  —Use appropriate hand signals
  —Respect traffic signs and signals
  —Stop at all stop signs and lights
  —Stop and look both ways before entering a street
- Is able to stop the bike by using the brakes.
- Doesn't ride at dusk or at night, when most fatal accidents occur. If she's still outside when it gets dark, she should turn on her bicycle light and she should be wearing reflective clothing.

Children under age 10 should be restricted to riding on the sidewalks and paths. Once reaching age 10, they should not be able to utilize the roads until they demonstrate how well they ride and how they observe all traffic laws. Adult supervision is needed until your child develops traffic skills and an appropriate judgment level.

SKATEBOARD AND SCOOTER SAFETY

An estimated 50,000 children are injured in skateboard injuries each year; more than 2,000 are injured in nonpowered scooter injuries. The increased use of these recreation modes is too new to make definitive recommendations, but you can use the following guidelines to keep your children safe:

Skateboard safety tips:

- Children under 10 should not use skateboards without adult supervision.
- Children under 5 should not use skateboards at all.
- Choose the correct skateboard–there are boards for slalom, freestyle, or speed riding. Some boards are rated according to the weight of the intended user. Talk to the salesperson about your child's needs.
- Buy and use safety equipment–helmet, elbow and knee pads, wrist guards, skateboarding gloves, and closed, slip-resistant shoes.
- Give your child a safe place to learn how to use the board. Learners have the highest rate of injury, so make sure she's away from traffic and where you can reach her in case of an accident.
- Encourage safe use of the board, and set rules about where and when the board can be used.
- Skateboards should never be used in or near traffic, or on steep gradients.
- Never hold onto a moving vehicle while riding a skateboard.
- Be careful of pedestrians.
- Carry the board to cross the street, and always cross at the crosswalk, stop sign, or traffic light.
- A skateboard can wear out over time, so take care of it. Check regularly for problems, such as a worn surface, loose, broken or cracked parts, sharp edges on metal boards, or nicks or cracks in the wheels.

Non-powered scooter safety tips:

- Children under age 8 should not use scooters without adult supervision.
- Always wear safety gear: helmet, elbow pads, and knee pads.
- Wear sturdy shoes. No bare feet or flip-flops.

- Don't lean forward; standing straight makes the scooter easier to handle.
- Always ride the scooter on the sidewalk or paved off-road paths–staying away from cars and other vehicles.
- Stay away from sand, gravel, dirt, and water.
- Cross streets only at traffic lights, stop signs, or cross-walks. Walk the scooter across the streets.
- Walk scooters down steep hills.

SHOPPING CART SAFETY

Yes, shopping carts. The number of children injured in shopping cart-related incidents has risen more than 30% since 1985, and five children have been killed from shopping cart-related injuries. Accidents can cause head injuries, lacerations, contusions, fractures, concussions, and intestinal injuries when children jump or fall from the cart, when the cart overturns, when they fall against the cart, or when they get pinched in the folding mechanism of the seat. Children are also at risk for injuries from running into or being hit by the carts, tipping over carts while climbing on the outside of the basket, and getting their fingers or toes caught in the wheels.

Falls from carts are the most common accidents because shopping carts have a high center of gravity and a narrow wheelbase. This makes them top-heavy and easy to tip over, especially when a child is placed in the seat. If the child stands, she increases her risk for falling or tipping over the cart. Eighty percent of falls occur when children are unrestrained, primarily because the cart did not have a safety belt or because the belt was broken. However, research shows that parents don't use belts, even when carts come equipped with them.

To keep your child safe on your next grocery trip:

- Always use the safety belt to restrain your child in the seat.
- Consider bringing a harness with you, in case the store's carts are unequipped.
- Always stay close to the cart.
- Don't let your child stand up in the cart.
- Never let the child push or steer the cart.
- Never leave your child in the cart unattended.

20

WATER

PENNSYLVANIA, 2003:
16-year-old boy drowns after being swept downstream by the rapid current.

SOME STATS

- 86% of drowning victims are under age 6, and 78% are male.
- 1,500 children drown each year.
- For every child that drowns, 6 to 10 suffer from near-drowning, and 20% of these children suffer permanent brain damage.
- 98% of drownings occur in freshwater; 60% to 90% of drownings in children 4 and under occur in swimming pools–50% of these in their own pool; 33% occur in a friend's or neighbor's pool.
- Infants are most likely to drown in their bathtub.
- 69% of drowning victims were being supervised by one of more parents, with a lapse in supervision of just a few minutes.
- Most adolescent drownings occur from boating accidents or in rivers and lakes, not pools.
- 40% to 50% of adolescent drownings involve alcohol.
- Diving accidents account for 1 in 8 spinal cord injuries.
- The CDC reports 59 new outbreaks of waterborne illnesses associated with recreational water use, that affected 2,093 people.

Undoubtedly, you know how dangerous water can be to small children. But did you know that the majority of young victims drowned while being supervised by one or both parents, with a lapse in supervision of just minutes? Drowning occurs in less than five minutes–less time than it takes for you to read this chapter or to answer the phone.

Did you know that a child can drown in just a few inches of water? All it takes is enough to cover her nose and mouth–the amount in a toilet, a bucket of water, or even a puddle.

Did you realize that 29% of drowning victims are teens? Drowning is the fourth leading cause of death of all children 19 and under. And teen diving accidents can result in permanent spinal cord damage, brain injury, and/or death.

Drowning is a silent killer. Young children can drown silently without any screaming or splashing.

Drowning isn't water's only hazard. Did you know that water-borne illnesses are on the rise? What is swimming in your pool along-side your children? What is lurking in your kitchen faucet? Clear water isn't necessarily clean water.

DROWNINGS

Childhood drownings and near-drownings can happen in seconds. The child loses consciousness two minutes after submersion and suffers irreversible brain damage in just four to six minutes. Ninety-two percent of the children who survive are found within two minutes of submersion, and 86% of the children who die are discovered after ten minutes. Nearly all the children who require CPR are left with severe brain damage or die. However, since CPR does benefit some children, it remains prudent for you to learn it. Contact your local American Red Cross or American Heart Association for a training program near you.

IN-HOME WATER SAFETY

Not all drownings occur in pools or lakes. Small children can drown inside their homes, and many of these deaths are associated with common household products. The Consumer Product Safety Commission provides these examples:

1. About two-thirds of the drowning deaths in the home occur in bathtubs. Some of these deaths happen when children were in bath seats or rings. Most of them occur when the parent isn't present. Stepping out to answer the phone, check on dinner, or grab a towel can prove fatal.
2. Five-gallon buckets, often used for household chores, pose a serious threat to toddlers, killing 58 children under 5 in 1999 alone. Their tall, straight sides combined with their stability

make it nearly impossible for top-heavy infants to free themselves when they topple in headfirst. Diaper pails also present
a drowning hazard for those of you who still use them.

3. Toilets are often overlooked as a drowning hazard in the home.
    The typical scenario involves a child under 3 years old falling
    headfirst into the toilet.

4. Spas and hot tubs pose another drowning hazard. A solar
    cover can allow babies to slip into the water while the cover
    appears to stay in place, hiding the child. Spas and hot tubs
    present other hazards to children, including burns from the
    chemicals used to clean the water, stress from higher water
    temperature to children under five, burns from the water tem-
    perature to very young children, electrical shock or electrocu-
    tion when an electrical current comes into contact with the spa
    or tub, and injuries from slips and falls.

Home ponds and fountains, both inside and out, and rain barrels create other drowning hazards.

PREVENTION

Don't assume your house is safe. Check around your home for
potential hazards, and correct them.

BATHTUBS:

- Never leave your baby alone in the tub, even for a few "sec-
  onds." Seconds turn into minutes without your realizing it.
- Keep the baby within arm's reach.
- Never leave the baby in the care of another young child.
- Gather your bathing equipment ahead of time, or better yet,
  store them near the bath site.
- Use infant bathtubs in the tub or sink, not on the counter-
  top where they can fall over.
- Don't use infant bath seats. Babies have drowned by slipping
  through or tipping over in them.
- Don't forget to test the water temperature to prevent burns and
  to keep baths short to prevent drying her delicate skin.
- If you use the bathtub to soak clothing or other items,
  lock the door to keep your child out of the bathroom to
  prevent her from falling into the tub and drowning or getting burned.

BUCKETS:

- Don't leave any bucket of liquid unattended when your young children are around.
- Stay away from the five-gallon size buckets. Use smaller ones that are less likely to pose a drowning risk because they are lighter and more likely to tip over when a curious child sticks her head in one. But realize that all buckets are dangerous, so empty them immediately and never leave a fluid-filled one unattended.
- Don't use a bucket as a drip catcher.
- Keep children away from ice chests. They can drown in the melting ice.
- Discuss these little known safety tips with grandparents, babysitters, and anyone else who watches your child.

TOILETS:

- Keep the lid down and install a childproof lock.

SPAS AND HOT TUBS:

- Don't allow children under age 5 to use the hot tub or spa.
- If your older child is taking medication, or if she has heart disease, diabetes, high or low blood pressure, or any illness, don't allow her to use the hot tub or spa without approval from your health care provider.
- Keep spa and hot tub chemicals locked and stored safely away from your child.
- If your spa or hot tub has a cover, remove it completely before use.
- Don't allow your child to play on top of the cover.
- Check to see if your cover complies with the American Society for Testing and Materials (ASTM) Safety Standard for Safety Covers. If it doesn't, consider purchasing a new one that does.
- Place a fence around outdoor tubs and spas. It should be equipped with a lock or a self-closing and self-latching gate, with a latch that is above the reach of children. Check to see if there are any codes that determine your fence requirements.
- Keep indoor spas and tubs in a room that can be locked when the tub isn't in use.
- Make sure your tub or spa's inlet and outlet fittings, grates, skimmer, and main drain are in working order and are not missing or broken. Don't use the tub until it's repaired.

- Assure that steps, ladders, and handrails are secured in place without broken treads or sharp edges.
- Check to see if your tub or spa is plugged into a ground fault circuit interrupter (GFCI) to help prevent electrical shock by cutting off the flow of electricity. If it's not, contact a licensed electrician and have one installed.

ARTIFICIAL PONDS, FOUNTAINS, RAINBARRELS

Ponds and fountains draw the attention of young children who can easily fall in and drown. Wait until your children are older to install them. If you already have a pond, fill it with sand until your child is older. If you insist on keeping it as is, follow safety guidelines and always supervise your child when she is near the pond area.

Since man-made ponds come in all shapes and sizes, safety covers don't exist. However, security grill suppliers and metal stock-holders can cut rigid steel mesh to fit. The mesh should ideally be heavy-duty and self-supporting, and have a grid size of no more than 80mm x 80mm: this size would ensure against entrapment. Depending on the size of the pond, a frame may also be required to provide stability and anchor points. Mesh that is on or below the surface isn't likely to prevent all drowning risks, and any method used to secure and lock the frame in place should ensure that there is no risk of entrapment between any moving parts. Keep the cover in place until your child can recognize and understand danger.

If fencing is used around the pond, it should be high enough so that it can't be climbed, and it should be securely locked in the same manner as fencing used for hot tubs and pools. Fencing material such as chicken wire is totally unsuitable, since children can crawl under it, get in the pond, and drown.

Rainwater barrels should be emptied regularly or sealed to prevent access.

WATER SAFETY

About 350 children under age 5 drown in swimming pools each year. Pools rank as the number one cause of drowning in preschool-age children and pose a danger to all children. Teens should know how to swim, but they are more likely to take risks, overestimate their skills, and use drugs and alcohol. They also underestimate water depth and current strength when swimming in water bodies such as rivers. To keep your child safe, use guidelines suggested by the American Red Cross, National Safe Kids Campaign, the American Academy of Pediatrics, and SafeKids.

GENERAL WATER SAFETY

- Learn to swim. If nothing else, you will be setting a good example.
- Learn CPR and how to help a drowning victim.
- Teach your child to swim when she's old enough, usually around age 5.
- Keep electrical appliances away from the water.
- Don't allow wheeled toys, running, or clowning around near the water area.
- Never let your child swim without adult supervision, and make sure that adult knows how to swim, how to get emergency help, and how to perform CPR.
- Never leave your child unsupervised near pools, spas, tubs, wells, open post holes, irrigation and drainage ditches, or bodies or water.
- Don't rely on inflatable toys and mattresses to assist her in flotation, and don't allow her to use them if she can't swim.
- Never use flotation devices or inflatable toys and mattresses in place of supervision.
- Discuss the risks of drowning by falling through thin ice in the winter.
- Obey the rules and posted signs.
- Pay attention to weather forecasts and disallow swimming when the weather calls for it.
- Watch for the dangerous "toos": too cold, too tired, too much sun, too far from safety, and too much strenuous activity.

Teen tips:

- Always swim with a buddy.
- Encourage her to take swimming, diving, and rescue lessons.
- Never swim under the influence of drugs of alcohol.
- Check the depth of the water and check the water for objects before diving.
- Make sure she wears waterproof sunscreen with a protective factor of at least 15, and limit exposure to direct sunlight between the hours of 10A.M. and 4P.M.
- Provide eye protection, using sunglasses with labels that indicate they absorb 90% of the UV sunlight.
- Provide foot protection; don't let her run around barefoot.

- Make sure you child drinks plenty of caffeine-free fluids to ward off dehydration.
- Watch for signs of heatstroke, which can be life-threatening: hot, red, dry skin; changes in consciousness; rapid, weak pulse, and rapid, shallow breathing. Call 911 or your local emergency number immediately and cool your child down by fanning and wrapping wet sheets around her body.

Know how to prevent, recognize, and respond to emergencies.

WADING POOLS

- Never leave your child alone. Don't even turn your head for a minute.
- Stay within an arm's reach at all times.
- Empty the pool and turn it upside-down when finished swimming.

HOME POOLS

- Keep the pool properly chlorinated to prevent the spread of infection.
- Install multiple drains to lessen the suction power of any one drain. Powerful drain suction can literally suck a child under and drown her.
- Know where the manual cutoff switch is for the pump in case a child is pulled down by a drain.
- Fence in your pool completely with a self-closing, self-locking gate. The fence should be at least 5 feet high with openings no more than 4 inches wide. If you use the house as part of the barrier, lock the doors leading from the house to the pool and protect them with alarms that sound when the door is unexpectedly opened. Latches and locks should be higher than children's reach. Realize that fencing alone can't prevent drownings.
- Power safety covers that meet the ASTM standards add to your child's protection, but should not be used in place of a fence.
- Don't leave furniture near the fence to enable climbing.
- Keep basic lifesaving equipment by the pool and know how to use it–personal flotation device (PFD), rope, pole, shepherd's hook.
- Keep a cordless or cellular phone by the pool, or have a regular phone installed there so that you can call 911 in an emergency.

- Remove toys from the pool after use to remove your child's temptation.
- Secure the pool after everyone is finished swimming.

LAKES, RIVERS AND OCEANS

- Swim only in designated areas.
- Use areas that are clean, well-maintained, and supervised.
- Choose water that has good quality and safe natural conditions. Murky water can contain hidden dangers and pollutants.
- Assure that rafts and docks are in good condition, typically a sign of a well-run facility.
- Stay away from strong tides, big waves, and currents, which can be more tragedy than fun.
- Avoid arroyos and drainage ditches. Both are used for run-off water, and can quickly become raging rivers that can drown the best of swimmers.
- Watch for aquatic life. Some plants and animals are dangerous.
- Check surf conditions before swimming in the ocean. Look for the warning flag or ask the lifeguard.
- Avoid piers, pilings, and diving platforms when in the water.
- For teens, if caught in a current, don't swim against it. Gradually swim out of it by swimming across it.

SNORKELING

- Know how to swim.
- Never snorkel alone
- Practice first in shallow water.
- Carefully check the equipment and know how it works.
- Be sure weather and water conditions are safe.
- Know how to clear water from the snorkel.
- Learn how to put mask on when treading water.

SCUBA AND SKIN DIVING

- Know how to swim.
- Never dive alone.
- Have your teen get a physical exam before diving.
- Take SCUBA and skin diving lessons from qualified divers.
- Know weather and water conditions.
- Tell her never to dive in rough or dangerous areas that she has not been trained for: ice, caves, and shipwrecks require special training.

DIVING SAFETY

Adolescents are more likely than any other age group to engage in reckless diving, which can result in brain damage, spinal cord injury and even death. According to the Cincinnati Children's Hospital Medical Center, diving accidents occur when teens: dive into shallow water; dive into aboveground pools, which tend to be shallow; dive into the shallow end of an inground pool, or spring upward from the diving board and hit the board on the way down.

To keep your teen (and younger child) safe, make sure she:

- Takes lessons to dive safely.
- Only dives in areas known to be safe for diving–water should be at least 9 feet deep.
- Obeys "No diving" and "No swimming" signs.
- Checks the water's depth and makes sure there are no objects such as rocks or debris.
- Doesn't dive into aboveground pools.
- Doesn't dive into the shallow end of inground pools.
- Doesn't dive when someone else is on the diving board.
- Never dives from docks or piers.
- Waits until the water is clear of other swimmers before diving.
- Never throws someone into the water headfirst.

WATERCRAFT SAFETY

More people die in boating accidents each year than in train wrecks and plane crashes. One-third of those deaths are alcohol-related, as are one-half of all boating-related drownings. Alcohol distorts judgment more on the water than on land, and can complicate "boater's fatigue," a condition where the wind, noise, heat, and vibration of boating wear a person down.

According to the National Electronic Injury Surveillance System, 38% of personal watercraft (PWC) injuries occur to persons between the ages of 15 and 24; 7% to children 14 and under. PWC are the only recreational watercraft where the cause of death is usually blunt trauma instead of drowning. These injuries result when PWC collide with other PWC or fixed objects, such as trees or docks.

BOATS

- Take a boating course to learn about navigation rules, emergency procedures, and the effects of wind, weather, and water conditions.
- Whenever in a boat, make sure someone on land knows where you're going and how long you will be out.
- If planning to be far away from shore, make sure to bring a two-way radio.
- Know how to swim.
- Stay away from alcohol and drugs.
- Make sure children wear Coast Guard-approved life jackets, and make sure there are jackets for the adults, too.
- Watch the weather and stop boating if you see or hear a storm.

PERSONAL WATERCRAFT

Rider should:

- Be 16 or older and should know how to swim.
- Know local laws and regulations, including licensing requirements and required safety equipment.
- Ride with a buddy.
- Wear a Coast Guard-approved life jacket.
- Obey wake and speed rules.
- Not use it around swimmers and surfers.
- Not jump wakes.
- Avoid other boaters.
- Avoid alcohol and drugs.

TUBING AND RAFTING

- Know how to swim.
- Wear Coast Guard-approved life jackets.
- Don't overload the raft.
- Don't raft after a heavy rain.
- When using a tour company, make sure the guide is qualified. Check with your local or your vacation site Chamber of Commerce for a listing of accredited tour guides in the area.
- Tubing behind a boat is similar to water skiing; two people should be in the boat, one to drive and one to spot the person in the tube.
- Make sure weather and water conditions are safe.

SURFING

Should your teen wish to surf, make sure she:

- Knows how to swim.
- Takes surfing lessons from an experienced professional.
- Never surfs alone.
- Wears a wet suit when the water is cold.
- Watches weather and water conditions.

WATER SKIING

Should your child wish to water ski:

- Assure that the boat and equipment are safe.
- Have two people in the boat, one to drive and one to watch the skier.
- Keep an eye on the water in front of you at all times.
- Turn off boat motor when approaching a fallen skier.
- During landing, run parallel to the shore when slowing and come in slowly.

Make sure your child:

- Knows how to swim
- Has good physical strength.
- Wears a Coast Guard-approved life jacket.
- Takes lessons from a qualified instructor.
- Uses the appropriate hand signals to signal those in the boat.
- Doesn't ski at night or in restricted areas.
- Checks the weather and water conditions

SAILBOARDING AND WINDSURFING

Should your teen wish to sailboard or windsurf, make sure she:

- Knows how to swim
- Has good physical strength.
- Wears a Coast Guard-approved life jacket.
- Takes lessons from a qualified instructor.
- Checks the weather and water conditions

RECREATIONAL WATER ILLNESSES

Did you know that recreational water illnesses (RWI) are on the rise? It just so happens that germy little organisms love swimming as much as humans do, and they are found in pools, spas, hot tubs, ponds, fountains, lakes, rivers, and oceans.

Pseudomonas aeruginosa can cause swimmer's ear; parasites cause swimmer's itch, and noroviruses cause diarrhea. The Centers for Disease Control and Prevention (CDC) reported 59 new outbreaks that affected 2,093 people. A toxin-secreting strain of *Escherichia coli* causes 30% of freshwater breakouts, while *Cryptosporidium parvum* accounts for 70% of swimming pool and other disinfected swimming venue breakouts. Giardia is emerging as a cause of waterborne illness in both recreational and drinking water.

What can you do about RWI?

The CDC states that healthy swimming behaviors are needed to protect you and your children from RWIs, and will help stop germs from getting in the pool in the first place.

Follow the six CDC "P-L-E-As" that promote healthy swimming:

Three "P-L-E-As" for Everyone

PLEASE don't swim if you have diarrhea. This is especially true for kids in diapers. Organisms will get into the water and cause others to become ill.

PLEASE don't swallow the water. Try to not get any in your mouth at all.

PLEASE carefully wash your hands after using the toilet or changing a diaper. Germs on your body end up in the water.

Three "P-L-E-As" for Parents with Young Kids

PLEASE take your children on frequent bathroom breaks. The words, "I have to go," may translate to, "It's too late."

PLEASE change diapers often and in a bathroom–not pool-side. Germs can spread to objects in and around the pool and spread disease. Swim diapers are not leak-proof, so don't allow her to soil them.

PLEASE wash your child thoroughly, especially her bottom end, before swimming. Invisible fecal matter and germs can spread disease.

THE WATER YOU DRINK

The United States has one of the safest water supplies in the world, and most Americans will never contact waterborne disease from their household taps. Nevertheless, when contaminants enter the drinking water system and are not eliminated by the treatment processes, people get sick.

There is no such thing as pure water. All natural water contains some impurities, some of which are harmless, and even preferred by people who enjoy drinking mineral water. However, at certain levels, minerals can become contaminants that can make water nasty and even unsafe.

Some contaminants come from the natural erosion of rock formations; others come from factories, farmlands, homes, and yards. Sources of contamination can be nearby or miles away. The Environmental Protection Agency (EPA) sets standards for more than 80 contaminants that might occur in drinking water and pose a threat to humans. Some of these are: *cryptosporidium, giardia, legionella, E. coli*, arsenic, cadmium, cyanide, and lead. The effects of these contaminants may be acute or chronic.

Acute problems occur quickly, within hours or days after consuming the contaminated water. Organisms (*cryptosporidium, giardia, legionella, E. coli*) have the greatest chance of reaching levels high enough to cause illness. They tend to not cause permanent effects, but can be deadly for children with immunosuppression, including children on chemotherapy or high dose steroids.

Chronic effects happen after a person consumes low levels of contaminants over a period of years. Contaminants most responsible for chronic problems include chemicals (such as pesticides, solvents, and disinfection by-products), radionuclides such as radium, and minerals such as arsenic. Examples of chronic effects include cancer, kidney or liver problems, and reproductive difficulties.

For a complete list of contaminants and their health effects, log on to the EPA's list at www.epa.gov/safewater/mcl.html#mcls.

What can you do?

You should receive an annual report on your water quality. Find out information about your local drinking water system. Contact your local water authority or log onto the EPA's local drinking water website at: www.epa.gov/safewater/dwinfo.htm. If contaminant levels are above those accepted by the EPA, find out what the local authorities are doing to remedy the situation. In the interim,—or if unsure as to your water quality, or if you have an immunocompromised child at home,—use bottled water. You can save money by ordering 3 or 5 gallon bottles from a bottled water supplier in your area. Check the

Yellow Pages of your phone book for listings. If you're curious, I switched to bottled water during the last drought because our water smelled and tasted terrible. The drought cleared, but I did not switch back to the faucet.

Boiling doesn't provide total safety. As a matter of fact, it may even increase the content of certain chemicals in your tap water. Since infants are particularly susceptible to waterborne illness, stick to breast-feeding or ready-to-feed formula until you know your water is safe.

Have a well?

Federal standards don't include private wells. Therefore, if your water comes from the well on your property, you're responsible for making sure your water is safe. Since some states do set standards for private wells, check their state requirements.

Make sure to check for copper, cryptosporidium, lead, nitrate, organic chemicals, pesticides, and radon. Contact your State Certification Officer for certified water testing labs in your state. You can find your State Certification Officer at www.epa.gov/safewater/faq/sco.html.

21

WORLDWIDE HATE

CALIFORNIA, 2002:
Four arrested in the killing of a transgender teen.

SOME STATS

- Law enforcement agencies reported a total of 9,730 bias-motivated incidents in 2001.
- Of the 11,451 offenses reported by the Hate Crime Collection Program, 67.8% were crimes against persons, 31.5% against property, and 0.7% against society.
- 5,290 offenses were motivated by racial bias.
- 2,004 offenses were motivated by religious prejudice.
- 1,592 offenses were motivated by sexual orientation bias.

September 11, the Holocaust, gay bashing, graffiti; hate is everywhere—in the deserts, on the battlefields, in the streets, in schools.

Depending on the jurisdiction, hate crimes involve criminal acts in which the victims are selected based on characteristics such as race, national origin, ethnicity, sex/gender, religion, sexual orientation, or disability. These crimes may be attacks on persons and on property, and include threatening phone calls, hate mail, physical assault, threats of harm or violence, arson, vandalism, cross burnings, destruction of religious symbols, bombings, and bomb threats.

The effects of hate crimes can reverberate throughout entire communities. Hate crimes don't just affect individuals, they can harm every member of the group the victim represents, creating fear, vulnerability, insecurity, distrust, and outrage. They can also launch ongoing retaliation and counter-retaliation.

To add to the disturbing news, most hate crimes are committed by teenagers and young adults. Almost two-thirds of hate-propelled attacks are committed by individuals under age 24, and the majority of these are young white males. Most of their victims are also young, with nearly one-third under 18. Frequently targeted victims include African-Americans, Jews, Arab-Americans and Muslims, new immigrants, lesbians, gay men, and women.

WHY TEENS COMMIT HATE CRIMES

Many are thrill seekers who randomly target specific groups out of boredom, seeking excitement; others are trying to impress peers by proving their toughness. Some feel that members of specific groups pose a threat to their neighborhood or way of life, and a small number believe they are ridding the world of some perceived evil. Most of the latter group are psychotic, suffering from some form of mental illness.

Most teen perpetrators of hate crimes don't belong to organized hate groups, but all are motivated by prejudice.

TOLERANCE, PREJUDICE, AND DISCRIMINATION

The good news is that no one is born hating. Hateful attitudes and prejudice are learned from family, schools, friends, the media, and society in general. Therefore, it's possible for all of us to learn how to appreciate and respect our differences.

Tolerance has two levels. On one level, all children must learn to be prepared to live and work harmoniously with people from various cultural and racial groups, abilities, and backgrounds. As for the other level, children need to learn how to deal with the teasing that all children go through, as well as prejudice.

Prejudice means pre-judging. It entails opinions or attitudes about a person or group of people made solely because the person or group belongs to a specific race, religion, nationality, gender, sexual orientation, or other group, or because the person is elderly, disabled, or obese. Prejudiced feelings are strong and difficult to change.

People discriminate when they act on the basis of their prejudices. Discrimination means demoralizing people, disallowing them to participate in activities, clubs, or events, forcing them to live in certain neighborhoods, limiting their access to educational opportunities or employment, or refusing them something they are entitled to by law. Prejudice and discrimination are unfortunately common in our society, with incidents happening on a daily basis.

Prejudice isn't inborn; it's learned. Youngsters make innocent generalizations about short or obese people, and they have an incredible knack for noticing anyone who looks different, such as an Amish farmer or a Buddhist monk, often commenting loudly on their appearance. They may even make quick assumptions about children who wear glasses or braces. But these judgments arise from their trying to make sense of the world, not from spite or bigotry.

Children learn prejudice through living in and observing a society where prejudice exists. Their opinions are influenced by what people, especially their parents, say and do. Even if you model tolerance, your child still may be exposed to the intolerance of other people who don't respect differences.

Books, television, and movies sometimes present stereotyped views of various groups. Stereotyping is the oversimplified generalization of a group of people—such as considering them all to be "cheap," "lazy," "stupid," "criminal," or "dirty." Every group has people who are cheap as well as people who are generous, people who are lazy, and those who are industrious. People in every group commit crimes. Labeling an entire group constitutes stereotyping. Stereotyping is always negative, even when the stereotype itself is a positive trait (blondes are popular, African-Americans are good at basketball, Asians with glasses are smart).

The media can present misinformation or exclude important information that highlights specific groups in a positive manner. Your child can be unduly influenced by books and television shows that expose him only to certain groups and not others. If your child has a poor self-image, he may try to bolster his self-esteem by finding a group to put down, making him feel powerful and more important than those people he's putting down.

Your child may exclude or make fun of other children because he thinks it's the popular thing to do. He may use thoughtless names for people of specific groups if he thinks it will make him more accepted by his peer group. These behaviors grow into prejudice and discrimination. All children notice differences, which by itself is normal. However, when they attach negative values to those differences, they move away from normal and toward bigotry.

Your child may notice that some people refuse to associate with members of certain groups, or that members of certain groups rarely occupy influential positions in the community, including his school. He may overhear people tell put-down jokes. If you don't address these biases, your child may grow up to believe that this is the way things should be, and that people who are discriminated against deserve such treatment because they are inferior.

Address issues of prejudice and discrimination every time they occur. Point out inequities, and teach your child that these ideas and actions are unacceptable. Tell him that there is no place for prejudice and discrimination in your home, in schools, in the work-place, and in society in general.

TEACHING TOLERANCE

Your child begins to notice differences between the ages of two and three years. He notices differences in size (short or tall, fat or thin), skin color differences, and gender differences. He begins to observe visible disabilities such as a person in a wheelchair. He's like-ly to point out his observations, usually causing parental embarrass ment"—Mommy, look. That lady is brown." "Daddy, how come that man's riding a chair." These result from his developing awareness of his own physical identity, as well as personal characteristics, appear-ance, and preferences. Be amused, not concerned by his observations. His focus on skin color isn't about race; that is too complex a concept at this age. It's about colors, like the blue sky and red balls, because that is what he's learning.

When he asks about differences, frame your answers in terms that he can understand. For example, tell your preschooler that his friend has brown skin because his mother and father have brown skin. Uncomfortable silence speaks loudly, so don't pretend that you don't notice differences. When you deny differences, you deny a person's uniqueness. Instead, show your child the differences in the world around him—flowers, trees, animals, rocks. He doesn't need or want details at this age; he just needs reassurance that being different is part of the beauty of life.

By school-age, your child becomes very concerned with fair-ness and justice as exemplified by how loudly he complains when his friends get to do something that he doesn't. If someone is treated dif-ferently in school, he will notice. This gives you a golden opportunity to discuss issues of fairness and equality.

Don't dance around issues of intolerance. Once your child reaches the school years, he warrants explanations. Simply saying that prejudice is wrong isn't enough. Your child needs to know what prej-udice is and why it hurts people. He needs to discuss the differences he sees to draw informed conclusions about people.

You can't view raising your child and understanding diversity as two separate tasks. But you can use the following strategies to teach your child tolerance:

- Set an example. Your child learns his attitudes from the adults around him, especially his parents. You have ways of thinking and behaving that may seem natural to you, but are not necessarily what you want to pass along to your child. If you don't examine these attitudes and actions carefully, you can be harming your child's understanding of the world. We all have our own prejudices. If you catch yourself making a generalization or voicing unsound assumptions, admit it. Let your child know that you're struggling with it. When you own up to your own biases and ask for help, your child is likely to do the same.

- Accept your child as special and unique. Demonstrate to him that you recognize and appreciate his individual qualities. If your child feels good about himself, he's less likely to be prejudiced. The ability to accept the differences of others is built on the firm acceptance of oneself.

- Raise him to be sensitive to other people's feelings. Empathetic children are less likely to be prejudiced. Share stories with him that help him understand other people's points of view. When conflict erupts, encourage him to think about how the other person feels.

- Teach him to respect and appreciate differences. Encourage play with dolls that reflect all races and ethnicities. Provide opportunities for interaction with people from diverse groups. When children play together and work toward common goals, they develop positive attitudes about one another. Encourage your child to join diverse sports teams, clubs, or community programs to help counter the effects of homogeneous neighborhoods. Use books, educational television programs, and other programs that show diverse groups in a positive manner.

- Hold brief conversations instead of long, boring lectures. Give him the information he needs at each stage of his childhood, but bring up the topic regularly. Let him know that he can discuss the issue without your getting upset.

- Be casual and openhearted. You can't force your child to be open and tolerant, but you can encourage him to see people from a different perspective.

- Don't be halfhearted, but don't worry if you don't know all the answers. Your child is more likely to pay attention when you talk specifically and answer his questions directly.

However, it's okay to admit when you're not sure of what to say. This provides the two of you with the opportunity to go to the library or surf the net to research cultural diversity and other differences. Just make sure that your source is accurate.

- Help him to recognize instances of prejudice and discrimination, and make sure he knows how to respond to them. Foster critical thinking skills, a good antidote to prejudice. Use the television as a source by examining shows, especially cartoons, which show diverse people in a negative fashion. For example, explore why bad guys seem to always have foreign accents, or why blonde women are frequently portrayed as being dumb.

- Be sure that he knows prejudice and discrimination are unfair. Create a house rule that no one be teased or excluded on the basis of their differences. Whenever you see discrimination, point it out and discuss it.

- Find out what he thinks so that you may correct his misconceptions. After you determine what he thinks, respond with something simple like, "I'm trying to understand why you said that, but I don't see it that way." Be direct and brief, using language that he will understand.

- Differentiate prejudice from dislike. Prejudice means having an idea or opinion about someone without really knowing them. Dislike bases feelings on information or experiences with a specific person.

- Don't tolerate prejudice language, including name-calling. Tell them that it sounds to you like he doesn't like someone (whoever was called the name) even though he doesn't know that person. Then explain that he can only like or dislike people he knows. If he doesn't know that person, he has no reason to not like him. He may not like playing with certain children, but it should not be because of their diverseness. Realize that your young child often doesn't understand the meanings of the words he uses, but that he does realize that some words get reactions. Teach him that words can hurt as much as hitting. If he uses a racist word or other slur, talk to him immediately. Tell him that such language isn't tolerated.

- Don't tolerate biased humor. If you laugh at an ethnic joke, you're giving your child the message that humor at the expense of someone else's background is tolerable. Teach him that this form of humor or language shows disrespect to people who are different. Remember that young children often use humor to test the limits of acceptable behavior. If you hear him use inappropriate language, don't get angry, but don't ignore it either. Tell him that you find the comment distasteful, and explain why.

- Foster his ability to create change. Help him to realize that he can make a difference. Encourage him to write to television producers who promote stereotypical characterizations, confront a peer's discriminatory remarks, or organize a clean-up group to paint over discriminatory graffiti.
- Create change yourself. Help your child with the above actions. If adults around you're bigoted, don't ignore it. Ask them to not talk like that in your or your children's presence. Hold yourself to the same standards that you want your child to follow.

HELPING YOUR CHILD DEAL WITH PREJUDICE

Differentiate normal childhood teasing from prejudiced remarks. All children get teased for being different at some point during their preschool years. Taunts such as "four-eyes," "metalmouth," and "freckleface" seem to hit each generation. Teasing is part of your preschooler's search for his own identity. It also helps him learn tolerance by experiencing the pain himself. If he doesn't experience it, it becomes difficult for him to understand the pain of others. When your child learns to accept and ignore the teasing that all children go through, he will be ready to respect the differences of others.

When your child becomes the target of prejudiced remarks, it's a different ball game. If your child is hurt by racial or ethnic cruelty, it's hard to restrain an emotional response. But don't give in to the temptation to fly off the handle. Your child needs your reassurance that he's a good person, and that the people who call him bad names are not nice people. Then tell him that all people of that particular group don't act like that, and that there are good people and bad people in all groups.

Acknowledge both his hurt and his anger so that he knows you respect his emotions. Clarify what happened by asking your child about the incident, as well as what he thought the other person meant. If he clearly misinterpreted a harmless comment, explain what the words really mean. The other person may have been trying to be funny or get approval from his peers. But if the comment was made with the intent to cause emotional harm, teach him how to handle it.

Your child needs encouragement to be assertive when this problem arises so that he will develop healthy coping mechanisms that don't compromise his dignity. He should at least tell the perpetrator to stop calling him names. Stress that he first try talking the problem out. If the situation gets out of control, adult intervention may be needed, and he should know that you will be there to back him up. But encourage him to first try to handle the situation himself. That way he will be able to handle the situation should it arise again.

EDUCATING THE EDUCATORS – WHAT SCHOOLS CAN DO

In its "Guide for Schools: Protecting Students from Harassment and Hate Crimes," the United States Department of Education notes that schools need to establish an environment free from harassment and discrimination that requires more than just punishing students who commit acts of misconduct.

According to the United States Department of Education, strong programs often start with developing and enforcing written policies and procedures that support the school's anti-harassment efforts. The school's instructional program, calendar of events, extracurricular activities, professional development efforts, and parent involvement initiatives are critical to establishing an environment where respect for diversity flourishes. Successful prevention strategies depend on the coordinated efforts of all school employees, as well as parents, students, law enforcement agencies, and other community organizations.

Schools should consider developing action plans both at the district level and at individual school sites that specify the steps each segment of the school community will take to implement a comprehensive anti-harassment program. The key components are as follows:

- Develop written policies that prohibit unlawful harassment that require staff to report incidents.
- Identify and respond to all incidents of harassment and violence.
- Provide formal complaint procedures.
- Create a school climate that supports diversity.
- Work with law enforcement to address and prevent hate crimes.

For the complete United States Department of Education document, go to www.ed.gov/pubs/Harassment/fundamentals1.html.

SECTION TWO

SAFETY TIPS FOR SPECIAL CIRCUMSTANCES

22

KIDS WITH DISABILITIES

Children with physical, cognitive, or psychological disabilities have higher rates of injury than children without disabilities. Sensorineural deficits, such as blindness or deafness, may also increase the risk of certain types of injury, while attention deficit hyperactivity disorder places children at greater risk from bicycle- and pedestrian-related injuries, head injuries, and multiple injuries than children without ADHD. Children with ADHD are also more likely to suffer more severe injuries and develop functional limitations as a result of their injuries.

Children with special needs are also at greater risk for abuse and from victimization from their peers.

PROTECT YOUR CHILDREN FROM INJURY

ADHD

The impulsivity and hyperactivity of ADHD tend to make children more susceptible to injury than average. Pay more attention to common dangers, such as those related to drowning and falling. Make sure he's supervised, and don't pair him off with another ADHD child and send them on their way. Use visual reminders, like the "Mr. Yuk" stickers, which may work even on older children with ADHD who are developmentally immature and have poor memories. Use "Don't touch" stickers on objects that can cause injury, including power tools, cellar and attic doors, the stove, and other potential sources. Make sure your safety rules are clear and specific, and establish exactly what is off-limits. Create a chart and post it in her room and in the kitchen as a daily reminder. Use role play about unsafe situations; play the tempting kid and ask, "Hey, do you want a cigarette?" Act out several different scenarios and explore their consequences.

MOTOR DISABILITY

Even if your child has minimal motor movement, take safety precautions to prevent falling. Don't leave him on a bed or other elevated surface. Falls are the most common injury in wheelchair-bound children. To prevent wheelchair falls, utilize suggestions from Parenting Special Needs:

- Make sure the chair fits your child's size and needs.
- Have the chair checked at least once a year by your dealer and have repairs performed by a licensed dealer.
- Make sure the brakes, locks, armrests, footrests, wheels, tires, and casters are in good working condition.
- Check the tires to make sure that the pressure is adequate.
- Don't use the wheelchair in a vehicle without proper tie-downs.
- Use the anti-tippers.
- Be sure that all locks are in place before the individual transfers to the wheelchair.
- Don't tilt a wheelchair without assistance.
- Don't use an escalator.
- When using stairs or a ramp with a steep incline, two people should be present to help the wheelchair user–one in the front of the chair, the other in the rear.
- When assisting a chair user, use the gripped handles. Don't attempt to use chair surfaces that could be slippery.
- Carry a cell phone, but note that cell phones and other electrical equipment can interfere with the performance of your power chair.
- Don't attempt to maneuver through ice and snow without assistance.
- Carry salt in a backpack to throw on icy spots.
- Don't travel long distances alone or without a travel plan.
- Make sure you have an accessible exit in case of emergency, and notify your fire department of the presence of a child with a disability in your home.

HEARING IMPAIRMENT

Hearing-impaired children can't rely on the lifesaving warning sound of a working smoke alarm to alert them of a fire. To keep your child safe:

- Install flashing or vibrating fire alarms on every level of your home and in your child's bedroom. Contact your local fire department for information on obtaining these devices.
- Make sure your TTY/TDD or phone is within arm's reach.
- Keep emergency phone numbers and hearing aids handy.

- Contact your local fire department to explain your special needs.

TOY SAFETY

For the most part, children with special needs can play with regular toys, occasionally with modifications. But toys should be durable, versatile, challenging, engaging, and most of all, safe.

Your child with physical disabilities should have toys that feature solid construction that supports his body, large buttons or levers that are easy to use, non-slide bottoms, and easy operation and maneuverability.

Your hearing-impaired child should have amplified or adjustable volume toys, or ones that feature: variable sounds and vibrations; bold, contrasting colors to visually stimulate him; interesting textures; and scented parts.

Your visually-impaired child should have toys that feature large or raised parts, realistic sounds, easy to activate components, various shapes and textures, and distinct scents.

LATEX ALLERGY

Latex allergy has become a way of life for many children, especially children with spina bifida and congenital urinary tract anomalies, and children who have had three or more surgeries. Exposure to latex for these children can cause anything from skin irritation to a life-threatening reaction. Unfortunately, latex is found in a number of objects. Therefore, parents need to exercise caution. Some examples of latex-containing objects and their alternatives are:

LATEX OBJECT	ALTERNATIVE
Latex balloons	Mylar balloons
Latex balls (koosh, tennis, bowling)	PVC and *Nerf* balls
Chewing gum	*Bubbilicious, Trident*
Diapers, rubber pants	*Huggies, Pampers, Luvs*
Feeding nipples	Silicone and vinyl (check the labels)
Toys	Many of the *Fisher Price* toys
Bathing suits	*Suits Me* swimwear
Wheelchair cushions	*ROHO* cushions
Zippered plastic bags	*Ziploc bags*

PROTECT YOUR CHILD FROM ABUSE AND VICTIMIZA-
TION

Children with disabilities are more vulnerable to abuse, bullying, and other victimizations. You need to take a proactive role and
teach your child personal safety. Follow the guidelines in the "Human
Predators" chapter as well as these tips from an article in *The
Exceptional Parent*, by Cema Mastroleo and Wendie H. Abramson:

- Discuss feelings such as confused, scared, angry, and safe,
  and provide examples of situations when these feelings
  may be experienced.
- Discuss various types of touches; ones that are appropriate (high fives from friends, goodnight kiss from parent)
  and ones that are inappropriate (pulling hair, slapping,
  touching one's private parts).
- Talk about safe ways to respond to hurtful or dangerous
  situations, including telling trusted adults, yelling for
  help, and saying, "no."
- Explain that she has rights; allow her to make choices and
  even say "no" to you once in a while.
- Talk about secrets. Tell her that children have secrets with
  each other, but adults don't have secrets with children.
- Discuss socially acceptable behaviors. Shaking hands in
  public is okay, undressing is not.
- Discuss and model family values.
- Use appropriate terms for body parts and discuss sexuality and puberty.
- Make arrangements if she needs assistance with personal
  hygiene at school.
- If she tells you she has been abused, talk to her about it
  and contact her health care provider.

23

RURAL KIDS

Children living in rural areas have a much higher risk from unintentional injury-related death than children living in urban areas. They are especially at risk from drowning, motor vehicle crashes, unintentional firearm injury, residential fires, and agricultural work-related injury. Higher injury fatality rates in rural communities are due in part to the high number of farm-related injuries. Children account for 20% of all injury-related farm fatalities, and represent an even larger portion of nonfatal injuries.

Injuries in rural settings occur in remote, sparsely populated areas that usually lack trauma care, resulting in prolonged response and transport times. The short supply of medical facilities, equipment, and personnel also contributes to increased risk.

Drowning, motor vehicle accidents, firearm injuries, and fires are discussed in chapters 20, 19, 7, and 6, respectively.

AGRICULTURAL SAFETY FOR CHILDREN

Children should always be supervised when performing work-related farming tasks, and should never perform tasks that are inappropriate for their age, size, strength, cognitive ability, or prior experience. They should also be prevented from entering hazardous areas.

The Centers for Disease Control and Prevention (CDC) National Agriculture Safety Base provides age-appropriate information for parents and grandparents regarding the safety of their children/grandchildren on the farm:

TODDLERS AND PRESCHOOLERS

Injuries to toddlers and preschoolers tend to occur when playing on the farm or when riding on farm equipment. Toddlers and preschoolers can climb, walk, and run. They have very short memories and like to test reality. Preschoolers have a fascination with moving parts, (for example PTOs, belts, and moving corn in an auger,) and children under five learn by trial and error.

Types of Injuries: falls from tractors; falls from heights, for example: silos, ladders, and hay holes; kicked and stepped on by animals; ingestion of chemicals.

Prevention

- Never have a child as an extra rider.
- Keep ladders out of reach.
- Keep chemicals in locked storage.
- Oversee their activities.
- Provide a fenced play area away from farming activities.

SCHOOL-AGE CHILDREN

Injuries to school-age children occur at both work and play. This is the age group when children like to explore and be creative, and when parental attention and praise are very important. School-age children generally try to complete any assigned task to please their parents, even though the task may not be appropriate for them. They don't feel they can tell their parents "No," even if they know the task is beyond their capability. This attitude results in many accidents. For example, a tired or weak child is more likely to become entangled in farm machinery.

Types of Injuries: falls from barns; auger amputations and entanglements; tractor rollover; suffocation in grain.

Prevention

- Restrict play areas.
- Evaluate your child's physical and mental maturity for a given task.
- Have proper protective devices on equipment, such as ROPS and shields.
- Place warning decals on hazardous equipment or locations.
- Set aside time to discuss farm dangers with your child.

ADOLESCENTS (AGES 12-16)

Most teens participate in farm labor. Therefore, their injuries are usually work-related. Teens are greatly influenced by peer pressure. They don't like to look like failures; they want to impress others and tend to believe they are immortal. Many risky behaviors, intended to impress, result in accidents.

Age should not be used as the sole measure of maturity. Some other variables that distinguish individual adolescents are judgment and body size. Experience and observation help to improve judgment. A parent who models proper safety precautions is the best teacher. Improper behaviors that parents perform automatically, for example stepping over a moving PTO, will likely be copied by their child.

There is a tremendous difference in the size of adolescents. Growth occurs in spurts and varies between siblings. A task that was appropriate for one son or daughter at age 12, may not be appropriate for his/her brother or sister at the same age.

Types of Injuries: tractor rollovers; amputations from PTOs; MVA (motor vehicle accidents) with farm equipment on roads; suffocation in grain bins.

Prevention

- Evaluate your child's physical and mental maturity for a given task.
- Install the proper protective devices on equipment.
- Have him complete the necessary safety courses for operating farm machinery.
- Teach him to use personal protective equipment.
- Set aside time to discuss farm safety with children.
- Be a good role model.

Be sensitive to the development and needs of your child. When assigning tasks, consider your child's age, maturity level, attention span, and physical size. If your child isn't physically ready for a task (for example, if he's too short), don't allow him to perform it. Don't alter machinery in an attempt to make up for your child's developmental state, such using blocks on tractor brakes.

Assess his level of alertness. If your child has been in school all day, he may be tired. Fatigue will increase the likelihood of an accident. A little time spent evaluating your child before assigning tasks may end up saving his life.

24

LATCHKEY (HOME ALONE) KIDS

Latchkey kids are children left at home to care for themselves, usually between the hours of 3 and 6 P.M.–the hours when children are most likely to experiment with alcohol and other drugs, and the hours when most children participate in violent activities. About 1.2 million of these latchkey kids live in homes with guns.

Inadequate supervision leaves these children at risk for both injuries and delinquent behaviors. Some feel more lonely, isolated, and fearful than other children who have supervision. To deal with their anxieties, they hide in closets or under beds, play the TV loud as a distraction to drown out noises and indicate that someone is home, and rely on pets for comfort. However, many enjoy the solitude, privacy, and responsibility, while others simply tolerate it out of necessity.

By all means, do everything possible to avoid leaving your child home alone. If both parents work during the after-school hours, or if you're a single parent, first try to find an after-school program for him. If that isn't possible, make arrangements for a relative or neighbor to watch him until you get home.

HOW TO TELL IF YOUR CHILD CAN HANDLE BEING HOME ALONE

Deciding whether and when your child is ready to care for herself alone at home is a difficult task for any parent. Most child care experts and specialists—including this one–recommend that children not be left home alone before the age of 12 (unless state law suggests an older age). However, there are other factors to consider, suggested by SafeChild:

- Ask yourself whether you can trust her.
- Your child indicates a desire or willingness to stay home alone.
- She can exercise good judgment and follow directions on serious issues, such as answering the phone and computer usage.
- Your child shows signs of accepting responsibility.

- The lines of communication between you and your child are open and running smoothly.
- She knows how to respond to an emergency.

You will also need to decide how long she can be home alone. Some children do well from the time they get home from school until their parents get home from work; others can only handle several minutes.

WHAT TO DO FOR YOUR HOME ALONE CHILD

Unfortunately, many parents have little choice but to leave their children unattended for those few, but critical, hours. If you have a latchkey child, follow these suggestions:

- Begin leaving her home alone progressively, for short periods of time, and stay close to home.
- Teach him to never display his keys and to always lock the doors. Give a spare key to a trusted neighbor.
- Instruct him to not enter the house if the door is ajar, a window is open, or if anything looks unusual. Tell him to go to a neighbor's and report his findings, because these signs mean that an intruder may be present.
- Tell him to not open the door for anyone, unless that person is approved by you.
- Leave emergency phone numbers where he can easily access them, preferably by the phone. Make sure he knows how to access 911. If available, use the memory feature in your phone so that your child can access you or emergency personnel with the touch of just one or two numbers.
- Establish clear rules as to what he can and can't do until you get home, and set up consequences ahead of time in case he breaks them.
- Instruct him to tell callers that you're busy, and NOT to tell them you're not home.
- Prepare a safety kit and teach him basic first aid.
- Teach cooking safety rules if he's expected to cook. Keep cooking to a minimum, and, whenever possible, have him use the microwave instead of the stove.
- Teach him fire safety rules, and make sure he understands them. Practice fire safety techniques regularly to assure that your child knows what to do in the event of a fire.

- Teach him weather safety rules, especially if you live in an area known to have bad weather.
- Reinforce water safety rules. If he must bathe younger siblings during this time, make sure he understands safe bathing methods.
- Make sure that your firearms are unloaded and locked, that the ammunition is locked in a separate area, and that he has no possible access to the keys. Utilize safety devices that prevent unauthorized users from firing the guns.
- Provide structured activities to fill his time until you get home.

No matter how "mature" your child may seem, he's still a child. Be punctual at arriving home, and talk to him about his day and how he's managing alone. Reinforce the rules periodically, and praise him for handling himself well.

25

BABYSITTER SAFETY

Sooner or later you have to get out of the house–without the kids. Choosing a sitter is a difficult decision, even when that person is needed for just a few hours a month. You want to know that your child is safe, even when you're not there to protect him.

You also want to know your child is safe when he's the one who is doing the babysitting.

HOW TO KNOW YOUR CHILD IS READY FOR A SITTER

Every child has his own temperament and personality, so each is different. But most children go through two normal phases that can impact on being left with a sitter–stranger anxiety and separation anxiety.

Stranger awareness begins around 3 to 9 months when your child realizes that everyone isn't mommy. It peaks around age 8 months. How your child reacts to "strangers"—grandparents, neighbors ,and sitters can count as strangers to babies—depends on a number of factors, including the presence or absence of a familiar figure, fatigue, and illness. Anxiety tends to intensify when in unknown surroundings, with the appearance and approach by the stranger, and due to the physical proximity of the parent during the new encounter. However, children who are exposed to many different adults during infancy usually experience less stranger anxiety than those who experience few.

Separation anxiety peaks around 18 to 20 months. Your now-mobile toddler wants to run and explore, but hates being away from mommy. Some children may even cry when mommy just leaves the room. Like stranger anxiety, the severity depends on a number of factors, particularly temperament and the number of adults the child is exposed to during infancy. And like stranger anxiety, it's a normal part of development that he will outgrow.

Both stranger anxiety and separation anxiety can be intensified by stress, including the addition of a new household member, a move, hospitalization, family stress, or your returning back to work.

To ease the transition to a sitter:

- Don't let him pick up on your anxiety. If you feel nervous, he will feel nervous, too.
- Keep his feeding and rituals the same.
- Practice short-term separations.
- Introduce "strangers," including the babysitter slowly, in your presence. Let your child see that the sitter is a safe person by having the sitter stand next to you as you approach your child, and don't forget to smile!
- Never sneak out on your child.
- For your toddler: Provide transitional objects (blankie, favorite toy), and tell him when you will be back, using terms he can understand ("when his favorite TV show is on;" "when he wakes up").
- Stop feeling guilty!

CHOOSING A SITTER

If you're looking for a full-time sitter, read Chapter 15 for more detailed information. For the occasional sitter, you still want someone trustworthy, responsible, and reliable. And plan ahead. Don't wait until the day you need a sitter to look for one.

To find a sitter, ask friends and family. You can also get names of sitters from the phone book and neighborhood bulletin boards, but be sure to check them out thoroughly–ask for and call their references. Interview several before making your choice, using these criteria from the National Safe Kids Campaign:

- Is at least 13 years old.
- Has experience with children, which can include younger brothers and sisters.
- Has taken a babysitter training course (usually at the YMCA or American Red Cross).
- Is certified in infant and child CPR.
- Knows what to do in an emergency.
- Is willing to accept your guidelines for taking care of your child.
- Understands the importance of constant supervision.

Meet with the sitter and watch him spending time with your children. Give him a tour of your home and show him the areas that are off-limits to the children, and to the sitter, if desired. Have him babysit while you're there so he can familiarize himself with your routine. If you have pets, make sure he meets them, too.

BABYSITTER SAFETY DO'S AND DON'T'S

DO:

- Childproof the house.
- Explain your expectations to the sitter–such as phone and friends off limits.
- Discuss her responsibilities:
    Children's bedtimes and routines.
    What the children can and can't eat, and when they can eat it.
    Allergies.
    Medical problems.
    Medications, if she needs to administer them. You should have her do this during her dry run to make sure she's capable. Explain what, how much and when to give the medication, and leave written instructions. HOWEVER, don't leave the medication where the children can reach it.
- Any other special directions.
- Make sure the sitter knows where you will be, what time you will be home, and how to reach you. Tell him what you will be wearing, in case he needs to identify you to someone over the phone.
- Post emergency numbers (911 or alternate, health care provider, poison control, trusted neighbor or relative) by the phone, show them to the sitter, and make sure he knows what to do in case of emergency.
- Give her a file with photos of your children. Include their names, birth dates, height, weight, and hair and eye color, in case the children get lost).
- Show the sitter where the smoke and carbon monoxide detectors, fire extinguishers, first-aid kit and emergency exits are located.
- Demonstrate the security system.
- Make sure the sitter has safe escort home.

DON'T'S

Make sure he knows not to:
- Let your children play in unsafe areas (near the stove or stairs) or with unsafe things (matches or outlets).

- Give your young child small objects he may choke on.
- Leave your children unattended.
- Give them any medication without your written instructions.
- Have his friends over while sitting or tie up the phone.

IF YOUR TEEN WANTS TO BABYSIT

You can certainly allow your teen to watch his younger brothers and sisters if he's capable. Just remember not to overdo it, which may lead to resentment or an uprising of sibling rivalry.

Babysitting for other people's kids is a great way for your teen to learn responsibility and make some money. However, you want your child to be as safe as the child he cares for; therefore, have him take a babysitting course (contact your local American Red Cross chapter or YMCA) and a CPR and first aid course (contact your local American Red Cross or American Heart Association chapter). Before he accepts a job, check out the family he will be caring for and find out what is expected of him. Make sure he only takes jobs he can handle, and if he feels uncomfortable, tell him to turn down the job.

When babysitting, have him do the following:

- Make sure he has all the emergency contacts he needs, and knows where the emergency equipment is located.
- Turn on the outdoor lights at night.
- Lock the doors and windows.
- Not tell anyone who calls that he's the babysitter.
- Not open the door to strangers, including delivery people.
- Not tie up the phone.
- Not have friends over.
- Always watch the children–never leave them unsupervised.
- Follow all directions and instructions carefully.
- Never use alcohol or drugs while caring for someone's children.
- Have a safe escort home.

26

CAMPING SAFETY

More and more Americans are heading for the outdoors. Whether camping out in the backyard with friends, in the woods with dad, or in a motor home campsite, you want your child's camping experience to be as safe as it's fun. The great outdoors hosts numerous wonders for your child to see and learn about, but it is also home to bugs, poisonous plants, wildlife, and the sun.

PLAN AHEAD

If you're inexperienced, don't set out for a week in the wilderness. Start small with day trips and work your way up. Read guide books, talk to park rangers and experienced campers, and learn about the terrain and weather of where you want to go. Learn about seasonal transitions so that you're not caught in storm or deep freeze by surprise, especially when camping in the mountains, where you may also have to acclimate yourselves to the altitude. Heat can be dangerous for children, since their sweat glands don't develop until adolescence. Plan to hike during cooler mornings and evenings, and spend time in the shade during the day.

Learn about the supplies you will need. Know how to erect a temporary shelter and give first aid. Know what to do if your child becomes unexpectedly ill or lost, and what to do if you come into contact with a wild animal.

Getting lost is a common problem, so plan ahead to familiarize yourselves with the area. Learn how to read a topographical map and pack a compass. Bring whistles for the children to wear in case they do get lost, and teach them the universal signal of three blows to call for help.

If your child has a medical problem, check with your health care provider to see if camping is appropriate for her, and pack necessary medical supplies. Makes sure you have access to emergency care should your child need it while on your trip.

Pack the right clothes to protect against sudden weather and temperature changes. Multi-layered polypropylene, wool, and cotton are best in layers of tank top, shirt, and sweater. Clothing should be bright and colorful to increase your child's visibility. Don't forget breathable, waterproof jackets and pants, as well as hats to protect against the sun and insects. Hiking boots should be comfortable to prevent blisters, and make sure to tuck your child's pant legs into the boots to protect against ticks. And don't forget the bug spray.

Lakes and streams may be inviting, but they also may be toilets for wildlife. Bring your own water. If you can't lug it along, bring water filters or iodine tablets created for water purification. Plan your meals and bring extra food. Bring portable food, such as trail mix, granola or cereal bars, protein bars, fruit, bread and peanut butter, and dehydrated meals that just require you to add water. Don't plan on foraging for berries, mushrooms, and other flora unless you're an expert at it.

Beside the above, also pack the following:

- Tent
- Sleeping bags
- Flashlight
- Radio with weather channel
- Emergency signaling device
- Lots of extra batteries and bulbs
- First aid kit
- Sunglasses and sunscreen
- Pocket knife
- Pocket mirror (signaling device if needed)
- Matches in a waterproof container, candle, or fire starter
- Foil (signaling device if needed)
- Nylon filament
- Space blankets
- Trash bags (can be used as ponchos)

The American Red Cross suggests that you pack separate "survival packs" for each hiker to have at all times. Place a pocket knife, compass, whistle, space blanket, nylon filament, water purification tablets, matches, and candles in waterproof containers for each family member old enough to use them. These kits increase survival chances in the wild.

For those of you not really roughing it, call ahead to see if the campsites require advanced registrations or permits. Find out their regulations, and don't go to campsites that are closed.

CAMPING SAFETY DO'S and DON'TS

DO'S

- Use sunscreen and bug spray, and check your child's skin for ticks.
- Be aware of potential dangers: fallen trees, forest fires, and man-made problems, including broken glass, discarded needles.
- Scout the area before pitching your tent.
- Know where the nearest telephone and ranger station are located.
- Remember that your child's body temperature changes faster than yours.
- Keep tabs on the weather.
- Teach your child water safety (see Chapter 20).
- Teach your child to stay away from river banks and cliffs and to be careful when climbing trees. Moss and dead branches can cause falls.
- Stay calm in the event of an emergency.
- Keep your children away from campfires and portable stoves.
- Stay clear of poison ivy and oak.
- Use portable heaters, lanterns, and vehicles properly to prevent carbon monoxide poisoning.
- Map hiking trails ahead of time.
- Teach your children to stay away from wild animals, even small ones.

DON'TS

- Don't feed the wildlife.
- Don't leave young children unsupervised.
- Don't let your child go into the water without testing the temperature and making sure it's safe. Calm water may contain strong undercurrents.
- Don't start fires in windy weather.
- Don't create campfires or use portable stoves, heaters, or lanterns inside tents, campers, or vehicles.

SECTION THREE

CHECKLISTS

27

HOME SAFETY CHECKLIST

Use this list to check your home for general safety measures. The list isn't inclusive, so don't forget to read the rest of the book!

EMERGENCY PHONE NUMBERS

- Do your children know how and when to dial 911 or other emergency number?
- Are emergency numbers available to babysitters?
- Are the following numbers posted?
  Police
  Fire
  Ambulance/paramedics
  Poison control
  Primary health care provider
  Electric company
  Gas company

FIRE SAFETY

- No frayed wires or overloaded sockets; don't run cords under rugs; don't use lightbulbs that exceed lamps' recommended wattage.
- Disconnect small appliances when not in use.
- Use only 300-watt bulbs and a protective wire guard on halogen torchere lamps.
- Keep lamps away from drapes/curtains and flammable material and fluids.
- Have your electrical system checked by a professional if any problems are found, such as warm outlets, flickering lights, blown fuses, or circuit breakers that shut off.
- Have your chimneys cleaned and inspected annually.
- Keep stove and dryer vent hoses, exhaust vents, and external vents free of dust and lint build-up.
- Set hot water heater at 120°F (49°C)
- Aim pot handles turned inward on stove; keep anything that can burn away from burners.
- No loose clothing worn near stoves/open flames.
- Use of cold mist, (not hot) vaporizers.

- Make sure your have an adult-only accessible fuse box, circuit breaker, gas shut-off valve
- Store gasoline in an approved, tightly sealed and marked container, and place outside, or in detached garage or shed. Store flammable liquids in tight containers, and never store oily rags, charcoal briquettes, or fireplace ashes (even cold ones) in bags; they can generate enough heat to cause spontaneous combustion.
- Have fire extinguishers on every floor, in the kitchen, garage, workshop, and basement. Check them periodically to make sure they are pressurized.
- Install at least one smoke alarm on every floor, especially in or near sleep areas. Replace batteries twice a year, and test alarms periodically.
- Provide fire escape ladders for upper floors.
- Make a fire escape plan and practice it regularly.
- Don't smoke. But if you do, don't smoke in bed or near children. Keep smoking equipment out of children's reach.

WATER SAFETY

- Learn CPR.
- Never leave young children alone in tubs or near water (pools, lakes, streams, etc.)
- Pools should be fenced in with locked gates.
- Keep proper safety equipment poolside.
- Teach children how to swim and and rules of water safety.

FALL SAFETY

- Use nonskid mats/surfaces in tubs and showers.
- Keep stairs, hallways, and exits free of toys and clutter.
- Install sturdy handrails on stairways.
- Make sure your stairs and hallways are well lit.
- Secure scatter rugs with nonskid backing.
- Keep walks, drives, steps, and carpet in good repair.

FIREARM SAFETY

- Keep firearms in locked cabinet, inaccessible to children.
- Store ammunition separate from firearms.
- Teach your children firearm safety.
- If older children hunt or target shoot, have them attend a safety course.

POISON SAFETY

- Call medications "medicine," not candy.
- Keep syrup of ipecac in home.
- Don't administer medications unless prescribed by health care provider.
- Use medications with childproof caps.
- Keep all medications and household poisons out of reach of children.
- Avoid use of poisonous plants, or hang them out of reach.
- Don't remove labels from medications and household poisons.
- Don't put household poisons in alternate containers such as soda bottles.

PET SAFETY

- Keep pets properly restrained.
- Keep immunizations up to date.
- Spay or neuter pet to decrease aggressive tendencies.
- Never leave infant or young child alone with pets.
- Properly socialize and train pets.
- Don't play aggressive games with the pet.
- Seek advice from veterinarian if pet shows aggressive tendencies.
- Teach children safety measures: don't disturb pet when sleeping, eating, caring for young; don't touch any strange animals; don't pet animal without allowing it to see and smell you first.

OTHER HOUSEHOLD SAFETY MEASURES

- Safely store knives, garden tools, and power tools
- Keep yards free of broken glass, nails, and other litter.
- Keep playground safe:
  —Keep equipment in good repair.
  —Have resilient surface under equipment to reduce impact from falls.
  —Use age-appropriate equipment.
  —Keep area free from broken glass, nails, and other litter.
- Remove or lock doors of unused refrigerators.
- Install sensor on garage door to allow it to rise if object is in its path.
- Never leave children alone in parked car, especially in summer.

- Secure large objects such as televisions, entertainment centers, and fireplace mantels, so children don't pull them down on themselves, causing severe crush injuries and death.
- Avoid exposure to loud noises.

28

AGE-SPECIFIC SAFETY CHECKLIST

To keep your child safe throughout her childhood, use this checklist as guide, but remember, it's not inclusive, so read the rest of the book!

YOUNG INFANTS (Birth to 6 months)

FALLS

- Raise crib rails.
- Never leave infant unattended on raised surface.
- Never leave infant unattended in infant seat or swing.
- Don't use high chair until child can sit without support. When used, never leave child unsupervised.

ASPIRATION/SUFFOCATION

- Keep plastic bags out of reach.
- Don't cover mattress with plastic.
- No pillows; no loose bedding or soft mattresses.
- Crib should meet federal guidelines: side slat no less than 2½ inches apart; no decorative cutouts; mattress fits snugly on all sides; drop sides have safety latches and lower only part way.
- Bumper pads should fit around entire perimeter and be secured in six places. Ties should be secured to prevent choke hazard.
- Use one-piece pacifier. Don't tie pacifier around neck, and remove her bib at night.
- Avoid baby powder. If used, don't shake near her face.
- Avoid bottle propping, and don't feed your infant lying down.
- Keep small objects out of reach. Toys should not have small, removable parts.

BURNS

- Use caution when heating formula, especially in microwave.
- Check temperature of bath water.
- Don't use hot liquids near infant.
- Don't leave infant in sun. Sun exposure should be very brief, and sunscreen should be used.

- Use flame retardant clothes and wash them according to manufacturer's directions.
- Check temperature of car seat before placing infant in it.
- Don't smoke or drink hot fluids while holding or caring for infant.

MOTOR VEHICLES

- Don't place infant in lap or seat.
- Use car seat properly. See Chapter 19 for instructions.
- Don't place carriage or stroller behind parked car.
- Don't leave infant alone in car.

OTHER INJURIES

- Never shake the baby.
- Avoid using sharp objects near infant.
- Keep diaper pins closed and pointed away from infant.
- Support the infant's head and neck when holding and carrying.

OLDER INFANTS (6 to 12 months)

FALLS

- Don't use infant walkers.
- Gate the tops and bottoms of stairs.
- Dress your infant in clothing and shoes that don't interfere with mobility.
- Install safety devices on windows.
- Make sure furniture is sturdy enough for child to pull self up on.
- Lower mattress and keep crib rails up.
- Don't leave unattended in high chair.

SUFFOCATION/ASPIRATION

- Keep balloons out of reach, and avoid latex balloons whenever possible.
- Remove all crib toys that are strung along crib.
- Keep small objects out of reach.
- No pacifiers or jewelry around neck.
- Keep plastic bags out of reach.
- Avoid overly-padded bedding, bean bags, and waterbeds.
- Keep cords secured and out of reach.
- Exercise caution with finger foods.
- Avoid foods such as peanuts that can be easily aspirated.

POISONING

- Furniture and toys should not be painted with lead-based paint.
- Store batteries in a safe place, and discard used ones.

BURNS

- Same as for younger infant.
- Place guards around stove and fireplace.
- Put plastic guards on outlets.
- Keep tablecloths out of reach.

MOTOR VEHICLES

- Same as for younger infant.

TODDLERS

FALLS

- Same as for older infants.

SUFFOCATION/ASPIRATION/POISONINGS

- Same as for older infants.
- Lock all medications and poisons in cabinets.
- Teach child not to run with food in mouth.

DROWNING

- Don't keep buckets of water within child's access; keep washer closed; lock toilet seat closed.
- Supervise children when near or in water.
- Don't rely on "swimmies" or other nonapproved flotation devices.

BURNS

- Same as for older infants
- Keep child away from stove, fireplace, curling iron, iron, heaters, etc.
- Teach child to not play with matches.

MOTOR VEHICLES

- Properly use federally approved car seat in rear seat of car. See Chapter 19 for guidelines.

- Supervise child when outdoors.
- Don't allow child to play near or in road.
- Supervise tricycle and other play vehicle activity.

PRESCHOOLERS

MOTOR VEHICLES

- Same as toddlers.
- Teach safety rules: (But still supervise!)
- Obey traffic regulations:
  —Stay back from curb until it's time to cross.
  —Use sidewalks. If no sidewalks, walk on left facing traffic
- Wear light colored clothes with fluorescent material attached at night.

DROWNING/SUFFOCATION/ASPIRATION

- Same as toddler.
- Teach basic swimming.

BURNS

- Same as toddlers.
- Have child participate in fire drills.
- Teach child to drop and roll if clothing catches on fire.

FALLS

- Same as toddlers.

OTHER TRAUMA

- Don't allow child to run with scissors or to run with lollipops in mouth. Teach how to handle scissors and knives.
- Teach personal safety:
  —Name
  —Address
  —Phone number
  —Who to ask for help (police, security)
  —Not to talk to strangers
  —Good touch/bad touch
  —To tell parents if anyone makes them feel uncomfortable
  —To say "no" in uncomfortable situations
- Sew identifying information inside child's clothing.

- Never put any personal identification on the outside of child's clothing. Avoid personalized items (hats, hair clips, lunch boxes, etc.).

SCHOOL-AGERS

MOTOR VEHICLE

- Use booster seats and seat belts properly. See Chapter 19 for guidelines.
- NO riding in the back of an open pickup.
- Keep car doors locked when riding.
- Reinforce traffic rules.
- Teach her to never hitchhike.

BICYCLES

- Wear properly-fitted helmet.
- Ride with traffic and away from parked cars.
- Ride single file.
- Use hand signals.
- Keep hands on handlebars except when signaling.
- Watch for road hazards (potholes, debris, etc.)
- Obey traffic rules.
- Make sure bicycle is correct size and properly maintained. Use reflectors and lights for night riding.
- Don't obscure vision with packages or decorations.
- Don't ride double.

IN-LINE SKATES/SKATEBOARDS

- Should not be used by children under age 5.
- Wear properly-fitting helmets and other protective equipment (wrists, knees, elbows).
- Never ride these near traffic.
- Don't "catch a ride"—connecting to another skateboard or even an automobile.
- Avoid homemade ramps.

DROWNING

- Select safe places to swim.
- Make sure water is deep enough for diving.

- Use approved flotation devices in boats and water.
- Encourage older child to learn CPR.
- Tell child to never swim alone.
- Instruct child to not play near drainage ditches.

BURNS

- Teach child fire safety.
- Teach child what to do in the event of a fire.
- Teach child safe use of equipment (matches, flammable liquids). Still supervise.
- Teach child safe cooking.

POISONINGS

- Educate child to not use nonprescription drugs, inhalants, tobacco, and alcohol. Teach them how to say "no."
- Keep dangerous products labeled.

OTHER TRAUMA

- Avoid use of fireworks.
- If firearms in household, teach firearm safety.
- Play in safe areas.
- Teach safe use of corrective lenses, contacts, and other corrective devices.
- Teach sports safety. (See Chapter 16 for guidelines)

ADOLESCENTS

MOTOR VEHICLE

- Use seat belts.
- Promote appropriate behavior when in motor vehicle.
- Don't drink and drive.
- Encourage driver's education.
- Specifics for your teen driver:
  —No riding with someone who has been drinking.
  —No using drugs and alcohol, especially in relation to motor vehicles.
  —Discuss how she would get home if she and her friends used alcohol, and she were in possession of the family car.
  —Teach her how to respond in emergency situations: tire blowout, skidding on ice or wet road.

ALL-TERRAIN VEHICLES (ATVs)

ATVs should be avoided, but if your teen uses one, follow these guidelines:

- Vehicle should be sturdy, stable, and properly maintained.
- Driver should receive careful instruction and not be allowed to use vehicle until driver demonstrates safe usage.
- Wear protective gear—helmet, trousers, boots, gloves.
- Avoid public roads.
- Avoid unfamiliar terrain.
- Avoid nighttime riding.
- Avoid carrying passengers unless vehicle equipped for same. If passengers allowed, they should wear protective equipment.

DROWNING/DIVING INJURIES

- Teach water and boating safety.
- Avoid use of alcohol when swimming and boating.
- Carefully choose swimming sites.
- Make sure water is deep before diving

BURNS

- Avoid excessive sunbathing, both natural and artificial, and use sunscreen.
- Reinforce careful use of hazardous objects.
- Reinforce fire safety rules.
- Discourage smoking.

POISONING

- Same as school-agers.

OTHER

- Watch for signs of depression and suicidal ideation. (See Chapter 17)
- Encourage sports safety. (See Chapter 16)

29

DISASTER PREPAREDNESS

Don't wait for disaster to strike your family. Always be prepared. Disaster can happen anytime and anywhere to anybody. And when it strikes, you won't have much time to respond. A highway spill or hazardous material could mean evacuation. A winter storm could confine your family at home. An earthquake, flood, tornado, or any other disaster could cut off water, electricity, and telephones lines for days. And we know the devastation a terrorist attack can bring.

Local officials and relief workers will be on the scene after a disaster, but they can't reach everyone immediately. You could get help in hours—or days. Be prepared to cope with the emergency until help arrives.

Create a family disaster plan to be used in the event of a disaster, and determine a safe place to go when needed. Establish escape routes from your home and places where family members will meet should you get separated. Choose several places (friend's house, motels, shelters) in case one doesn't work out. Take CPR and first aid, and disaster preparedness classes (contact your local chapter of the American Red Cross).

Keep emergency phone numbers posted by the phone:

- 911 (where appropriate; police, fire, and ambulance in other areas)
- Local emergency management service
- Family contacts
- Work numbers
- Your children's schools
- Neighbors

Assemble a disaster supply kit. The United States Department of Homeland Security Federal Emergency Management Agency (FEMA) suggests the following:

1. Gather the supplies that are listed. You may need them if your family is confined at home.
2. Place the supplies you would most likely need for an evacuation in an easy-to-carry container, such as a covered, wheeled trash container, a camping backpack, or a duffel bag.

3. There are six basics you should stock for your home: water, food, first aid supplies, clothing and bedding, tools and emergency supplies, and special items.

WATER

Buy bottled water or store water in plastic containers such as soft drink bottles. Avoid using containers that will decompose or break, such as milk cartons or glass bottles. A normally active person needs to drink at least two quarts of water each day. Hot environments and intense physical activity can double that amount. Children, nursing mothers, and ill persons will need more. Store one gallon of water per person per day, keeping at least a three-day supply of water per person (two quarts for drinking, two quarts for each person in your household for food preparation/sanitation).

FOOD

Store at least a three-day supply of nonperishable food. Select foods that require no refrigeration, preparation, or cooking, and little or no water. If you must heat food, pack a can of sterno. Select food items that are compact and lightweight, including ready-to-eat canned meats, fruits, and vegetables.

FIRST AID KIT

Assemble a first aid kit for your home and one for each car. A first aid kit should include:

- Sterile adhesive bandages in assorted sizes
- Assorted sizes of safety pins
- Cleansing agent/soap
- Latex gloves (2 pairs)
- Sunscreen
- 2-inch sterile gauze pads (4-6)
- 4-inch sterile gauze pads (4-6)
- Triangular bandages (3)
- Nonprescription drugs
- 2-inch sterile roller bandages (3 rolls)
- 3-inch sterile roller bandages (3 rolls)
- Scissors
- Tweezers
- Needle
- Moistened towelettes

- Antiseptic
- Thermometer
- Tongue blades (2)
- Tube of petroleum jelly or other lubricant
- Nonprescription drugs
- Aspirin or nonaspirin pain reliever
- Anti-diarrhea medication
- Antacid (for stomach upset)
- Syrup of ipecac (use to induce vomiting if advised by the Poison Control Center)
- Laxative
- Activated charcoal (use if advised by the Poison Control Center)

TOOLS AND SUPPLIES

Additional supplies that may come in handy:

- Mess kits, or paper cups, plates, and plastic utensils
- Emergency preparedness manual
- Battery-operated radio and extra batteries
- Flashlight and extra batteries
- Cash or traveler's checks, change
- Nonelectric can opener, utility knife
- Fire extinguisher: small canister ABC type
- Tube tent
- Pliers
- Tape
- Compass
- Matches in a waterproof container
- Aluminum foil
- Plastic storage containers
- Signal flare
- Paper, pencil
- Needles, thread
- Medicine dropper
- Shutoff wrench, to turn off household gas and water
- Whistle
- Plastic sheeting
- Map of the area (for locating shelters)
- Sanitation
- Toilet paper, towelettes
- Soap, liquid detergent

- Feminine supplies
- Personal hygiene items
- Plastic garbage bags and ties (for personal sanitation uses)
- Plastic bucket with tight lid
- Disinfectant
- Household chlorine bleach
- Clothing and bedding
- Include at least one complete change of clothing and footwear per person.
- Sturdy shoes or work boots
- Raingear
- Blankets or sleeping bags
- Hat and gloves
- Thermal underwear
- Sunglasses

SPECIAL FAMILY MEMBERS

Remember family members with special requirements, such as infants and elderly or disabled persons:

For Baby:

- Formula
- Diapers
- Bottles
- Powdered milk
- Medications

For Adults:

- Heart and high blood pressure medication
- Insulin
- Prescription drugs
- Denture needs
- Contact lenses and supplies
- Extra eyeglasses

PETS

Most humans shelters don't accept pets; therefore, you need to make alternate plans for your pets ahead of time. Have a 4 to 7 day supply of pet food, sanitation, and other supplies ready. Have any medications handy (prescription, vitamins), as well as comfort bedding and toys ready to alleviate anxiety.

ENTERTAINMENT

- Store a supply of nonbattery operated games and books to keep the kids busy.

IMPORTANT FAMILY DOCUMENTS

Store these records in a waterproof, portable container:

- Will, insurance policies, contracts, deeds, stocks and bonds
- Passports, social security cards, immunization records
- Bank account numbers
- Credit card account numbers and companies
- Inventory of valuable household goods, important telephone numbers
- Family records (birth, marriage, death certificates)

Store your disaster kit in a convenient place known to all family members. Keep a smaller version of it in the trunk of your car. Keep items in airtight plastic bags. Change your stored water supply every six months so it stays fresh. Replace your stored food every six months, and rethink your kit and family needs at least once a year. Also, replace batteries and update clothes as needed. Ask your physician or pharmacist about storing prescription medications.

For more up-to-date information on preparing a disaster kit, check the American Red Cross Disaster Kit site at: www.redcross.org/services/disaster/beprepared/supplies.html.

REFERENCES

PRINT

American Academy of Pediatrics, Committee on Injury and Poison Prevention. (2000). All-terrain vehicle injury prevention: Two-, three-, and four-wheeled unlicensed motor vehicles (RE9855). *Pediatrics, 105* (6), 1352–1354.

American Academy of Pediatrics, Committee on Injury and Poison Prevention. (2000). Snowmobiling hazards (RE0006). *Pediatrics, 106* (5), 1142–1144.

American Veterinary Medical Association Task Force on Canine Aggression and Human-Canine Interactions. (2001). A community approach to dog bite prevention. *JAVMA, 281* (11), 1732–1749.

Anonymous. (2002). Carbon monoxide poisoning resulting from exposure to ski-boat exhaust–Georgia. *Morbidity and Mortality Weekly Report, Atlanta, 51*(37), 829–830.

Anonymous. (2000). Tips for toy safety. *The Exceptional Parent,* 30(12), 66–68.

Bailey, M. (n.d.) Protecting your children from abduction: age-appropriate guidelines for keeping kids safe. *Ladies Home Journal.* www.aol2.lhj.com

Bard, G., and Haney, T. (2003). Cybercrime Lecture. Week 18, from May 17, 2003. Wecht Institute of Forensic Science and Law at Duquesne University, Pittsburgh, PA.

Biagioli, F. (2002). Proper use of child safety seats. *American Family Physician,* 65(10), 2085–2090.

Blaschke, G., and Lynch, J., [Guest Editors] (2003). Terrorism: Its impact on pediatrics: Part I. Pediatric Annals, 32(2).

Blaschke, G., and Lynch, J., [Guest Editors] (2003). Terrorism: Its impact on pediatrics: Part III. Pediatric Annals, 32(4).

Bull, M., Agran, P., Laraque, D., Pollack, S., et al. (2000). Children in pickup trucks. *Pediatrics, 4* (1), 857–859.

Burgstahler, S. (2002). Keeping kids safe on the Internet. *The Exceptional Parent,* 32(9), 94–99.

Center for Disease Control. Youth Risk Behavior Surveillance United States, (1997). MMWR Surveillance Summaries, August 14, 1998, Vol. 47, No. SSB3. http://www.cdc.gov/epo/mmwr/preview/ss4703.html.

Cieslak, T., and Henretig, F. (2003). Ring-a-ring-a-roses: bioterrorism and its peculiar relevance to pediatrics. *Current Opinion In Pediatrics*, 15(1), 107–111.

Clemens, P. (2001). Terrorism in America: How do we tell the children? *Journal of Psychosocial Nursing & Mental Health Services*, 39(11), 8–10.

Committee on Environmental Health and Committee on Infectious Diseases. (2000). Chemical-biological terrorism and its impact on children: A subject review. *Pediatrics, 105* (3), 662–670.

Committee on Injury and Poison Prevention. (2000). Personal Watercraft Use by Children and Adolescents. *Pediatrics, 105* (2), 452–453.

Committee on Injury and Poison Prevention and Committee on Sports Medicine and Fitness. (1999). Trampolines at home, school, and recreational centers. *Pediatrics, 103* (5), 1053–1056.

Committee on Injury and Poison Prevention, and the Committee on Adolescence. (1996). The teenage driver. *Pediatrics*, 98(5): 987–990.

Committee on Public Education. (2001). Children, adolescents, and television. *Pediatrics, 107* (2), 423–426.

Committee on Public Education. (2001). Sexuality, contraception, and the media. *Pediatrics, 107* (1), 191–194.

Committee on Sports Medicine and Fitness. (2001). Medical conditions affecting sports participation. *Pediatrics, 107* (5), 1205–1209.

Committee on Sports Medicine and Fitness and Committee on School Health. (2001). Organized sports for children and preadolescents. *Pediatrics, 107* (6), 1459–1462.

Cvijanovich, N., Cook, L., Mann, N., and Dean, J. (2001). A population-based assessment of pediatric all-terrain vehicle injuries. *Pediatrics, 108* (3), 631–635.

Duchin, J. (2003). Bioterrorism. Medscape: www.medscape.com/viewarticle/448589.

Elkind, D. (1967). Egocentrism in adolescents. *Child Development,* 38:1025–1034.

Fagan, P., Wise, T., Schmidt, C., and Berlin, F. (2002). Pedophilia. *JAMA, 288* (19), 2458–2465.

Farrell, A., and Crimmins, D. (2001). Coping with disaster: A second guide for parents and other caregivers. *The Exceptional Parent,* 31(12), 38–44.

Finkelhor, D., Hammer, H., and Sedlak, A. (2002). Nonfamily abducted children: National estimates and characteristics. *OJJDP NISMART, October.*

Fisher, L., and Laskowski, L. (n.d.). Rattlesnake bite – Treatment or mistreatment? *Nursing Spectrum Career Fitness Online.* www.nsweb.nursingspectrum.com/ce/ce1167.html.

Flatter, C., Barnard, K., and Heller, L. Fear: A through the years look at fear. Sesame Workshop. www.sesamestreet.org/parents/advice.

Greydanus, D. Editor-in-Chief. (1991). *Caring for Your Adolescent.* New York:Bantam Books.

Hammer, H., Finkelhor, D., and Sedlak, A. (2002). Children abducted by family members: National estimates and characteristics. *OJJDP NISMART. October.*

Hanze, D. (2002). Collaborative practice: How to help children and adolescents deal with the threat of terrorism. *Journal for Specialists in Pediatric Nursing, 7* (1), 42–43.

Heights, R., Fieldman, J., and Crespi, T. (2002). Child sexual abuse: Offenders, disclosure, and school-based initiatives. *Adolescence,* 37(145), 151–160.

Henkel, J. (2002). For goodness snakes! Treating and preventing venomous bites. *FDA Consumer Magazine.* www.fda.gov/fdac/features/995_ snakes.html.

Herringshaw, D., Longo, M., and Zies, S. (2000). Healthy kids: Germ free. *Journal of Nutrition Education,* 32(4), 233A–233B.

Karen C. McNally, "Earthquake," *World Book Online Americas Edition,* http://www.worldbookonline.com/ar?/na/ar/co/ar171680.htm, March 5, 2003.

Kilpatrick, D., Saunders, B., and Smith, D. (2003). Youth victimization: Prevalence and implications. *National Institute of Justice Research in Brief,* April, 1–14.

Johnston, J., and Girdner, L. (2001). Family abductors: Descriptive profiles and preventive interventions. *OJJDP Juvenile Justice Bulletin,* January.

Johnston, J., Sagatun-Edwards, I., Blomquist, M., and Girnder, L. (2001). Early identification of risk factors for parental abduction. *OJJDP Juvenile Justice Bulletin,* March.

Major, E. (n.d.) Children and eating disorders: A review of the literature. www.vanderbuilt.edu/AnS/psychology/health_psyhcology/children andED.html.

McLean, F. (2002). Marketing and advertising: Harmful to children's health. *The Lancet,* 360 (9388), 1001–1002.

Meier, E. (2002). Effects of trauma and war on children. *Pediatric Nursing,* 28(6), 626–629.

Mental Health Report of the Surgeon General. Depression and suicide in children and adolescents. www.surgeongeneral.goc/library/mental-health/chapter3/sec5.html.

Miller, K. (2001). Television viewing time increases risk for obesity. *American Family Physician,* October 1.

Moran, R. (2003). Breaking the cycle of childhood obesity. *The Clinical Advisor,* February, 62–67.

Muscari, M. (2003). What can I do to help a child who is being bullied? Medscape for Nurses: Ask the Experts. http://www.medscape.com/viewarticle/451381.

Muscari, M. (2002). *Not My Kid: 21 Steps to Raising a Nonviolent Child.* Scranton, PA: University of Scranton Press.

Muscari, M. (2002). Media Violence: Advice for Parents. *Pediatric Nursing.*28(6), 585–591.

Muscari, M. (2002). Effective management of adolescents with anorexia nervosa and bulimia nervosa. *Journal of Psychosocial Nursing*,40(2), 22-31.

Muscari, M. (2002). Preventing Teen Violence. *Advance for Nurses*, 4(5), 31-33.

Muscari, M. (2002). Sticks and Stone: The NP's Role in the Management of Bullies and Victims. *Journal of Pediatric Health Care*, 16(1), 22-28.

Muscari, M. (2001). *Pediatric Nursing, 3rd Edition*. Philadelphia: Lippincott, Williams, and Wilkins.

Muscari, M. (2001). *Advanced Pediatric Physical Assessment: Skills and Procedures*. Philadelphia: Lippincott, Williams, and Wilkins.

Muscari, M. (1999). Prevention—Are We Really Reaching Today's Teen. *MCN*, 24(2), 87-91. (Solicited)

Muscari, M. (1999). Teen Driving: Getting the Maximum Mileage from the Drive's Physical. *Advance for Nurse Practitioners*, 7(2), 61-62.

Muscari, M. (1998). Adolescent Angst: When Should You Really Worry? *AJN, 98* (3), 22-23.

Muscari, M., and Mills, D. (1998). Preventing Sports Injuries. *AJN, 98* (7), 58-59.

Muscari, M. (1998). Screening for Eating Disorders. *AJN, 98* (11), 22-23.

Muscari, M. (1998). Walking a Thin Line: Managing adolescents with anorexia and bulimia. *MCN 23* (3), 130-141.

Muscari, M. (1996). Primary Care of the Adolescent with Bulimia Nervosa. *Journal of Pediatric Health Care*, 10(1), 17-25.

Murray, J. (2002). Collaborative practice: Helping children cope with separation during war. *Journal for Specialists in Pediatric Nursing*, 7(3), 127-129.

Nadler, E., Coucouslas, A., Gardner, M., and Ford, H. (2001). Driveway injuries in children: risk factors, morbidity, and mortality. *Pediatrics, 108* (2), 326-328.

Pfefferbaum, B., Nixon, S., Tucker, P., Tivis, R., Moore, V., Gurwitch, R., Pynoos, R., and Geis, H. (1999). Posttraumatic stress response in bereaved children after Oklahoma City bombing. *Journal of the*

American Academy of Child and Adolescent Psychiatry, 38, 1372-1379.

Pfefferbaum, B., Seale, T., McDonald, N., Brandt, E., Rainwater, S., Maynard, B., Meierhoefer, B. and Miller, P. (2000). Posttraumatic stress two years after the Oklahoma City bombing in youths geographically distant from the explosion. *Psychiatry, 63,* 358-370.

Piacentini, J., and Roblek, T. (2002). Recognizing and treating childhood anxiety disorders. *Western Journal of Medicine,* 176 (3), 149.

Poster, E. (2002). Helping children respond to 9/11. *Journal of Child and Adolescent Psychiatric Nursing,* 15(2), 43-47.

Preboth, M. (2002). Preventing injuries and deaths in schools. *American Family Physician,* 65(10), 2167-2168.

Preboth, M. (2000). Anxiety disorders in children and adolescents. *American Family Physician,* 61 (11), 3472.

Ressel, G. (2002). AAP issues guidelines for selecting and using the most appropriate care safety seats. *American Family Physician,* 66(3), 509-512.

SAMHSA's National Mental Health Information Center. Anxiety disorders in children and adolescents. www.mentalhealth.org/publications/allpubs/CA-0007/default.asp.

Simpson, E., Moll, E., Kassam-Adams, N., Miller, G., and Winston, F. (2002). Barriers to booster seat use and strategies to increase their use. *Pediatrics, 110* (4), 729-736.

United States Consumer Product Safety Commission. *Your Home Fire Safety Checklist.*

Walsh, K., et al. (2000). National Athletic Trainer's Association Position Statement: Lightning safety for athletics and recreation. Journal of Athletic Training, 35(4), 471-477.

Whalen, B. (2000). Preventing animal bites in children. State Medical Society of Wisconsin. www.medem.com.

WEB SITES

ABC News: www.abcnews.go.com

Agency for Toxic Substances and Disease Registry: www.atsdr.cdc.gov

American Academy of Child and Adolescent Psychiatry: www.aacap.org

American Academy of Family Physicians: www.aafp.org

American Academy of Family Physicians Family Doctor: www.familydoctor.org

American Academy of Pediatrics: www.aap.org

American Association of Poison Control Centers: www.aapcc.org

American Cancer Association: www.cancer.org

American Kennel Club: www.akc.org

American Lung Association: www.lungusa.org

American Medical Association Medical Library: www.medem.com

American Psychiatric Association. www.psych.org

American Psychological Association. www.apa.org

American Red Cross: www.redcross.org

Baby Center: www.babycenter.com

Brain Injury Association of America: www.biausa.org

California Poison Control System: www.calpoison.org

Campaign for Tobacco-Free Kids: www.tobaccofreekids.org

Canadian Paediatric Society: www.cps.ca

Centers for Disease Control and Prevention: www.cdc.gov

Child Care Online: www.childcare.net

Children, Terrorism and Disasters Toolkit: www.aap.org/terrorism

Children's Hospital at Westmead: www.chw.edu.au

Children's Hospital Medical Center of Akron: www.akronchildrens.org

Children's Hospital of Pittsburgh: www.chp.edu

Cincinnati Children's Hospital Medical Center: www.cincinnatichildrens.org

City of Cotati Public Safety: www.ci.cotati.ca.us/safety

College Drinking Prevention: www.collegedrinkingprevention.gov

CT ParentsPlus: Connecticut's Parenting Resource. www.ctparentsplus.org

Consumer Product Safety Commission. www.cpsc.gov

Cybercrime: www.cybercrime.gov

DC Military: www.dcmilitary.com

Disney Online Family Fun. www.familyfun.go.com

Division of Human Resources, UC Davis: www.hr.ucdavis.edu/childcare

Dr. Paul's Child Health and Wellness Info Site: www.universalhealth online.com/DrPaul

Environmental Protection Agency: www.epa.gov

Erie County Department of Health: www.ecdh.org

Exceptional Parent: www.eparent.com

Family Education Network: www.familyeducation.com

Family Practice Notebook: www.FPnotebook.com

Federal Emergency Management Agency: www.fema.gov

Greater Dallas Council on Alcohol and Drugs: www.gdcada.org

Hanford Fire Department. www.hanford.gov

Hearth, Patio, and Barbeque Association. www.hpba.com

Humane Society of the United States: www.hsus.org

Injury Prevention: www.injuryprevention.com

IVillage: www.ivillagehealth.com

KeepKidsHealthy. www.keepkidshealthy.com

Kids and Traffic: www.kidsandtraffic.mq.edu

KidsHealth: www.kidshealth.org

KidsSource: www.kidsource.com

LimiTV: www.limitv.org.

Lucile Packard Children's Hospital: www.lpch.org

Mayo Clinic: www.mayoclinic.com

Media Awareness Network: www.media-awareness.ca

Medem Medical Library. www.medem.com

National Agriculture Safety Database. www.cdc.gov/nasd

National Association of Pediatric Nurse Practitioners Keep Your Children Safe and Secure Campaign: www.napnap.org

National Association of School Psychologists: www.nasponline.org

National Center on Addiction and Substance Abuse at Columbia University: www.casacolumbia.org

National Center for Injury Prevention and Control: www.cdc.gov/ncipc

National Center for Missing & Exploited Children: www.misingchildren.com

National Eating Disorders Association: www.nationaleatingdisorders.org

National Fire Prevention Association. www.nfpa.org

National Institute on Drug Abuse: www.nida.nih.gov

National Safe Kids Campaign: www.safekids.org

National Center for Injury Prevention and Control: www. http://www. cdc.gov/ncipc/

National Oceanic & Atmospheric Administration: www.noaa.gov

National Youth Violence Prevention Resource Center: www.safeyouth.org

National Weather Service: www.nws.noaa.gov

New York City Fire Department. www.nyc.gov/html/fdny/html

North Carolina State University Cooperative Extension. www.ces.ncsu.edu

Northwest Baby and Child. www.nwbaby.com

Office of National Drug Policy Control: www.whitehousedrugpolicy.gov

Otto World Scooter Safety Tips: www.aaa-calif.com/otto/kids/learn/scooter-tips.asp

Parenting Teens: www.parentingteens.com

PNN Online: www.pnnonline.org

Royal Society for the Prevention of Accidents: www.rospa.com

SafeChild: www.safechild.net

Safekids: www.safekids.org

Safe Parks: www.safeparks.org

Sexuality Information and Education Council of the United States: www.seicus.com

Soundvision: www.soundvision.com

Stormfax: www.stormfax.com

Texas Department of Public Safety: www.txdps.state.tx.us

Tri-State Fire District. www.tristatefire.org

United States Department of Education: www.ed.gov

United States Department of Justice: www.usdoj.gov

United States Department of Justice Drug Enforcement Agency: www.usdoj.gov/dea

United States Fire Administration. www.usfa.fema.gov

USA Today: www.usatoday.com

University of Maryland Medicine: www.umm.edu

University of Michigan Health System: www.med.umich.edu

Washington State Attorney General: www.wa.gov/ago/violence

Washington State Coalition to Reduce Underage Drinking: www.clearing-house.adhl.org/ruad

Water Quality and Health: www.waterandhealth.org

WebMD with AOL Health. www.aolsvc.health.webmd.aol.com

West Virginia University Extension Service: www.wvu.edu/~agexten

Word on Health: www.nih.gove/news/WordonHealth

World Water Council: www.worldwatercouncil.org

INDEX